2009

COACH OF THE YEAR CLINIC NOTES

LECTURES BY
PREMIER HIGH SCHOOL COACHES

Edited by Earl Browning

COACHES ≡ CHOICE™

www.coacheschoice.com

ISBN: 978-1-60679-065-6

ISSN: 1945-1202

Telecoach, Inc. Transcription: Earl Browning, Jr., Kent Browning, Tom Cheaney, Dan Haley

Diagrams: Steve Haag

Book layout and cover design: Bean Creek Studio

Front cover photo: Tulsa World Newspaper

Back cover photos: Tulsa World Newspaper and Tulsa Union High School Athletic Department—Union County Public School

Special thanks to the Nike clinic managers for having the lectures taped.

Coaches Choice
P.O. Box 1828
Monterey, CA 93942
www.coaceschoice.com

Contents

Contents

FIFTEEN POINTS IN TURNING THE PROGRAM AROUND

Tesoro High School, California

We did have an outstanding year this year. We got beat 20-17 in our last game. I am proud of our team's ac-complishments. We did have some big offensive linemen, but we did not have anyone on the team that was any better than the next guy was.

I have been at two places in my coaching career. I was at Estancia High School in Costa Mesa. It was a school of 1000 kids. We only had 25 players in our varsity and junior varsity programs combined. Including the freshmen, we had close to 40 players.

Going to Tesoro High School is a different world. I was hired there two years ago. We have 133 varsity players, and, counting the others, we have close to 300 kids in our program. It is from one end of the spectrum to the other.

Tesoro is an influential commu-nity. I do not know how many of you have seen the TV show *The Real Housewives of Orange County*. Two of my players have mothers that are on that show. I bought a new Denali™ automobile for Christmas, and I still drive the cheapest car in the school parking lot. It has its good and bad points living in Tesoro.

I have only been a head coach for four years. The first year at Estancia High School, we were 2-9. The next year, we were 7-4. That was the third best record in the school's history. At Tesoro High, our first year, we won seven and lost four games. We did beat Mission Viejo that year. They are in our league. They had not lost a league game in 10 years. We beat them for the league championship and went to the playoffs. We did lose to Mater Dei High School in the playoffs.

This past year, we had a 13-1 record. We were in the finals of the state. We played in Anaheim Stadium in the playoffs. We ended up with Orange County who was the number six ranked team in the state. Going into the state finals, we were rated number one in the state. We did finish 23rd in the country. We were back-to-back Orange League champions. I did win several coach of the year awards.

My topic today is *Fifteen Points Vital to the Success of a Program*. My staff has turned around two programs in four years. I think we do have some credentials to back us up. My lecture is to take you through those 15 points.

FIFTEEN POINTS VITAL TO BUILDING SUCCESS

- Build relationships.
- Establish goals with a vision.
- Establish an off-season workout program.
- Hire quality coaches.
- Keep it simple.
- Find your passion and help your players and assistant coaches find their passion.
- Take risks on the field in big games.
- Schedule games you can win.
- Believe in what you are doing and stick to your guns.
- Have fun.
- Establish discipline.
- Remember that it is the little things that count.
- Practice hard and upbeat.
- Hold a mandatory summer camp.
- Emphasize team bonding and unity.

I want to go into each of these points to give you a better idea of where I am coming from.

Build Relationships

I am a big believer that this is what life and football are all about. If you want to be successful, you must build relationships. We shake hands and we hug our players. When we get off the bus going to a game, I am the first person to stand up and get off the bus. I shake each player's hand. When I see them on campus, I shake their hands.

You can give kids hugs. It does not matter if they are from low-income homes or high-income homes, the kids are the same. Kids need love, and they need respect. Coaches should care about their players, regardless of what they are doing for your program. When the kids understand that you love them, they will buy into what you are doing for them.

You must deal with parents, and you must be open to them. Most of the parents want what is best for their kids. Treat them with respect and show it, and that will make things better.

Establish Goals With a Vision

Have goals and talk about them often. We make our goals simple. The first day I meet the kids at Tesoro High School, I give them a list of our goals and visions. We want to make sure everyone knows what our goals and visions are. Each day in the weight room, I am asking the kids what goal number one is. I want them to be able to recite the goals to me when I meet them in the halls. We only have five goals. The first year, we only had four goals. We added the goal of winning a state championship.

Have the goals on a board, and have them where everyone can see them. I tell them to put them on their refrigerator doors at home and to put them on the backs of their bedroom doors. I want the players to be able to see those goals as much as possible. They must be able to see them in order to envision them coming true.

In 2008, I gave every kid a goal sheet. Our first goal was to improve every day. When I became the head coach at Estancia High School, they were 1-9 the year before. I could not put up a goal that we wanted to win the state. After thinking about the situation, we picked our first goal: We can get

better every day. That was our first goal. I asked them to pick one thing and to work to get better at that one thing. By the end of the season, they were much improved. The way it is now, we are a lot better at the end of the season than we are at the start of the season.

Our second goal is to beat our rivals—that is Capistrano Valley and Mission Viejo. We beat Mission Viejo on the last play of the game last year. This year, we want to beat both of them again. They are our rivals, and in practice and in the weight room, we want to have the players respond with: Beat Capistrano Valley and beat Mission Viejo.

Our third goal is to win the league championship. That is why you play. Our goal is to win the South Coast title and go 5-0.

The fourth goal is to win the CIF Pac-5 championship. We only had four goals last year. If we want to be the best, we need to add a goal. Our fifth goal this year is to win the California state championship. We ended up short in the championship game this year. Our goal next year is to get back to the championship game and to win it this time. Because we are a public school, we do not get to reload like some of the private schools do, but we are all in the same boat. We have to compete and play to win.

Next, I give the players a copy of the vision of our program. This is what I expect our program to be. We all have our vision of what we expect our program to be. I believe we are going to be the toughest players on the field. We never want to be outhit.

In our locker room just before we go out for the game, we have a moment of silence. If a player wants to say a prayer, he can. Then, after the minute is up, I call out, "Tesoro Titans," and the kids all respond with "I am never outhit." Then, we go on the field for the game.

Continuing our vision, we are going to play with great passion. Our kids play with passion, and they play hard. If they do not play with passion, they do not play. We do some crazy things on defense. We are going to take chances. Nevertheless, we are going to play with passion. We buy the best equipment possible. We are all going to look the same. This is what makes us special.

We do not allow the kids to alter the equipment. Players cannot wear earrings around the practice area. The players must have a decent haircut. I had a Samoan kid that had hair down to his butt when I came to Tesoro. I told him I could not change the rule, even though I knew it was part of his culture. He was playing football for Tesoro High School, and that made it special. We are not a private school, but we feel it is a privilege to play football for Tesoro High School. I expect the players to look the part of football players. When you look at the NFL players when they come out on the field for the kickoff, they are all dressed the same. They look professional on the field, and that is what we want.

We are going to execute to perfection. I know a lot of teams are not perfect, but we are going to strive to be perfect. That is why we play the game. We are going to be great players, and we are always going to be on the attack. We are going to be exciting to watch. When people come to one of our games, we want them leaving with the feeling that they had a fun night at the game.

We are going to play with great confidence. We teach our kids to play with confidence. They may not always know the right answer and know what to do, but I want them to be confident, to play hard, and to have fun.

We are never going to beat ourselves. So many teams and so many coaches go out and beat themselves. They turn over the ball, and they make mistakes. We are going to play to the best of our ability, but we are not going to beat ourselves. Some coaches play *not to lose*. We play *to win*.

We are going to respect each other. We do not use profanity around our players. If we hear a kid cursing, we make them do push-ups. If I hear a coach cursing, we are probably going to get rid of him. I am not going to say we are perfect because sometimes a word may slip out in the heat of battle, but we do not use profanity. I have never cursed a player. Kids are there because they want to be a better person. There is no reason to curse the kids.

We never give up. If we get behind by 50 points, we are going to keep playing. We have great character. A big point for me is this. From the day I was hired at Estancia High School, this is a quote that I use often: "*The territory you choose determines your destiny.*" I remind players of this often—especially if they get into trouble. If you want to be great, you must choose great character. If you choose to be a bum, then your destiny is to be a bum.

We want winners. We want kids that play the game because they want to win. They want to have fun and they want to win. No one wants to play on a team that never wins. We are playing to win.

Establish an Off-Season Workout Program

We want to establish an off-season program, and we are going to make it demanding. I believe the off-season program at both schools where I have coached was a big part of our success. It is a five-day-a-week program. On Mondays, Wednesdays, and Thursdays, we are in the weight room. On Tuesdays and Fridays, we are on the field during our seventh-period class where we are doing football-related activities. By the time we get to spring practice, we are ready to play a game. We may not be in top physical condition, but the kids know the plays and the defense.

We have a grueling push-up/sit-up routine. It helps make the kids mentally tougher. We have what we call *1,000 sit-ups Thursday*. We do 1,000 sit-ups every Thursday. Every day, we do a minimum of 500 sit-ups. We do 200 push-ups every day. After 200 sit-ups, they are crappy, and after about 50 push-ups, they are crappy. However, doing the last reps of each is what is making that kid mentally tough. It teaches them they can do it. We feel this has made our players tough.

I am a big believer in the fundamentals in weight lifting. We do the bench press, the squat, and the cling. We did hire a strength coach this year. It is nice to have someone else in the weight room with me. I told him what I wanted, and we added some of his ideas. We do bench presses, squats, and clings. We do some curls as we get into the program.

As I said, every Thursday we do 1,000 sit-ups. We do them in sets of 100. This takes from 15 to 20 minutes. The kids lift with a partner who helps keep his reps. As the kid who is doing the sit-ups gets to his jersey number, he calls it out, loud enough so everyone can hear him. If he is #75 and he gets through doing the 74th sit-up, he is going to call out "75" very loud. Each kid counts out his own number. This is a little thing, but that is what counts.

We also have competitions on Thursdays. Our practice does not take as long so we have some time to play some crazy games. We may go on the tennis court and play dodgeball. We may divide them up and play 5-on-5 basketball. We only play for 20 minutes or so in these games. This teaches the kids to compete. It teaches them to have fun. If they are not having fun, the kids are not going to enjoy the workouts.

The off-season is a good time to talk with your kids and get them to buy into your program. Every day after workouts, I am preaching to them how they are to act and what we want them to do. We talk about their dreams and their visions.

Hire Quality Coaches

We want to hire quality men as coaches. It is important to be a good coach. Being a good person is more important than being a good football coach. We all know that I do not know as much football as a lot of you here know. However, we are going to treat our kids well, and we are going to work hard. We do the things we know how to do, and we get very good at it.

We have to check the backgrounds of coaches before we hire them. I like to meet coaches three, or four, and even five times before we hire them. Have them come to practice. Get to know them. Go to lunch with them. I do not think it is good to hire a coach without getting to know all you can about that person before you hire them.

You have to get assistant coaches to believe in your philosophy and what you are trying to do. We all have our own philosophy. If the head coach and the assistant coaches cannot get together on what

you are doing, you are not going to be successful. Everyone has to be on the same page.

I am a big believer in having coaches with great character. We do not use profanity, and we believe in being a person with character. Assistant coaches must know football. They must be willing to put time into the program. We are not crazy about what we do. We never work on Sundays. We work on Saturdays during the season. We usually play on Friday night. We go to the coaches' office at about 8:00 a.m. We work until we get the job done. We do not spend a lot of time shooting the breeze. I know coaches that meet on Saturday, then come back on Sunday, and still do not get what they want done. I believe you must allow the assistant coaches some time off.

We did have two Sundays where we had to work this past season. We had two Saturday night games in the playoffs and had to come in on Sunday to be ready for the kids on Monday. However, we gave the kids off on Monday. In the playoffs, they do not give us the schedule until Sunday.

On-campus coaches are a must to survive. Yet, we all have off-campus coaches. That is the direction high school football is going. I am in a unique situation in that I have nine on-campus coaches. I see the trend where this is fading in many of the schools. It is good to have those on-campus coaches because you can have meetings during lunch, and you can keep track of your kids better. However, I do believe the teacher/coach breed is dying. We all have to depend on off-campus coaches to be successful.

Keep It Simple

Do what you do best. Our best play was our stretch play. We ran it very well. We do not make things complex. We do run four or five other run plays. They may look complex, but they are simple for us. We run four or five pass plays. We have other plays in our playbook, but we do not run them. We do what makes us successful.Keeping the routine is another point we stress. Our practice plan is about the same every day. One day I tried to change it because things were starting to get a little dull. When we started practice on the new schedule, the kids could not function. I saw what was happening, and we switched back to the regular routine.

Normally, our practice goes like this. We do pre-practice, stretching, agilities, individual drills, and then team drills. On that one day, we started out with team drills, groups, and then individual drills. The kids could not pick it up. Therefore, we changed back to the old routine. It was early in the season, and it did not hurt us.

If you look at our game film, you will see the first couple of plays in each game are the same plays. Those were the plays we ran well. In our win over Mission Viejo, we ran the blast play 23 times. It is the simplest play in football. They could not stop us, so we kept running it. We won the game 31-14. In another game, we ran the stretch play 20 times. We are going to do what we do best. If you cannot run a play successfully, you need to go to another play.

The power and counter are great plays, but our kids could not execute those plays. We did not run those plays. It is important to stick to the basics and stay with them. We use the same plays, and we use the same game plans. Why change what works?

Find Your Passion and Help Your Players and Assistant Coaches Find Their Passion

Passion is a big word in our program. To be successful in anything, you must be passionate about it. I talk to the kids a great deal about finding their passion. If you want to be successful in business, you must be passionate about it. If you want to be successful in coaching, you must be passionate about it. I explain the situation to the players like this: If you want to find a girl to date steady or if you are serious about a young lady, to be successful about this relationship, you must be passionate about it. If you are not passionate about the situation, it is not going to work. The players laugh about the analogy, but they get the picture.

The job of the head coach is to help the assistant coaches and the players find their passion. You can see by the way our kids play that they are passionate. You can look at all the teams around the country, and you can see the teams that are passionate about their team. They play hard, they play physical, and you can see they enjoy what they are doing.

There is a difference between passion and being crazy. Some coaches out there think being passionate means being crazy. Crazy is not passion—they are two different things.

Take Risks

I am a big believer in this statement: *Any play, any time, from anywhere.* We are going to take risks. For example, before one game, we said we were going to onside kick the ball after our first touchdown. We scored early, made the onside kick, and recovered the ball. The opponents were not ready for that onside kick that early in the game.

We run the pressure defense. If you watch us, you will see that we are wild and crazy. We blitz a lot. At first, it drove me nuts. I let our coaches coach. I do not try to micromanage them. If things are way out of line, I will say something to them. I am concerned with the offensive line in the games. I do not watch what the other coaches are doing because I am working with the line.

I can give you several examples where we have used plays that were a complete surprise to the defense to win some big games. We play to win, not to tie or lose. You have to play to win. If you are playing to lose, you are never going to win. We are aggressive—offensively and defensively.

Schedule Games You Can Win

I believe this is an important part of winning. Winning is important in building a program. If you lose enough, you are not going to have a job very long. I am not saying to schedule teams that you are going to beat by 100 points. You need to schedule teams that are going to be competitive. When we first arrived at Tesoro High and Estancia High School, we played teams that were too tough for us, and we could not compete with them. The next year, we scheduled teams that we had a chance against. Playing teams that are much better than you does not make you tough. It makes you feel bad, and it can get the players hurt. It can demoralize the players and coaches.

Our goal is to play 15 games a year—that includes the state championship. At the end of the year, no one cares who we played—they care that we were 13-1 and we played in the state finals.

We want to schedule games where we can get a lot of the kids in the game. If you have a lot of kids in your program, you need to get them in the games. If we have kids that come to practice every day and work hard but are third- and fourth-string players, I want to reward them by getting them into the games. Some of those kids work just as hard as the starting team. To get them in a game is a big thing for us. For those kids to get into a game with the game on TV, it is something they are going to remember for the rest of their lives.

Believe in What You Are Doing and Stick to Your Guns

You have a game plan, and you need to stick to it. I have had to dismiss players, including starters, for different reasons. Kids do some stupid things around the campus. You have to set the rules and stick to your guns. If you are doing something that is horrible and you realize it, then you do have to change. If you change the program just because some parent is not happy, then you will be in trouble. You do not change what you are doing if that is what you believe. If you believe in it, do it.

Have Fun

When I was hired at Estancia High School, it was a dying program. However, it was a place that gave a 25-year-old a chance to be a head coach. I realized you must make football fun. Football is hard work—it is hard. Think about all of the times when you were a player and how you hated to go to practice because of the hard work involved. Nevertheless, you have to do those things to be successful.

We play a game called "cover the bodies" at the end of practice. It is similar to the king-of-the-hill

game. We line up inside the hash marks, facing each other. We set a limit on the length of the area we work in. We may pit the seniors against the juniors or the offense against the defense. The players are down on their knees. The objective of the game is to pull the opponent out of the square the players are in, between the hash marks. When a player is pulled out of his area, he must move over to the side and do push-ups. Those kids are gassed when they are finished. It is a fun drill.

We do a field-goal contest with the linemen. We do contests for conditioning. If we are running sprints at the end of practice or running other conditioning drills, we stop the action and bring up a lineman to attempt a field goal. If he makes the field goal, we take off a certain number of sprints. If he misses, we continue the drill. If you feel good about the work the team has done for the day and if the field goal is good, you may want to cancel all of the remaining drills and call it quits for the day. That is a fun practice. The thing I am shocked about is the fact that we have a couple of linemen who are not bad as kickers.

We have a wrestling contest at the end of practice. We pick out a player, and he can challenge another player to wrestle. We do not let them pick our quarterbacks. The team makes a circle, and the two players wrestle. In the spring, it is a free-for-all.

This year for the playoffs, the coaching staff ran 40-yard sprints for conditioning. Our goal for every Monday was to have 10 perfect plays. Monday is a light practice day for us. At the end of practice, we set our goal for 10 perfect 40-yard sprints. Usually, at the end of practice, it would take us 40 tries to get the 10 perfect plays in.

You know the drill here. Everyone must have their mouthpieces in, their stances must be perfect, and they must run hard on the play. For every win, we took one 40 off the required number of perfect plays. We did this for the entire year. When we reached week 10, the players did not have any 40-yard sprints to run. Early in the year, the kids wanted to know what would happen if they won 10 games and did not have any sprints to run. We told them if they won 10 games, the coaches would start running the sprints.

The kids won the 10 games, so the coaches ran the 40s for conditioning. It was tough on us when we got to the championship game because we were horrible. We were just not in very good shape. I had never seen a coach pull a hamstring muscle after running five yards. It was a lot of fun for the players.

I started something at practice last year. We get in our stretch lines to warm up. The kids all clap on a certain count. One day, it was a slow and lazy type practice, and the kids did not have much pep. It was during two-a-days, it was hot, and they were just dragging. I am still a kid, and I am trying to have fun. So, I started on a gesture to interject some fun into the practice. I said, "Stick your right hand in the air." The kids all responded. I said, "Stick your left hand in the air." Again, the kids responded. I do not know what hit me, but I continued those absurd directions. "Flap your arms like a bird. Put your hands together as if you are drinking water from a river in the Sahara Desert." The players yelled, "Coach, there are no rivers in the Sahara Desert." I just passed that off and continued. "Now, drink the water. Start clapping your hands." The players all followed along with the antics.

The next day when we started stretching, the players wanted to know if we were going through the Sahara experience again. So, we did that silly drill again. Now, it has become an everyday thing. It did get kind of old, but the kids loved that part of practice.

This year, after the fifth game of the season, things were getting tedious. I got a CD that one of the kids had made. It had all of the rap stuff, but it was appropriate. I went up in the press box, and we played the CD over the loudspeakers. We practiced to rap music during the entire practice. If we had a good Monday and Tuesday practice, we played music for our Wednesday practice. It was a lot of fun. On game night, it is loud in the stadium. It gave us a game-type atmosphere for that Wednesday's practice. It helped get us over the hump, as the kids were loose and enjoyed the change of pace on Wednesday.

We started doing some of these things when I was coaching at Estancia High School, and I have continued to do them at Tesoro High School. It does not matter where you are coaching—these things are always good to help the kids have fun. The kids know when to have fun, and they know when it is time to turn it on. There is a difference. There is a time to have fun and joke with the kids, and they know when it is time to be serious. We kick their butts, and we love them, and we treat them well.

Life is about relationships. We have great relationships with our kids. This is one of my goals as a coach. I want these kids to come back to see me in 25 years, and I hope I am still coaching at Tesoro High School. I want the kids to come back and tell me what good husbands and fathers they are. I want them to tell me they are good businessmen, good policemen, or whatever they do in life. I am hoping the football experience has given them a good stepping-stone to accomplish their goals in life. I hope football teaches them more about life than it does about the game.

Establish Discipline

We must establish discipline in our program. We are a "Yes, Sir" and a "No, Sir" football program. We do not accept "Yeah" and "Nah." If a player comes into our office and gives us a "Yeah" for an answer, we say, "Excuse me!" We expect them to say "Yes, Sir" or "No, Sir." It is "Yes, Coach" or "No, Coach." I go back to my statement on character. "The territory you choose determines your destiny." We are firm and we are strict on our kids, but we treat them very fair. You must realize the point when you are overdoing something or when are doing it. You must be firm, but you must be fair.

You must know the types of kids you are dealing with. The things that went fine at Tesoro High School with 130 kids weren't true at Estancia High School. Estancia was a low-income school. If it was a holiday, you could not practice because the kids had to work on those days. They had to make money for their families. At Tesoro High School, on holidays, every kid is at practice.

I may be hard on the kids, but it is what I think we need to be successful. If you believe it, do it.

We make the players do punishment exercises for poor grades or if they are late to practice. We could not do this at Estancia because a few players would have to miss a practice during two-a-days. One player would have to get up and go to work with his father in the morning. Sometimes, he would get up at 5:30 a.m. and go to work with his dad. Then, he would come to practice at 8:30 a.m. Then, he would go back to work with his dad after practice. He would come back to our 5:30 p.m. practice, and, occasionally, he was a few minutes late. That did not upset me that he was late. He was doing a great job because playing football was important to him, but he had to help the family first.

At Tesoro, if a kid is a minute late to practice, we are all over him. I give the kids a grade each week. Every Thursday, I make out my grade sheets. The teachers did not like me for this at first, but now they like it.

On the report is a note from the player explaining that he does not want to do "bear walks," so he wants to get a good grade report. The teachers list the grades for each player that is in their class. For every D, the player has 300 bear walks after practice, and for every F, it is 500 bear walks. Some kids are out bear crawling the entire weight-lifting period. If they do not bring in the grade sheets, I assume they have all Fs. That is a lot of bear crawls. Each kid has six classes. That comes out to 3000 yards of bear crawling. I make them do the bear crawls. They hate me when they are going through the bear walks. I may even get a call from some of the parents. We are trying to establish discipline, and we are trying to make academics an important part of our program.

Every player must look the same. We talked about having a decent haircut. I make our kids wear white shoes. You can pick what you want, but I am not going to have our kids wearing 10 different colors of cleats. It has to be a white cleat. We do get a good deal with Nike® on the cleats. I am a big believer in being loyal. The Nike rep I deal with helped

me out at Estancia and he has helped me at Tesoro. He has been good for me. His name is Larry Woods, and he is the greatest sales person there is. He gets the equipment for us. We will continue to work with him.

We do not allow the players to alter or change the team uniforms. We give them nice, quality equipment, and there is no need to alter it. We make the players buy their practice jerseys. The players must be clean-shaven. In the off-season, I am not as big on this point. During the season, I do want them to be clean-shaven. I do not allow the players to wear earrings. I explain all of this to them at the beginning of the year. I tell them how I expect them to act when we win and when we lose. I do not want some kids throwing a fit on the sideline when we lose. That makes the program look low-class. You have to tell them how to act. If you do not tell them, they do not know. We tell them how we want them to dress. I stress how to tuck the jerseys in their pants. I tell them how I want their socks worn.

We consider it a privilege to play football at Tesoro or any other school. It is not a right to play football. It is a privilege, and the players need to act like it is a privilege.

I have never had to ask a player to play football. They are playing because they want to be there. They must do the right thing to be a part of the program. This is one fact we are proud of at our school. If I call a kid in to talk about some problem, I will ask him if any of the coaches asked him to play football. He will tell me they have not asked him to come out for football. I ask, "Why are you out for football?" At times, they will cry and say it is because they want to be out for the team. If they want to be out for football, they will find a way to be successful. If they want to be successful, they must find a way to be passionate.

Remember That It Is the Little Things That Count

The little things count. You do not have to spend a million hours to be successful. It is important to get to know the players and their families. In the off-season, I have "Lunch With Coach Barnes." One day a week, I pick four players and have lunch with them. I bring my lunch and the players bring their lunches, and we sit and talk in my office. We talk about their families. I ask them about their parents, their brothers and sisters, and anyone else who may be in their lives. I ask them to tell me about the things they like. The kids enjoy this.

We let players out of conditioning drills if they give great effort. We have "Turnover Tuesday" that we stole from USC. If they make an interception or force or recover a fumble, they get out of conditioning. The kids love practice on Tuesday. They really go after each other in practice that day.

We have a film-and-picture night. We do this early in the year. We give the pictures to the players and the parents to let them know we want to do something for them.

We have a great banquet. We give a lot of awards. We say nice things about every kid. We want people to leave that banquet happy so they are excited about the next season. I want every kid excited after our banquet. When you have a lot of kids and you go to the state finals, the banquet is going to be longer, and it should be. No one complained about the length of our banquet this year. It lasted close to five hours this year. They all left happy.

Practice Hard and Upbeat

The key to practicing hard and upbeat is the pace. We use a clock for everything we do. We give the coaches a practice play for every session. I do not worry about what the coaches do in their individual periods. I expect the coaches to know what they need to do. We kick their butts, but we love them later when we get off the field.

Hold a Mandatory Summer Camp

I do want to touch on our summer camp. It is one of the big secrets to our success. We run for five weeks, Monday through Thursday during the summer. We do not go on Friday, and we want to make sure we give them three days off. We work out from 7:45 a.m. to 10:00 a.m. If they want to get a job or hang out at the beach, they can.

It is two hours of hell. It is a big part of our success. We work for one hour in the weight room in circuits and one hour on the field. We split linemen and skilled players up. The linemen will start on the field first, and the skilled players start in the weight room. They work for one hour. Then, we come together and do a team period at 8:45 a.m. They switch at 9:00 a.m. with the line going in the weight room and the skilled players going to the field.

The conditioning and the weight room is brutal training. On Mondays and Wednesdays we do upper body, and on Tuesdays and Thursdays we do lower body.

We do not work on strength that much in the summer practices. We are working on quickness and making the kids tougher. We want them to do 20 days of the summer camp. I do not want them to come out for two-a-days until they have done the 20 days. We have everyone check in for the practice. If they miss a practice, they have to make it up. If a kid is in summer school, they have to come at 6:00 a.m. They have to get 20 days of the camp. If a kid goes on vacation, he has to make up any days missed. We have some kids that will come at 6:00 a.m. and do two days in one. They know they have to make up any days missed, so, at times, they may be doing two sessions to get their 20 sessions completed.

We alternate the days a coach has to be at practice at 6:00 a.m. I think I did it three times last summer. The other coaches split up the number of days they have to be at early practice. This program makes the kids accountable.

Emphasize Team Bonding and Unity

We stress team unity. We have our kids wear their jerseys to school on game day. I want the kids to be comfortable on game day.

We have team dinners on campus on game day. You would be surprised at the number of businesses that will donate meals for the team. We have people donate meals every week. We have a sit-down dinner for 150 people counting the players, coaches, and others.

The kids may hate me, but we have pasta, garlic bread, salad, two sodas, and two cookies. It never changes. This is a good meal for them. I do not want them to eat a big steak and be bloated all night. We want them to get quick carbs and something that will be easy on them that night. If they do not want soda, we have Gatorade® for them.

We have postgame parties on campus. It keeps the kids from drinking and getting into trouble after the game. We get pizzas for them and feed them before they go home.

If our line does not give up a sack on our quarterback, he has to take his linemen to dinner. This year, we had eight games where he had to take the linemen out to dinner. He was going broke, but they all chipped in and made it work.

After a win, the coaches buy donuts on Saturday morning. I get them for the offensive team, and the defensive coaches buy them for the defense.

We do not bring in the whole team for film on Saturday morning. We have a list of 80 players that we dress for the games. That group comes in on Saturday morning.

If the defensive player scores a touchdown from an interception, they get a steak dinner from the defensive coaches. This past year, we had 15 touchdowns from interceptions. This is not against the rules the way we work this. We are inviting the defensive players to dinner, and we eventually spread it out to the entire team so everyone is equal in getting those dinners.

If I can help any of the young coaches, I would be glad to tell you what we do in all of our programs. I have enjoyed visiting with you. Thank you very much. I appreciated the experience.

COACHING LINEBACKERS AND TACKLING DRILLS

Crater High School, Oregon

Thank you. I think coaching is the best profession in the world to be in. I am just thankful to be a part of it and to be able to impact kids' lives. I have been coaching for 25 years, with the last five at Crater High School. We have a great staff. Half of them are guys who played for me. We are like an extended family to each other.

I am going to talk about linebackers. I played linebacker at Southern Oregon University, and I have coached linebackers for 25 years. I will talk about our philosophy, some of the things we like to do, and some of the drills we use. I am going to try to give you the biggest overview I possibly can on developing linebackers.

FANTASY VS. REALITY

Let me set this up by talking fantasy versus reality. Fantasy is having linebackers in your high school who are 6'4", 220 pounds, run a 4.6 40, and are all Division I prospects. The reality is, when you are at Crater or some other places I have been, those are few and far between. The reality is having those 5'8", 180-pound kids whom you coach up the best you can. We hope they can run, and you can get them to be students of the game.

QUALITIES WE LOOK FOR IN A LINEBACKER

We want our linebackers to be playmakers. I have had kids who had all the looks of a linebacker but could not make plays. I have also had the kid who does not look the part but is always around the football making plays. I will take the playmaker over the prototype athlete any time.

Next, I want kids at linebacker who really want to play defense, have a desire to learn, and want to become students of the game. They have to be coachable, develop a great work ethic, and of course, they have to love to hit.

Lastly, physical size does not matter, but size of heart does. You are going to see a film clip in a moment of one of our backup linebackers who comes in. In reality, he is too small to play, but he has the heart of a lion, and he does make plays. He will be a senior this next year.

BEING ABLE TO COMMUNICATE IS ESSENTIAL

If you take one thing away from this session besides any footwork stuff we do, it is our communication keys, and that is where students of the game come in to play. Teach them how to communicate. We have had kids whose communication skills were not very good in the beginning, and they were very quiet and shy. We teach them to talk. In all of our drills, our linebackers talk. You will see film clips of our drill work in which all the linebackers are talking. They learn how to communicate on the field, and that is essential for us.

LET THE PLAYERS KNOW YOUR EXPECTATIONS

We expect our players to take a positive attitude into every practice and every game. We also want to make it clear to them the speed at which we practice and play, and the quality that we expect in our practice drills. We have one speed. It is always full speed, unless otherwise stated. We will do full speed, or we will do walk-through speed. There is no in-between speed. That is about it, and players have to understand that.

We want them to understand their lineup rules and responsibilities. We have progressed from a 4-4 defense to a combination 3-4 defense. We will roll up into a 4-4 and even play some 4-3. Our linebackers have to understand the difference between their alignment in a 3-4 base and a 4-4 G-front. That takes a lot of learning and some time.

We like to say, "If you think, you are wrong." We want all our communication done before the quarterback's hands go under center. After his hands go under center, our linebackers' play is all reaction, and there is no more thinking involved. As soon as our kid says he thought this or he thought that, we know he has handled the situation the wrong way.

We want our players to know that it is okay to be mad. We push our kids hard. We try to push their buttons in practice and make practices harder than games, and they are going to get mad at us. We want them to know it is okay to be mad at us, so long as they understand the rules and the boundaries of being mad. You can be mad at me for pushing you, and pushing the pace with you a little, but I am still going to care about you. We talk about unconditional love. I am going to be mad at you, too, when you miss tackles, so it is a two-way street.

We want our players to know that we are willing to listen to them. I once had a player ask me about an ineffective way I always used to try to fire them up for a game, and he had a point of view that made a lot of sense. After I thought about it, I changed my whole philosophy on the approach to motivation. Players usually see things as they really are, so be willing to listen to them.

We want to teach communication. You will see in this film clip where our linebackers are recognizing formation tendencies, communicating those tendencies before the quarterback goes under center, and then making plays by ignoring fakes and playing the tendencies. It is all reaction when the ball is snapped, and it comes because of studying our opponents.

AS A COACH

As a coach, you have to have a variety of drills that fits your scheme. Because we run a three-man front and a four-man front, we have a lot of drills to pick from. Make sure you have a variety that fits what your opponent is showing offensively. We coach technique in every drill we do, and in every rep, all the time.

STANCE AND FOOTWORK DRILLS (EDDS)

We start our linebackers out every day with stance and footwork drills, called everyday drills, or EDDs. We do not take any read steps or any false steps in our reads. We have what we call a buzz-and-go drill, where we buzz our feet, keep them within the framework of our body, and go on command. That is buzz and go. We also run a buzz-wave-and-go drill, and we will show you all of those.

We do a big wave drill over the bags. We do a shuffle drill over the bags. We do a scoop-and-score drill along with a fumble-recovery drill. We do what we call "high knees over the bags" and we do a box drill. If you get a couple of things out of this talk, one would be communication, but the other would be the footwork that we do in these drills.

STRIKE-AND-SEPARATE DRILLS

After the footwork drills, we do strike-and-separate drills, which we will cover in strike progression: triangle and angle strike, get over the top, zone drill, and skate drill. All of those drills build a base for tackling, so the next set of drills will be a variety of tackling drills.

POPSICLE DRILLS (HANDS INSIDE)

We went to a 50 front recently because there are so many spread teams now. Our linebackers are not covered up like they are in our G-front. That makes it more important to get our hands inside on our strike-and-separate technique. We now use a popsicle dummy. We want to teach our linebackers to take on half a man and cancel our gap. We are going to strike and separate with our inside hand on the breastplate and our outside hand on the shoulder, sliding the inside hand to the neck. The popsicle dummy has helped us with that more than anything else has. We have a couple of different drills for that.

PASS-COVERAGE DRILLS

For our pass coverage drills, we have cone drops, cone drops and angle out, and a quick neck drill that I got from Oregon State. On the quick neck drill, the linebacker does an angle drop and then spins back to the inside instead of opening back to the inside like we have traditionally taught.

We were taught never to turn our backs on the quarterback. But people are running so many under routes, double under, and dig routes behind linebackers. It is a lot quicker to throw your elbow, turn, and get flat than it is to open step and then open back up and try to run with a dig or an under route.

Okay, we also have a special drill, which is a break-flat-to-the-ball drill. Then, we do play-action bites and third-key reads, all of which you will see.

READING RUN VS. PASS
(LINE-BACKS-QUARTERBACK)

Our reading run versus pass drills are all line reads in combination with the line and running backs. We do an inside drill with defensive tackles and/or defensive ends, which is a group drill. We do a perimeter drill, which is an outside group drill. Of course, we also do a team period.

STUDYING OPPONENTS

We look for several things when we study our film and scouting reports. On individual alignments, we will notice the linemen spacing, especially on teams that like to run traps. We check running backs' depth on different plays. We try to pick up line calls, cadence, and audibles with our guy down on the field before the game.

Team wise, we record formation tendencies, down-and-distance tendencies, and hash field tendencies. We also chart any trick plays and go-to plays. We want to know when and where they like to run them.

STANCE AND FOOTWORK DRILLS

The first drill is our footwork drill called the buzz-and-go drill. We simply put our linebackers four

across, buzz our feet, and then do not take a false step as we drive out on the coach's command. Then we do a buzz-wave-and-go drill in the same setup. It is the same drill, except we move them laterally back and forth in a wave drill, and then they drive out. The coaching point here is to keep their feet in the framework of their body as they move laterally.

The next drill is a reaction drill that we call our box drill. We put two linebackers in the middle of a 10x10-yard square. On signal, they will work laterally, pass drop each way, and then finish by hitting on their stomach and bouncing back up. Again, they have to keep their feet within the framework of their bodies.

The other footwork drill we have here is shuffle over the bags. On command, the players shuffle laterally over four separate bags, recover or scoop a football, and finish by driving up the field. It is a great drill for working on pad level. They will touch each bag while keeping their eyes up, staying square, and maintaining solid lateral footwork, and then finish with a scoop and score.

STRIKE-AND-SEPARATE DRILLS

We do a three-man strike drill to get kids to strike the inside breastplate or the outside breastplate on a side (Diagram #1). We want to make sure we step with our inside foot, roll the hips, and keep ourselves in good position.

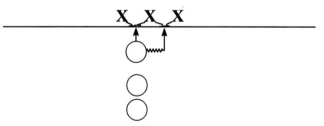

Diagram #1. Three-Man Strike Drill

We want a six-inch power step when they strike. We say to put toes on their toes. The problem kids have at first is stepping too early and stepping too big. If they can put toes on toes and strike half a man, the offensive man should be lifted off the ground.

The next drill is the three-man strike progression drill (Diagram #2). This is one of our main drills. We get three different blockers at three different depths. The linebacker shuffles, strikes, and separates off the outside half of the first man, then stays on that same plane so he gets to defeat blocks from three different depths. He gets a block from line depth, then a block like a fullback lead, and third he gets a deeper perimeter block.

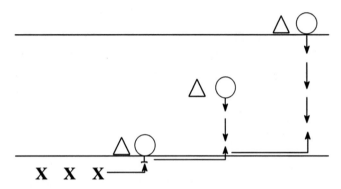

Diagram #2. Three-Man Strike Progression Drill

We are working here on your strike and separate half a man, on shuffling, on hand placement, and playing blocks from different depths.

This last strike drill is the angle strike drill (Diagram #3). We take a lead blocker head on, and then we shuffle to the right and to the left. We see a lot of zone blocking and comboing up. We have to get our hips out and get around to the outside. We take the lead guy on here, strike and separate, and shuffle back to the original depth. Then the coach will point at a blocker, on one side or the other, who will try to block us at an angle. We want to club over the top, get our hips out and around, and then we will shuffle back for the next part of the drill.

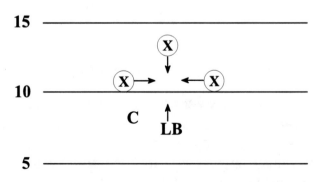

Diagram #3. Angle Strike Drill

TACKLING PHILOSOPHY

Tackling is the most visible attribute a defensive player can display. It does not matter how fast you run, how hard you hit, how great a pass rusher or pass defender you are, without the ability to tackle with confidence and control, you will not be considered a great player. Conversely, be known and respected as a force on the defensive unit.

WHAT MAKES A GREAT TACKLER?

As previously discussed, outstanding physical ability is not essential. What is essential is an intense burning desire and determination to get to the ballcarrier and bring him down to the ground in the most advantageous manner for the defense.

TACKLING AXIOMS

There are certain physical constants in outstanding tackling that we must always emphasize. We want chest and eyes up, a low pad level, and Zs in the knees. In making contact, we want the eyes across the bow, we want to strike on the rise, and explode the hips and eyes on contact. When ready to tackle, we want to take one more step, wrap arms, dig fingers into cloth, drive our feet, and square our hips.

FORM TACKLE

We want to close on the ball with the proper attack angle. In the open field, we will break down with low pad level, but if not in the open field, we will attack on the rise with low pad level. Our eyes are up and across the bow. We explode our eyes on contact, wrap up and lock fingers, and dig into cloth. Finally, we want to drive our hips and keep driving until ballcarrier is down.

RUN-DOWN-THE-LINE DRILL

In the run-down-the-line drill, we want the running back to change speeds three different times (Diagram #4). We want to go at walk speed, jog speed, and run speed. We want our linebackers to stay half a man behind the ballcarrier. They keep their shoulders square at walk and jog speeds, and they have to turn their hips at run speed. However, we want them to keep that half-man angle.

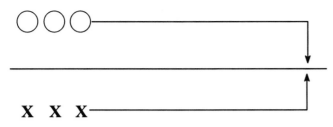

Diagram #4. Run-Down-the-Line Drill

SIDELINE TACKLE DRILL

In the sideline tackle drill, we are working to keep a good angle and use the sideline as our friend (Diagram #5). We use a one-cutback rule on this drill. We go at about three-quarters to half speed, and we are about seven yards from the sideline.

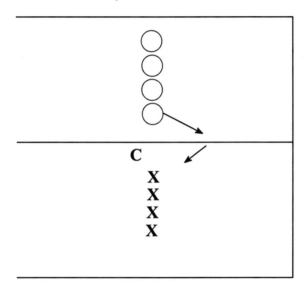

Diagram #5. Sideline Tackle Drill

We do several other tackling drills, which I will just briefly describe. We do an Arbuckle drill, which is an open-field tackling drill. It starts 10 yards apart. At five yards, the ballcarrier makes a move right, left, or straight ahead. We run this drill at half speed.

Our skate drill is like the strike progression. The linebacker has to take on a blocker at the line of scrimmage, who is trying to hook him. Then, he works outside and plays upfield through a second blocker, who is coming out of the backfield at about five yards. The third guy is the ballcarrier, and we take him on at about 45 degrees. This is a good drill in preparation for option teams.

The last tackling drill I want to mention is the score drill. This is a competitive, open-field tackling drill. We just face off a ballcarrier and a tackler across a line. The ballcarrier can move back and forth, then take off, and he tries to score across a line within a five-yard area. It is a lot of fun for our players.

PASS DROPS

In our pass coverage, we are a spot-drop team. We like to spot-drop and then find work. We drop our inside and outside linebackers at a 45-degree angle, with the head on a swivel, looking for inside threats first. We want good communication with our defense. When the quarterback settles, we backpedal out.

On a three-step drop, we drop at 45 degrees, and as soon as the quarterback settles, then we backpedal. On the five- or seven-step drop, it is the same thing. It is just a bigger angle picture, and then we settle.

Our first drill is a simple spot-drop drill. We set up four cones at the depth and angles we want. We drop our four linebackers toward them, with the coach simulating quarterback action. We follow up on that drill with a break-to-the-ball drill. The coach will go ahead and throw the ball to one of the linebacker areas. We want to make sure on this that the other three linebackers are transitioning on the interception.

We do a drill we call "reading the third key" (Diagram #6). The first key is always the line. The second key is the backfield, and the third key is the quarterback. We start with a three-step drop, and we get our angles in a walk-through. We work on a five- to seven-step drop and get our angles. We work on a sprint-out and keeping our angles.

Our outside linebacker on the playside is pushing to the deep flat. Our inside linebacker on that side pushes deep curl, and he will force if the quarterback breaks containment. The backside inside linebacker mirrors the quarterback, and the backside outside linebacker covers what we call "trail dig."

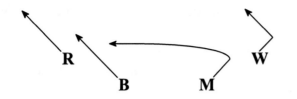

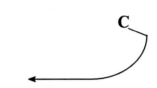

Diagram #6. Reading the Third Key Drill

SECOND KEY READ DRILLS

Next are the second key read drills that we do. We read trap, belly, zone, counter gap, toss, and then pass and draw.

Guard vs. Trap (Diagram #7)

Also run to other side.

Coaching Point: Mike and Backer must fill quickly.

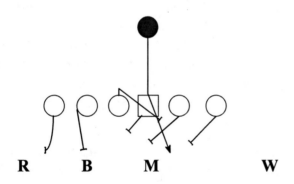

Diagram #7. Guard vs. Trap

Guard vs. Belly and Reach (Diagram #8)

Also run to weakside.

Coaching Point: Mike and Whip should watch their backside leverage.

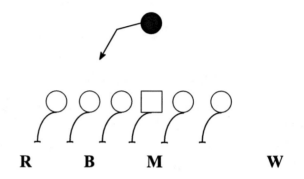

Diagram #8. Guard vs. Belly and Reach

Guard vs. Controlled Trap (Diagram #9)

Also run to weakside.

Coaching Point: Watch for Backer and Mike biting on backs' first steps.

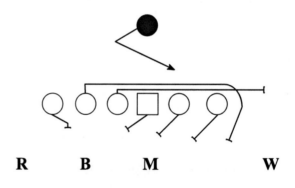

Diagram #9. Guard vs. Controlled Trap

Guard vs. Toss With Crack (Diagram #10)

Coaching Point: Whip must force quickly or get cracked.

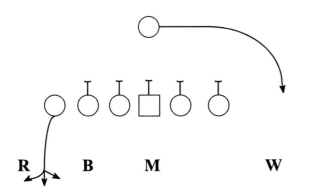

Diagram #10. Guard vs. Toss With Crack

Guard vs. Pass (Diagram #11)

Coaching Point: Look for proper drop angles of 45 degrees. Emphasize derouting the tight end, and communicate crossing route by yelling out, "Cross, cross."

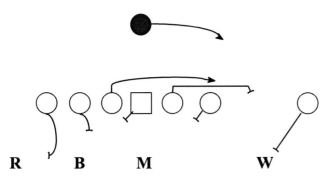

Diagram #11. Guard vs. Pass

Guard vs. Draw (Diagram #12)

Coaching Point: Look at reaction to pass and then run reads.

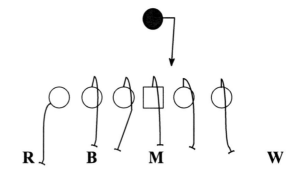

Diagram #12. Guard vs. Draw

We do this group work every day. Of course, we emphasize the plays and blocking schemes that we are preparing for that particular week. We have a lot of good game film, which shows the impact of these drills on our linebacker play.

Thank you for your attention.

Shawn Berner

THE COMPLETE OPTION GAME

Fort Campbell High School, Kentucky

First, let me thank Coach Browning and the Nike clinic people for allowing me the opportunity to talk to you guys. It is a real honor to speak in front of a lot of great coaches.

We have great kids at Fort Campbell. It is a unique place. It is the home of the 101st Airborne Division in the United States Army, and you all know the special work that they have done for our country in recent years.

Our situation is also unique. I have no affiliation with the military at all, but I took the coaching job there right during the 9/11 situation, and to see the transition of the Army and the way our kids handled things then was absolutely amazing. Without a doubt, it is because of the kinds of kids we have and the types of players they are that has allowed us to be successful coaches. Not only are they good athletes on the field, but they are also high-character kids. They believe in what we tell them, and they make it a truly rewarding place to work.

I am going to talk today on our stretch play and how we adjust our offensive scheme to fit our personnel. I will show you some of the drills we use to prepare to run our zone option stuff. I will talk about the way we run the outside zone and show you how we incorporate our inside zone, outside zone, and some other things in one particular drill. Finally, I will show you a few of the complementary things we do off of the outside zone.

Incorporating the zone play a couple of years ago was one of the best things we ever did, and I am going to talk about the reasons why. Before, we found ourselves constantly trying to outscheme people and come up with creative ways to put the football in our athletes' hands. Now, over the last couple of years with the zone scheme, we are able to simplify more than ever from what we had been doing before. Before, I never was a zone guy, but now, I am only a zone guy, so to speak.

We are a spread offensive team. Often, when you see a spread offensive team you think that is a team that is going to throw the football a lot, but that is not our philosophy. We rushed for over 4000 yards and threw for over 2000, but our passing game is not a vertical passing game at all. What we do in the run game opens up some of our screens and our quick passing game, but we averaged 412 yards per game, and the majority of our yardage came off of this particular stretch play I am going to talk about.

First, I think you have to develop a philosophy. With our military situation, we sometimes have a kind of revolving door with our kids, and sometimes, we do not know exactly who will be there. What we are doing allows us to have very simple rules, especially with our offensive line. You will see with some of our other plays that we are going to be able to run the exact same thing with different plays and in different ways, so it creates simplicity for us in our offense.

It also saves us scheme time. We meet on Saturdays now and get our game plans made in much less time than before. During the week, the same is true for practice planning, so it keeps us fresher and gives us more time for other things.

Our scheme allows us to control the football. My mentality is that we want to run the ball first, we want to run the ball second, and we want to run the ball third. We want to run the football. We do throw it some, but essentially, we are a running team and our scheme allows us to do that. With our zone-blocking scheme, we are essentially a triple-option offense, but now doing it in a different way.

In our philosophy, we want to utilize our athletes as much as possible, especially our quarterback. He will always be one of our best athletes on the field. Unlike most of the under-center offenses, in our scheme, the quarterback is in the gun and he is a threat on every single play. In addition to that, our tailback is a threat on every single play, and our slot receivers are also a threat on every single play as well.

We use multiple formations and various motions to move these guys around and get them the football in different ways while staying within the simplicity of the scheme and staying exclusively in the shotgun set. At the same time, that simplicity allows us more practice repetitions.

In our shotgun formations, a one-back set has the firepower of a traditional two-back set because the quarterback in the gun position can assume the role of a running back. In essence, he becomes a bonus player. Beyond that, we actually gain an additional one-player advantage because we do not have to block certain people in the zone-read play. It is an added bonus to our offense that those players we do not have to block are the edge players, who are usually among the best and most physical players on the defensive line.

The last point to be made about our scheme has to do with tempo. We are a no-huddle team, and we can set a tempo that can put a defense back on its heels. We have several things that we do.

We will "sight adjust" the offense at the line of scrimmage and run what we call a regular tempo, or we can run what we call a speed tempo. Where our opponents have huddled their defense all season, now, they cannot huddle. It forces different practice habits for them and a tempo they are not comfortable in. It also allows us to get tons of offensive practice reps in, literally hundreds of reps, during our practices. I will be happy to give details of all that in the breakout session that follows. We used to be a big gap-blocking team. We used the down-down-kick scheme along with the inside trap, the speed option, and that type of stuff. I was against the zone play because of penetration.

We tried every spring for the past five years to run the zone play, and we studied how others ran it, but when we ran the inside zone, the 1 technique would penetrate, hit us in the mouth, and it was a done play. After about two days of practice, I would give up on it and we would go back to a gap-blocking scheme.

Finally, we visited West Virginia and we visited Western Kentucky. We took a lot of the things they do, tweaked them to fit our personnel, and now, the way we run it allows for penetration not to affect the mesh of the play or the reads. I am going to talk more about that later on.

When you run the zone-read scheme out of a shotgun formation, the shotgun snap has got to be in the strike zone. That is one of the most important elements of the play. Off-target snaps will distract the quarterback and hinder his reads.

This scheme also causes you to create different practice habits and come up with different drills. We run the old two-ball drill that we once used when we ran some option from underneath, but now, we use it with the shotgun snaps to run the inside zone, outside zone, and other parts of our offense. We can do all that in our group period and get a lot of things accomplished. I have some of that on film for you.

This is our stretch play versus the 4-4 defense (Diagram #1). You can see that we are in two-back, but we will run it out of everything you can possibly think of. We will run regular stretch out of two-back and out of one-back, we will use motion to run it, and we will use different tight end formations. We will also run a quarterback stretch out of empty, which I will also show you.

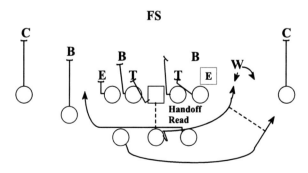

Diagram #1. Stretch vs. 4-4 Defense

What we are doing is running the old triple option. That is all it is. We are zoning everything to the left, we are reading the backside 5 technique, and the triple is coming off of the outside Will backer.

I want to talk first about some of the drills that we have come up with. I take the quarterbacks first. We work through a progression of just steps, reads, and throws, and then, we will come together as a group and do our two-ball drills where we work quarterbacks, running backs, and receivers all in one drill that emphasizes mechanics and scheme.

In this first setup, I have the three quarterbacks that I work with (Diagram #2). I have one snapping, the number one quarterback is up first, and my freshman quarterback is back here. I stand just outside the dummy, and if I have an extra defender, I will put him at outside backer and use him to read the triple.

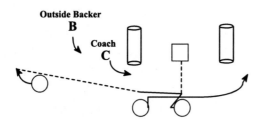

Diagram #2. Quarterback Bubble Mechanics Drill

All we are trying to do here is work on steps and making simple throws. The way we run the triple off of the outside zone play is the bubble screen to the slot, away from the zone. I will just put the younger kid out there and let him simulate the bubble route.

There are several steps to the quarterback's technique that we teach. His eyes are up as he secures the snap, and his first step is with the opposite foot back just to get off the mesh. He gets the ball to the front hip, rides it to the back hip, and then, shuffles out and throws the bubble. While he is doing that, I am just holding up a number. He has to tell me that number so I know his eyes are on me the whole time. I will talk more about his technique as we get into the actual scheme. That is one of our individual drills that we do with our quarterbacks.

After that, we will come together for a two-ball drill. I will bring up our receivers coach with his guys, and we will work on one side of the ball together with the running backs and quarterbacks. On the defensive side of the ball, we will have our defensive backs coach and our linebackers coach along with their players.

Now, one thing we have done that I think is really important is to take the philosophy that we are going to put our best guys on defense. We have finally gotten to a point in our program where we have enough kids that we can take kids that are maybe not quite as aggressive, maybe not our very best football players, and bring them over to offense. That creates two platoons for us.

Of course, we do not two-platoon every single person on the field because we just do not have that kind of personnel, but the way we structure our practice allows us to keep one kid on one side of the ball as much as possible. I mention that now because, when I get into this drill, I have my starting defensive personnel over on defense working against our two-ball drill (Diagram #3). I think, for obvious reasons, that has made us a better team. Here is what the drill looks like on film.

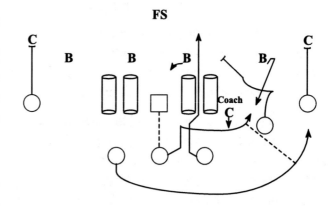

Diagram #3. Blast, Two-Ball Drill

The two inside backers are not going to work a lot of stuff, but the outside guys can get some good work. The receivers and corners are working stalk blocking the whole time, and then, the safety is going to run the alley and get a look.

What you see first here is our inside zone, which we call blast. The back who is running the inside zone is our F-back, and the back running the pitch route is our H-back. We will flex our F-back in and out of the backfield so he has to be one of our better athletes.

On our inside zone play, we are running a backside-A/backside-B read, so what you see here is blast left, and we actually hit it on the backside. I talked about penetration earlier, and this is why we run it on the backside. If the 1 technique penetrates, he does not become a factor. In fact, we want to run it to the 1 technique if we can.

In this drill, we are getting running back reads on the inside and pitch reads on the outside. The F-back reads the inside backer for his A-to–B-gap cut. I hand the quarterback a second ball, and he and the H-back run the pitch read off of the outside backer. Our quarterback is not getting the handoff read from a 5 technique in this drill. We have already gone through that drill as far as getting his eyes up. We will progress to that, and he will get more work on it during inside period and also during team period.

Now, one thing we do, probably differently than most option teams, involves our pitch mechanics for the quarterback. We do not pitch with one hand because we have had so many inconsistent pitches in the past. Several years ago when we visited Western Kentucky, they were teaching the two-hand basketball chest pass. We thought that was a more consistent way to do it, so that is what we have done since, and it has improved our ball security.

If we go to the right to pitch the ball, we have the ball securely in both hands up high, we step with the right foot, and we pitch chest to chest. We extend our arms with thumbs down, and then, we trail the football just as is done with the one-handed pitch.

Here are a couple more reps of the drill and you can see that our coaches will mix up the reads, we will run it in both directions, and we will alternate our kids through the drill. We spend a lot of time with our kids on this film. At the end of the day, we bring this in and try to make sure that we are all coached up.

Notice, on that inside zone, I was on the line of scrimmage just off the bag for the two-ball drill.

Now, this is our outside zone, and the way we create the triple option on it is to throw the bubble screen (Diagram #4). To work the two-ball part of this drill, I just come up high and hand it to him quicker so he can avoid bobbling the ball and stay in rhythm.

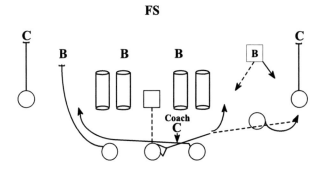

Diagram #4. Stretch, Two-Ball Drill

The quarterback steps back and then slides with the running back. As they mesh, the ball tip goes up and down. In this drill, obviously, he hands the ball off every time, and I give him the second ball to throw. The coaching point for the quarterback is to ride back hip to front hip and snap the football.

If he is a right-handed quarterback, he has to flop his hips around to square himself, and then, he has to sprint for three steps high. He has to stay up three steps past the mesh, and that is one of the keys to this play because of the threat of penetrating defensive linemen. Off of that third step, he throws the screen, right foot to left foot. For a right-handed kid throwing to the left side, he makes a crossover step off of the mesh, then goes three steps, and throws.

He is reading the outside backer to make the throw or keep the ball. So, he has to make the choice by the third step to keep the advantage we gained from the misdirection that the play provides. If the outside backer turns his shoulders to the outside at all, the quarterback is pulling the ball down and running. If he just sits in no man's land and shuffles his feet, the quarterback will throw the bubble because our slots can outrun the outside backer once he gains that relationship. That is how we teach the read.

Now, this is just the one-ball drill that we run (Diagram #5). It is a misdirection off of our stretch play where we are pitching off of the 5 technique. I will go through that in more detail in the breakout session.

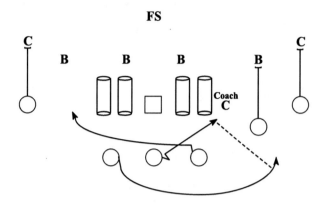

Diagram #5. Stretch, One-Ball Drill

After we do these group drills, I will bring the offensive line down and we will mesh with them for five minutes, mainly working gap scheme (Diagram #6). We will work against the same personnel that we had in the previous drills, adding two 5 techniques to the drill but no other down linemen. It is still a kind of group drill for us.

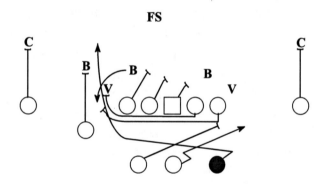

Diagram #6. Mesh With Offensive Line

All we are doing here is working reads with our quarterbacks, and we are also working different ways of running the gap play, whether it is counter or dart. We will play games with the defensive guys and make sure that we are kicking and sealing against the various looks they can give us.

On our stretch play, the quarterback, the H-back, and the F-back all align their heels at six yards. The running backs put their outside foot on the inside foot of the tackle, or we may put a faster back all the way behind the tackle. I have one back

who is really fast, and to get the mesh the way we want it, he has to bump out over the tackle because we want to go full speed when we mesh on the stretch play.

Our X- and Z-receivers in the spread alignment will normally align on the bottom of the numbers on the shortside of the field and the top of the numbers on the wideside. The Y- and F-receivers in the slots will split the difference between the #1 receiver and the offensive tackle. These are our normal spacing rules.

The splits of our offensive linemen will go from one foot to two feet, based upon who we are playing. In this regard, we would consider their athleticism and their style of play.

On the stretch play, we teach the quarterback to step off the mesh because we teach the running back to run through the quarterback's heels. The quarterback then rides the running back from front hip to back hip.

When we first started running this play, we would teach the quarterback to read the 5 technique, but we started seeing all kinds of games being played off the edge by the defense. So, we started teaching him to just read the C-gap defender. We do not read a guy, we just read the C gap.

The H-back steps lateral, opens, and goes right through the quarterback's heels. When he gets the ball, he goes three steps past the mesh on the same plane, and that is a big key in the success we have had with the play. We want to get it to the 1 technique, but that does not always happen. We often end up running it toward a 3 technique and a 5 technique who are trying to penetrate and get upfield. In the past, we taught the ballcarrier to work downhill, sink it into the tackle's tail, and then, make a read. That did not work so well against penetration.

Now, with our running back, we go three steps past the mesh on the same plane, and we read the tackle's hat. If the tackle can hook up, we are getting downhill and reading the block of the slot and making the cut off of the second defender in.

If our tackle cannot hook up, and 9 times out of 10 he cannot, then, we stick the outside foot in the ground and we are working cutback right now. Then, the next thing we are looking for is the second-down defender, the defensive tackle who is covered up by our guard.

If our guard can hook up, we are banging the B gap right now. If the guard is kicking, we have faith that our backside guys are doing their jobs, and we are banging it all the way back. This is almost an inside run for us. Even though we call it outside zone, we run this in our inside period because, probably 9 times out of 10, it hits in the B gap or to the backside. We can bang it all the way back because the quarterback's read removes the C-gap defender from the play.

If we are in a two-back set, our F-back steps at 45 degrees and also reads the hat of the tackle. He is the lead blocker. If the tackle hooks up, he is going to the edge player or force player. We would like for him to hook up too, but, if not, he gets a hat on a hat and creates lanes. If the tackle kicks, then we are banging the B gap, and we will likely double-up on the Sam or Mike backer.

Our slot away runs bubble screen, and the wideout on his side blocks bubble screen. The wide receiver on the side of the zone simply stalk blocks the cornerback, and that is it.

The offensive line has a couple of different techniques. We do not teach the inside zone the same way we teach the outside zone, so I am talking outside zone here. If we get a playside shade, we are going to step laterally on the same plane, actually four inches laterally and climbing four inches, or 4x4. Then, we are going to go three steps. We will fight three steps, get to that third step, turn, and create a running lane. We will run him all the way to the sideline if we cannot hook up on him, and if he gets a little penetration, we are still okay with that.

Against a backside shade, we do what we call a pop step. We do a pop step, skate, and get up to the next level as the backside technique works underneath the block.

If we are uncovered, we will drop laterally and lose ground to gain ground in the zone scheme. Then, on the backside, if we have a 3 technique, we will just make a *come-through* call and cut him off with our backside tackle because we want the backside guard getting up on the backside backer for the cutback play.

Now, I want to show you some video and you can see how this thing works.

I think my time is up now. I will be happy to answer any questions you may have in the breakout session. Thank you.

PLAY-ACTION PASSES OFF THE ZONE OPTION

Greenville High School, Alabama

It is good to be here today. Greenville High School is located in a low-income county in Alabama about 40 miles south of Montgomery. We are in the 5A classification. The top class is 6A in Alabama. The enrollment of our school is in the middle to low in our classification. I have been there two years. During the nine previous years, they have had their ups and downs. They did win a state championship in 1994. When they got to 2000, they had some rocky roads. They had a number of turnovers in the head coaching position. I took the job in July of my first year, and I am beginning my third year as head coach.

I hope you can get something out of this lecture. What we do, we feel we do well. I do not profess to know everything. I have been coming to clinics since 1995. I father ran the Nike Clinic in Birmingham before we moved the Nike Mid-South Clinic to Tunica. I started coming to the clinics when I was a senior in high school to learn football.

In 1996, I remember sitting in the back of the room listening to Hayden Fry speak. At that time, I did not know if I wanted to be a coach. He said something that caught my attention. He said, "There are two kinds of coaches. There are those who want to be called a coach, and then there are those that want to coach." Those that just want to be called "Coach" are the ones you see sitting in the halls, talking to their friends. They are in the casino gambling and are always looking for other jobs. They never seem to want to learn and improve their knowledge of the game. That is why I appreciate you being here today. You are trying to learn and want to coach football.

We try to be good in everything we do, but we have not seen the results we would like to see. We keep working every day to improve. It is not the X's

and O's that make you successful. It is the people you have on the field playing for you. I learned that the hard way.

When I went into the job with the offense we were using, we were going to be good. We ran the West Coast offense and struggled. We simplified what we were doing. We are in the shotgun spread, but we have only five running plays and one protection. We use that protection in all of our passing game. You can learn a great deal, but what you have to do is get something that fits your program and do it well.

A turning point in my life occurred at this clinic. I met Dennis Parker, and it changed the way I looked at coaching. He talked to me about character education. He talked about what players need to be successful. They need a male role model. In Greenville, Alabama, the mothers run the home. There are not many male role models for the players to follow. We use the program that Dennis Parker advocates. We talk to our players every day about some important topics in their life. To me, football is more than a game. We have to teach our players how to be men. I feel we are doing that.

I got a technique from Coach Jeff Tedford from the University of California. I listened to him speak at this clinic last year. I coach the quarterbacks at Greenville, and this is something you can do with them. In the off-season, he plays checkers with his quarterback. He takes a checkers set, uses a white marker, and writes the positions of the offense and defense on them. He sits his quarterback down and gives him the red checkers, which are offensive positions.

He takes the black checkers, which are the defensive positions. The quarterback lines his checkers up in an offensive formation. Coach Tedford lines up the black checkers in a defensive alignment. They run a play, using the checkers. He moves his checkers around and asks the quarterback what he does in each situation. I started doing that, and it worked well with our quarterbacks.

OFFENSIVE PHILOSOPHY

Let me talk about our philosophy. I know coaches do not like to hear other coaches talk on philosophy, but this is what we are trying to do.

- Force the defense to defend the entire field.
- Use the triple and double option to keep the defense honest.
- Utilize screens and draws.
- Effectively throw the ball off play-action, quick game, and sprint pass.

Our offensive philosophy is simple. We believe we have to run the football first before we can throw the ball. We feel we must run the triple and double options along with some kind of jet sweep. We try to get the defense going one way and run back the other way. When we started to run the option game, the defense did not blitz us as much. We use the play-action pass, quick game, and sprint pass. This year, we did not throw a straight dropback pass.

2008 Offensive Statistics

- Rushing: 396 carries for 2,548 yards (6.4 per carry)
- Passing: 110 completions of 190 attempts for 1,593 Yards (62 percent)
- Total: 4,141 yards / 11 games = 378 yards per game and 32 points per game

When I was the quarterback coach at Opelika High School, I used to challenge our quarterbacks to throw for 60 percent pass completions. Sixty-two percent is a high percentage when you throw the football. Our quarterback next year is a two-year starter. He started as a sophomore and again last year. He runs the 40 in 5.0 and was our leading passer and rusher. He is not very fast, but he makes the right decisions.

The first year we came into the program, we overloaded the players with a new offense. We tried to do too much. This past season, we had 12 seniors on the team. Of the 12, only three of them had played football from the 9th grade through the 12th grade. We had six first-year seniors play on last year's team. We have reloaded the program. We have 111 players and 26 seniors coming back. We return 16 starters from last year's team.

Our base runs are zone, stretch, dart, speed option, and midline option. We are a shotgun team. We went under the center one time last year, and that was a quarterback sneak. We run the zone play, but we are actually running the triple option (Diagram #1). We read the zone play and run the triple option with motion or two backs in the backfield.

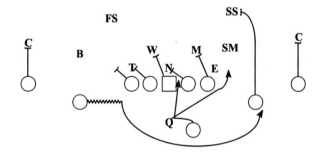

Diagram #1. Zone

We also tag the play and run the bubble screen as part of the play. We picked up that series from Fort Campbell gh everything they did. We installed it this past year, and it was one of our better plays.

We block back with everyone on the callside of the play. We try to build a wall to the backside. The important thing for them to do is not let anyone cross their face. The back opens up and aims at the onside leg of the center. The back presses the A gap. If he feels pressure, he has to be prepared to cut the play back. The quarterback reads the man over the playside offensive tackle. If he steps down the line of scrimmage, he pulls the ball and runs the triple option with the Sam linebacker as the pitch key. We call this a zone play, but it is the veer out of the shotgun.

We can motion the slotback as the pitch man or align him in the backfield. We can use the slot receiver to the callside as the pitch man. We snap the ball, and the slot backs up, delays, and becomes the pitchback. We can run the scheme for the pitchback a number of different ways.

We call the play 35 zone, even though the play goes to the right. The five tells the offensive linemen to step to the left. In the beginning, we veer released the playside tackle for the linebacker. As we got better at running the play, the defense tightened the defensive tackle down to prevent the tackle from veer releasing on the linebacker. We told our tackle to take the best release. If he can get inside, he goes inside. If he cannot get inside, he releases behind the defensive tackle for the linebacker. He jab-steps inside and arc releases behind the defender. That gives the defender a clear shot at the running back, but the quarterback pulls the ball and runs the triple option. With the tight tackle alignment, the option becomes a double option because we do not get the read on the back.

The stretch play we run comes from West Virginia (Diagram #2). I listened to Rick Trickett talk about the blocking and backfield mechanics. We installed that play also. On the stretch, the playside tackle will determine where the back runs the ball. We want the offensive tackle to reach the defender. We tell the back he must stay high for three steps. He reads the tackle's butt. If his butt is outside, we run the ball to the outside. If his butt is inside, we cut it back.

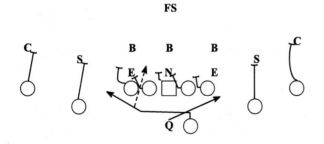

Diagram #2. Stretch

The defense in the diagram is a 3-3 stack. The playside guard and tackle zone for the outside stack. The tackle reaches on the down lineman. If he goes inside, the tackle steps up for the linebacker.

The guard zone steps for the down lineman. If he comes inside, the guard blocks him. If the linebacker blitzes the B gap, the guard blocks him.

We teach the back to bounce, bang, or bing his cut. He bounces the ball to the outside if he reads that the tackle has reached the outside. He bangs it into the hole if he reads the tackle's butt inside. If he bings the ball, he goes backside with the run. The back is making one cut and not dancing around trying to find a hole. He cannot get in a hurry to cut the ball up. He has to be patient and let the blocking develop. When we ran this play in the spring, the best gains came on the cutback play. The back's aiming point is the inside leg of the tackle.

The running back's alignment on the zone play is in the B gap. We widen him somewhat on the stretch play. He straddles the inside leg of the tackle. We try to spread the defense with a double slot or trips formation.

If we run the play with two backs in the backfield, the playside back reads the same thing the ballcarrier sees. If the tackle's butt goes outside, he goes outside and blocks the force on the run. If the tackle's butt goes inside, he has to get inside and isolate on the linebacker.

We tell the playside tackle to reach to the outside. If on his third step he does not have the defender reached, he jams his inside hand on the hips of the defender and runs him to the sideline. If he can do that, it creates a gap for the back to cut.

We align the quarterback with his toes at five yards from the line of scrimmage. The tailback lines up on the heels of the quarterback. When he steps to receive the ball, he uses a J-step. That puts him on the proper angle to receive the ball. He steps forward at about a 45-degree angle to get in front of the quarterback. The quarterback drops the leg to the side of the running back to give him room to make the mesh. This allows the quarterback a one-step ride on the tailback.

If the quarterback finds the backside defender closing hard down the line of scrimmage, he can pull the ball. We tag the play and give him two options.

He can run the ball out the backside or throw the bubble to the inside slot receivers.

We had a wide receiver with decent speed. We began to bring him in motion and run the jet sweep using the stretch blocking scheme. We run the dart play and the speed option. We felt if we were going to run the triple option to the outside, we had to put add the midline to give us an inside option play.

We read the zero-technique player on the center all the way outside to the 3 technique on the offensive guard. We have to teach the backs the aiming point on the different alignments. The blocking and mechanics are the same.

Showing you the base runs allows you to understand our passing game. The two base runs are the zone and the stretch. Our play-action passes are based on those runs.

We have one pass protection we use on all passes.

PROTECTION

- 200: Half slide right; #1 and #2 on the left; back fills inside-out off the play-action.
- 300: Half slide left; #1 and #2 on the right; back fills inside-out off the play-action.
- 34/35: Back will fake zone.
- 36/37: Back will fake stretch.

We call different plays in our passing game, but we protect only one way. The protection concept is the same. If we call 234, the center right guard and tackle slide protect to the right (Diagram #3). They are responsible for the A, B, and C gaps to that side in a zone-protection scheme. On the backside, the guard and tackle block the first and second man on the line of scrimmage. To the backside, the #1 on the line is anything head-up on the center to the outside. We block big-on-big. The running back is set to the left of the quarterback. He fakes the 34 zone play and blocks the left side of the protection. He is picking up linebackers on a blitz.

If we call 237, the protection is the same thing to the other side (Diagram #4). The center left guard and tackle slide protect to the left. The right guard

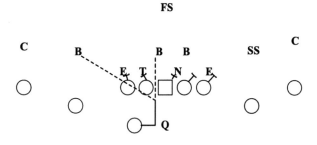

Diagram #3. Protection 234

and tackle block big-on-big on the line of scrimmage. The center calls the defensive set of the defense. He calls the set by verbally calling out 4-2, or 4-3, or 3-3, or whatever the front they are playing. The running back aligns to the left of the quarterback, fakes the 37 stretch, and blocks to the right side of the line.

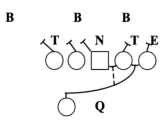

Diagram #4. Protection 237

If the center has a nose aligned on him, he blocks him if he slants into his frontside gap. If he slants into the backside gap, he belongs to the guard. He punches the nose to slow down his reaction to the backside if that is the way he is going. However, his gap is to the playside and not backside. In the play-action, the line takes one play-action step before they start into their protection scheme. We do not full slide because of the size our backs. A full slide puts that small back on a defensive end.

We are a double- or triple-formation team, which eliminates a lot of the running backs' blocking. We always want the backs to block from the inside out. If a back gets a two-linebacker blitz, he blocks inside first. If the linebacker walks up into the backside B gap, we give a "danger" call. On that call, the tackle blocks down on the linebacker, and the back takes the first to the outside. That is the only time we have a back on a defensive lineman.

To the backside, we pass off line stunts. If the guard's defensive tackle loops to the outside, he lets him go and sets for the defender coming to the inside. If the tackle's man slants down on the guard, he rides him until the guard takes over and then reacts back outside.

I am going to ask our passing game coach take you through our passing game. He was a great player, and he is a great coach. He was the all-time leading receiver at Jacksonville State University. I am proud to have him as our wide receivers coach, and he coordinates our passing game. Here is Joey Hamilton.

JOEY HAMILTON

There are three main points I want to touch on. I am going to go over the routes we use in the play-action passing game. The second thing is an abbreviated version of how we teach those patterns. The third thing is to look at the cut-ups of these routes.

The first play is our 234 slant (Diagram #5). The quarterback action is the 34 zone play to the right. This is a double slant into the trips side. Our goal on this pattern is to put some defender in a bind. We align in a trips set to the right. The first inside receiver runs a bubble pattern to the outside. The middle slot runs a two-step slant pattern to the inside. The outside receiver runs a four-step slant to the inside. The player we want to put in the bind is the strong safety or the flat defender.

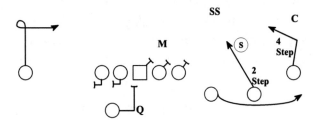

Diagram #5. 234 Slant

If the strong safety jumps the bubble route, we throw the first slant behind him. The middle slot runs his two-step slant at the strong safety. If the strong safety sits on the slant, the outside slant is open. The backside pattern can be a tag call or a pivot in route.

If the quarterback gets a bad snap or reads the blitz coming from the outside, he does not fake the zone and gets the ball out of his hands immediately.

The second pattern is 234 switch go (Diagram #6). This pattern is a four-vertical route. We teach landmarks on the vertical routes. The outside receivers are running on the bottom of numbers, and the inside receivers are up the hash marks. When we run switch and go, we switch the responsibilities of the inside and outside receivers. The outside receiver goes first, and the inside receiver comes underneath him. When they get 10 yards down the field, they should be on their landmarks.

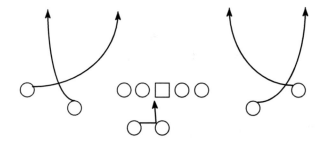

Diagram #6. 234 Switch Go

This is a good pattern against one high safety. If it is cover-1 man, we get the natural run with the switch of the receivers. With one high safety, the quarterback is thinking inside seam pattern. With two high safeties, he has to read the field.

The 237/336 pop is a backside throwback (Diagram #7). The action is the stretch play. We like this pattern against two safeties. We want the backside slot or tight end to get between the two safeties in the middle of the field. If there is one safety, the receiver wants to run away from that safety. We are pushing deep with all the other patterns. If we are in a 3x1 look, we want the action away from the formation, and hit the middle slot on the post route. The inside slot in a trips set runs the bubble route.

As soon as the pop receiver comes off the line of scrimmage, he has to read the safeties. If it was a two-safety look at pre-snap, they may roll the coverage. If the coverage stays two-deep, he wants to get down the middle between the safeties. If they roll out of the two-coverage look

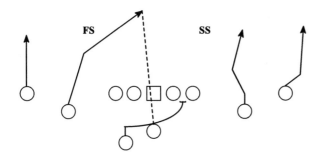

Diagram #7. 237 Pop

into a three-deep coverage, he wants to work away from the single safety, going to the middle of the field.

The 237 jet post/wheel is designed off our jet sweep action (Diagram #8). In the diagram, we run it from the trips set right with the inside slot running the jet motion. The single receiver runs a post cut at the corner, hoping to take him inside. The jet motion comes out of the backfield and runs a wheel route up the field. The middle slot receiver runs an inside dig, and the outside receiver runs a go route.

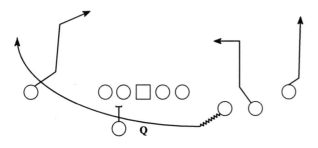

Diagram #8. 237 Jet Post/Wheel

We throw the bubble pass to the backside of the play-action pass. This play is 36 bubble (Diagram #9). The wide receiver blocks the man over him, and we throw the ball on the play-action to the slot receiver. This can be a tagged play off a running play. The ball is thrown behind the line of scrimmage, so it does not matter if anyone gets down field. At the beginning of the season, I called 336 bubble. At the end of the season, I called 36 bubble, and the quarterback could read the play off the backside defensive end. If the end closed on the stretch play, the quarterback pulled the ball and ran the bubble pass.

When the receiver runs the bubble, he can stay flat to the line of scrimmage toward the sideline. He does not have to belly back to run the pattern. If he

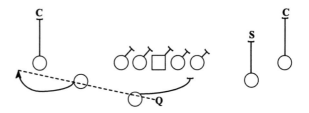

Diagram #9. 36 Bubble

catches the ball, we want him one yard behind the line of scrimmage. We coach him to open, take three steps, and look for the ball.

The last play is the 36 slip (Diagram #10). The outside receiver takes three steps down the field and retraces his steps. The inside receiver pushes three vertical steps up the field and blocks the corner. The playside tackle blocks his assignment and releases for the flat defender. The offense line and backs are running the 36 stretch play.

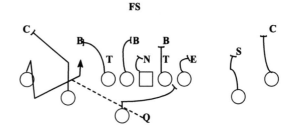

Diagram #10. 36 Slip

When we start to teach the receivers, we go back to the basics. We teach stance, start, and release. In our stance, we align with our outside foot back. When we leave the line of scrimmage, we explode off the ball and make up the cushion on the defensive back as quickly as we can.

When I teach the receiver, the first thing I have to teach him is how to get off the line of scrimmage. If the defender presses the wide receiver, he can take three releases. The first one is a single-move release. On that move, all he does is jab-step to the inside or outside before he releases. If he is going to the outside, he jab-steps to the inside and gets his outside release. As soon as the receiver gets his release, he gets back on top of the defender and gets back on his line.

The next release is the double release. We align with our outside foot back in our stance. On the double release, he fakes to the outside on the first step, fakes to the inside on his second step, swims over the defender, and gets back on his line. I hope you understand this is not all we do. This is an abbreviated version of some of the things we teach.

The third release is to drive hard at a 45-degree angle to get the defender to move his hips. That allows the receiver to get across the defender's path and back on his line.

If you need anything, let us know. If you want to stay around and talk, we will be around. I appreciate your attention. Thank you.

STAFF ORGANIZATION AND PLANNING

Cherry Creek High School, Colorado

Coaching at Cherry Creek High School is a very unique situation for me. My father is a former head football coach at Cherry Creek. In addition, he is on the staff with me now. I am the head coach in both football and basketball. I have been the head basketball coach for 18 years. We are the largest high school in the state, and we play in the highest class in sports in the state.

I do want to give you a few points about my background. I did play quarterback at Cherry Creek High School. My dad was my coach. He has been a head coach for 25 years. I am lucky to have him on my staff as I said before. Because of my background and the passion I have for Cherry Creek is part of the reason I accepted the challenge of being the head coach of both major sports. It is a very unique situation at Cherry Creek. I know there are a few grads of Cherry Creek that are here today that are head coaches at other area schools. I am sure they could tell you that Cherry Creek is a different place to be as a student, teacher, or a coach.

When you look at Cherry Creek from the outside in, you can list several things that set Cherry Creek apart from other schools. I will tell you from the beginning, we do have a lot going for us even as seen by outsiders. We have a great deal of advantages. But I think the biggest advantage we have is the fact that our school and our community demand excellence in every area of our school. They do not cheat athletics, they do not cheat activities, and they do not cheat academics. I think this is important in the backing we receive from our administration.

The first point I want to stress is the philosophy of Cherry Creek as it relates to the athletic program. I do want to tell you about something Cherry Creek High School was doing back in the 1970s that no other area schools were doing. We had a fall camp before the two-a-day practices started. We did a lot of testing, and we did weight lifting. I do not remember many other teams that did this type of program.

Today, everyone does testing and weights. We all may be doing as much as we need to do today. A coach must go with what their philosophy is in this matter. Is it all about winning? At certain times it is. Is it all about getting kids out for the team so you can have high numbers? What is important to your school? The thing I say is this: "Everyone wants to win on Friday night." The question is: "Are you, your kids, and your staff willing to win Monday through Thursday? Most coaches know games are won Monday through Thursday. Each coach must set his course on that Monday through Thursday track to enable the team to do their best.

I think the most important program in the entire school is the freshman program. When I talk about staff organization and where to put coaches, I want two or three of our best coaches at the freshman level. I think this is very important. I will ask the head coaches here, do you go to your freshman games? Do the freshmen know that you, as a head coach, know who they are?

A lot of my coaching philosophy is based on things I learned coaching basketball. It is a totally different program. Because of the equipment necessary and the cost of equipment, at a lot of schools, football is placed on the back burner.

You hear basketball coaches talk about playing 999 games, and playing in 48 summer leagues and camps. You hear baseball coaches talking about playing 425 games on Sunday. They can! Football does not have that luxury. Football is a different sport. When you talk to your kids, staff, parents, administrators, faculty, and coaching staff, you must be able to tell them what is important for you.

At Cherry Creek High School, it is very important that we win football games. It is extremely important that we win. I know it is important to win at other schools. It is important to win at all of your schools. I will tell you that we have the support system in place that will allow us to win in all areas. We are very fortunate in that respect. We work very hard to get all of this in place.

The first thing I had to do when I took the football job as head coach was to make some decisions about the staff. I had to place the assistant coaches at the different levels in our program. We are very similar to most coaching staffs in that we get a certain number of paid assistants and a certain number of nonteaching extralegal coaches. I had to figure out where to place the staff.

I had to answer several questions in making those decisions. Where were our best teachers? We do not have the luxury of having every coach in the building anymore. We had 15 staff members. Again, not all of them were paid. We only had four of the 15 staff members in our building. On our basketball staff, I have six members and five of them are in the building. We had to figure out what we could do in football as far as placing the staff.

We have one thing that I would encourage all of you to do. We have a staff member on the freshman team that is a teacher at the feeder middle school on campus. I cannot tell you how valuable this is in terms of getting information out, in terms of letting kids know what is going on, and in terms of having a familiar face when the kids go there. If there is a way to get a staff member at your middle school, it will help you in the long run. We want our kids to know what is going on in our program.

When we started to look at the staff and how we would place them, the first thing I did was to hire my father as the offensive line coach. I think that is the most important position in the game.

We hired the strength and conditioning coach as our defensive coordinator. He was in the building, and it made sense. However, more importantly, we wanted to make defense our number one priority to start out. He was an excellent coach, and we could not have been successful without him. He had been on the staff before. From there, we made our assignments like most other schools. We have a running backs coach, a defensive backs coach, a receivers coach, and all of the other aspects of a good coaching staff.

We wanted to keep our freshman staff. Our head freshman coach had 22 years experience at the varsity level. We felt good about this situation because we felt we could expect our freshmen to be taught the fundamentals when they came to the high school level. As most head coaches at the high school level, you are responsible for all of the programs. It is a good feeling to have someone that is capable at the freshman level. Head coaches have enough to keep them busy, and if you have to spend a lot of time working with the freshman team, it can be a drag on the system. Having an experienced coach at the freshman level is a worthwhile project.

Another important aspect of hiring a staff is to look at different personalities. I cannot be a control freak in football like I am in basketball. In football, if you do not trust what the assistants are doing, then you had better get new assistants. You must have that trust factor, and the assistants must have confidence in the head football coach.

You must know how to handle the situations where the assistants give the kids enough information to cause the parents to be upset with the head coach because their kid is not playing. Most parents want their son and the best 10 players to start each game. When staff members start talking behind the head coach's back, this information gets to the parents. You need assistants that will come to the head coach and let him know what is going on and make him aware of certain situations. The assistant coaches can stop a lot of problems by doing this.

We have 172 players out for football. Not all 172 of those players like our coaching staff. Our staff must have a relationship with those kids and the other coaches where they can talk with each other. They must be able to communicate. The game is all about communication and how you make these kids feel.

I am an old-school coach, but the fact is that the kids want to feel good about themselves. In this day and age, with all of the things that go on, it is important to communicate with the players and to get to know them. They want to feel good about themselves, and they want to hear it from the coach.

Coaches are the most important people in the school. The scores of our games are on TV on Friday night and in the papers on Saturday morning.

Before I took over as the head football coach, we never had a weight-lifting class at Cherry Creek High School. When I talked with the principal about taking the head job, I told him we could not build the program without a weight-lifting program. We are on a 5x5 schedule. Now, we meet three days a week during the zero period through first period. Our athletic director and principal did that for us. That has been the biggest change in our program. We lift from 6:45 a.m. to 8:10 a.m., they finish up, take showers, and are ready to go to their second period by 8:10 a.m. Every varsity player we had except one was in that early morning weight class.

How many of your assistant coaches stand out in the hall and shake kids' hands when they come into the hall? How many times do you call a player in to see you just to say, "Tom, how are you doing?" We do not have to be their friend, but we do have to be their coach. At times, we do need to be their friend and let them know we care about them, not only as a player but also as a person. There are different ways to do that.

With 15 assistant coaches, it is difficult to make everyone happy. We want assistant coaches that can discuss the situations in the proper time and place. If they disagree, they need to sit down and work it out. When they leave the coaching office, they must agree upon the way they are going to address certain situations. I want coaches to have

input. It has to be done in the proper and professional manner.

We had seven penalties because the officials ran into our assistant coaches on the sideline this year. I can tell you, that does not go over well with the principal. The athletic director calls me in when I get a technical foul called on me in basketball, and when we get a penalty on the sideline in football, I can assure you we are going to correct that problem.

We feel it is important to practice sideline procedures. That is one way to eliminate some of the penalties on the staff. We are going to practice "game day" where we work with the headsets, and we work on all the other aspects related to what we do in a game. We are going to have an organized sideline next year. I realize that is my responsibility.

It is very difficult when you lose that first or second game to start the season. But I can tell you this, it sure is fun to win football games in November. I know one outstanding basketball coach that does not even coach his team during the summer. They are not at tournaments, but they do play 15 summer games. In a couple of weeks, his team will be playing for the championship. We want to win in November. We are not interested in being 7-on-7 champions. Some of you may like the 7-on-7 games in the summer. It all depends on your philosophy. We want to win the state championship the first week of December.

The question is: How do you get there, and how do you handle the situation once you get there? That is a difficult thing. There are coaches who are having their teams run plays in the gym in the winter programs.

The point I am making here is that we want to win when it counts. I think too many coaches want to win all of the time. We do not go to the passing camps or the other all-star games because once they start keeping score, you are teaching the players that winning takes priority. By doing that, the fundamentals and proper techniques are overlooked and not covered as they should be. That is because coaches are concentrating on winning. They do not have time to teach the fundamentals. We want to just go for two weeks of spring football and not worry about all of the other summer programs.

The off-season program is an interesting topic. This is what we do in our off-season program. Our seventh, eighth, and ninth graders lift in one group, and our tenth, eleventh, and twelfth graders lift in another group. They lift and condition in two different groups. We think it is important for our feeder kids to be involved in our program.

At Cherry Creek High School, we have three or four organizations that compete. Whether you like it or not, we are not supposed to be at the young kids' games because that could be viewed as recruiting. Even though we cannot go to some of those games, the feeder kids need to know who we are. They need to know our staff, and they need to know what our program is all about.

When a seventh grader comes into our weight room to lift, one of our coaches will make sure that person knows who he is. Our assistant coaches will assist those young kids in teaching them the proper techniques of lifting. When that young seventh grader goes home, he can tell his parents that Coach Jones helped him with weight lifting today. I am sure all of the coaches in our program have the same impact with the kids that come from their feeder school.

We work out three days a week during the summer. We go Mondays, Wednesdays, and Fridays. Some people do not like to lift on Fridays. We lift three days a week in conditioning and speed camp. We have a very stringent routine that we follow in this program. We make sure the football players and parents know we have a year-round weight lifting and conditioning program. In basketball, we have a year-round skill-development program.

You can say what you want, but I think coaching is a 365-day-a-year job. The landscape has changed. Right or wrong, it is what it is. If you are not doing anything to make your program better, you are not going to be around much longer. We have camp three days a week, and we change our routine from time to time.

One thing that is clear to me is that football is so different in practice than basketball is. I asked the players what was the most difficult thing about football. Most of the players said, "Practices are boring." That is one reason I will not chew out a player on July 5, for not zone blocking properly when it does not matter at that time. Come September 10, I want to make sure he is zone blocking correctly. Then, I can chew at him when it really matters.

We did take part in one 7-on-7 last year and that was out of sheer boredom for our kids. It was a chance to go against someone different than our own players.

When we get through lifting, from 12:15 p.m. to 1:00 p.m. we have either offense or defense with the kids. It is a special time for us to work with them. I will tell you that sometimes our kids will go out on their own and throw. In general, we do not do a lot of installation during this summer workout period. I want the kids fresh when they come into fall practice. I do not want them to run zone coverage 487 times in July. Some teams may believe in that, but we do not.

In terms of weight lifting, our kids became stronger during the off-season. I am not sure if we are going to tweak it some for this year or not. We do not tell the players that if they do not attend a certain number of sessions in the summer program that they will not start in the fall. Our starting safety was an All-Colorado Team player, and he only came in to lift twice. He played in 92 baseball games. He will get his college education through baseball. Was he there for football when it mattered and when the kids needed him? Yes, he was. He had built a relationship of trust with the kids over the last four years.

Your hardest worker has to be your best player. I am a firm believer in that statement. He needs to be your best worker and you need to talk to him about that.

I have talked with a lot of coaches about going to summer camps. In the old days, they did not have the contact camps as they have now. Wyoming used to have basketball camps. They would have over 298 teams in camp at one time. The coaches could get out of town and be with the kids. All of the bonding took place with the coaches and players. However, coaches are with the players almost every day now. If you have a problem with a kid, you need to go see him and get things straight. Coaches are with the players too much as it is now. Players get tired of hearing the same voice over and over again. They want something different.

I have heard coaches say they wanted to go to a team camp so they could get the players away from their parents. In football, you cannot do that. They will follow you no matter where you go. We do our own contact camp with ourselves. The entire program is designed for teaching. Last year, we did it in June, and we had close to 70 percent of the players present. We are going to do the camp in July this year. Football practice will officially start after the camp is over. We will go into practice from there, and the players will be ahead of where we were last year. We will go one day of two-a-days and continue from there.

The old two-a-day practices are just about over. Because not only is school starting earlier, but we also do not really need two-a-day practices any more. We do conditioning and weight training all year so we do not need the two-a-day practices. In the old days, we had two-a-day practices because we did not have summer camps and conditioning programs. If you do two-a-days, you end up running drills and plays you worked on back on June 3. In addition, you run the risk of players getting hurt in two-a-day practices.

Last year in our contact camp, we allowed the players to play the positions they wanted to play. That takes care of a lot of problems. In the contact camp, we found where kids could and could not play. Our emphasis was on teaching and implementing our system. We wanted to find players that fit our system. We placed the emphasis on teaching and on implementing the way the practices and the program were going to run. We were not trying to beat anyone. We were trying to find the identity of our team for that season. That is one point we also emphasized in work ethic and the way we practiced.

We do run a SAC camp. That has changed in terms of what we do. We used to do all station work. Now, we do one hour of station work and one hour of football. After nine days, we test them. When we do the camp, the weight lifting routine suffers because of the time we take to test.

The year before I took the job as head coach, we had 12 players that were in the 70s club. The 70 is the highest you can get in our eight stations or testing areas. We called all the colleges around us, and we decided to test the way colleges test. We found out what a high school kid should have on his vertical jump and the other test items.

We made the freshmen accountable at that level or that score. We did not water the program down for freshmen. We wanted them to see the kinds of scores they could get on the test. Our test scores were the lowest in the history of Cherry Creek High School. Our strength and speed was much better than a lot of teams at Cherry Creek High School. We made the test extremely difficult. I will send you a copy if you drop me a note.

We do vertical jumps, bench presses, and the other lifts. We do not test to see how much they can lift. We work on reps as much as we can. We try to make it like the Combine as much as possible.

We get kids that come in and tell me they are going to a quarterback camp. I ask them how much they are paying to attend the camp. They tell me they are paying $250 per week. I tell them I can make them throw just as poorly as the camp will make them.

A lot of the players are going to the outside coaches today. They think those coaches know more than the high school coaches. They make the kids think they are going to be on the next McDonald's® All-Star team. We have to address those issues and let the kids know what is really taking place. They get the mothers and fathers to pay all of that money because they think those guys have something that is going to make them special.

In our SAC camp, our seniors lead the groups. Throughout the entire program, kids of all ages are mixed together. I cannot tell you how important this is to our program. Every kid in our program from the freshmen, to the sophomores, to the varsity players gets the same equipment in terms of sweats, spirit packs, and other items. Last year, we bought new jerseys for our freshman team, and we did not buy them for our varsity team.

This did two things for us. First, it highlighted the importance of the freshman team, and second, the parents of the freshman team were more likely to join the booster club. A lot of schools spend all of their money on the varsity team and the freshman team only gets hand-me-downs. We think it is important to take care of that freshman program.

After testing, we give the kids two days off, and then, we start our two-a-day practices. It is not as easy to do two-a-day practices anymore. Coaches are out of the building, and some of them are teaching and coaching at different schools. It is important to establish what you want to accomplish and what you want to do in the two-a-day practices. We were able to have one week where we had two-a-day practices last year.

Cherry Creek High School did not win a state championship until 1982. The year they won was the first year they ever went to platoon football. They used the platoon system from 1982 until last year. We played seven and sometimes eight kids both ways last year. Some of you may be thinking we have 180 players out for football and we were playing eight players both ways. We decided we were going to play the best players even if we had to play them both ways. We wanted to win and we needed to play our best players to do that.

When you start planning your practice, you need to know what you are going to do as far as playing the best players. Our quarterbacks coach does not want to spend time with our quarterback playing defense. Our defensive coordinator does not want our defensive back to take any snaps as a wide out. How do we handle those situations? The head coach tells everyone what they are going to do before the

season starts. Everyone must know the situation before they get into one of them. We have to plan for these situations before the season begins.

How many coaching staffs meet on Sunday? Raise your hands. How many of the wives of those coaches that meet on Sunday are in favor of this?

After the games on Friday night, the film coordinator gives the coaches their DVDs, and we go home. The modern technology has made things a lot better for everyone. The coaches take the films home, and since they cannot sleep anyway, they look at the film. On Saturdays, we have a short coaches' meeting. Then, we meet as defensive groups with the backs in one meeting and the line in another meeting. Then, we do the same with the offense. We have the line in one room and the backs and receivers in another group. We only look at the films for 45 minutes. We feel if you are in meetings with the kids watching film for over one hour, you are wasting your time. I go from room to room, and I find them asleep in every room. They are tired because they just played a game the night before.

How many of you think the kids go to bed early after games? Don't kid yourself. The kids stay out late. We tell them we are going to bring them in at eight o'clock, and they still stay out. They do not care about going to bed early. They want to wind down. They get to practice or to the meeting the next morning, but they are not worth a darn. They do not want to watch film for two hours. They are just as tired as the coaches.

After we watch film for 45 minutes, we stick the kids in the swimming pool to relax and soothe their wounds. The coaches get cut-ups of the opponent for the next game, and then we all go home. We have found that the shorter we make the film sessions the better. You have to be a great teacher in the film session—shorter is better. If you watch the films with all of your players and coaches together, you have too many coaches talking and making corrections.

After the film session on Saturday, we go home and the coaches do not meet again until Monday. At Cherry Creek, Monday at practice is fundamentals day. We do not game plan on Monday—we work on fundamentals. We hit the sled, we do daily drills, and we stress the fundamentals.

After practice on Monday, the head coach provides dinner at the office. We get the dinner delivered to our office, and we start our game planning. By doing it this way, we accomplish two things: we are fresh as coaches, which relates to the kids being fresher. You are better as a coach when you are fresh. If you know what you need to work on, you can get it done in less time. More does not mean better in terms of time when it comes to planning.

We meet for three to three-and-a-half hours on Monday evenings. We practice on Tuesdays and Wednesdays, and we go in full pads on Thursdays. If we are not in pads on Thursday, we have found that the kids think that they do not have to practice. So, we wear pads and pants on Thursdays. I do not want a thigh bruise because some kid was careless in practice. We want them focused all of the time, so we go out in pads.

We do a few things different in terms of how we plan practice. I got some of the ideas from basketball. We get out of school at 3:00 p.m. Most of our kids do not have class for the eighth period. We are able to get them on the field at 3:10 p.m., taped and ready to go. They report to their position coaches and do some stretching. We do not do a ton of stretching. We probably should do more stretching.

We do one special teams drill per day, and sometimes we may do two special teams drills. This year, we had such a great kicker that we did not have to work on that phase of the game that much. We kicked off 68 times, and we only had four kicks returned upfield on us. We did not waste a lot of time on our kickoff game. We did work on it on Thursdays. We spent more time on the punt and punt return because that is the special teams play you do most often in the kicking game.

The question came up about doing drills in practice that show up in a game. I think coaches are terrible at that. A lot of coaches do drills to do drills. I can tell you now that we do basketball drills to be doing drills. They may not have any game purpose at all, but we do them. If you can get just one point out of this talk, do drills that are integrated into what takes place on Friday night. Our line coach wants 30 minutes a day to run line drills. Our offensive coordinator wants to have 30 minutes of 11-on-11 each day. How does the head coach handle those coaches' requests and make out the practice schedule?

I keep a chart on the time we spend in practice. I keep each minute of time spent in each phase of the game. As we go through the season, the individual time becomes smaller and the team sessions become larger. We divide our time into three basic areas. We work on individual drills, we work against dummies, and we work live a large part of the time.

One way we break up the practice sessions to keep the players interested is to do "situations" that occur in the game of football. We do one drill which is very interesting for us. We call it *five-on-the-five*. It is the first 11 on offense against the first 11 on defense. We go five plays from the five-yard line. We want to see if we can score. We do the drill every other week for one period. The kids really get excited about the drill. This is a live drill all the way.

Another thing we do is to have a situation where we have 20 seconds on the clock—time for three plays. The drill could come in the middle of practice. We call the situation and tell the team, "We have no time-outs, 20 seconds on the clock, no time-outs, and time for three plays." We do this drill to break the monotony and to practice those situations.

We know practice is not like the games, especially in football. The game is not like practice. We ran a drill we called BMAC, which stood for Big Man At Creek. The player got to wear a special jersey. It was for the offensive line. We lined up at the 50-yard line with the offense on one line and the defense on the other side of the 50. We went 1-on-1, and everyone participated. The coaches selected one player that knocked the opponent off the line and did the best job in the drill. One player was selected for the BMAC, and he wore a green jersey for the week or until someone defeated him or someone did better in the drill the next time. The kids did a lot of whooping and hollering during the drill. They really would get after each other during the drill.

Another drill that we did that was very good we called *thrill drill*. It was just a continuation of the Oklahoma drill. We would go to the line running the Oklahoma drill.

In addition, kids like doing two-minute drills with the 1s going against the 1s. They are competitors, and they want to see who can win. I suggest you could incorporate more situations in this drill. You can insert the field goal and the blocked field goal, along with other kicking situations. You can add conditions to the drill. For example, you can tell the offense if they make the field goal, then practice is over for the day. Those types of things keep things interesting for the players. Football coaches do not think about this enough because we get caught up in too much detail.

We talked about winning the game on Monday through Thursday. You do not win games on Friday night. If you are coaching fundamentals on Friday night, you did a poor job through the week. You may have to make adjustments on Friday night, and that is where your mind-set should be.

Work very hard on not making any adjustments that you have not practiced. Do not expect the kids to execute something on Friday night that you have not drilled on Monday through Thursday. Do not just draw up plays in the sand.

How do you plan for the playoffs? To me, less is more. You must keep the kids fresh. They are beat up and need to slack off on the heavy work. We practiced for an hour and a half during the playoffs.

We were fortunate to go all the way to the state championship doing this.

The times you have to play in the playoffs can be a problem. Most teams are used to playing on Friday night. The worst time to play a playoff game is on Friday at 4:00 p.m.—there is no worse time. You have to take the kids out of school early. If the game is on Friday night, everything stays consistent. It is inconsistent on Friday at 4:00 p.m. The coaches have to adjust to that schedule as well as the kids. Kids do not do well when there is a time adjustment involved.

If we have an in-service teacher workday on a Friday and we are playing that night, we have our players come into school as they would on a regular school day. We have them do something to keep them occupied. We do the same thing when we play a Saturday night game. We have the players come in at 10 a.m. for a meeting. We have a short practice, and then we get off the field in one hour.

It has been an interesting experience in seeing the football aspects of practice and the basketball team's practice. I have respect for football coaches because football coaches work tremendously hard. The thing I see about football coaches is the fact that there are so many more technicians. I think football coaches are teachers more than basketball coaches are at times. In basketball, you do not have to force kids to come to practice.

One point I want to make about football coaches and trading films. Coaches should not be so reluctant to trade films. Coaches are going to get them anyway so you should trade films.

I appreciate your time. Thank you very much.

THE ZONE BLITZ PACKAGE

Don Bosco Prep, New Jersey

It is good to be in this area. I know you play good football here. I am from Don Bosco Prep High School in Ramsey, New Jersey. Recently, we have had a lot of success. We are 20 minutes out of New York City. I want to go into our fire-zone package and give you some of the reasons we went to this scheme.

REASONS FOR FIRE ZONE

- We want to eliminate the big play not only in the pass, but in the shotgun run game, also.
- Too many plus-25-yard plays in zero pressure.
- We want at least one deep-middle defender on pressures.
- Gives us the opportunity for more turnovers because we are all looking at the ball, not the man.
- Can be physical on the #2 receiver trying to get vertical.
- Enables us to do things that are complex for the offense, but simple for us.
- We can attack the protection from anywhere.

We played with a lot of zero-pressure schemes. When you do that, you have the opportunity to give up big plays. We went back and looked at the plus-25-yard gains. We found that most of them came when we were in some type of man coverage with no middle safety. With the middle safety, you have someone there in case we miss a run fit or make a mistake in coverage. In the last two years, we only gave up two plays of 25 or more yards in our zone-blitz package.

When we play this scheme, we get more turnovers. We are all looking at the ball instead of the man. If the ball is being run, everyone can gear up and get downhill at the ball. We like the three underneath and three-deep scheme. That is what I am going to talk about today.

This package allows us to look complex to the offense, but is simple for us. We can run the same pressure out of many fronts. We call the set to eight different strengths. We study the protection scheme of teams and can attack it from anywhere. This is a great way to create turnovers on second and third down in long-yardage situations. It allows us to get a free hitter on the quarterback or back. This scheme is like all other schemes: it is great, but the players win the games. They have to play, but we feel this package makes it simple for them.

- Scheme is great, but in the end players win the game. Let them play fast.
- Not much thinking.
- No paralysis by analysis.

The players have to execute and do their job. However, this scheme keeps it simple for them and does not require a lot of thinking. We do not want to analyze to the point that they cannot move. The rules are simple and allow you to play against any defensive formation.

CHECKLIST

- Be draw- and option-proof.
- Study protections, get free hitters, and get your best blitzers on their worst pass blockers (backs).
- Find what fronts force certain protections.
- Find the waist-benders up front.
- Have answers for backside isolation routes.
- Get violent on #2, or walk out of the stadium.
- Get close to your work; time it up.
- Use the quarterback's snap indicator.
- Use the sticks, and know the situation.

The first thing you need to do is make sure you are draw- and option-proof in this scheme. If you play a team that runs a lot of option, you must know the pressures you want to run and the ones to stay away from. That comes from the game plan. We want to study the protections and get one of our blitz runners on the tailback. You have a chance to make the tailback block your best blitz defender and give him a headache all night long.

The other thing you are doing is preventing him from releasing out of the backfield. You are making him stay in and protect. If they do release the back, you can still cover him. If we want to get the offense in a certain protection, we know the front we have to run that puts them in that protection.

We want to match our good rushers against the waist-benders. That reference is to the offensive linemen who are not flexible and cannot bend their ankles and knees. We study the personnel of the opponent and find those types of linemen. Those are the players we want to match our best rushers against.

We have to be able to cover the backside isolation routes, because that is the way the offense attacks you. A trips team will try to use the single receiver on isolation routes against the zone blitz. To the trips side, they run combination routes. Whatever you are playing against those teams, you must have an answer.

We want to show the offense different alignments and disguise what we do. However, when they snap the ball, we have to be in our proper alignment. If we are not, the defense is in trouble. We use the quarterback-snap indicator to move the defense. We study the quarterback, particularly in the shotgun, to see when he is going to snap the ball. This year, we played a team whose quarterback always snapped the ball when he dropped his hips. We did not rotate the secondary until he dropped his hips to take the snap. Teams do it different ways. Study and find out how they do it, and move off that key.

Know where the first-down marker is on every situation. You do not want to drop 10 yards if they only need eight yards for the first down. Know each situation, and react accordingly.

FIRE ZONE RULES

- There are always six defenders to the callside and five defenders away.
- Nose, end, Mike, Sam, free, and field corner to the callside.
- Rover, tackle, backer, weak safety, and bench corner away from the callside.

The first front I want to show is the Eagle front (Diagram #1). To the callside or tight-end side, we align the Sam in a 9 technique on the outside shoulder of the tight end. The end is in a 5 technique on the outside shoulder of the offensive tackle. The nose aligns in a 1 technique on the inside shoulder of the guard, and the Mike linebacker is in a 30 technique over the offensive guard.

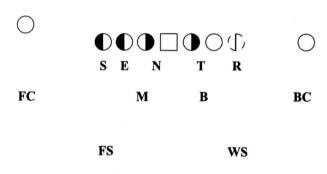

Diagram #1. Eagle Front

To the backside, the tackle aligns in a 3 technique on the offensive guard, and the Rover or rush end is in a ghost 6 technique. If he has a tight end to that side, he is in the 6 technique. With no tight end, he aligns in a position as if there was one. The backer linebacker aligns in a 30 technique over the guard.

We have the boundary corner to the backside of the formation and the field corner into the callside. The free safety aligns over the #2 receiver at a depth of 10 yards. The weak safety aligns over the backside offensive tackle at a depth of 10 yards. We give a cover-2 appearance in the secondary.

FIRE ZONE RULES

- We will always make the call in this order: strength, front, stunt, and coverage (e.g., field Eagle Seattle Magic).

- Field is the strength, eagle is the front, Seattle is the stunt, and Magic is the coverage.
- There are many different strengths, fronts, stunts, and coverage's that we can mix and match together.
- The six-to-and-five-away method still applies.
- The base coverage that we teach with our fire zones is Magic.

The first call is "field," which means six field defenders align to the field and the five boundary defenders align to the backside. The front is the Seattle Eagle front in the diagram. The stunt is Seattle and the cover is Magic.

The strength calls we use are field, bench, tight, split, strength of formation, weakside of the formation, back, or a player number (lineman or skill receiver). When we refer to the strength of the formation, we mean passing strength. If we have the wide slot to one side and a tight end and flanker to the other side, we align to the slot. That is the passing strength of the formation.

If we play a shotgun team, we can match the front to the alignment of the running back in the set. We found out that shotgun teams do not bring the back to the opposite side in his alignment enough. Therefore, you can key on his alignment and set your front to the back. If the back is set to a particular side, that is usually the big-on-big side of the protection scheme. That is the side we want to attack. The offensive guard and tackle to that side are blocking the defensive linemen, and the back is double-reading the linebackers. That is when we match the linebackers on the running back.

The player number means we roll the defense to wherever that player aligns. We can call the front to a lineman. That is how we get the best rushers on the waist-benders. If we want to match up on the right tackle, we call his number in the place of "field" in the example call.

The fronts we run from the Seattle are Owl, Eagle, Hawk, and Bear. The Owl is the Okie front (Diagram #2). On that front, we move the nose head-up on the center and play with two 5 techniques by

the end and tackle. The Rover and Sam play 9 techniques on the offensive ends or ghost alignments.

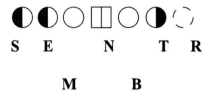

S   E   N   T   R

M   B

Diagram #2. Owl

The Eagle is the front in the example. The Hawk front is a 3 technique to the callside by the nose (Diagram #3). To the backside, we move the 3-technique tackle into a 2i technique on the guard, and the Rover moves down to a 5 technique on the tackle.

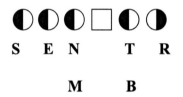

S   E   N   T   R

M   B

Diagram #3. Hawk

The last front we run from the Seattle package is the Bear front (Diagram #4). The end moves into a 3 technique, and the nose moves to a zero technique on the center. The Mike linebacker tightens his alignment to the line of scrimmage. All the players need to know is where they have to align because the stunt never changes. They always go to the same spot, but they start from different alignments.

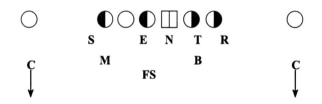

Diagram #4. Bear

Magic is the coverage that goes with the zone blitz. It is an acronym for "missing a guy in coverage." We try to use acronyms with the players because it allows them to understand things quicker.

- Five-yard, no-cover zone, rally down.
- Hold the disguise as long as possible.
- Movement on the quarterback's snap indicator in order to minimize audibles.
- Consists of a deep middle player.
- Corners reading #2 receivers.
- Two wall/flat defenders.
- One hole/#3 defender.

I will try to talk about some of the coverage's if I have time. We run Magic and tag Conor, which stands for "corner on number-one receiver." If there is a bunch formation, we play box. I will cover that if I have time. We play a coverage called 2-Z, which is a fieldside roll to the Z-receiver. We play sink/lock and white peal. We also have ability to play zero coverage with a double-team on a receiver. We call "black-#." That is the zero coverage and the number is the receiver we double. The free safety has a double coverage on that receiver. I will cover as much of that as I can.

In Magic coverage, we have a deep middle defender, two corners keying the #2 receiver, two wall/flat defenders, and a low-hole defender.

I am going to draw up the Seattle stunt so you will know what I am talking about (Diagram #5). The "S" in Seattle means the Sam linebacker on the stunt. This stunt is good against the run as well as the pass. The defensive front is tight Eagle to the tight end with Magic coverage. The Sam linebacker runs a stick inside through the C gap, working to get to the B gap. He reads the block of the tight end. If the tight end blocks down, he closes behind the tight end and spills everything. If the fullback or guard comes to kick him out, he gets inside them.

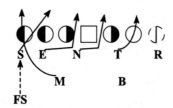

Diagram #5. Tight Eagle Seattle

The 5-technique end runs a long stick into the A gap. If the guard blocks out on him, he has to get

inside of him. If the guard blocks down, he comes off his butt. The nose runs a NOA stunt, which means nose into the opposite A gap. The 3-technique tackle runs a punch contain. He steps outside reading the offensive tackle.

These movements are lateral, vertical steps. They back off the ball a bit, and lateral-step inside and get vertical into their gaps. We play in more of a square stance instead of getting the inside foot back in the stance. They keep their pads down and the chest square to the line of scrimmage.

If there were no #2 receiver, we send the safety for contain. In this case, we have a #2 receiver, and the Mike linebacker runs the contain blitz off the edge. If the offense runs anything in that direction, all the defenders spill the ball to the Mike linebacker.

The free safety drops down and becomes the wall/flat defender to that side (Diagram #6). To the backside, the Rover end is the wall/flat player and the backer linebacker becomes the #3 hole player in the low middle. The weak safety has the middle third, and the corners are playing their read technique.

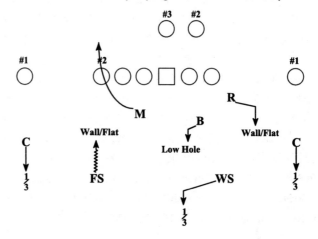

Diagram #6. Magic Coverage

In this formation, the free safety and Rover are the wall/flat defenders.

WALL/FLAT DEFENDERS

- Collision the vertical route at five yards (outside-in with a tight end and head-up on a detached #2 receiver).
- Never pedal back. Use a nose catch technique, and pop your feet (inside=wall, outside=funnel).

- Keep him off of the hash.
- #2 to flat leverage him through the curl.
- #2 to flat carry him through the wheel intersect point.
- If #2 is vertical, collision until #3 takes you to the flat (backside receiver or back).
- If #2 is on an immediate "in" cut, pass him through to the hole player, yelling "In, in, in," and look for the slant behind you or a crosser coming back.

The wall/flat defender does not jump the flat route; he keeps leverage and drops through the curl area. If the flat becomes a wheel, he runs with it. If the #2 receiver goes vertical, he has to keep him off the hash mark and play him until the #3 receiver goes to the flat. If the receiver is inside, force him to the inside or funnel him to the outside. Never let him run up the hash mark.

The backer linebacker is the hole player. He reads the #3 receiver in the backfield. When we talk about the defender pushing to the final #3 receiver, he is not following the #3 receiver to the flat. He works the next inside receiver working to the inside. If #3 goes to the flat and #2 crosses, he takes the #2 receiver as the final #3 receiver.

HOLE #3 DEFENDER

- Works off of the #3 receiver.
- #3 goes flat. Wall/flat player takes him while the hole player pushes to the final #3.
- Run game. Key #3 through offensive line. Play fast when the ball is run to the movement, and tempo the back when he runs away from the movement.
- Versus trips, alert #3 on the vertical route.
- If there is a crosser, leverage him (don't run at him because he will run by you).
- Hole call with the weakside end exchanging responsibilities.

If the #2 receiver to the weakside is in the backfield, we play the way I just described. However, if he detaches and moves into the slot, the backer linebacker goes outside, aligns on him, and becomes the wall/flat defender. He aligns at one yard inside and a five-yard deep alignment. The free safety would make that same adjustment on a slot receiver to him. The Rover is now the hole player, working off the #3 receiver in the backfield.

The corner in Magic coverage aligns on the #1 receiver and reads the #2 receiver. The corner to a single receiver climbs from a press to an 8x1 inside alignment, reading the three-step drop. If #1 goes outside, do not get stemmed out because he is coming back in to beat the corner on the skinny post route, and the Safety cannot make that play at 18 yards outside the hash (never give up the inside).

The corner to a two-man surface should read the #2. If #2 goes vertical, he midpoints his zone, which is one yard inside the numbers, when the ball is in the middle of the field. If the ball is on the far hash, the midpoint is four yards outside the hash.

CORNERS

- With #2 vertical, open with your butt to the sideline so that you can still make a play on the inside vertical. If the ball is thrown outside of the hash, it is yours.
- If #2 isn't vertical, then you have all of #1. Get your eyes to him, and break up through his inside shoulder.
- The corner must also relay the split of #1 down to the wall/flat player. This will help the wall/flat player to drop under the intermediate route by #1.
- If you are away from a 3x1 formation, squeeze the three-step (alert weak press call).

The corner to the single-receiver side relays information to the Rover. If he calls "Cut, cut, cut," the Rover has to get a wider drop to stop the out cut. If he calls "Wide, wide, wide," the receiver is probably going to run a slant. If the corner is away from a trips set, he squeezes the #1 receiver because he does not have help. The #3 receiver is declared to the frontside and the hole defender is pushed to that side. In those situations, we might play locked man coverage on the single receiver.

The middle safety has from seam to seam and reads the quarterback's front shoulder. If it is a running play, he stays on the same path as the tailback attacking inside-out. He accelerates his pedal so that he can attack every ball downhill. We will only ask the deep-third player to cover one third of the distance that the ball is in the air. If it is a 21-yard throw, he can cover seven yards to break that up.

He must defend the post at all times; everyone's technique is catered to him. He is probably the most important player on the field. The three-prong philosophy for the defensive backs in the zone blitz is to never let anyone behind you, allow no yards after the catch, and don't let a receiver make a play on or against a ball in the air.

Let me give you something on the weakside end quickly. He is going to be in pass coverage on this scheme.

WEAKSIDE END

- Align in a ghost 6, and take a shuffle-step outside, reading the offensive tackle.
- If it is pass set, work back off of your inside foot to get underneath the weakside three-step.
- Should the back release to the flat weak, play with leverage over him through the wheel intersect point.
- If it is a run play, you cannot be reached no matter what. Down block box the ball back inside.
- On run away, fold back inside and become the backside cutback.

If the #2 receiver detaches, he becomes the inside hole defender. The backer walks out and calls "Hole, hole, hole." If there is a trips away from the weakside end, there will be no hole call. However, if the back goes away, there will be a crosser coming back to him.

The universal answer for offenses against zone pressure has become the three-step game Along with the vertical/crosser package, the spread is often trying to find ways to beat the pressure and get receivers free or locked up on a linebacker. Other offenses may try to maximum protect in order to give themselves enough time to throw the three-step passing game They want to isolate your corners on athletic wide receivers.

Sink/lock coverage is a coverage that is implemented in order to take away the three-step game weak and give the defense a different coverage to the frontside against 2x1 sets.

SINK/LOCK COVERAGE

- On the frontside, the corner aligns outside at seven yards and reads #2.
- If #2 is flat, the corner hangs and jumps down to the flat. If #2 is vertical, the corner is locked man on #1, and he will sink back to the deep third with him.
- The deep middle-third player is now also reading off of #2 at 14 yards. If #2 goes flat, he works his kickpedal over #1 with width and depth.
- If #2 releases vertically, he should be walled out by the wall/flat player, and the safety would then have him vertically.
- The wall/flat defender can now be extremely physical on #2 because only #3 can take him to the flat now.
- The original hole #3 defender cannot allow anyone to cross him (seek depth, and catch the first crosser; if no cross, look to curl). If #3 releases vertically, you run with him.
- Dropper to the weakside, and look to get under three-step weak with no threat from #2.

You can play this coverage to either side, meaning to or away from the blitz. We usually prefer to call the blitz to the single receiver and sink the coverage away to the two-receiver surface. The key to this coverage is communication. When the secondary recognizes the two-receiver surface, they must echo the sink call around the field. If the offense comes out in any 2x2 or 3x1 formations, we check Magic coverage

I want to show you the stunt from the splitside. If we call split Eagle Seattle, we run the stunt from the split-end side (Diagram #7). The Sam linebacker has no tight end so he walks off the line of scrimmage. The Rover aligns on the tight end. He can never get reached on a running play. If he gets reached, the defense is dead. If it is a pass, he is the wall/flat defender. Everyone does exactly what he did on the stunt the other way. What we get is the Sam and Mike linebacker on the running back. The Sam attacks on the inside, and the Mike attacks outside.

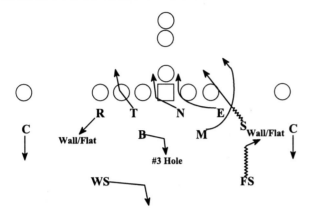

Diagram #7. Split Eagle Seattle

We have terms that we tag to the stunt. We run nose, switch, and cat. We can run them all at once. The nose stunt is between the nose and tackle. The nose jets into the A gap in which he is aligned. The tackle comes from the other side and penetrates the callside A gap. On the switch call, the Mike and Sam linebackers switch their responsibilities. The Mike blows the C gap, and the Sam linebacker comes to the outside. The cat stunt is the corner switching responsibility with the Mike linebacker on the Seattle stunt. The corner is the blitz containment, and the Mike linebacker becomes the wall/flat defender to the weakside.

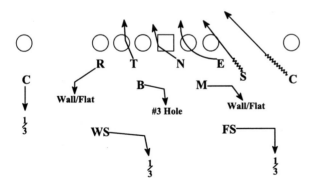

Diagram #8. Split Eagle Seattle Cat

If we ran the split Eagle Seattle and added the word "cat," we get a corner blitz for the contain rusher (Diagram #8). We never run a cat stunt from a two-receiver side. If we have two receivers, we call off the stunt and run regular Seattle. On this call, the free safety plays over the top into the outside third. The Mike linebacker becomes the wall/flat defender to that side. If the offense runs to the field, that is the way we are stunting.

If we change the front to a field Owl, we are in the Okie front (Diagram #9). The nose is head-up on the center. His opposite A gap is away from the call. We run the Seattle stunt, and nothing changes.

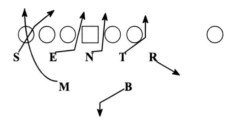

Diagram #9. Field Owl Seattle

We can run the same stunt from four different fronts and eight different directions. If we play the shotgun team, we want to run the Seattle to the back. If the back aligns left, we call "Left, left," and make him block. If we do not get home on the quarterback, we can knock his block off.

We like this stunt from the Okie front because it takes advantage of a slide protection moving away from the tight end. Since there is a zero technique on the center, the guard to the tight end has to stretch down to the nose because of the threat of the nose coming behind the center's block. When the guard goes down on the nose, it isolates the tackle on the defensive end. The tackle has to go down on the defensive end and shortens the edge to the back. The Sam linebacker goes under the back, the Mike comes over the top, and someone will get home.

The offensive guard is supposed to work down and back out when the nose goes away. However, the end's stick stunt speeds up the reaction time for the guard. The tackle and guard do not have time to switch up their blocking assignment.

We can run the stunt out of the Bear front. The reason we like to run the stunt out of a Bear is we get a full slide from the offense instead of the half slide. There are too many twists in the defense for the offense to block man protection. If we call tight Bear Seattle, the end moves to the 3 technique, and the nose moves to the zero technique. The Mike linebacker tightens his alignment. The front looks different and the defender starts from different alignments, but they end up in the same place.

If we called split Bear Seattle cat nose, we get the same stunt (Diagram #10). The only difference is the corner is the contain rusher from the boundary, and the Mike linebacker becomes the wall/flat defender to that side. We run the nose stunt on the inside with the nose and the end. The nose jets the A gap to the split-end side, and the end lone sticks into the awayside A gap. The free safety is over the top into the outside third, and the weak safety rolls into the middle third.

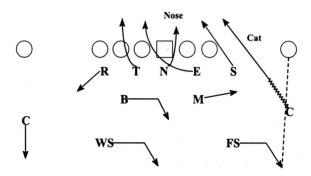

Diagram #10. Split Bear Seattle Cat Nose

I know this may seem like Chinese math to some of you, but it is not a tough package to install and run. Before I stop, I want to show you one stunt that has been good for us. If you are thinking about using the zone-blitz package, you might want to consider this stunt.

We run this stunt from the Hawk front. We align the tackle to the backside in a 2i technique on the guard. The nose to the callside moves out into a 3 technique on the offensive guard. We call back Hawk Salem (Diagram #11). This is a good pass-rush scheme. We take the 5-technique end and jet him up the field. We run a long stick with the nose. He keys the center. If the center goes away in his protection scheme, the nose beats the guard into the A gap. If the center comes to the nose, he crosses his face

into the backside A gap. The Sam and Mike linebacker run a double-team on the back in the backfield.

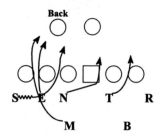

Diagram #11. Back Hawk Salem

If the tackle kicks out on the pass rush of the end and the guard stretches down on the stick by the nose, there is a big gap. With the center sliding away, the guard has to respect the move of the nose to the inside. The Sam linebacker comes behind the end jetting up the field and blows into the B gap. The Mike linebacker scrapes off the edge. The back cannot block both the Sam and Mike linebacker, which means someone will be free on the quarterback.

We still have a three-underneath pass coverage with three deep behind that. The reason we run the stunt from the Hawk front rather than the Eagle is the technique of the nose. If the nose aligns in the shade technique as he does on the Eagle, the guard will pass him off to the center and not stretch inside. If the guard has a 3 technique aligned on him, he has to respect him because it is not the center's job to pick up the A gap to that side. The center is responsible for the A gap to the other side.

If you play a team that throws the ball, study their protection scheme. The way we play the game, there is nothing wrong with knocking their best player out of the game. That is the way this game is played. If they do not like that, they should have played soccer.

I see my time is up. I thank you for your attention.

OFFENSIVE OVERVIEW AND THE STRETCH PLAY

Lakeland High School, Florida

I want to thank Nike for having us here. They put a lot of money in high school football. High school football has really grown over the last five years. There are more and more games on TV each year. It has been a tremendous experience for players. They are getting to go to more out-of-state games and have the excitement of being on television. We have been fortunate enough to play in a couple of those nationally televised games. It is good for the kids.

I know you have some of the same kinds of players that we do. We have a lot of players who come from single-parent homes. It is fun to watch them get on an airplane for the first time. High school football has grown, and so have the players who are playing the game.

What I am going to do today is give you an overview of our offense. After that, I want Coach John Flath, our offensive line coach, to come up and talk about our most successful play. That play is the stretch play. For years and years, we ran the option as our best play. However, the defense has caught up to that play, and it is not as consistent as the stretch play. He will tell you how we install the play and how we run the play.

I want to start with some offensive thoughts. We are not great at anything we do. We work hard and try to improve a little every day. We have had some good players.

• Mirrored offense.

• I-backs depth from the line of scrimmage.

• Multiple formations with motion.

• Everyone touches the ball.

• Make first downs.

• Do not be outnumbered at the point of attack.

• Have an answer for the fourth man on the blitz.

• Big plays come from play-action.

We are an I-formation team. I like it for two reasons. I like it because it is a mirrored offense. You can run the same play at the line of scrimmage on either side. The other thing I like about the I formation is the depth of the tailback. He has a chance to adjust his running path if things are clogged up at the line of scrimmage.

We run the same plays out of the one-back offense. We use the shotgun, and it gives you a two-back set with the quarterback as a viable runner. That allows you to keep the receivers in the game and still have a two-back offense. It gives you a two-back offense, but the defense has to account for an additional receiver on the field. That may require them to take a run defender out of the game and use another defensive back.

We are a multiple-formation team with numerous ways to motion from those formations. We use the motion to try to find soft spots in the defense. That gives us a chance to dictate schemes to the defense instead of them dictating how we adjust. We get many big plays during the course of the year because teams do not get aligned properly.

Everyone in our offense touches the ball. In some years, the tight end is almost nonexistent. That was what happened to us last year. However, over the years, the tight end has been the biggest playmaker of all the receivers. Some years, you do not have the exact personnel you want. We may have to play a fullback at the tight end or a tailback at a receiver position. That is what happened to us last year, and we did what we had to do.

On offense, we must make first downs and move the chains. Everything we do on offense is predicated on keeping the ball moving down the field. Big plays just happen in a game. We want to concentrate on getting the tough yards and moving the chains.

We do not want to be outnumbered at the point of attack. The object of our offense is to get a hat on a hat. We want to get man-on-man at the point of attack and give the back chances to make a play. You cannot make yardage if you have three blockers and they have five defenders at the point of attack. It is hard with today's defenses to get into running formations and have an equal number of blockers and defenders at the point of attack. That is where the multiple uses of formations are an advantage.

When you throw the football, you have to know how to account for the fourth man to a side on a blitz. We have to avoid the bad play by taking the sack. You have to develop a hot system, adjust your protection, or throw the ball away. You must have an answer for that type of situation.

Last year, we did not have a tailback who was a breakaway threat. In the past, we had backs that could go the distance on any given play. Last year, our big plays came off the play-action pass. Most of the big plays were made by the wide receivers.

Our offense is broken down into five parts. We run power, option, toss, passing game, and goal line. The power phase consists of inside and outside zone, power, counter gap, and isolation. The outside zone and the stretch are the same plays in our offense. In the past, our option game was our number-one play. However, in the last three or four years, the stretch play has become our number-one play. Next year, that may not be the case. Our offensive line for next year is very small.

I am going to show you some examples of the zone schemes and the stretch concepts. I am not going to give you the details because Coach Flath will talk about that later. I want to show you some examples of how we use different personnel and run the same scheme (Diagram #1). We can run the play from two tight ends, which is the formation in the diagram. We can also run it from trips, three

wide receivers and two backs, one tight end and two backs, or any number of formations. The blocking scheme is the same on any formation we run.

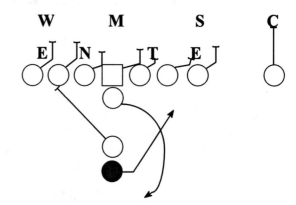

Diagram #1. Stretch/Two Tight Ends-One Back

We run the inside zone at the frontside A gap (Diagram #2). The aiming point is the inside leg of the playside guard. We can hit the play there or take it to the backside. Against the 4-3, the tackle and tight end run a combo block on the defensive end and Sam linebacker. The center and playside guard use a combo block on the defensive tackle and Mike linebacker. The backside guard and tackle zone-step into their gaps. The backside guard zones to the nose, and the tackle zones the B gap up to the Will linebacker. We use the fullback in this set to block the backside defensive end.

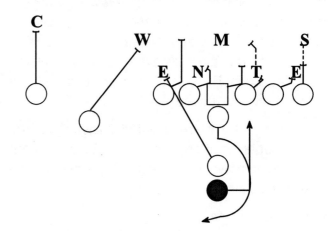

Diagram #2. Inside Zone Vs. 4-3

We can run this play from all our formations. When we go to the one-back set, the quarterback reads the backside end with an option read. We can use the same blocking scheme with the quarterback reading the backside end.

We run the power off tackle with the fullback kicking out on the outside linebacker (Diagram #3). We block down and kick out at the point of attack. We pull the backside guard for the frontside linebacker. There is nothing earth-shaking about the play. We can run this play from multiple sets, also.

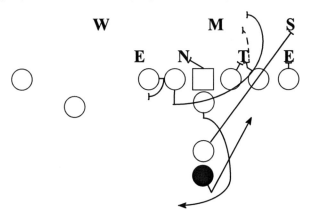

Diagram #3. Power

The counter gap is a traditional scheme (Diagram #4). The frontside blocking is like the power play. Instead of the fullback kicking out the outside linebacker, the backside guard pulls and traps him. The backside tackle pulls and turns up for the frontside linebacker. The fullback cuts off on the backside for the pulling tackle.

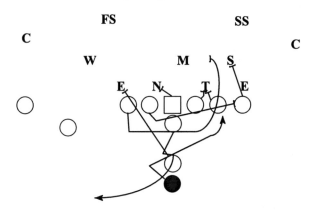

Diagram #4. Counter Gap

The isolation play is a simple play. It is the fullback lead-up on the inside linebacker. When we run the draw, we use the isolation blocking scheme. We can run the quarterback isolation using the isolation blocking scheme. That puts the quarterback in the shotgun, and he is getting the lead block from the one back.

The option game has become a supplementary play in our running game. We run multiple options as part of our packages. We run the option because you do not need great athletes to do it. Another factor is it makes the defense play assignment football. The pass off the option play is good because it requires the defense to use base coverages. If you have an option game, it eliminates a number of the combination coverages teams like to play. To be option sound, they cannot play a lot of man coverage. We run a lot of our play-action passing off the option game.

The option controls the blitzing game. It puts the ball in the hands of your best athletes. You do not need a great offensive line to run the option attack, and it is fun.

We run a number of options. However, you must match your options to the defense you play. The one that has been the best for us is the freeze-trap option. The option play has a lot of carryover value in the offense. We have run the option since I started coaching and have been able to carry it over with the new schemes we are running. If you can carry over the teachings to the offense, it allows you to spend less time drilling things because your players know it.

I like the trap option against a 5-2 alignment (Diagram #5). I like the inside veer to an A-gap player. We run the midline option to a B-gap defender. The speed option is a double option with no fake. It is a down-the-line option. It is good against an Eagle defense. The zone option is good against teams that play a 7 technique and play inside-out on your tight ends. We like to run the G-option against a 4-3 team that plays a 9-technique defender over the tight end. I know some of you may not be familiar with the freeze-trap option or the G-option.

We are a running team, and our passing game comes off many play-action passes. We are not the type of team that throws the ball 50 times a game. I do not like to throw the ball but four or five times a game, unless I have to. When we start to work our passing game, we work on the hot patterns, bubble patterns, and automatic throws. We have the three-step and five-step passing games. We throw the play-action and screens.

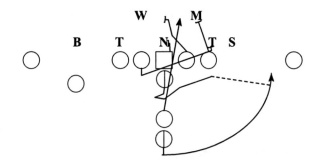

Diagram #5. Freeze-Trap Option

When we get into our goal-line offense, we align in two tight ends and three backs in the backfield. Goal-line offense is an attitude thing. We start it in spring practice. We go every day in a one-on-one goal-line drill. We begin it every day in our fall practices. It is not necessarily the package we run with the power I. It is the mindset our players develop. They know when we get into the five-yard line, we are going to two tight ends and three backs. It is something our players believe, and it has been good to us over the years.

I am going to turn the program over to Coach John Flath and let him tell you about the stretch play.

JOHN FLATH

I grew up in Orlando and have been coming to this clinic for three years. Coach Castle hired me three years ago. In that time, I have learned just how great a coach he really is. If you think we meet all the time and work into the wee hours of the morning, there is nothing farther from the truth. We meet once a week as a staff for two hours.

Talking about the stretch play, we have to get off the ball and keep what we are doing simple. We have to run the entire playbook, but we do not have to worry about the formations. In practice, we run 85 reps of team plays every single day. We have 20 minutes of individual work in a drills period. We follow that with an option period. We run all our options during that period. We get anywhere from 18 to 20 reps during that period. After that, we flex, stretch, and get ready for practice. We do team agilities for two minutes. Then, we do team take-offs and go through all our reverses, screens, and gadget plays. There are 16 of those plays in our offensive package.

We go dummy stretch drill for five minutes. That is the period when we run all of our zone, stretch, and screen plays. During those five minutes, we get 8 to 10 repetitions.

The next drill is the offensive line against the defensive line and linebackers working together. We work team runs. We do all the isolations, power, counter games, and sweeps. We run goal line for five minutes. We get 10 reps during the goal-line period. After that, we get a short break. After the break, we go to team pass drill. I hate this drill because the scout team knows we are going to pass every time. From there, we go to kicking game and conditioning. That is what we do every day.

Before I came to coach with Coach Castle, I do not know how he did things. Coach Castle has never had a losing season in 33 years of coaching. He has never had a losing season. After I came to work for him, I found out.

These are the things I have learned from Coach Castle in the three years I have been here. The number-one thing we have to do is coach the team. All the ordering of uniforms and scheduling and all the other stuff, he handles. When things get hectic, he stays calm. He never coaches anything in a negative way. He has a statement he uses all the time. He just says, "Move on." Do not dwell on things. Move on to the next play.

The first year I came to work for him was 2006. During that year, we did not do a single up-down the entire year. We did not do an up-down for being late off the ball or fumbling. The attitude was not to dwell on mistakes but to move on to the next play. If you saw us play this year, we won some games we should have not have won. That was all because of Coach Castle. We never ran a play twice in practice in 2006. We simple moved on to the next play. He wins because he has the competitive passion it takes to win. It is all about being prepared to win and never dwelling on the bad things that happen.

I am going to try to give you the particulars about the stretch play. We ran the stretch play 88 times this year. We gained 563 yards for a 6.4-yard average per play. We scored eight touchdowns. We ran for it for 15 yards or more 11 times. We went 14 yards 33 times for almost a seven-yard average. One out of two times, we called the play, and we gained seven yards or more. Only 12 times out of 88 times did the play fail to gain yards. That type of play keeps you on schedule to move the chains.

This is a play in our offense which we describe as a catch-all play. We can run the play against any defense. We ran the play against 50 fronts, 40 fronts, and schemes that had eight men at the line of scrimmage. It is a zone-blocking play. The key to the play is everyone is on a track. It is not only the offensive line on a track but the running back, also. The running back has to stay on track until something happens.

It is essential that your linemen stay on their track. I have had offensive guards who have not touched anyone for as many as 10 steps into the play. The thing you have to convince your linemen is to trust the track. They all want to lock onto a defender with their eyes and go get him.

The aiming point of the running back is the butt of the playside offensive tackle. He takes a drop-step and sprints on that track. The running back coach teaches the track by placing a fire hose we use as the alignment guide in the passing game on the ground. He lines it up from the tailback's position to the tackle's butt, and the running back uses it as a guide to the tackle.

After he teaches the track, he adds the first read. The running back is reading the hat of the defender on the tackle. If the hat is inside of the offensive tackle's hat, he goes to the next open gate because that gate is closed. The back knows if the defender's hat is inside, he is outside. If the hat is outside, he is inside. From there, he goes to his second read. The second read is the inside man.

Three things can happen on the play. If we get the reach on the #1 defender, the ball goes outside, and nothing else matters. If the hat is outside, he reads the second man. If the hat on the #2 defender is outside, he goes vertical inside the offensive guard. If the guard has the reach block, he goes vertical from

there. The key to the entire scheme is tracks and to keep the running back sprinting on his track.

Our blocking rules on this play are very simple. We are going to reach the playside gap (Diagram #6). To the playside, we talk about the first and second defenders. We number them from the outside to the inside. On a 37 alignment to the tight end, the 7 technique is the #1 defender, and the 3 technique is the #2 defender.

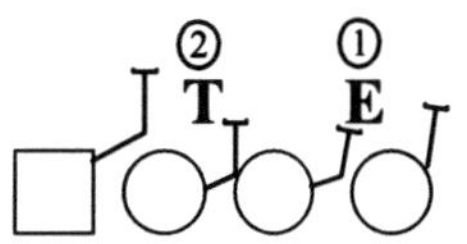

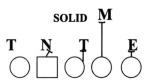

Diagram #6. Playside Gap

The aiming point for the offensive blockers is the armpit of the defender. We use covered and uncovered rules. The offensive lineman knows if he is covered, his help is the man inside of him, and he is going to work to the next linebacker. If the lineman is covered and the man to his inside is covered, they become solid and lock onto those defenders (Diagram #7). The combination block goes to someone inside of them. If we get a double Eagle Bear front, we man up on the frontside. The backside runs the scoop scheme to the inside.

Diagram #7. Solid

At the point of attack, if we get the #1 defender reached, the ball is going outside regardless of anything else. If we cannot reach him, the offensive lineman wants to cover him up and allow the running back to make a two-way cut off of him. If we cannot reach the defender, the blocker wants to wall the defender. We did a good job of this technique this year. On the fourth step, the blocker wants to throw the defender.

On this play, if the guard can knock the 3 technique off the ball, that is where the big plays come from. The 3 technique is the #2 defender in the scheme. The backside has to cut the first defender to the backside. It does not matter whether it is a zero, 1, or 2i technique. We want the first defender to that side on the ground. The backside tackle has to gap-step and try to cut off the backside linebacker. If we cannot get the backside #1 defender cut, we want to run him down the line and not give up penetration.

At times, we do not get the playside linebacker blocked. We have someone assigned to him, but for some reason he does not get to him. The linebacker is too fast, or the offensive blocker is too slow. However, the playside linebacker is never the defender who makes the play. It is always the backside linebacker. He is the one who keeps the play to a three- or four-yard gain, when the play could have easily gone to the house. A good percentage of the time, the playside linebacker overruns the play.

The tackle and tight end will work on the 7-technique defensive end. The tight end has him leveraged at the start, but he has to work up to the Sam linebacker. The offensive tackle reaches from the inside, working to get his hat in the armpit of the 7-technique defensive end. We do not want to overreach and have the defender come inside the tackle's block. On the tackle's second step, he wants to be into the defender. If by the fourth step, the tackle has not reached the 7-technique end, he walls him to the outside. He takes his inside arm, locks out, and throws the defender outside. That walls the defender to the outside, and he cannot fall back into the play as the ball cuts inside.

The offensive linemen use a zone into the playside gap on the first step. He wants his helmet working outside on the first step. The second step is into the crotch of the defender and gaining ground toward him. On the third step, we want to be into the defender and working vertical to keep him from crossing his face. That is the three-step takeoff. We are looking for the breast over the knee. Most of our offensive linemen are not great athletes, but if they will work on their track, they can make the blocks.

When you watch your game tape, you should be able to find the drills you work in practice. If you cannot see your drills on the game tape, you need to get rid of them and try other drills.

If the offensive tackle has a 5-technique defender on him, he has to know whether the guard is covered or uncovered (Diagram #8). If the guard is uncovered, the tackle knows he has help inside. He does not worry about an inside stick by the defender. If the defender runs a stick stunt to the inside of the tackle, the tackle stays on his track and lets him go. The playside guard runs his track and expects the defender to come down. He works his head across the stick and work to get vertical. If the tackle had not come down, the guard would stay on his track until the linebacker attacks the line of scrimmage.

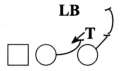

Diagram #8. Inside Stick

When the 5-technique defender stunted to the inside, the tackle released him and ran his track. That eventually will lead him to the inside linebacker. The trick is to make your linemen trust their track and not lock his eyes on the linebacker. They have to believe when the defender slants, there is another defender coming from somewhere. If they stay on their track, they will find him.

The best drill I know to teach the track technique is the gunny drill. I paint two lines, 30 inches apart. On those lines, I line up the left offensive tackle across from the right offensive tackle. They are going to block each other. One of them is blocking the stretch right play, and the other is blocking the stretch left play. They are both working in the same direction. This is a competitive drill.

If the right tackle gets the left tackle reached, he rips vertical and pins him inside. If he cannot reach him, on the fourth step, he takes his inside arm and throws the other tackle outside. Both tackles are trying to do the same thing to the other.

When they finish with that part of the drill, they come back and work the second part of the drill. They are the backside tackles working for a cutoff block on the backside 3 technique.

Teaching the cut block causes some tense time between the offensive and defensive line coaches. The defensive line coach does not want his player cut in practice. However, the head coach is on my side. He says if they are going to get cut, they have to learn how to play the cut. The defensive line coach starts yelling at me, and I yell at him. It looks like we are going to fight, and the players get all jacked up, and it becomes a good drill.

High school players think they take one-step and dive on the ground. The cut has to occur no sooner than the third step. If you watch good college players, they run five steps and cut. Before we cut, we want to get leverage. We punch the outside fist through to the far or inside knee of the defender. We follow that with the elbow to the far knee, followed by the shoulder to the far knee. We get the third step in the ground and roll up the defender.

The key to the cut block is to get vertical with your pads. If the hips are turned to the sideline, or the blocker gets flat to the line of scrimmage, the defender will flatten the blocker down the line of scrimmage and play off the cut block with his hands. The blocker has to zone-step for leverage and keep his pads vertical. That gives him a chance to make the block.

When we install the track, you talk to your players before you try to do these drills. You talk about the technique and what you want them to do. The first time we try this in practice, the uncovered man never gets to the overtake position. He gets hit in the mouth every time. When we run the drills, we start with the first two steps. If he sees the outside number of the 7-technique defender, he thinks about overtaking the block. If he does not see the outside number, he stays on his track to the next level. The first time I go through the drill, I tell the dummy player to keep leverage and stretch to the outside and the linebacker to close. That allows the tackle to make the proper track and block on the play.

Then, we reverse the movements and let them work on that part of the block. We bring the defender inside and scrape the linebacker over the top. The tackle sees the outside number because it is coming to him. He knows he has to overtake the defender, and the tight end comes off for the linebacker.

You must understand, when your linemen start to do this for the first time, they will not be successful. You have to continue to rep and work on the techniques, and it will eventually come. They have to get the feel for what is going on. They can grasp it in the walk-through, but when we go full speed, they think too much. It takes time and reps to perfect the scheme.

It has been a privilege to be here. I appreciate Coach Castle giving me the chance to speak. Thank you very much for your time and attention.

SCREEN PASSING GAME FOR RUNNING BACKS

Jonesboro High School, Arkansas

It is a pleasure to be here today. I know a lot of you feel as I do about clinics. Coaches want to hear X's and O's and not philosophy. I am going to spend a large part of this presentation on strictly X's and O's, but, in order to get to that point, I am going to start with a little philosophy behind what we do.

The screen game has been big for us. Today, I am going to talk about the screen game for running backs.

Out of 374 passes this year, we only gave up five sacks. I believe a lot of that is because of the emphasis we place on the screen game, which slows the rush of the defensive linemen.

OFFENSIVE PHILOSOPHY

We think pass first. We ran 610 offensive plays, and 62 percent of those were passes. When we talk about 62 percent being pass plays, 50 percent of that was three-step passing and sprint-out passing. That is 50 percent of what we do. We run the ball 38 percent of the time, and the remaining 12 percent of our offense is screen-passing plays. The reason I list pass plays and screen plays separately is because I do not think of our screen passes as passing plays. They are seen as runs to us.

Second, we want to put kids in the best position to do the best they can do. With the situation where the wishbone had been the offense the year before, we had to put running backs, tight ends, and even some linemen into different positions so they could play their best in our system.

One of our receivers had spent the two seasons prior as a fullback. I am guessing he had never caught a football in a game before. This year, he caught 50 passes for over 700 yards and 10 touchdowns. He was a big threat for us as our Z-receiver. We spend time trying to find a place for each kid where he can play his best on Friday nights.

Third, we want to figure out who our best player is and get that player the ball. It is going to change from year to year. A couple of years ago at another school, it was our quarterback. He ran, he threw, and we did anything we could think of to get him the ball. This year, it just happened to be our running back, and we are fortunate enough to have him coming back next year.

We think pass first, but our best player is a running back. We have to figure out ways to get him the ball besides just handing it to him. We will split him out some, motion him some, and try to get him involved in our screen game. It is interesting as a pass-first team, last year, our running back had way more touches than anybody.

Let me describe our running back in our offense. The first thing he has to do is pass protect. If you think that 62 percent of our offense is passing, then he is going to spend a majority of his time blocking. He has to get it in his mind that he is going to pass protect first.

Number two, he has to be football smart. If you ask his teachers, they may not brag on his performance in the classroom, but, for us, he knows our offense. He knows the formations, the protections, and all the assignments of everybody.

The third thing he has to do is get positive yards rushing. Negative plays kill the spread offense. Negative plays allow the defense to attack. If we can get just one or two yards on a run, we consider that a positive play. Positive plays tend to limit somewhat what the defense is able to do. Finally, because we are a pass-first offense, he has to catch the ball.

STATISTICS 2008

This chart will show you some of our statistical breakdowns. I want to talk about them briefly. We had 610 offensive plays.

POS	RUSH	YDS	TDs	REC	YDS	TDs
X	0	0	0	68	964	8
Y	7	79	0	48	647	9
Z	1	7	0	60	834	12
H	31	154	1	38	423	4
QB	30	210	2			
F	206	1217	15	46	419	3

You can see the balance among our X-, Y-, Z-, and H-receivers on touches. We distributed the ball to all receivers. However, our quarterback did a decent job of making sure our running back (F) had, by far, the most touches.

The receivers each touched the ball about 10 percent of the time. Our running back touched the ball over 40 percent of the time. He averaged 16 to 17 carries per game. We needed to get him the ball in other ways. We wanted to get him close to 25 touches every Friday night—part of that would be through our screen game.

The last point in our offensive philosophy is that we consider screens as runs. We believe they slow down the blitz. In addition, this gives athletes the ball in space to use their ability to make plays. This year, we were fortunate to have athletes who could take a two-yard screen pass and turn it into a 50-yard touchdown. In addition, most of the time, our screens are safe plays. I say most of the time because we did have one intercepted and returned for a touchdown.

When we get to the game clips, you are going to see that I did not just put in the plays that were 100 percent successful. I also put in plays that went the other way, but I hope you will see the mistakes our kids made that led to that. If you implement this into your offense, you can avoid those mistakes.

At Jonesboro High School, we have 11 screens—six are wide receiver screens, four are running back screens, which is what we are going to talk about today, and we have one double screen. On each of those, there is a sister play to the other side, so we have some variety in the ways we can get the ball to our athletes in space with our screen game.

We practice our screen game for 15 minutes every day. Some people say that two hours is about as long as a practice ought to be, but we are not like that. We practice probably three hours a day, but we try to build it up. We spend 30 to 40 minutes individually at the beginning of practice, and then, the next hour going tri-team where everyone is together without a defense. Then, we spend the last hour in scrimmage-type situations.

Our screen drill is the first drill we do every day. We can practice the 11 screens four times, or twice to each side for two quarterbacks, in 15 minutes. We are running four or five plays per minute. I do not like running sprints, so this also serves as a conditioning drill as well. There are players moving all over the place and it is a very intense 15 minutes.

RUNNING BACK SCREENS

We have four different running back screens. We have an *off-tackle screen*, and we have a *middle screen*. We have a *one-man screen* we use to combat a particular blitz. Finally, we have *fast screens*, which are catch-and-throws by our quarterback to get the ball to our running back on a flair-type route.

Off-Tackle Screen

The off-tackle screen has to be sold. There has to be somewhat of an acting job done by all 11 offensive players for a screen to be successful. This is more so with our linemen than with the other players. They have to sell the look of a regular pass. They have to show their hands, get a good kick-slide, and get depth before they get upfield as part of the screen.

- *Left Tackle:* Kick-slide, try not to contact the defensive end.
- *Left Guard:* 60 set; show hands, engage, two count, pull by, release right to trash.

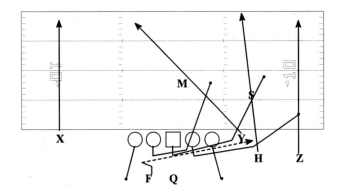

Diagram #1. Off-Tackle Screen Right

- *Center:* 60 set; show hands, engage, two count, pull by, release right to alley.
- *Right Guard:* 60 set; show hands, engage, two count, pull by, release right to corner.
- *Right Tackle:* Kick-slide, try not to contact defensive end.
- *X:* Go outside, run to cornerback's outside shoulder and through.
- *Y:* Go try to get to safety's toes.
- *Z:* Go outside, run to cornerback's outside shoulder and through.
- *H:* Go to seam.
- *F:* Slide to inside leg of backside tackle at snap, check blitz, when guard leaves, you leave and work down the line of scrimmage, catch, and score.
- *Quarterback:* Read, three-step drop out of gun, go through two reads of route, retreat and draw rush in, and throw screen to the F-back.

The quarterback has to use his eyes to go through the progressions of the pass play called. Typically, our routes are mirrored routes. He picks a side and lives with it. He goes through two reads, and then comes back to the screen. In a perfect world, if we are in a 2x2 set and we want to throw the off-tackle screen to the right, then it would be perfect for him to pick the left side to go through his progressions. In using his eyes, he may influence a secondary player or a linebacker for one or two steps. This gives us a bit of an advantage.

Our wide receivers do not block on this. They run the route called. They are not as good at blocking, so we want them to run their routes. We really want them to show they are going to get the ball. If

four verticals is the pass play we called to go with our screen, then they need to get downfield deep. Any kind of block they might throw would be a peel-back block, if our running back is getting downfield with the ball.

Let me get to the plays. I will go through the assignments in detail, then diagram it, and then show some game clips of the play.

For our tackles, it does not matter if the call is left or right because they are going to do the same thing. They are trying to get as much depth vertically as they possibly can before they make contact with the defensive ends. If you tell them to try not to contact the defensive ends, they will probably have to contact them about two or three yards in the backfield.

The defensive ends' feet tend to stop on contact. When that happens too early, it allows them a better chance of retracing their steps, trailing the play, and making the tackle. We do not want to hit them too early.

The guards and the center are the most important part of this play. The playside guard, in this case the right guard, does two kick-slides, which we call a 60 set. He will show his hands, engage by just touching the defensive lineman, and if he has to, he will throw him by. Typically, we do not have to do that because they are trying to get up the field.

The important part here for both guards and the center is to not try to release out to their landmarks over the defensive linemen. By that, I mean they should not cross their face. They have to release under them toward the line of scrimmage before they get to their landmarks.

The playside guard's landmark is the corner. It amounts to blocking the flat defender, whether that is the outside linebacker or the cornerback. It is very important that he goes flat down the line of scrimmage. If he heads up the field too far, he will run past his man.

The center sets for two counts, releases flat down the line, and he blocks the alley. The backside guard kick-slides twice, releases flat down the line, and blocks any trash coming from the inside.

We can get a better picture of it looking at this diagram. If we are seeing cover 1, the flat defender may be well off the line of scrimmage, so when the playside guard gets to his landmark, he needs to turn and get his butt upfield. The alley player may be the safety trying to fill, and the center is responsible for that alley. Now, as the backside guard approaches the alley, he needs to have his eyes looking back so he can cut off the linebackers that are coming from the backside. As he gets into position, his hips need to start turning where his butt is facing the sideline. He is catching any trash.

The running back steps up as if he is in pass protection. His landmark is the inside leg of the backside tackle. As soon as the guard leaves, he leaves with him and works flat down the line of scrimmage.

Our quarterback takes a three-step drop with his eyes on his progression for the pass play called, and then he drifts. If he feels pressure but does not have a good passing lane yet, he has two options: he can bounce it at the running back's feet or he can scramble to the playside.

Before we get to the film clips, I want to show you one more slide. A lot of times, we will throw this screen away from the strength of the formation (Diagram #2). The running back will just step up and go the other way. There are fewer defenders, typically, on that side.

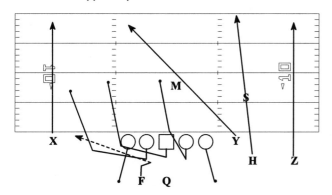

Diagram #2. Off-Tackle Screen Left

Middle Screens

Middle screens also must be sold by the blockers (Diagram #3). Our offensive linemen have to invite, allow, or throw defensive linemen or blitzers upfield. We are going to kick-slide, get our hands inside, grab them, and throw them upfield. Now, if they are better athletes than we are and they are really beating us upfield, then we just let them go.

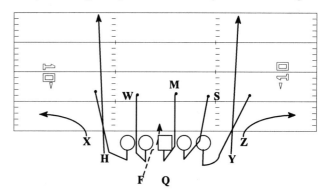

Diagram #3. Middle Screen

- *Left Tackle:* 60 set; show hands, engage, three counts, release left to flat defender.
- *Left Guard:* 60 set; show hands, engage, three counts, release left to Will.
- *Center:* 60 set; show hands, engage, three counts, release to Mike.
- *Right Guard:* 60 set; show hands, engage, three counts, release right flat to Sam.
- *Right Tackle:* 60 set; show hands, engage, three count, release right to flat defender.
- *X:* Speed-out.
- *Y:* Go seam.
- *Z:* Speed out.
- *H:* Go seam.
- *F:* Slide to inside leg of playside guard at snap, check blitz, when guard leaves, you leave and find throwing lane, catch, and score.
- *Quarterback:* Read, three-step drop out of gun, go through two reads of routes, retrieve and draw rush in, and throw screen to the F-back.

The quarterback has to be patient on this play a little more than others and keep his eyes upfield. All five offensive linemen are getting downfield, so every defensive lineman and blitzer is coming right at him. He has to find an alley to get the ball to the running back. He may have to change the plane he is throwing on, or he may have to change his arm action and throw sidearm. He may have to jump, but he has to get the ball to the back. As before, the wide receivers have to run the route called—they do not block.

Again, you will get a better idea of it if I draw it up for you. We have it here out of a 2x2 set, which is rather compact. It is my responsibility to call a play that will influence some of the secondary defenders in a way that puts our guy in the best position to make a touchdown rather than a 10- or 12-yard gain. Sometimes, a good way to do that is to compact our formation, run speed outs, and get the corners to turn their backs.

Our offensive linemen all take their 60 set, show hands, engage for a three count, and release. The tackles release to the flat defenders, and the inside three release on the inside linebackers.

The outside receivers run speed outs, and the inside receivers run go routes. The running back is a little different. He is stepping to the inside leg of the guard on this screen. When the defensive linemen pass him, he turns around. He should be about two or three yards behind the line of scrimmage at that point.

One-Man Screens

We had to come up with a way to beat a backside blitz when we went to our 3x1 formation, so we put in a one-man screen (Diagram #4). Since our running back is always on the backside of that formation, it just made sense to put the ball in the large area where the blitzer left.

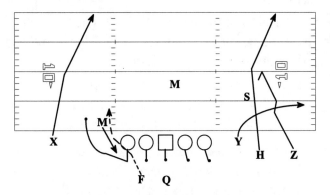

Diagram #4. One-Man Screen Left

- *Left Tackle:* Kick slide and get to the flat defenders.
- *Left Guard:* 60 set.
- *Center:* 60 set.
- *Right Guard:* 60 set.
- *Left Tackle:* 60 set.
- *X:* 10 post.
- *Y:* Speed out.
- *Z:* 10-8 inside curl.
- *H:* 10 corner.
- *F:* Slide to inside leg of playside tackle at snap, when tackle leaves, you leave and get flat down the line of scrimmage, catch, and score.
- *Quarterback:* Read, three-step drop out of gun, use eyes to look away from play, retreat and draw rush in, and throw flat screen to the F-back.

All we do is slide our back to the inside leg of the tackle, which is his normal landmark for pass protection, and when the tackle leaves, he leaves and gets flat down the line of scrimmage. The only guy that is getting out is our backside tackle. He will kick slide, let the guy go, and it is one lineman with our running back. We are just trying to get it to him with that lineman running interference or blocking.

In the shotgun, we like to hook the end, get the guard to the alley, and quick pitch the ball to the running back. This screen is similar in philosophy to that running play.

We are trying to get a guy to the alley, run off the cornerback with our receivers, and get the ball to the back as fast as we possibly can, in the vacated area, with one guy blocking. Our quarterback's eyes need to go to the strength of the formation. He needs to do his two reads and then come back and throw the one-man screen.

We only ran this play four times this year, but if you can catch people who do not see you consistently, possibly in the playoffs, and they like to bring backside pressure away from your trips formation, then this is a good play to get your best player out there with the ball. Now, I have a few film clips of it to show you.

Thank you for your attention

THE PASSING GAME MADE SIMPLE

Wilson Area High School, Pennsylvania

Some of you may not know me, but I am the guy who thought it would be a good idea to throw the ball 53 times to try to win a state 2A championship in 2005. We throw the ball quite a bit at Wilson High School. However, statistically, we are almost even in our runs-to-pass ratio. We had so much success throwing the ball that people thought we threw it every down.

I come from a little town north of Harrisburg called Newport. I have been spoiled throughout my life as a player and a coach. I have been around really good people and have seen great examples of what to do. When I played for Newport, Coach John Zeigler was hired as the head coach. I was a sophomore, and we had not had a winning season in 25 years.

When he came in as head coach, he had one formation. The double slot formation was like the Delaware wing-T. That was the formation we used 95 percent of the time. I say that to you because it is important as to where we are today. We have a formation we stay in about 90 percent of the time unless we get into a short-yardage situation.

The first year, we went 5-6. The second year, we had our first winning season in 27 years. The first high-five we tried, we missed. We were so unaccustomed to winning; we did not know how to handle success.

After Newport, I went into the Marines for four years. The Marine Corps plays football. It was eight-man football, but it was football. In the eight-man football, you do not have two tackles. You have two guards and a center. The field is only 80 yards long and 40 yards wide. It is a very wide-open style of football.

I was stationed in California. That year, California had some bad wildfires in Yellowstone Park. The Marines were called in to help contain the fires. Our two coaches went to fight the fires, and I became the player/coach of the team. My first experience at coaching was a player/coach for that Marine team.

From there, I went to school at East Stroudsburg University. Denny Duds was the head coach there and was an institution at that school. While I was there, Jim Pry came in as our offensive coordinator. I did not know how to take him. I thought he was insane. He wanted defenses to cover every inch of the field. He put together schemes and packages that caused a lot of dilemma with base defenses.

One of my backups, when I was at ESU, was James Franklin. He is the heir apparent at University of Maryland. After I graduated for ESU, I was an assistant coach for four years before getting the head coaching position at Wilson. I have been there since 1998.

We started as an I-back team and evolved into what we are today. The reason we went to the offense we run now was personnel. We had a good quarterback and a bunch of wide receivers. We have many philosophies of why we do what we do. We have been very successful. Our quarterback, Tyler Smith, threw for almost 3,000 yards last season. We put a lot on his shoulders.

I am unorthodox in the way I do things. I am going to show you the schemes and work backward from there. That may drive some coaches crazy, but we have had success teaching our receiving corps and the quarterback that way.

The formation we use 90 percent of the time is a double-wide slot set. We call it "air raid." I have not invented anything. I have stolen everything I have heard from other people whom I mentioned earlier. We have the West Coast element in our passing game. We have a lot of ideas built into our scheme.

Most of what we do is mirrored patterns. It creates mismatches and makes it simple for the quarterback to read defenses. One of the most popular routes today is the hitch route by the outside receiver and the takeoff by the inside receiver (Diagram #1). We call the streak route a zero pattern. We want to know how the flat defender is going to play. Are they going to the flat immediately, or are they going at an angle? The free safety in the middle is watching the quarterbacks. The quarterback has to look off the free safety and linebackers. He knows he has the same pattern on both sides and looks for a move by the free safety or linebackers to determine the side he works.

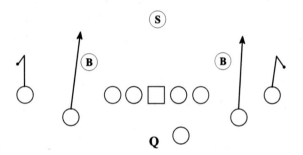

Diagram #1. Air Raid

If he finds the safety favoring one zero pattern over the other, he throws to the opposite zero pattern.

The corners in a cover 3 are there to stop touchdowns. They will let you have the underneath routes. They do not want to be beat deep. We massage the defense and get them moving around, and hopefully we've undisciplined them before we throw the ball. That is what we are trying to take advantage of.

The hitch is one combination we run. We also run the slant/quick out (Diagram #2). It is a mirrored route. We run slants by the outside receivers and quick outs by the inside receivers. The quarterback

keys the outside linebacker. This pattern is nothing earth-shattering, but it puts the defense in a coverage conflict.

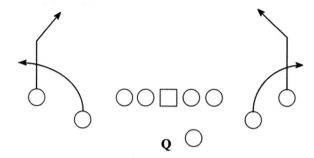

Diagram #2. Slant/Quick Out

We run the eight patterns by the outside receivers and a five-yard out by the inside receivers, which is good against a cover-2 secondary.

This next pattern I learned from Jim Pry. We call it "bingo" (Diagram #3). It is another mirrored route. On this pattern, the single back in the backfield runs a checkdown pattern in the box. The inside linebackers are hook/curl players. The outside linebackers in a cover-3 defense should be flat players. The first problem for the defense is the running back in the box. If the inside linebackers drop to their responsibility, we throw the pattern to the back in the box between the inside linebackers.

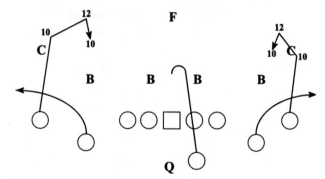

Diagram #3. Bingo

We will give the ball to the running back as long as the linebackers drop to their hook/curl responsibility. If you hit the back and he stumbles for three yards, it becomes second-and-one-yard for the first down. Sooner or later, one of the linebackers will cover the back coming into the box. When one of the linebackers covers the box receiver, there is no one in the hook/curl area to that side. The outside receivers push hard to 10 yards and break to the post for two yards. They snap the pattern off and come back down to 10 yards in the curl area. The inside receivers run a flat pattern.

When we originally taught this pattern, the receivers pushed to 10 yards and curled to the inside. As the receiver became more experienced, we added some moves to the route. We want to drive the corner and make him play deep. When we drive to the post, it keeps the corner from coming back on the curl. After two steps to the post, the receiver snaps the pattern back into a 10-yard curl pattern. That leaves you two receivers on one defender. The flat defender has to play the flat in most coverage situations.

It is a simple read for the quarterback. The quarterback reads the back in the box. That is where the play starts. If one of the linebackers takes the back in the box, that is the side he throws. If the right linebacker takes the back, he throws the right curl pattern. The only thing he has to see is a different-colored shirt on the receiver. If there is a defender on the curl, the flat has to be open because there is no other defender in the area.

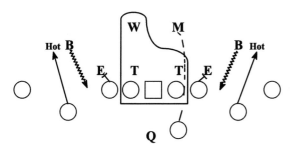

Diagram #4. Protection Scheme

This pattern creates a conflict in the coverage and is very useable. It takes time to get the quarterback to this point. It takes discipline in the quarterback to understand and see all the things you ask him to see. We have built-in hot routes for the quarterback (Diagram #4). The back is going to the box on the pattern. In our protection, we have the center and both guards on the two defensive tackles and one linebacker. They will designate who that linebacker is. The tackles block the defensive ends. We block big-on-big, and the center takes the Will linebacker. If the right linebacker blitzes, the

running back picks him up, and the quarterback throws to the right curl route. The blitz pickup is built into the pattern.

The inside receivers are looking at the outside flat defenders. If one of them blitzes off the edge, he yells, "Hot, hot, hot," to the quarterback. The quarterback is five yards deep in the shotgun set. When he hears the hot call, he turns and throws to the flat receiver. It does not matter what pattern we have called. When the receiver sees the linebacker blitz, he runs his hot pattern. It is a sight-adjust pattern.

Bingo has been good to us over the years. It is a good call in a third-and-eight-yards-to-go type of play. If they want to blitz, you have the hot reads built into the play. If they want to sit back and cover, you can put pressure on the linebackers to cover the back in the box.

This is an adaptable play to the I formation (Diagram #5). That is the offense we were before we began to spread the field. You can run the curl routes with the split end and flanker. The tight end runs one of the flat routes, and the tailback runs the other. The fullback becomes the back in the box.

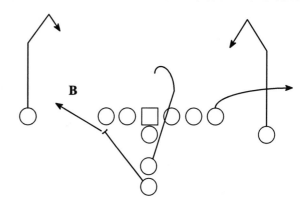

Diagram #5. I-Formation Bingo

The difference is the protection scheme. When the tailback releases to the flat, he has to read the outside linebacker blitz. If he is coming on the blitz, he has to block him instead of running the flat route. The tight end is a different story. If the outside linebacker on his side blitzes, he runs his pattern because he is aligned on the line of scrimmage and can get to the flat quickly. Because of his proximity to the line of scrimmage, he releases.

From this set, if both inside linebackers blitz, we have an adjustment we can run. We call that "bongo" (Diagram #6). We can switch up the routes of the tight end and fullback. That gives the fullback a check-out release and puts the tight end between the linebackers on the box route. The fullback runs the flat route unless his outside linebacker blitzes, in which case he picks up the blitz.

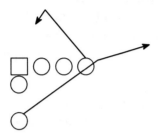

Diagram #6. Bongo

When the wide receiver sees the linebacker blitz, he bends his pattern instead of running the sharp cuts. He has to be aware of the safety to his side in a two-safety or four-across look. If the coverage is a quarter-type coverage with the safety sitting on the inside curl, he may have to convert his pattern. If he reads the safety robbing the curl, he can take the pattern deep behind him. If the fullback goes into the box, we call bingo. If the tight end goes into the box, we call bongo. It is not a different play; it is an adjustment.

Against a cover-2 look, we run a route called Gator (Diagram #7). It is named Gator because we learned it from Jim Pry, who was a disciple of Steve Spurrier when he was at Florida. If we steal something, we make sure we tag a name on it and give credit to the originator. So much of our passing game comes from Steve Spurger's days at the University of Florida.

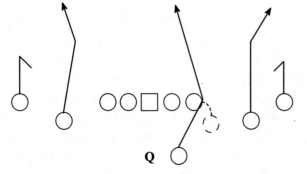

Diagram #7. Gator

With this pattern, we want to create a dilemma in the middle of the field. It is better run from a 3x2 formation, but we can run it from this formation. In the empty set, the back has a freer and quicker release down the middle of the field. The outside receivers run five-yard hitch patterns. The inside receivers run eight, which is a corner route. The third receiver runs from the backfield, or the slot in a trips set, down the middle of the field.

We try to put the half players in a bind. As soon as one of the safeties start to lean toward one side or the other, that declares the side for the quarterback. The scheme is good, but we have not had much success because of the quarterback. They are like most quarterbacks. They are greedy and selfish. They want to throw to the deepest receiver. I do not have a problem with that as long as he is the deepest, most open receiver. They get greedy and forget to take advantage of what the defense gives us.

We have a complement to the play. We bring one slot receiver in motion to give us a trips set and work a 2-on-1 deep route on the half player to that side. In our league, there were teams that did not adjust to the third receiver in motion going vertical. The free safety stayed on the far hash, and we worked on the half player to the trips side. The inside receivers running the eight routes still key the outside linebackers. If they blitz, the receiver has a sight adjustment to a hot route.

When we send all the receivers vertical, we refer to that as "crocodile." That is what we call in the huddle. We are a silent-snap team. We are not a no-huddle team, but we go at a no-huddle pace. We run this against a two-deep look. When we go to the 3x2 set, we put another receiver in the formation. We do not set the fullback or running back in that third-receiver formation. We still read the hot routes and try to hit the areas that anyone throwing four-vertical routes tries to hit.

When you run a four-vertical route, the quarterback has no bail out for a failed route beside tuck the ball and run (Diagram #8). We call an under pattern to one of the outside receivers. The way we call the play is to use the receiver's name. The quarterback calls, "Crocodile Brian under." We have a wide receiver named Brian. He goes down the field as if he were going to run a five-yard out pattern. He plants, opens his hips and eyes back to the quarterback, and pivots back to the inside. He runs a pivot route, coming back hard into the middle of the field. We still have to threaten the deep-half players. The slot receiver to the pivot-route side widens his deep pattern to keep pressure on the two-deep coverage.

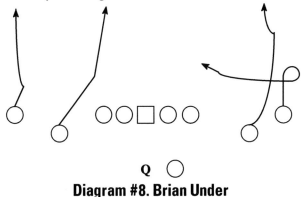

Diagram #8. Brian Under

We can designate any of the four receivers to run the under route. The other receiver to that side has to make an adjustment in his pattern. He has to make up for the lost deep pattern to that side. If the inside slot receiver ran the under, the outside receiver has to bend his pattern to the inside to keep the pressure on the deep zones.

We have had a lot of success with this pattern, mostly because of the teenage boys running the coverage. There is an undisciplined nature about them because they have all kinds of distractions. Sometimes, they misalign and get outside the hash mark by a step or two. That means something to our quarterbacks. We take advantage of those misalignments by bending our patterns away from them. We put a lot of pressure on the shoulder of the quarterback and the receiver. I think the neatest thing is the number of catches our receivers have. The four receivers caught 34, 27, 29, and 22. We do not have one receiver catching all the balls. We spread the ball around, and they all take pride in running their patterns. Our receivers run their routes at 150 miles per hour because they do not know where the ball is going.

We sort of keep them in the dark because we hate them to take a play off. If they know the ball is not going to be passed to him, he may not run the pattern as hard. The only one who knows where the ball is going is the quarterback. With his pre-snap read, he knows with 90-percent effectiveness where he will throw the ball. Our league is a running-dominated league. The defenses align to stop the run. However, they are starting to do some crazy things because the offenses are spreading out.

We are a one-back set, and I am excited about our waggle pass from the play-action (Diagram #9). We have rules that go along with this pattern. The wide receiver to the side of the waggle runs a zero pattern and clears the deep coverage. The opposite wide receiver runs a hard post at eight to nine yards. It is not deep to the post by something that brings him across the field. We want the quarterback to see this receiver. The running back aligns to the side of the waggle and runs a trap fake to the opposite side.

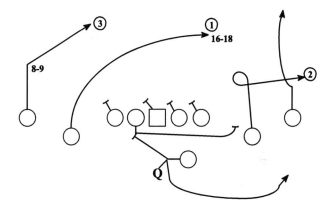

Diagram #9. Waggle Pass

We block away from the waggle side and let the uncovered lineman to the backside pull as the personal protector for the quarterback. If the center is the uncovered lineman, he pulls. The quarterback has to feel the containment. If the containment is outside, he stops and sets his feet. If he is outside the containment, he continues to run. The quarterback determines that part of the play. We try not to overcoach that too much. After he makes his fake, the tailback cleans up the backside for anything chasing the play. He initially fills for the pulling lineman and works outside.

The inside slot to the backside is the primary receiver. He screams across the field, trying to get to a depth of 16 to 18 yards. The playside slot runs a pivot out pattern at five to six yards. The quarterback reads the first crosser to the flat pattern. We run this pattern very effectively. Defenses will try to stop the crossing route with the safety dropping down on him. Before our receivers gained experience, we called the play "waggle throwback."

With experienced receiver, they can see the safety jumping the crossing route and automatically know the ball is coming to him. His job is to lose the corner and get into the post area behind the safety. We have fast and smart receivers who read those types of situations. We can call the route or let the quarterback read it.

We have a rule about the zero-route to the outside receiver on the side of the waggle. We do not throw to him unless it is a touchdown. If it is only a 65-yard gain, I yell at him for throwing it. However, I do not yell too loud [laughs]. Unless it is a touchdown, do not throw the ball. Try to keep them from being greedy. Being greedy and selfish will affect them later on with their touchdown-to-interception ratio.

If the play is covered, do not force the ball into some place it will not go. If you have lots of green grass in front of you, run the ball. Throw the checkdown instead of trying to hit the home run. There are several things you can do, including throwing the ball away. The interception is not one of those choices.

We want the backside post receiver's pattern at the correct angle rather than the correct depth. We are not as concerned with the depth as we are the angle. I tell them eight to nine yards, but I want to make sure their angle is flatter than a deep post. I want separation over the under crossing route but I do not want a tremendous amount of depth. That lets the quarterback pick him up quicker and gives him great vision on the receiver. The best weapon for a good quarterback is their eyes.

From an I-formation set, we can run the same pattern (Diagram #10). The tight end runs the cross pattern at the 16- to 18-yard depth. The flanker runs the flat post route over the top of the crosser. The split end clears the top off the coverage. The fullback sifts through the line and becomes the pivot flat pattern. The tailback counter-steps and fills for the pulling guard to the backside. The quarterback fakes and brings the ball out on the waggle. It is the same pattern.

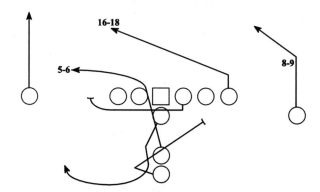

Diagram #10. Waggle I Formation

If you see the fourth rusher creeping up to the line of scrimmage from either side, you want to check out of the waggle if you can. If you cannot check, call time-out. You cannot protect this play very well with the fourth rusher coming off a side. We would check out of the play to a slant or hitch to the side of the blitz.

We fell into the waggle screen by accident. We ran the waggle and everything broke down on the play. Our tailback has a tendency to stand around on the play. He was standing there watching the play, the quarterback threw him the ball, and we gained 12 yards on the play. One of my assistants said that would be a good play to install. We started to run the play, and it has been a successful play for us (Diagram #11). The tailback chips off his blocking assignment and turns around. He sits and makes himself a big target. Our quarterback is a great salesman and makes the play go.

When you run a play-action screen, you do not want to get in too big a hurry to throw the pass. You must let the defense take the handoff fake and begin to scramble to get back into their pass responsibility. If you throw the pass too quickly, the defense does not have time to feel the panic of being out of position. Make them scramble to find receivers, and throw it when they least expect it.

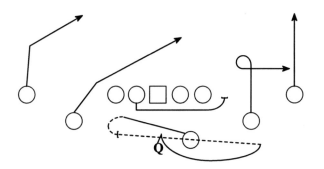

Diagram #11. Waggle Screen

Our running offense is about three plays. We are a shotgun team and run a trap, a quarterback power off the trap, and a dive play. We rush the ball for about 130 yards a game. We run it effectively because all week long the defense works on our passing attack and not so much on the running game.

The teams in our league do not play much cover 2 or cover 3 anymore. Most of them are playing us in a loose man-to-man coverage. Before I run out of time, I want to show you some drills we do with our wide receivers. We have a JUGS® machine, we use in our machine gun drill.

MACHINE GUN DRILL

Purpose: To get as many repetitions to all your receivers as possible in a very limited amount of time.

Key Points:

- Eyes on the ball.
- Use your hands.
- Hand position.

Logistics:

- We do not allow our quarterbacks to throw this drill.
- Several balls will be needed.
- Quarterbacks, managers, or walking wounded can be used to reload the gun.

BOMB DRILL

Purpose: To become highly effective at throwing and catching the deep ball.

Key Points:

- Full speed on post pattern.
- Quarterback's awareness of different wide-receiver abilities.
- Wide-receiver concentration on a ball that has a lot of air and flight time.
- Use your legs to get to the ball. Avoid "the Frankenstein 40" (running with your arms outstretched).

Logistics:

- Quarterbacks should do this drill.

WRONG SHOULDER

Purpose: To give the wide receiver the skill and knowledge to go after a poorly thrown pass.

Key Points:

- Half speed in a straight line away from the quarterback, looking over the designated shoulder.
- Ball is thrown purposely over the incorrect shoulder.
- Wide receiver turns only his upper body to find the ball; may have to increase speed.

Logistics:

- Several footballs will be needed.
- Use managers to feed balls; this drill is a progression of the machine gun drill.
- Quarterback should not throw this drill (builds bad habits).

EENIE, MEENIE, MINEY, MO

Purpose: To create an atmosphere where the wide receiver cannot cheat a hook or hitch route by looking back early.

- To teach the wide receiver to make break quickly.

Key Points:

- Taking the last step in the pattern.
- Snapping the hips, shoulders, head, and eyes around while bringing hands up to make the reception
- Wide receiver should not duck his head, lean away, or use his body to make the catch.

Logistics:

- Wide receivers should be about 10 yards and with their backs to the passer.
- Each wide receiver is called individually by name or number.
- When the passer calls out the wide receiver, that wide receiver executes the technique.

WINDOW DRILL

Purpose: Progression from Eenie, Meenie, Miney, Mo drill.

- To allow wide receiver to make himself open.
- To not allow an under-covering linebacker to get between the wide receiver and the passer on a hook or hitch route.

Key Points:

- Looking for subtle movement form the wide receiver.
- Quick feet and judgment.

Logistics:

- Have wide receivers stand at a points close to the top of the curl route with their back to the passer.
- Place two cones one yard in front of and on either side of the wide receiver.
- Tell them whether the intent is inside or outside.
- Give command to move.

FOCUS DRILL

Purpose:

- To have wide receivers develop concentration on the ball.
- To distract wide receiver in order to test his concentration.

Key Points:

- Make sure technique is not breaking down because of the distraction.

Logistics:

- Have several other wide receivers standing with their arms in the air and about three or four yards apart.
- Have one wide receiver at a time jog about five yards behind the line of wide receivers.
- Passer throws the ball so that it barely clears the arms of the other wide receivers.

HIP FLIP

Purpose:

- To take immediate advantage of a defensive back who commits to the angle of the wide receiver too early.
- To create separation from the defender before the actual break in the pattern.

Key Points:

- Wide receiver should attack a shoulder of the defender from his get-off .
- Wide receiver should make break on pattern when he sees the defender flip his hips.
- Anticipation and quick reaction are key.

Logistics:

- Have a defender across from the wide receiver with varying coverage looks.
- When the wide receiver sees the defender flip his hips, he should accelerate into his break.
- Wide receiver learns that the route on paper and the route on the field are not always the same. We do not want our wide receivers being robots.

STALK BLOCK

Purpose:

- To develop a blocking technique that is sound, effective, and understood.
- To make wide receivers aware that this is the majority of their job.
- To motivate wide receivers.

Key Points:

- Angle to a point midway between the defender and the plays design.
- Maintain quick feet and a coiled posture.
- Let the defender come to you.
- Deliver a blow to the breastplate and recoil, moving the feet to better position yourself for another blow.
- Keep hands inside the framework of the defender.
- If the defender turns away, disengage until he turns back around.
- Go till you hear a whistle.

Logistics:

- Place a defender in front of the wide receiver.
- Make sure the defender is taking "recognition" steps to keep the drill realistic.

The last thing I want to show you is our passing route tree (Diagram #12). All even routes are run to the outside, and all odd routes are run to the inside.

Coaches, I hope I have given you a couple of things you can take back and use. It has been my pleasure, and I thank you for your attention.

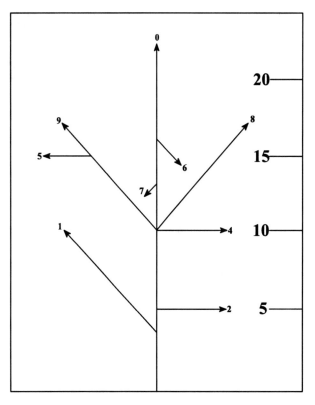

Diagram #12. Passing Route Tree

Greg Dempsey

THE 4-3 DEFENSE: FIRE ZONE BLITZ

Toledo Central Catholic High School, Ohio

First, I want to give you some background information on our defense. We used to be a *slant-50* defense. Now, we are a 4-3 quarter-coverage team with press corners. We evolved into this defense just as most of you are doing. We see one offense one week and another offense the next week. We see the wing-T and the double wing-T, and then, we see the spread offense and the flexbone. The 4-3 defense gives us a better chance to adjust on a week-to-week basis.

The other aspect relates to the practice situation. We have always wanted to bring more pressure on the offense, but I was afraid we would have some kid trip in man coverage, or get rubbed off on a crossing route, or get picked and the offense would get the big play. This is how we became a very heavy fire-zone pressure team. We are bringing a lot of pressure, but we are bringing it in a safe manner.

I want to cover a lot of different pressures. First, I will cover it on paper, and then, I will show it to you on film. I will show you some plays that worked well, and I will show you some plays that did not work so well. Keep in mind that everything we cover today, we have tailored it to the teams we play. We play the same seven league teams each year. We have four nonleague games per year as well. We cater the things we do depending on the teams we will be facing.

We are a formation defense. The defense is dictated by a tight end call. We have strongside defenders and weakside defenders. Our Sam backer goes to the tight call, and the Will backer goes away from the call. We have a 3-technique tackle that goes to the tight callside. We have a nose tackle that goes away from the tight call. The strong safety goes to the tight call, and the free safety goes away from the call.

It has been different with our corners depending on what type of offense we face. If we face a wing-T team, one corner is always going to go to the tightside or the wingside. He is going to help on the Buck sweep, the off-tackle play, and other plays similar to those two plays. If we face a fast, spread team, we put our best corner to the field as a base rule and the slower corner to the boundary. Sometimes, we will place our best corner to the best receiver's side. We do switch the corners around depending on the team we are playing. Everyone else plays either strong or weakside. Even the ends are flip-flopped. That works into a tight end trade a lot.

In our front seven, we are in a base 4-3 about 90 percent of the time. We have used the over-and-under concepts about 10 percent of the time. We do that by bringing our Sam backer on the line. We are in a two-deep shell look 90 percent of the time. If we play cover 3, which is the weak fire zone, we are going to do it off the press-quarters look.

We do play some man coverage. If you get into our red zone and if we are desperate, we are going to man up and bring pressure.

Our best players play defense—the rest play offense. We can manufacture scoring opportunities through field position, big plays, trick plays, special teams, or turnovers. You cannot manufacture good defense. Our goal is to hold our opponents to scoring less than 14 points per game.

An important aspect of our defense comes into the teaching of the blitzing we do. We are a wrong-arm, redirecting team. We redirect blocks. We force the ball to bounce to the linebackers and the safeties.

Each of the front four down linemen takes on the blocker with his outside shoulder and makes the play spill out to the linebackers or safeties. We want the ball running sideways. We are not just a team where the defense can take out the pulling man, take out the kick-out man, or trap the trapper. We want to take on the blocker and wrong arm him, and then, take the upfield shoulder and rip under the man. He wants to fight uphill when he does that. If the back does not bounce outside, we are in a position to fill the running lane.

The question is: Why quarter-coverage play? It is because we want to stop the run.

QUARTER-COVERAGE PLAY

- Gets nine defenders involved in the run game
- Easy to disguise coverage from a two shell
- Easy to spin safety in box for fire zone
- Easy to do a variety of schemes from the same look

We do not want to give our defense too much to do. We do not list the number of different combinations we could line up in on defense. We line up the same way 9 out of 10 plays. We want our players to be able to line up.

The way we name things is to keep them in an organized fashion. We use family names and names of trees so the learning process can be a lot easier for them.

Our base front is our *shade front* (Diagram #1). To the tight end side, we have a 9 technique on the tight end. If there is no tight end, he is going to play a wide 5 technique on the tackle. We have a 3 technique to the callside. The nose man is going to shade the weakside of the center. That is where the term shade defense comes from. It is a weak shade on the center. The backside end is in a 5 technique.

If we would get a double-tight-end formation, we have several adjustments. At times, it could be a personnel adjustment. Our base default that we teach from day one is this: The nose would kick over into a 1 technique, and the end would play an inside shade on the other tight end. That is a 7 technique.

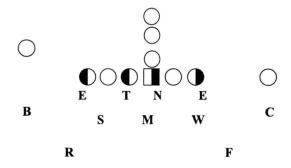

Diagram #1. Base Nose Defense

The Sam linebacker is in a 50 technique. He lines up over a 5 technique or the outside shoulder of the offensive tackle at linebacker depth. The Mike linebacker lines up over the center and the ball. This could change, depending on who the linebacker is. Sometimes, he is shaded to the weakside, and sometimes, he is shaded to the strongside. The Will linebacker lines up with his inside foot on the outside foot of our defensive end.

The corners are in press-cover-4 alignment. We want our safeties to play eight yards off the line of scrimmage. In high school, we believe the hardest passes to complete are the deep passes. In our area, you may see two quarterbacks that can make the big throws deep.

Next, is our *uno front*. It is exactly the same except that the nose tackle on the weakside moves to a 1 technique. That is why we call it uno (Diagram #2). Everyone else aligns the same as the base nose lineup.

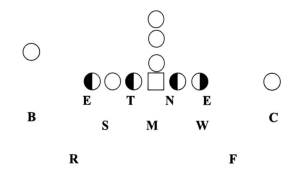

Diagram #2. Uno Front

This is a change-up front. We may use it with a blitz, or it may be to occupy the guard. Against the wing-T teams, we like to load the guards and key on their moves.

Our next front is the *I front*. We work this front off the shade front. It is a shade front for everyone except the 3-technique tackle (Diagram #3). He moves into a 4i technique. He is a B-gap penetrating player. We use this defense against the zone run game when the defense is handling our 3 technique with the lead or outside zone play with a back leading the play. If the offense is getting a good shot on our Mike linebacker, we switch to the 4i to force that tackle to block our down man to help free up the Mike linebacker.

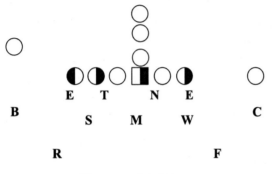

Diagram #3. I Front

Now, the offensive guard has to block the Mike linebacker, and that gives us a better chance to get over the top on the zone play. It is a change-up call. It is not something we live with, but it is something we can go to for an adjustment.

Next is our *G front* (Diagram #4). This front works off the uno front on the backside. The weakside looks like the uno front. On the strongside, it is a gap-responsibility alignment change between the strongside defensive end and our Sam backer. Our end will kick into a 7 technique. He is going to be a penetrating player. He is not going to read the tight end from the inside shade. We move our Sam backer outside into a 90 technique outside the tight end at linebacker depth.

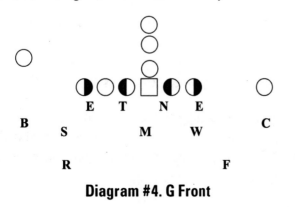

Diagram #4. G Front

It is a way to change things up on our front. Sometimes, we will do it by stunting. With the G front, we do it by alignment.

Our next front is the *Eagle front* (Diagram #5). This is another change-up front. We move our tackle to the weakside 3 technique to help on that side. We have the end in a 5 technique outside our tackle. The nose moves to the strongside of the defense. We have the end inside the tight end. Our Sam backer is in the 90 alignment at linebacker depth.

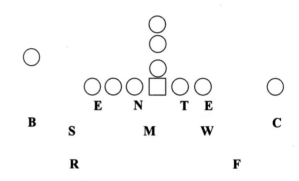

Diagram #5. Eagle Front

I want to move into our *fire-zone package*. Besides being a strong/weak defense, we have the capabilities of becoming a field/boundary defense by calling *bench*. We are telling our kids we are going to set the strength of our defense into the bench. If the tight end would be into the boundary, we could play our normal shade front.

This is the way we line up in our bench. We are playing shade to the boundary (Diagram #6). We always stem on the call.

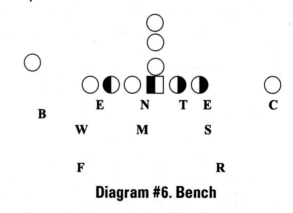

Diagram #6. Bench

If we want to set the strength to the wideside of the field, we call f*ield* (Diagram #7). If there is no tight end, our end slides down to a 5 technique on the tackle. Our nose is in a 1 technique on the backside. We are playing our shade front to the field.

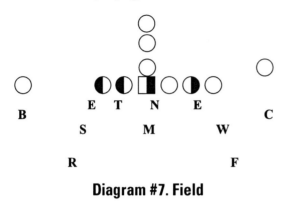

Diagram #7. Field

We are not going to plug every hole. We feel we are safe in this defense. We guess right sometimes, and we guess wrong sometimes. We want to be sound in what we teach. We believe in the old saying, *If we try to defend everything, we will stop nothing.* We know we are not going to plug every hole. We are 99 percent sure we are going to be safe in what we are doing on defense.

We can get into our 50 front. We run our *fire-zone blitzes* out of that look. We use this against a team that uses a tight end. We do not use the defense against a spread offense.

Our *over front* is like our uno front (Diagram #8). It depends on what we want to do with the nose tackle. We can put him in a shade or leave him in a 1 technique—it depends on what we are working off the front.

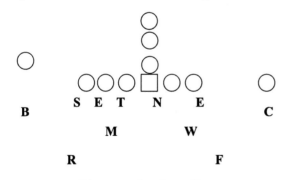

Diagram #8. Over Front

We bring the Sam linebacker up on the line of scrimmage. He plays a two-point position. He is playing a 9 technique. We kick our defensive end down into a 5 technique. The 3 technique and nose man play our uno front.

We try to play Sam on the line, and we tell him he is a wrong-arm player. We play that way on the line of scrimmage. Even when we put our best linebackers on the line, they forget to play the wrong-arm technique. We prefer to wrong arm and make the play bounce to the outside. It depends on the ability of the linebackers on picking up that wrong-arm technique. It comes down to the ability of each player on this situation.

If we are going to play our 50 defense, I prefer to play our under front (Diagram #9). It makes us gap sound to both sides of the ball. We want to bounce the play to the Will backer and let him run the play down. On plays away from the Will, he can protect the A gap away from his side.

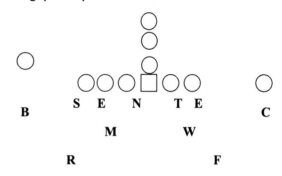

Diagram #9. Under Front

It is the same alignment for the end, Sam, Mike, and Will backers. We put the bubble to the strongside of the field. Our 3 technique goes to the weakside. We play the nose in a 1 technique or we can play him in a shade alignment.

I want to get into some of our fire-zone alignment rules. You hear a lot of teams talk about fire zones played with three deep backs and three underneath players. We do play some of that type of zones. Two years ago, we started playing with the concept of only bringing one linebacker and defending with four deep. We say that we "dated" the concept two years ago. This year, we "married" the concept. We want to play a cover-4 concept. That is our preferred coverage. It is our five-man pressure fronts plus bringing those four men along with one linebacker. That allows us to play four deep in our secondary.

Let me cover our weak pressure with cover 4 special (Diagram #10). We call it our *cat-and-dog package*. We want to play with the cover-4 concept. That is where we "tag" 4 special. Our fire-zone package is a color. What that means is that we are going to run a weakside cat call. If we run cat or dog, we are going to play 4 special. We play press man on the two wide outside receivers. Our Sam linebacker is a #2-match player. He matches the #2 receiver from the outside. Our *Rover*, who is our strong safety, is reading the #2 man. If the Will backer is not running a cat, he is a #2-match player. The Mike backer is a #3-match player. We are a route-reading team. We give them an area to cover, but we are matching men. We do not want to guard grass. We are playing with tight pressure forcing the quarterback to be accurate.

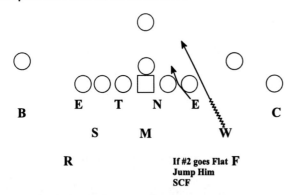

**Diagram #10. Weak Pressure
With Cover 4 Special**

If we call 4 special, it tells the free safety he is losing his linebacker to his side. It means he lost his #2-match player underneath. He is running the blitz. If we call strong pressure 4 special, it means the Sam backer is going to be included in the blitz (Diagram #11). The Rover knows if the #2 receiver goes to the outside flat, he must jump and defend him. He must protect the *wheel* and proceed with caution.

If the offense is willing to nickel-and-dime us down the field for 80 to 90 yards, good! We do not want them getting 80 yards quick and cheap on us. We tell the Rover to "jump the flat," but defend the wheel. We know the #2 receiver is a skilled player.

From that look, we move to our five-man pressure. This is the true fire-zone blitz. Now, we

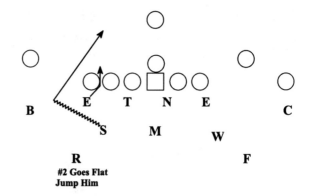

Diagram #11. Strong Pressure 4 Special

are going with three linemen and two linebackers. We play with three under players and three deep in the secondary. This is the fire-zone blitz that all of the college coaches talk about. It is bringing four defenders from the field.

I do need to backtrack and talk about cat again. When the offense gets in an *edge pass*, we want to line up in our base alignment and look for quarterback indicators. Once we see the quarterback is ready to take the snap, we stem down one man to the line of scrimmage. We line up three yards from the end man on the line of scrimmage. He comes hard off the edge going for the quarterback. We do not want to blitz from that depth. You think about it. If you are five yards back from the line and the quarterback is going to drop back five yards, or he lines up in the shotgun, we have 10 yards to make up. We want to get up on the line of scrimmage and get after him.

At times, we show up on the line of scrimmage and bail out of there on the snap of the ball. The other thing we do is to make sure our safety does not tip his move before the quarterback takes the snap. If the quarterback sees the defense creeping down toward the line, they know it is a blitz. They can read the defense just as we make every effort to read the quarterback. We tell our backers to "hold your water." We want to stem down to the line and surprise them with the blitz. This is what takes us to the four-from-the-field concept.

We are going to bring four from the boundary on the fire-zone blitz. We are bringing the outside linebacker and the corner on the boundary side. We call it *boundary outside linebacker/corner pressure* (Diagram #12). The corner stems down on the line of scrimmage just before the snap. On the snap, the corner comes hard. The Sam backer times his move and comes over the outside eye of the offensive tackle. The end on that side steps into the tackle and drops to the flat.

We run the same concept to the field. First is the field safety/outside backer, single width (Diagram #14). Our end must get back and outside on the snap of the ball. We want the safety to stem down and come hard from the outside. The nose is going to the backside A gap, and the end has contain on the backside.

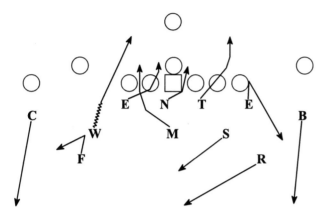

Diagram #12. Boundary Outside Linebacker/Corner Pressure

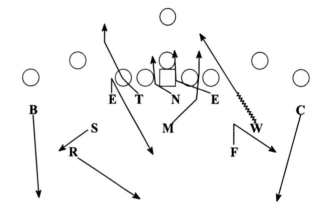

Diagram #14. Field Outside Backer/Safety Pressure, Single Width

We have five men on the rush with the end, nose, tackle, outside backer, and corner. The Will and Mike backers and the backside end drop and play the three under players. The corner and two safeties play the three deep zones.

A change-up to the boundary pressure is our boundary outside backer/corner pressure, double width (Diagram #13). We show the cat and bring the outside corner down. The Will backer comes down inside to the B gap. He needs to make sure the Mike backer knows he is going to the B gap. The end on the wideside must play contain and get upfield on the snap.

The corners are dropping deep to their landmarks. The free safety is covering deep middle. He must get depth on the play as soon as possible. He must not get beat on the dig route. He is the last line of defense.

A quick look at the field outside backer pressure to the weakside and we see the free safety and the Mike backer running the blitz. It is the same concept to the weakside of the formation. The safety must stem down and come hard on the outside. The Mike backer goes off the outside shoulder of the tackle. The nose is in the A gap, and the tackle is in the B gap.

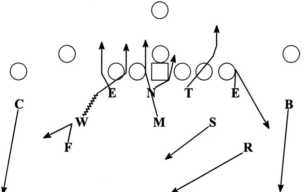

Diagram #13. Boundary Outside Backer/Corner Pressure, Double Width

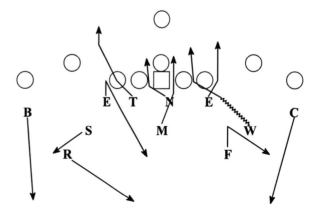

Diagram #15. Field Outside Backer/Safety Pressure, Weakside

My favorite blitz is the double A-gap blitz (Diagram #16). It is the most difficult to teach. In the huddle, we make the call and we know who we are going to have on the blitz. However, when we get to the line of scrimmage, the formation dictates a change. That is what makes it so hard to teach. Our double A-gap blitz, by rule, is a blitz for the Mike and Will backers. We run the blitz out of our uno front. We have our nose to the 1 technique on the weakside. The ends play their regular 9 technique rules.

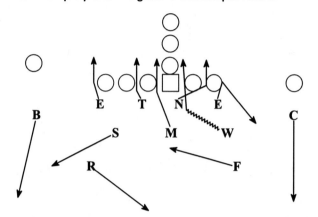

Diagram #16. Double A Gap, Mike/Will

We tell the tackle and nose to "speed to B gap." We want them to get upfield and turn the guards outside. We want them to try to get the guards to go with the tackle and nose. The Mike backer takes the strongside A gap, and the Will backer takes the weakside A gap. This is good against the pass and the run.

The corners press and then bail to their landmarks on the snap. Here is the rule breaker on the play: The free safety is dropping into the middle hole. His backer is blitzing, so he is dropping down. He must be aware of the draw play. If the backers miss the draw, the free safety must be there to make the play. He is going to follow the blitz in the hole. We do not want him to get caught up in the trash. If the backers miss the draw, we will live with the rule breaker. We want him to keep the play in front of him. We can live with the six-yard play. If the backer is not going, the safety on his side is the middle-third player.

Here we run the Sam and Mike backers (Diagram #17). Notice that the Will backer is displaced. It is the same for all of the other players.

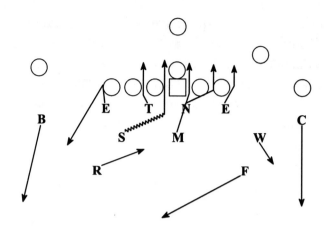

Diagram #17. Double A Gap, Sam/Mike

If we think it is going to be a pass, we can cross the two blitzing linebackers. Who do you send first on the blitz? This year, we sent our Mike first because he was not a good blitz man. We wanted to get him out of the way. He was a sacrificial blitz man so Will could come clean on the play and make the tackle. We want to find out which backer works best and that is what we will do. We think the first man on the blitz will take up the blocker, and the second man on the blitz will get to the quarterback. We call the double-A blitz a "band" play. One of the schools' bands will be playing after this blitz is called, and I would prefer that it be our band playing.

We can also bring our defensive backs on the blitz. This is our *bird* package (Diagram #18). We run the boundary outside backer and the corner on the blitz. Our end on the boundary who is lined up on the tight end must drop and cover the flat.

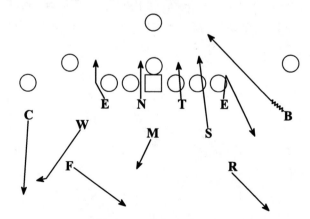

**Diagram #18. Boundary Outside Backer/
Corner Pressure**

We run the same blitz on the fieldside. We have the outside backer and safety in the blitz. The formation is set to the field. Our defensive end on the tight end must drop and play the flat. The two corners and the free safety cover the deep one-thirds.

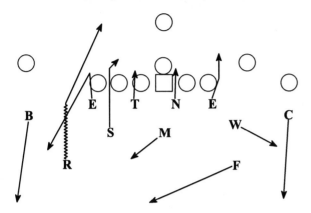

Diagram #19. Field Outside Backer/Safety Pressure, Single Width

If we want to run the same blitz from the weakside, the free safety and Mike backer are involved (Diagram #20). We bring the defensive end back into the middle area as the Will backer has the outside.

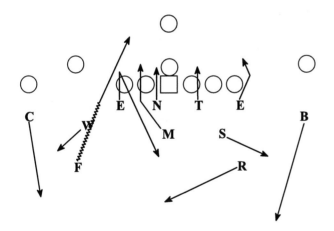

Diagram #20. Field Outside Backer/Safety Pressure, Weakside

I am covering three different concepts. I know you must be thinking there is no way we can run all of this. We do run all three packages. We work hard on this. We have a lot of walk-throughs. We get seven coaching days in the summer. For us, those days are all install days. We do not go to any passing tournaments or passing scrimmages. We have four-and-a-half-hour practices on those seven days. We spend two hours on offense, two hours on defense, and one half hour on special teams.

We give the players cut-up films on the plays we are going to use. When the players come back to our two-a-day practices to start fall practice, the kids that have studied the cut-ups are the ones that are ahead of the other players, and they are the ones that play for us.

In the fall pre-season, we have two scrimmages. In the first scrimmage, we play our base defense with a few stunts up front. We do not blitz in that first scrimmage. We play base defense playing cover 2 and cover 4. We will play some cover 3.

In our second scrimmage, which is a week before our first game, we go two sets of 10 plays versus our opponents with 1s versus 1s. Next, we go into the fourth-quarter-situation scrimmage. The first half is for our starters, and the third quarter is for our second team. The fourth quarter is for our junior varsity team.

In that first half, we blitz every play. What a perfect way to practice. One, I cannot get fired over the score in the scrimmage. Two, you are not scripting the scrimmage. It is easy to script a practice to put the team in a bad spot—you just stop practice and tell the defense how to cover the play. Here, we are seeing the plays live, and we play it like a game. We get burned a few times, and we are successful a few times. Then, we have tape on Saturday morning to correct the mistakes.

We will do the same in our second scrimmage on offense. We will throw the ball 70 times in that scrimmage. We are going to work on our passing game, and we are going to be a better passing team as a result. It does not matter what the score is in that second scrimmage. We may get beat 35-0, but I hope we are not that bad. That is OK because it teaches us what we need to throw out of the system, what we need to use more, and what we can teach better so we can use it more.

I covered the defense in the order in which we teach all of the calls and the blitzes. If the players are not good enough in our base defense, we cannot get to some of the blitz calls.

We do bring our corners from the boundary. We bring one linebacker and one defensive back. We know when we bring a defensive back on the blitz, the other three defensive backs are the three deep players. We know we must cover the three deep zones. We run the dog concept in this scheme.

From the field, we bring the safety on the blitz. We do not blitz the corner from the field. It is the same concept, but it comes from the field.

Timewise, that is all the time I have. Good luck to everyone this season. Thanks for having me.

PRESSURE DEFENSE ON THIRD DOWN

Doss High School, Kentucky

Good afternoon. First, I want to thank the Nike Coach of the Year clinic for the opportunity to stand in front of you today. Thank you to everyone for coming.

I am from Louisville, Kentucky. I went to Louisville Male High School where, I can honestly say, I spent 85 percent of my four years there on the campus. I tried to be involved in everything. I had the honor of playing for Coach Bob Redman who really taught me the meaning of pressure defense. I played college football at Kentucky State University. There, I played under George Small and defensive coordinator Wesley McGriff who is now the secondary coach at the University of Miami in Florida. If anyone knows Wes, they know he is all about pressuring people out of the 4-3 defense.

I had a few tryouts on the next level, but that didn't pan out. I started my coaching career at Kentucky State during my senior year. Because of an injury, I had to sit out of a makeup game against the University of Tennessee at Chattanooga. The circumstances of that game allowed me to have my first coaching experience. That day, I ended up calling the defense and subbing players in and out of the game. We lost to say the least.

I started my high school career at Iroquois High School, where I was the defensive coordinator. I then went to Ballard High, where I coached the defensive line, which was one of the greatest learning experiences of my life. Tommy Acklin was the defensive coordinator. He has taught me a lot over the years, and I appreciate him. I moved on to Fern Creek Traditional High School and was defensive coordinator there. After a year there, I got the head coaching job at Doss High School.

Today, I want to talk about applying defensive pressure on third down. We all have heard the saying that pressure can bust pipes or make diamonds. How true is that? How many times have we watched games and witnessed an offense just get destroyed by a defense? Or watched a defense make a quarterback so uncomfortable that he makes the worst decisions ever? That's busting pipes on the offensive side and making diamonds for your defense. On every level, press defense must win first and third downs to be successful.

- Know situations and offensive tendencies.
- On normal downs (first-and-10), stop the run.
- On medium downs (second-and-six or less), stop the run or pass.

Designing the pressure you bring by the tendencies of the offense is very important. In essence, it can dictate what the offense does during the game. Today, I will break down how to create pressure and win major downs on defense.

EVALUATE YOUR STOCK

- Find the most aggressive players.
- Find the most athletic players.
- Find your big hitters.
- Realize they don't have to be Rhodes Scholars to play.

As you go through spring ball and summer practice, find your most aggressive, athletic players that you can put on defense. The funny thing is that they don't have to be Rhodes Scholars.

KEEP IT SIMPLE

- Allow your players to be as aggressive as possible.
- Simplify your scheme.
- Players play better when they don't have to think.
- Put the best players for positions in the right spots.

You want your guys to be as aggressive as possible, so don't make your scheme so complicated. Players play better when they don't have to think about what to do. Put the best players for the position in the right spots. Use kids with good fundamentals and techniques.

PLAY THE DEFENSE THAT SUITS YOUR PLAYERS

- It doesn't matter what defense you play.
- How does pressure fit into your defensive philosophy?
- Believe in what you decide to do.

It doesn't matter if you play a 4-3, 3-4, 3-3-5, or a 5-2; make sure that you have the athletes to run the scheme effectively. Always ask yourself, "How does the pressure fit into my defensive philosophy?" If you believe in it, let it become a core part of your package. If you don't believe in it, don't mess with it.

DISTURB THE PEACE

- Disrupt the timing of the offense.
- Destroy blocking schemes while securing the secondary.
- Force opponents to accelerate their execution.

The major purpose of pressure is to cause disruption in the timing of the offense. Second, destroy blocking schemes while securing the secondary's coverage. Penetration into the backfield can eliminate the pulling and trapping lanes. Third, force opponents to accelerate their execution.

When we commit the front seven or front eight on the blitz, it is important to make sure our defensive backs know how they are covering the receivers. They must communicate with each other to prevent the mistake of allowing a receiver to beat us deep.

Some teams run a slow-developing offense. The wing-T is a good example. They want the defense to penetrate so they can run the traps. You need to figure out a way to speed those teams up to give your defense an advantage. We tell our defensive linemen not to get too far upfield. We tell the linemen to pick out the offensive lineman and aim for his near hip. Once he gets to that hip position, he needs to find the football.

CREATE CONFUSION

- Limit the number of pass protections and blocking schemes you see.
- Make the quarterback overthink plays.
- Make the running back doubt the blocking of his offensive line.

The benefit of pressure versus the run or pass is primarily designed to cause confusion. Ideally, it will limit the number of pass protections and blocking schemes you see. You want to confuse the protectors to the point that it creates doubt on blitz pickups or run-blocking keys. Just think of what that does to the quarterback. I remember in high school, we created so much pressure that the quarterback would be so mad about being hit every pass play. I've even witnessed a few cry. That is honestly the greatest benefit of bringing pressure, especially on third-and-long situations. You want to be very problematic for offensive coaches when you add disguise and bluff concepts to what you normally do.

DON'T BE AFRAID TO GAMBLE

- Bringing pressure and blitzing is a gamble.
- Understand that you may give up the big play.
- Know that you will make more big defensive plays.

The blitz defense is a gamble all day. You are going to lose some downs when you blitz. You may lose on one or two plays, but you are going to make more plays on defense than the offense will make if you bring the pressure and bring it to the right places. You have to know the defense will make big plays.

Again, anytime that you blitz, you are gambling. There are times that you may bring pressure and the offense will make a big play off of it—they may even score. So what! A wise man once told me: "One doesn't beat you." When applying pressure, you may give up a big play here and there, but you will make more big plays on defense. A lot of us get caught up in being conservative and not trusting our players to make plays. That's all part of the gamble. I am willing to allow my guys to make plays, but I also remember they are not perfect, and they will make mistakes.

STUDY YOUR OPPONENTS

- Try to understand what their offense is trying to do.
- When watching film, record the offensive formations and plays.
- Find your opponents' weaknesses.
- Look for tips in alignment and/or body language of the players.
- Establish who the missing link is and attack him or them.

We watch film every day. We take film home and study our opponents as much as possible. We are looking for the opponents' weaknesses. Our secondary coach does a great job studying the pass receivers. He checks the hands of the receivers when they come off the ball, how many steps they take before they make their break, and any other tendencies.

Every time that you lead your team on the field, each player should know what the offense is going to try to do. They should know what you know. Nothing should surprise them. What that means is that you, as a coach, must study your opponents' every move. I can't tell you the number of hours that I spend watching and breaking down film and drawing up the other teams' offensive formations. I am blessed to have assistant coaches that are film rats like me.

Record all the formations and plays the offense runs and the down-and-distance situations in which they run the plays. This might take a while, but it is worth the time involved. Line all your defensive formations up to their formations. Make sure every gap and man can be covered.

Go back and watch for weaknesses in the offense because they all have some weakness.

- Watch the linemen for:
  ✓ Footwork
  ✓ Hand placement
  ✓ If they tip off run or pass
  ✓ How active they are
- Watch the backs for:
  ✓ How well they pick up blocks
  ✓ How they react when the pressure is on
  ✓ If they tip off run or pass
  ✓ If they show if the ball is coming to them or not
  ✓ If they run hard on every play or take plays off even with the ball

A lot of backs have certain things that they do that give the play away. Be sure to watch them closely.

- Watch the receivers for:
  ✓ How they come off the ball
  ✓ How many steps they take going into their breaks
  ✓ If they tip off run or pass

They tip off run/pass all the time. Watch their body language before the snap. Sometimes they give it away.

Now that we have scoped out the entire team, we determine who the weakest link is and attack him. If there is more than one weak link, send the crib at them. Don't hold back—exploit them.

If we find a guard that is slow coming off the line or if the center gets his head up slow after the snap, we are going to attack that area of the line. We blitz a linebacker or a safety to put the pressure on those two players. We can bring a man off the edge to force their protection all the way across the line. We want to create matches that will favor the defense. It is no different than what the offense does in trying to find mismatches they can exploit.

DON'T STAY IN ONE PLACE

- Give the offense different looks.
- Keep the offense on its heels.
- Use and disguise different coverages to confuse the quarterback.

We use a lot of different fronts. We play all types of fronts, but it is the same defense. We are walking players up on the line and backing them off the line so we do not give the offense the same look all of the time. The offense must respect what you are doing. By changing the alignment, we want to confuse the blocking schemes for the offense. So, we want to be creative in our defensive scheme. A wise man once told me: *"If you sit in one place long enough, they will find you."*

Give the offense different looks at different times in the game. Try to be very strategic in your attack. Move your defensive line around. Again, we align head-up, in shades, or in the gaps. We try to figure out the best way to attack the line of scrimmage.

We can send someone different every time, from a different place every time. Keeping the offense off-guard and on its heels is very important. This also causes the quarterback to get "happy feet" if he doesn't know where the extra man is coming from. Use different coverages to confuse the quarterback. Show cover 2, and play cover 3. Send your backer or safety—do something that he is not used to seeing. We may drop all three linebackers and send someone else on the blitz. Our corners must be disciplined enough to play pass first.

GAME PLAN VS. THE RUN

You must work hard on the game plan. We have a list that we consider when making the game plan. We must make sure we are not confusing anyone on our team. The coaching staff must know what the front line is reading on each play. These are the points we consider in making the game plan versus the run.

- Make sure the pressure maintains proper run support.
- Try to overload the point of attack.
- Isolate a blocker.
- Affect the rhythm or timing of a play; speed up a slow-developing play.
- Attack or eliminate pulling and trapping by penetrating the gaps and lanes on offense (disturb the peace).

We can take one player or position and overload him. We can put a man inside on his shoulder, line a linebacker on his nose, and put a man on his outside shoulder. We want to apply the pressure on him so he does not know who is coming after him. We can bring any one of those defenders, or we can bring any combination of those three players on the blitz. We want to force him to make a decision about which man he is going to block. It is confusing as it is, and if we can create a mismatch, we feel we can gain an advantage. We want to disrupt the offensive line's blocking scheme.

If we feel we have a better athlete than they have, we can line him up 1-on-1 with a defender and gain an advantage. We put a second player next to that matchup and force the defense to decide who they are going to block. If they do not bring help, we are going to blitz both men and get to the quarterback.

GAME PLAN VS. THE PASS

Pressure must maintain the integrity of deep coverage, while the front seven are attacking the protection.

- The pressure has to disrupt the rhythm and the timing of the passing game.
- Overload a certain area in the protection to create 3-on-2 situations.
- Isolate a specific protector by creating a 2-on-1 match-up.
- Create a missed assignment by stunting or exchanging running lanes.
- Create a missed assignment by disguising or bluffing the pressure.
- Try to get a free rusher by a technique error in passing off, or picking up a stunt, or by setting to a dropping defender and allowing a backer or a defensive back to come free.

WINNING DOWN-AND-DISTANCE

- Defense must win first and third downs to be successful.
- Know situations and offensive tendencies.
- On normal downs (first-and-10), stop the run.

- On medium downs (second-and-six or less), stop the run or pass.
- Design the pressure you bring by the tendencies of the offense.

As you watch film, see if your offense or defense is showing tendencies on certain downs. If you can pick up a tendency from the offense, the pressure you can apply on that down to the area that is the weakest, the better chance you have for success. You must make your kids aware of those tendencies. Let them know what to expect in certain situations. That is a key to winning the first two downs.

Now, we will talk about the third down. There are two downs that a defense needs to win—the first and third downs. Limiting offenses to getting no gain or taking a loss on first down is a major goal. Knowing the situation and the offensive tendencies will always determine what pressure that is used.

We want to force teams into third-and-long situations. The quarterback knows he must get rid of the ball quickly because you are bringing pressure. Make sure you harass the quarterback enough so he is not comfortable on third down. If we can apply enough pressure on third down, 9 out of 10 times, they are not going to be successful.

On normal downs, like first-and-10, most teams run the ball on first down, so we plan to stop the run, and our pressure dictates it. We also call our coverage according to what the offense's tendencies are. Beware of play-action later in the game; that is the offense's way of trying to counter the pressure. Make sure your defensive backs play pass first. The more the defense can stop the first down, the easier it will be to stop the third down.

On medium downs, you will get equal run or pass threats from the offense. Therefore, you have to be creative in what you do and how you bring your pressure. This and third downs are the perfect downs to fall for the screen play. Be prepared for that play. The pressure will attack the quarterback and the timing and rhythm of the run blocking as the plays develop.

If any of you are interested in seeing what we do and the way we line up on defense, let me know.

I will be glad to visit with you. For the Kentucky high schools, I am on the list server as well.

Thank you for your attention.

Kirk Fridrich

DEFENSIVE CONCEPTS AND MULTIPLE COVERAGES

Tulsa Union High School, Oklahoma

Each time I get a chance to speak, I take the time to let everyone know what I consider important. From the coaches I have heard speak here today, I can tell you that I have been impressed with the X's and O's, but more impressive has been the concern for coaching character and the influence that has on kids. I know the schools in this area do a great job in that regard We feel the same way in our area about teaching character.

A motto I have used for a long time comes from John Maxwell: *"Am I building people or building my dream and using people to do it?"* As an assistant coach, it is easy to say, "I want to be a head coach." Or you may say, "I want to win the state championship." You work hard and really push yourself to reach those goals. You need to stop and ask Maxwell's question of what you are doing. *Am I building my dream, or am I building the kids?*

The other point I like to stress comes from St. Peter: *"Everyone should use the gift he has received to serve others."* I believe we have been given a gift as coaches. We have been gifted with the time we get to spend with those kids. We need to serve them and not just ourselves.

I am going to talk about our defense, but first, I want to build a foundation so you can see why we do the things in our defense. This is the time of year that coaches talk about philosophy. You can use that as an evaluation tool.

- What we do is who we are.
- Who we are is what we do.

What is your philosophy for your program? It may be what your defensive philosophy is. You can use this as an evaluation tool. This is what I challenge you to do. This is what we do in our program.

What is it? What does it look like? What do you do? My point is this: If your philosophy isn't producing what you say it is, then you need to change what you are doing or change your philosophy. It must be emphasized. How do we communicate it? How do we know if we are successful?

Here is our program mission statement:

"The purpose of the Union football program is to produce and develop good, moral, and productive citizens. Our goal is to teach each athlete the importance of attitude, self discipline, and strong work ethic both in the classroom and on the field."

That came from our team handbook. That is our mission statement. You can't just put that statement in a handbook—it needs to be emphasized. You can't just say those things one time and expect them to take place. They need to be emphasized. How are you going to communicate this message? How are you going to know if your philosophy is successful?

How do we emphasize this statement? You can ask any kid in our program how we emphasize it. He will tell you that we emphasize the statement, "Live like a champion!" We do not say to *play* like a champion; we say to *live* like a champion. We believe being a champion is a habit. It is not something you can turn off and on. You can't decide to turn it on when it is third down with two yards to go for a touchdown.

If you do things right all of the time, there is a good chance you are going to do it right when it is fourth-and-two for the score. So we talk to our kids all of the time about living like a champion, not just playing like a champion. After you develop yourself to be a champion, then you can win a championship. We teach the players to live like champions.

I want to continue with our mission statement. How do we communicate developing good, moral, and productive citizens? We do it by stressing those types of activities throughout the year.

This year, our theme for our T-shirts was the letter V or the Roman numeral V. The V stood for winning the school's fifth state championship. I elaborated on the V logo with the idea that the V stood for having a *vision* about *victory* and about obtaining goals. It was not just a dream, but a vision with a plan to obtain our goals and about being successful in life.

I want to talk about mental training. We run a weekly program where we give each assistant coach the assignment of teaching a lesson about character each week. It could be on responsibilities, goal setting, or anything the coach chooses. We go through four days, Monday through Thursday, with those goals. On Thursday, we recap the theme. On Friday night, my pre-game talk will have something to do with that topic. We take about five minutes a day and rap on that given subject.

One part of our mission statement says something about academics. We want to know what we are doing in this area. Are we helping the kids that need help in academic areas? We have a program called our Redskin Academic Tutoring (RAT) session. We tell our kids they do not want to be a rat. We do play on that theme, but we have a system for our kids that need the tutoring.

You want to know if you are being successful in the programs within your program. Last year, we decided to run a survey on the internet to see how we rated with the players, parents, and community. Over half of our team and their parents took part in the survey. We asked them questions to give us some feedback on how we were doing with our program. We had them rate the different questions 4 to 1, with a 4 being the highest score and 1 being the lowest score.

We got the survey back, and, for the most part, we ranked very high in almost every category. One area that we did not rate very high on was community service. That identified one of our problems that we needed to improve on.

We developed a program called Redskin Aid. It was our community service program. We have just gotten started in the program, and it is a great thing for our community and our team. We have been to the children's hospital. Yesterday, we went to a homeless shelter and entertained the kids while their parents were getting help in another area. We are going to be involved in some Special Olympics programs later in the year. We are consistently looking for things in the community that can help our kids.

Earlier, I mentioned that you need to look at your program to figure out what some of the problems are. Every year, coaches are going to have problems. What is the one thing that keeps hitting you in the head every time you turn around? Is it players being late to practice, late to class, or some other problem? Whatever the problem is, you need to improve on that problem for the next year.

We have a big rivalry with one school in our area—Jenks High School. We get together and have friendly competitions. We have had a number of blood drives to see which school could get the most blood donated.

Last year, I received a call from the Salvation Army. They wanted to know if I would go ring the bell to help raise money during the Christmas season. I said I would be glad to do it. The next thing I know, they have Coach Alan Trimble of Jenks High ringing the bell. Now it was a matter of which coach and school was going to raise the most money by ringing the bell. As coaches, we did not feel we had the time to be involved with that project. We turned it over to the team, and the kids took ownership of the project. We had a lot of problems with the weather and the fact that we were out of school, but the kids did a great job with this project.

This was a way we could measure our program in terms of becoming involved in the community. The kids had taken on a responsibility, and they got the job done. We felt we were making strides with the kids in this respect.

I think it is important in your philosophy for you to evaluate your coaching staff. I have to communicate with them and let them know what is important to me. For example, I do not allow kids to use profanity. That is important to me. It may not be important to a staff member, but I want him to know it is important to me. It is important to the team. How do you control this with the assistants? The first thing is that you are the one that hires them. You need to hire great guys. I feel we have one of the top coaching staffs in the country. I could not ask for a better deal.

I do not look for a linebackers coach. I look for a coach that has outstanding character. I can help him coach linebackers. It is hard to coach a guy that does not have integrity. What is important to you must be important to them. Search out great men, not just great coaches.

We throw a quote by Albert Einstein into our playbook: "Concern for man and his fate must always form the chief interest of all technical endeavors. Never forget this in the midst of your diagrams and equations." We cannot forget about the kids when we are doing the X's and O's. We must always keep the kids first.

I saw this quote by Max Frisch in The Changing Times: "We hired workers and human beings came instead."

The challenge is not coaching the great athlete. We were very fortunate this year in that we had six players sign Division I scholarships. We had 12 kids that signed scholarships overall. That was an outstanding year for us. The challenge was not coaching those Division I players. We all know it is a challenge to coach the other kids and make them better. Is this not true about the athlete that has a problem with self-discipline? Coaches often say certain players are not disciplined and so-and-so is unreliable. They want to get rid of those types of players. This is where real coaching comes into play. You can coach someone to be more responsible and more reliable. Coaching is not just about coaching the better players.

Use your philosophy to evaluate your program. Is there a better way? We start with our defensive philosophy.

DEFENSIVE PHILOSOPHY

- Fundamentals—schemes are overrated
- Tackling
- Great effort
- Be disciplined with responsibility
- Dominate the running game
- Stop the offense immediately (first down)
- Force the offense to throw the ball
- Take away the offense's strength by playing percentages by formation
- Keep it simple
- Be great in critical situations

Every year, I ask each position coach to give me a list of the fundamentals his players need to master in order to play the position he coaches. They each give me a list of things the players need to do to play for them. When a player comes to me and asks me, "What do I need to do to play more, Coach?" I give him the list the assistant coaches gave me and tell him, "This is what you must do to play more."

We do not do drills just to be doing drills. We want to drill the fundamentals. We have told the player what he had to do to play, and now we must drill him on the fundamentals.

The fundamentals of our defense consist of three categories: pre-snap, technique, and effort. The players need to know their snaps, alignments, and assignments.

How do we teach all of this? We start every day with a circuit drill for our defense (Diagram #1). We do not skip this drill, regardless of the ranking of the opponent we are playing each week.

We take an area of the practice field and set up the circuit. We call this area the *big cage*. At the first station, we work on defeating the blocker and escaping the blocker (Diagram #1). We have a coach that teaches this phase of the defense to the kids. Our defensive line coach runs this drill. We feel he is the expert in teaching this drill. If he is not the expert, he is expected to be and he must go find out how to teach it. He teaches this drill to everyone on the defensive team.

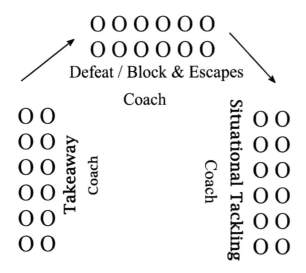

Diagram #1. Tackle/Takeaway Circuit

The second station is what we call situational tackling. Our linebackers coach is at this station. We do all types of tackling drills at this station. Again, everyone on the defensive team goes to this drill.

The third station is a takeaway drill. It could be an Oskie, strip, or a scoop-and-score drill. We only spend three minutes on each drill. That is only nine minutes on the drill. Then, we jump to our pursuit drill. We spend four or five minutes on that drill. That is 15 minutes to start each practice.

Each practice, the drills are changed to give them a different fundamental in regard to tackling. They practice those fundamentals each day and everyone is getting the same instruction.

We teach fundamentals each session of practice. We work on both sides of the ball. The offensive team has its drills to include fundamentals. What we stress in all of our drills is for the players to learn the fundamentals of the game.

One thing we do is to grade the players in scrimmages and in games. If a coach tells me that one of his players graded out at 61 percent and he wants to find another player to take his place, I tell him that the 61 percent is *his* grade. If he cannot teach the player to do any better than 61 percent, then we need to look at the techniques he is teaching the player. I would like to tell this to some of the English teachers that keep pounding our players in their classes.

We like to grade on effort when we grade the films. In addition, we want to grade productivity. We post the grades we give the kids. They fight to get the best scores possible. We give two points for a tackle, one point for an assisted tackle, and three points for a tackle that results in a loss. To encourage hustle, we give one point for the first man to get to the ball. A missed tackle is minus two points. We give points for forcing a hurry, a big hit, a forced fumble, an interception, and we give a minus for loafing on a play. We tally up the points for the scores. Players are rewarded for how many points they scored rather than how many percentage points they received.

Another part of our defensive philosophy is to be disciplined with responsibility. How do we teach discipline? We do that by making sure our kids communicate over and over again. They all have responsibilities on each play. They are constantly talking to each other to let everyone know who has what.

I said part of our philosophy was to take away the offense's strength by playing percentages by formations. Let me cover what we do with our front defenders. If we call an *under* call (Eagle or hawk), we move the nose to the A gap and play the end in a 3 technique on the split end side (Diagram #2). The Mike backer plays over the center and the R backer plays on the outside shoulder of the tackle on that side.

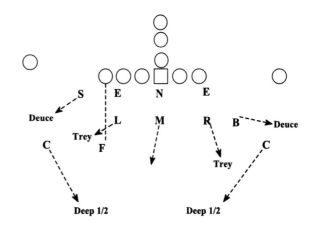

Diagram #2. Under (Eagle or Hawk)

On a *heavy* call, we play the nose on the center and the two ends both play 3 techniques (Diagram

#3). The Mike backer is stacked behind the nose. The L and R backers play in 5 techniques off the line in their normal backer positions.

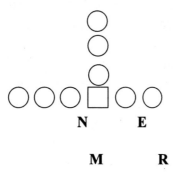

Diagram #3. Heavy

If we want to slide the defense, we call *slide* on the under call. The R backer moves up on the line on the split end side (Diagram #4). The end on the tight end side is in a 5 technique, and the nose slides over to the 1 gap. The Mike backer slides over to the outside shoulder of the center in a linebacker's position. The L backer plays over the 3 technique to the tight end side.

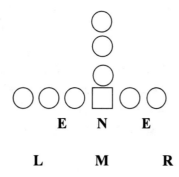

Diagram #4. Slide, Under

If we call *slide over*, the nose goes to the 1 gap on the backside. The end goes out to a 5 technique on the tackle (Diagram #5). The end on the other side goes to the 4i technique. The L backer moves up on the line in a 6 technique if the tight end is there. Mike and the R backers play on the outside shoulder of the guards in a linebacker's position.

We have what we call "I-am-here" players. Any time we have two backs, we are always going to have two I-am-here players (Diagram #6). Those two I-am-here players allow us to get an extra man

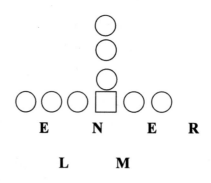

Diagram #5. Slide, Over

in the box. That tells the linebackers they have someone behind them. They know they can spill the ball, and if the ball goes away, they can fly over the top. They do not have to worry about cutback. They are constantly communicating. They are disciplined with their responsibility. It all starts from the sideline and goes to the safeties and corners, to the linebackers, and to the line.

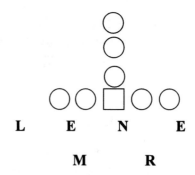

Diagram #6. I-Am-Here Players

If we have a linebacker that has an I-am-here player on flow away, he can get over the top of the center anyway he can. If the defense pulls the guard, he may get a run through. He does not have to worry because he has a safety behind him.

Let me repeat this: Part of our defensive philosophy is to take away the offense's strength by playing percentages by formations. We keep it simple in everything we do. We want to stop the offense on first down. We want to force the offense to throw the football.

You can have a good defense, but if you can be a great defense, then you need to be great. We talk about that in our Live Like a Champion program. If you can be good at something, we think it is good, but if you can be great, you need to be great. We sell that concept repeatedly.

I want to talk about our multiple coverage concepts. We want to create numbers mismatches versus tendencies. We want to pressure the point of attack.

The reason we have multiple coverages is because we want to get a mismatch at the point of attack. How do we do that? We do it by tendencies. We roll our coverages to where you are going to go. We roll safeties and linebackers to where they need to go. We created multiple coverages so we could pressure the point of attack.

In the time I have left, I will show you how we roll our coverage. I will show you a roll toward the left side of the formation against the twins look. On the right side of the offense, we roll the corner down low to play a hard corner (Diagram #7). The free safety must cover the outside deep one-third. The Bandit must rotate to the middle of the field and play the deep middle one-third. The corner on the backside of the call drops back and plays the deep outside one-third on his drop. Both the S and R backers play the deuce or the second receiver. Mike and the L backer play the third receiver or the trey player. That is our three-star coverage.

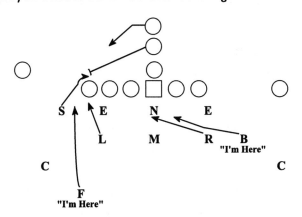

Diagram #7. Three-Star Coverage

If we want to play the 3 coverage against the doubles or twins, we can roll the other way. Now, we have both corners playing the deep outside one-third. The free safety plays the deep middle one-third (Diagram #8). The Bandit is playing the deuce,

and he is an I-am-here player. The Mike backer plays the hole, and the L and R backers play the trey. That is our 3 coverage against doubles.

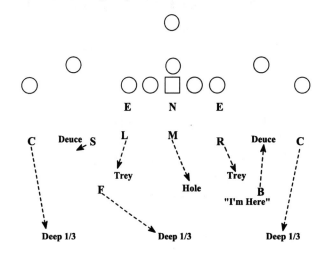

Diagram #8. 3 Coverage vs. Doubles

The last look is our 3 spoke coverage (Diagram #9). Again, the two corners have the deep outside one-thirds. The Bandit has the deep middle one-third. The free safety and the R backer have the deuce on their side. We are bringing the S backer on the outside rush.

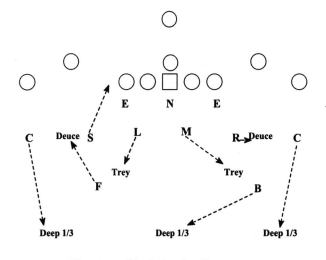

Diagram #9. 3 Spoke Coverage

I am out of time, but before I go, I want to remind you of this point. It is about developing young men and teaching them how to be champions. If you have a team full of champions, you are going to win games.

I appreciate your time. If you ever get to Oklahoma, come by to see us. Thank you very much.

ESSENTIALS IN INSTALLING THE SPREAD OFFENSE

Columbus East High School, Indiana

Thank you. It is a pleasure to be here. I want to talk about how we implement our spread offense, and then finish by showing you some cutup action of what we do. As we go along, if you have any questions, I will be happy to tell you the way we do it.

THE WAY WE DO IT

Our spread offense emphasizes the pass. People who play us would say that they have to stop the pass first. So, when we train in the off-season, a lot of the things we do just emphasize throwing the ball, catching the ball, and all of the things that go along with it. We will start with our kids in March, one morning a week. They come into our open facilities, and they start throwing the ball around and catching it.

They will throw it and catch it all summer. We go to 7-on-7 competitions, and we go to camps that emphasize pass offense and pass defense. Kids like it and because that is what we want to do.

We want to throw the football, but there's another thing about the spread offense that I think is important. We learned this when we installed the offense. We want to run the ball when we need to and when we want to. We learned a lot of that by trial and error.

When we switched to the spread offense from the I formation, we were a power team that really wanted to run the ball. We had to change the way we thought. We had a lot to learn, but one thing we learned quickly was that you cannot be too soft when you run the spread. You still have to be able to run the football. Getting the ball downhill, by running the ball hard, and hitting up in there, north and south, is an important factor that I think has made us better in the last two or three years in the spread.

CONCEPTS

I am going to give you some concepts and ideas that we used in getting to the things we think we have to do to be successful. Then, I am going to show you our best pass and our best running play.

First, you have to stretch the field vertically and horizontally. Your kids need to understand what that means. We can throw the ball coming out of our opponent's red zone. In practice during team time, we want to put our kids in those positions. We go from the 20-yard line in our own red zone, we will go middle of the field, and then we will work coming out of the opponent's red zone. We will do that every time we practice offense. We want to spread it vertically and horizontally.

The first concept we teach in the summertime is four-vertical. You have to make four-vertical a threat, but it does not mean that you have to throw it every down. You may not throw it more than one or two times a game, but it has to be a threat.

What that means is that you want to see if they are going to commit four defensive backs to defend the four deep quarters of the field. Are they going to put four guys back there, or are they going to put three guys back there? If they put four back there, which we see most of the time, then that dictates how many they can put in the box and how many guys they can put in the flats. It is all dictated by you being willing to throw the football down the field on four-vertical.

In our offense, we can run a four-vertical play from a dropback, or it can be out of play-action. The concept is the same either way.

We decided to go to the no-huddle offense most of the time. We really like it. We can huddle, and we do, but not very often. We work on the no-huddle in practice, and then we run it in on game night. We can yell out plays to the quarterback. We have very few plays on the quarterback's armband. On some of them, we disguise with words. Sometimes, we might not do a good job of disguising them. We tell our guys we want to make sure we know what we are doing when we try to communicate in the no-huddle. We are not too much concerned what our opponents are doing.

The other thing I think that happens with the no-huddle is that you make the defense show their hand early. Defensive coordinators have gotten a lot better. They will have their kids just stand and watch us get the plays from the sideline. If they see spread, they have three choices. They can change their defenses. However, if you are really going fast, then they have to get lined up to play. A lot of times, they may give you a vanilla look, especially at crunch time. You might get them into a vanilla look, and you know where you are going to be able to attack them to be successful.

The other important thing is giving your quarterback the ability to change the play and live with it. We probably change the play 50 percent of the time. You have to coach him on why you are doing it and what you are trying to do. However, if he makes a mistake, I do not think you can jump his tail end for it when he comes off the field. If he makes a mistake, I might just ask him what he saw. If he has a good answer, we would move on to the next time, and that would be it.

COMMUNICATION

Communication is important in any spread offense. How are you going to communicate? How are you going to identify defenses? Everybody has to be on the same page, including your whole staff and all of your kids. We want to know if a linebacker is a flat player or a hang backer. Is he a middle backer, a Mike backer, a Sam backer, or a Will backer? What are you going to call him?

Is he a corner? Is the corner hard, or is he soft? Is the safety on the hash, or is he in the middle of the field? Are you going to call it middle open or middle closed? Those are the points you have to figure out. You must decide on how you are going to communicate, and how you are going to identify defenses. The thing I think you find out when you run the spread is that defenses have some choices, but they do not have many choices. You are either going to see five or maybe six guys in the box, and then the secondary comes off of that.

We teach our guys to read from the secondary down. If there are two safeties, they probably cannot get six guys in the box, and so on. You have to figure out how you are going to identify defenses, what you are going to call a front, what you are going to call a stunt, and what you are going to call the coverages.

We do not have many players who go both ways. We do not have that many who practice both ways. We try to make our offensive terminology the same thing we are hearing on defense. If we call it a 5 alignment on defense, we call it a 5 alignment on offense. We want to be able to communicate where players line up.

Players need to talk and communicate on the field. When we are in no-huddle, we want them to talk. We tell them what we want them to communicate. It does not really matter to me how they get it done. On the running play I am going to talk about, they have to be able to tell each other if the guy is in a 3 or a 1 technique, and if they are in an even or an odd front. They need to say that, but they might have different words to do it. It does not matter, as long as they can figure that out. We want them to talk on every single play.

SPEND TIME

As I said before, we spend a lot of time throwing and catching the football. In Indiana, there are no rules in the summertime, and we could practice every day if we wanted to. We throw once a week in the springtime and once a week in the summer, and then we go to all the 7-on-7s, but they need to throw and catch the football and get good at it.

I think it is important to pick a protection that you can teach. We do not want a protection that we can draw up on the board, but one that we can teach. Pick a protection that works for you, and rep it up. For example, our protection will not work with the quarterback under center. It will not work because we pick up the A-gap blitzes with a back most of the time, and the quarterback would get sacked if he was under center.

You have to be able to draw up every blitz imaginable and have a chance to pick it up. I am sure you understand that no matter what formation you are in, they can always bring one more guy than you can block. They can always do it. It does not matter what you are in. So use the protection that works for you against every front and blitz.

Here is how we do it. When we go to skelly in practice, our linemen are doing pass protection the whole time. We set it up with five offensive linemen and one back against every front imaginable. In the pre-season, we show them every front, and then we bring out the fronts and blitzes we will see from week to week. Then, we prepare specifically for them. They need to identify them, call out the blitzes, and then protect against them. We start out being able to protect three on each side but we can kick four one way and two the other, just as everyone running the spread offense does.

The thing is, you need to have an answer. What is your answer going to be if they do bring one more guy than you can block? You have to have an answer, and you need to do that in practice. We man up in practice and bring one more guy than we can protect. We see what our quarterback is going to do with it. I hope that he is going to change the play and get the ball out quick, or check to some kind of screen. That would be our answer.

We spend a lot of time teaching routes. We do not have a lot of routes, but we want to be able to get good at them. We spend a lot of time just teaching kids how to cut. We want them to get their foot down, get their nose over their toes, push off that foot, and make cuts.

We want to teach them how to shake guys. Sometimes, when we get on the board, we draw routes with just straight lines. Then, we tell them straight lines do not get open. You have to learn how to shake a guy, attack his technique, and flip his hips. We spend a lot of time on this, and we teach adjustments they can make in their routes.

We do a lot of sight adjustments. We call routes on each play. If we have a deep route on against a guy we know is playing us very deep, we will not go deep if we want to get him the football. He changes his route at the line of scrimmage. In addition, our quarterback can change it. It does not matter how they change it. Sometimes it is visual, sometimes it is with words, and sometimes they just look and nod to each other, and they know they are going to change it.

SPREAD FORMATION

Here is our formation. We are in a spread formation with two wideouts and two slots. The X and Z are the wideouts, and L and R are the slots. L and R are for left and right. Our tailback just has to know where to line up. It takes too much verbiage to tell him. When we teach alignment, we just teach alignment to the play.

Cover 3

For us, this would be a cover 3 (Diagram #1). If the safety is in the middle of the field, two things can happen. It can be either cover 3 or cover 1. We tell our guys, the man in the middle is going to tip off if it is man or not. If he is deep, it is probably a cover-3 look.

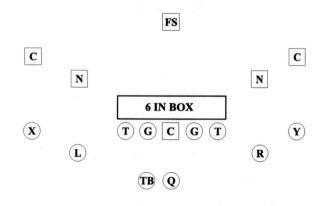

Diagram #1. Spread Vs. Cover-3 Look

We do not see a cover 3 very much. If we get it, we are throwing the ball down the field. I guarantee you, if our quarterback sees cover 3, he is jacking it deep. He is going to try to get the football out because they have six in the box and we can get 4-on-3 now.

We call the guy in the flat a nickel defender. It does not matter if he is a Sam linebacker or a strong safety. If he is in the flat, we call him a nickel defender. If he is over a wideout, he is a corner. If he is in the middle of the field, he is either a free safety or a half safety.

Cover 2

This is a cover-2 look (Diagram #2). How do we identify a cover-2 look? If the two safeties are on the hash marks, it is a cover-2 look for us.

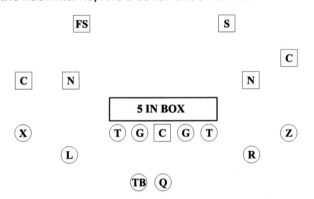

Diagram #2. Spread Vs. Cover-2 Look

The corner can be a hard cover-2 player, or he can be soft cover player. If he becomes soft, that would be a cover-4 look for us. The inside guy is still a nickel for us. They can only have five guys in the box. We think we have them outnumbered there, and we should run the football.

If the nickel starts walking down and he is going to blitz off the edge, we call that a storm. When he moves inside, our slot will yell inside to "Watch storm; watch storm!" Our linemen are in a two-point stance, and they stand up and look at the defense. Our quarterback will look at the defense as well looking for the storm blitz. They are all pointing at it and identifying it.

If one backer in the box comes, it is a blitz, and if two of them come, it is a Hawk. If a backer and a nickel are coming on the same side, to us that is a combo, and we will turn our protection to the side it is coming from.

PICK YOUR BEST

These are the things we have been able to do the best out of our spread offense. Our best run is the dash play. I will tell you why we like it. The play most everybody is running is the zone play, and we run that play, too. However, if we see the 4-1 front, we will probably run the zone play. If we think we can knock guys off the ball, get them covered up, and let our tailback just be a player, then we will the run zone. However, we cannot always do that.

Dash is back to the old isolation concept. The spread offense is viewed as a pass-first offense. Because of that, those 5 techniques are going to really get their tails upfield. They want to make the line of scrimmage come at the offense. We have to get the football going north and south right now.

We have to create a horizontal seam and get vertical. We do not want to take a long time reading zone and then going. The dash play gets the ball up the field right now. It is a power back play away from the play, and it is a zone-type play to the play. It is as simple as that.

Our best pass is four-vertical. We run several routes off it. As I said earlier, we want the defense to have to commit four guys deep. We will run some routes to take advantage of the areas that they give us.

DASH BLOCKING

The playside guard will recognize the defense and call out the technique in his area. If he calls out a 3 technique, then he and the tackle on that side will take a zone step, and they are blocking zone. Everybody else is picking back like the old isolation play. You are going to get a double-team back on the nose with a step off on the backside linebacker. The backside lineman who is uncovered pulls to the 1 technique area. On a 3 call, he pulls inside the 3 and leads the tailback just like on isolation.

Finally, the quarterback is still running an option read on that backside end. You can also take the play and let the quarterback fake it to the tailback, who would go block that end, and then let the quarterback run the same play. That is our best running play, and I will show it to you on the tape.

To finish up on dash blocking, we pull the uncovered lineman on the backside. If the playside guard calls 3, he comes to 1. If the playside guard calls 1, he comes to 3. It is not real hard. If the backside tackle is not the puller, he takes an inside zone step and looks for the run-through backer on the backside. He is not worried about the 5 technique. He will punch him and look for the backer running through.

Our receivers block alley to support. If we get a storm call to the frontside, it means we will also get a slant to the inside gaps. The quarterback will change the play. It is no good into that defense, so the quarterback may run the toss sweep outside of it. He may change it to a different direction and keep it himself, but he has to understand what that means.

Here is the dash versus the 4-1 (Diagram #3). We have a 3 call on the right. The guard and tackle are zoning out. The center and guard are doubling, and the backside tackle pulls. The quarterback just puts the ball in the tailback's belly and reads that defensive end.

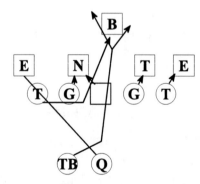

Diagram #3. Dash Vs. 4-1

Here is the same play with the quarterback carrying the ball (Diagram #4). If we want to have the quarterback keep it, everything looks the same. Nothing changes with the blocking scheme, but the tailback has to take care of the defensive end. If they run some kind of twist, the tailback has to keep his eyes up and get a piece of the edge player.

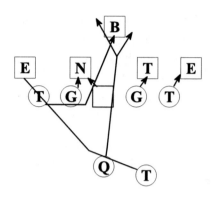

Diagram #4. Quarterback Dash Vs. 4-1

If the defensive end is any good and is coached up, he may try to run the track and get down inside. If he does that, our quarterback can still pull the ball. If our tailback can beat him and get a piece of the end, we can still get the ball north and south.

At times, they turn the defensive end loose, sit back, and play the quarterback with the nickel. That is why four-vertical is such a great play off this look. They cannot get any collision on the slot, and he can run free right down the field.

We see a lot of 3-2 and 3-3 fronts. Here is dash versus 3-2 (Diagram #5). This is what it should look like. The guard has called an odd front, so he gets to pick back and double with the center. If they get some kind of twist with the backside backer, they pick that up. The backside tackle should step up and take any kind of a run-through. The frontside tackle will zone out. We pull the guard around and get right up in the backer's face, and the tailback follows him. The quarterback still makes the decide read on the end.

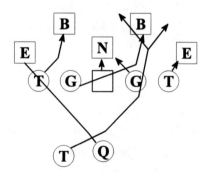

Diagram #5. Dash Vs. 3-2

When they play cover with a nickel player on one side in the flat, to control that nickel we run a bubble on it. If we want to run a bubble, we put a tag on the play. For us, the dash play is simply a 4 call. If we call 4 bubble, the slot runs the bubble, and we have a triple option. The quarterback can give it, keep it, or throw it to the slot. If the nickel is jacking around inside, the quarterback puts the ball in the tailback's belly and then throws the bubble.

We do not block the nickel. We do not crack block. We just take our X-receiver and block the corner. The only time we throw the bubble is when we think our slot can outrun the nickel.

Here is the dash versus the 3-3 stack (Diagram #6). This is the hardest one to block. They have six guys in the box. Theoretically, we should not be running the ball in there, but we need to have a way to run it on this front.

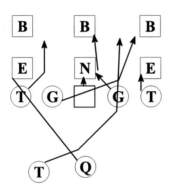

Diagram #6. Dash Vs. 3-3 Stack

If we tried to run outside zone on this, our offensive line would have some disadvantages. At least, when we run the dash, we get a chance to double the nose. In other words, you are not asking the center to catch that backer. We will go ahead with the same blocks with our tackles. The quarterback still has his decide read on the end. However, our playside tackle will not take his zone step against that 4 technique. He steps with his inside foot and does battle with anybody who comes inside. The other thing we do on this play is take big splits. We split them way out.

FOUR-VERTICAL

I am going to go through four-vertical and the other routes quickly. As I said earlier, we want to stretch the field, and present the threat of four-verticals on every snap we are in spread. We throw it off dropback or play-action, and then come back to our variations. When we make the defense think we are running four-verticals, we can throw it somewhere else. If they are going to play man on us, and blitz us, then we have to do something else.

This is our four-vertical against cover 3 (Diagram #7). It is run like everybody else in America runs it. We tell the guys to the field that they are not coming off the hash. If the ball is in the middle of the field, then our R would be on the hash. We are just going to stretch them with 4-on-3. That is easy.

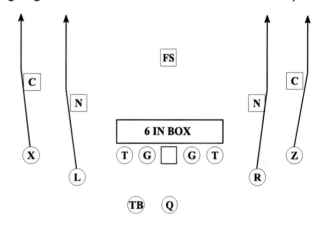

Diagram #7. Four-Vertical Vs. Cover 3

If we get cover 2, here is how we do it (Diagram #8). If the ball is in the middle of the field, then R stays on the hash and works vertically up the field. Our L receiver then becomes the reader. He will read the free safety and try to get to that soft spot in the middle. If they line him up 18 yards deep and just bail him, then we cut our L receiver off right there at 17 or 18 yards and let him try to work to the hole.

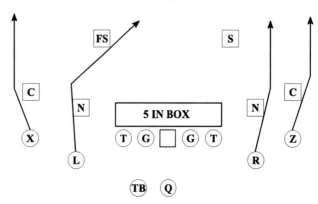

Diagram #8. Four-Vertical Vs. Cover 2

VARIATIONS OFF FOUR-VERTICAL

One of our best plays off four-vertical is what we call hitch (Diagram #9). We are running the same four-vertical plays. The inside men are running their vertical routes. The outside guys make it look like verticals, and then they sit the hitch down.

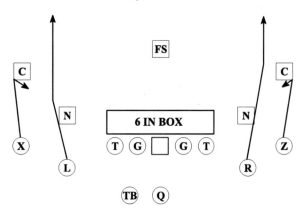

Diagram #9. Hitch Vs. Cover 3

We tell the outside guys to get six yards on the hitch. The nickel is the guy who can stop the route, so we keep the thing away from the nickel.

Here is the hitch versus cover 2 (Diagram #10). If we see cover 2, we are not running the hitch. We convert it and go back down the field. It is now just like four-vertical again. If the safety gets too deep, our R receiver may set down at 17 or 18 yards.

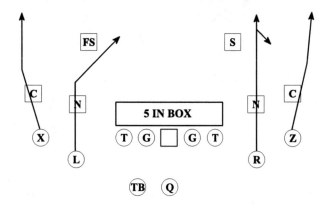

Diagram #10. Hitch Vs. Cover 2

Smash is an excellent route off four-vertical (Diagram #11). When we teach smash, L is our first read. He has been our reader a lot of times. He comes inside, looking at the quarterback. He is trying to get that safety thinking he is coming to the middle of the field. Then, he plants his foot and

takes it back to the corner. We want to make it look like we are adjusting four-vertical.

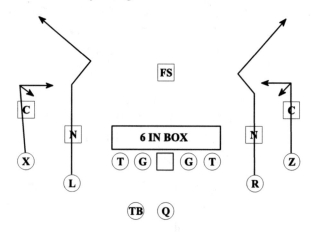

Diagram #11. Smash Vs. Cover 3

We tell the outside receiver to get open at eight yards, plant his foot, find the nickel, and stay away from him. If it is man coverage, he just plants his foot and runs.

All of our routes are mirror routes. If we do not want to mirror them, and work the backside, we call left or right (Diagram #12). If the ball is in the middle of the field and we run smash, we might call a smash right. We get a double post on the other side. The safety cannot be right. It is good against cover 2, and it is like stealing against cover 3, because the post will be wide open.

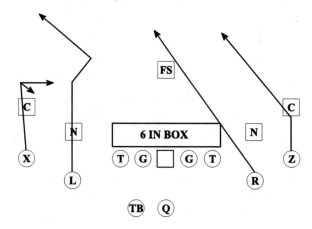

Diagram #12. Smash Post Vs. Cover 3

We read the smash, look at the smash, and find the free safety. If the free safety runs with R—and Z flips that corner's hips as I mentioned earlier, and shakes him a little bit and takes it to the post—if that happens, the quarterback has an excellent alley to throw the football.

Another route we really like that comes off of four-vertical is choice. We do not make it any harder than it is. When we run choice, our inside guys get open. They simply attack the nickel's technique and run away from him. If he is inside, run outside. If he is outside, run inside. If he is right on you, get him off you as if you are running vertical and squirrel it down.

Against cover 3, our outside guys run out and up routes. Against cover 2, they run fades. That is it.

We are going to work those choice routes off of those nickels.

One of our best routes is our squirrel play. On squirrel, all four receivers run a base route of 12 yards and back to 10 yards, coming back to the outside. It is a great route to run on third-and-five. Just get past the sticks, get open, and get the ball out on time. If they think you are running vertical, it is a good route.

I want to thank you for being here today. Thank you very much.

THE 3-3 STACK FIRE ZONE BLITZ PACKAGE

Anderson High School, Ohio

It is a great honor to be here. This is a great clinic. I want to thank the Nike Coach of the Year Clinic for having me. At one time, I coached at Franklin, Indiana, and we came to this clinic several times. This clinic has always been a place where you could learn football.

Last year, I spoke on offense at another clinic. This year, I am speaking on defense. I will never speak on special teams because I do not know enough about that part of the game. I realize that special teams is an important phase of the game, but I have some good assistants who help with that phase of our game.

Our defense has evolved over the last several years. When I came to Anderson in 1988, we were in a 50 defense. Five years later, we switched to the 4-3 defense. We were a 4-3 team for about 10 or 11 years, and we had a lot of success with that defense.

Five years ago we were 5-5 and we struggled on defense. The reason we struggled was because we did not have enough defensive linemen. We switched to the 3-3 and one of the reasons was the fact that we did not need to have as many defensive linemen.

The thing about changing is the fact you should always evaluate what you are doing on offense and defense. You need to look at the things you have been doing and see if you can change a few things to make you a better football team. You must be willing to change what you are doing if there is something you can do to make your team a better team. You do not have to make drastic changes, but you can get an idea or two, and it helps. I have taken other ideas from many coaches.

I think it is important to note: the longer you coach, the more you realize the game is more about player development and their attitudes than it is about X's and O's. To learn the X's and O's is not that tough to do, but coaching kids' attitudes and getting them to play as they can is much more important.

In my bio, it was mentioned that we were state champions in my first year as a head coach. That was a great accomplishment, but we had 15 seniors on the team. We had lost 38 seniors the year before, and we were just hoping to survive that next year. Our players stepped up for us, and we got some breaks along the way. This year, we went down to the last 32 seconds before we lost in the state finals. We have been successful in this game in the last two years.

The thing I have been able to look at in the last two years is the fact that it is not just the end results that matter. The result is not always going to be the most important thing in the game. Working with the players every day and developing a relationship with them and the other coaches is a big part of the game.

I think it is important for coaches to find out what works best for them in football. Not all of the things we do are going to fit in for you, and that is fine. You must make an evaluation of your kids is selecting an offense or a defense.

If you are looking for defensive players, you do not want those who cannot make plays. You must find players on defense who will make plays. You must make an honest evaluation of the knowledge of the defense you are switching to run. You have to ask the question of how much you know about the defense. You need to know the weakness of the defense.

It is important to study your opponents and know whom you have to beat on your schedule. Can you beat them with the defense you are selecting? You must select a defense that will give you a chance to get into the playoffs. Once you get into the playoffs, then you have a chance.

In Ohio, we are a large Division II school. We were in Division I for a long time. We were in a district with Moeller, Colerain, Elder, and St. Xavier. These schools are great teams. We could never get out of the first round of the playoffs. Now that our enrollment has dropped, we are in Division II. Now, we are a large Division II team in Ohio. There is a big difference in playing those teams in Division I and the teams in Division II.

You must have assistant coaches to go along with the other things needed to be successful. I am fortunate in that I have 9 out of 10 coaches who are in the building with me. I know that is not the case in most schools, but that is a big plus for us. Two of our three freshman coaches are in the building.

I want you to know that I am not bragging when I tell you about our program. I am just telling you some of the things that have worked for us over the years.

You must have a philosophy to start out with on offense or defense. Here are our objectives on defense:

• Prevent our opponent from scoring.
• Get the ball back.
• Score, or set up scores.
• Execute all defenses perfectly.
• Everyone is on the same page.

We need objectives when we put the defense into place. We want to prevent teams from scoring. We do not shut teams out from scoring. Now, we are giving up more points than we did before, but we are winning more games. The most important stat on defense is the number of points scored against you. It is not first downs or yards given up. It is the points scored against you.

We would like to get three-and-out every time if possible. We know that is important to the offense as well as the defense. We know third down is the money down, and we must get off the field on third downs.

We must be able to communicate to the players. Players have to communicate with each other and to their coaches. When our players come off the field, they go to their position coaches to let them know what is going on in the game. There is a lot of communication between the press box and the field. The style of play for us is as follows:

• Physical
• Relentless
• Attacking
• Recognition
• Communication

We want to be physical. This can be developed in the off-season. We lift weights four days a week. Our staff does a great job in the weight room. We develop leadership by physically attacking each other. The players go through a series of exercises that are tougher than anything they do in two-a-days. They keep coming back for more. They build confidence in these drills. You can see as they go through the program.

The players develop camaraderie as they are going through some difficult workouts together. They help each other through some difficult times. They learn to care about their teammates, and they care about their teammates' success. This is very important in developing teamwork.

They have to learn to be relentless. They just cannot quit. They must be willing to work through problems. Gaining confidence in what they are doing helps a great deal here.

Recognition is important. It is important to match up with personnel. Communication is important in dealing with all phases of the game.

Good defenses are always going to align correctly. This is what we base our defense on, and this is what we want on every play.

• Align correctly.
• Diagnose plays and schemes.
• Separate from blocks.
• Run to the ball.
• Tackle.

- Great attitude ("The most important choice ever made" –Hal Urban).
- Great habits that show up in stressful situations.

The good defensive players line up correctly. They know their responsibility, and they know their gap. They know the depth they need to be off the ball. They know their shade techniques.

They must be able to diagnose plays and schemes. It is important for the players to come off to the sideline to tell the coaches what they are doing. It is important for players to be able to communicate with the coaches when they are out of the game.

We want to find players who can separate and get off blocks. It does not have to be technical and playbook style, but players must get off blocks. Find players, for some reason, get to the football. Find players who can find the football, and who do not let other players get in their way.

We want players who can tackle the football. Tackling is getting tougher to teach more and more. You see a lot of articles that state tackling is getting worse over the years. I am not sure if it is or not. It may be the offensive-skilled players are becoming more athletic. Tackling is something you must work on all of the time.

It is important to have a good attitude. Hal Urban wrote a book about attitudes: *Choices That Change Lives*. I read his book, and I got a lot out of it on attitude. He said, "The most important choice you will ever make is your attitude."

Coaches can tell the kids who are going to step up and be leaders. Those players have a great attitude. Bad things can happen sometimes when you are playing defense. How does the player react to a bad situation? Does he have his head down for the next four plays? If he does that, he is not the kid you want as your leader. Most of the time, when the offense sees that player with his head down, that is the person they are going to run at for the next two or three plays. Eventually, he figures he better get his head up and play tough. This is especially true with secondary players.

Great habits show up in stressful situations. In the long run, to be coached on what players need to do will pay off when the players get in a stressful situation.

Why play the 3-3 stacked defense? We have had three Division I players in the last 15 years who have gone on to college to play defense. We have not had many good defensive linemen. This is one reason we like the 3-3 alignment. Here are some reasons we play the 3-3:

- Only three defensive linemen are needed
- Six in the box to stop the run
- Five defensive backs
- Variety of fronts and looks
- Bluffing and deception
- Adjustments and flexibility
- Aggressive downhill defense
- Creates turnovers

We would like to have six defensive linemen to rotate into those three down positions. Those three positions are very demanding positions.

We like the idea of always having at least six men in the box to stop the run. We are very hesitant to break our stack. We want to leave the six defenders in the box. If the offense starts to outflank us, we will move some defenders outside.

We like the idea that we have five defensive backs. That puts more speed on the field. It allows us to give the offense a variety of fronts and looks. It is difficult for the opponents to learn a lot of different looks each week. We disguise the defense as much as we can. Walking up into a seven-man front is easy to do in this defense.

This defense allows us to mess up the offensive scheme by moving around. We have the ability to adjust the defense. It is very flexible in that we can change the defense without disrupting the rest of the defense. The adjustments are very easy, and we have a wide variety of defensive looks we can line up in.

You do need to have some ideas on how you are going to play against certain formations. One of the first things you need to decide on is how you are going to play against a double-tight-end set. Teams will line up in two tight ends and try to run the ball right at you. You need to decide how you are going to handle a wing-T set. How are you going to play on the wing? Are you going to walk the linebacker, or dog as we call them, down to the line and play on his outside shoulder? There are a lot of ways to play that set, but you need to decide how you are going to play it before you get in to the game.

You have to look at your personnel in making these decisions. You may have to make a personnel change against certain offenses. You need to have a certain amount of adjustments in your package that will help against certain offensive looks.

Our defense is an aggressive downhill defense. Those inside linebackers are running to the football. We like the defense because it helps create turnovers. This past year, we had 18 interceptions and recovered 9 fumbles. I think one reason we get the turnovers is because of the hesitancy of the offense by our crashing defense. The offense is looking for the blitz, and they make mistakes.

The keys to our success are as follows:

• Execution
• Play recognition
• Communication
• Fun

We feel you must make football fun for the players. You cannot just scream and yell at them all of the time. It can be tough on the players after they have been in school all day. They come to practice, and they have problems on their mind. It may be a problem at home, a problem with a girlfriend, or something that is keeping them from performing at a high level. It is up to the coaches to get them going. In the time that you have with the players, it is your job to make it fun for them. You want them to enjoy practice and want to come to practice every day.

In our base alignment, we line up head-up with the nose man (Diagram #1). We line up in heavy 5 techniques with our tackles. We are close to being head-up on the tackles. Our Mike backer may shade just a little to the strong A gap. The backers will

shade one way or the other, depending on the boundary and the field. They still are stacked behind the tackles. We try to play the five backs across the back line. We do not line up in 4x4 alignments. We can move them around and drop them back between seven and eight yards deep. They can still cover anything in front of them.

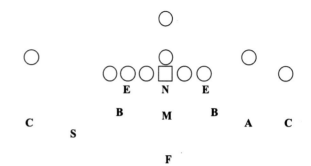

Diagram #1. Base Alignment

It is easy to disguise who the robber is going to be, and to disguise the coverages, or to determine who is going to be the run support at times. We can play a variety of three-deep out of this defense. All of our linebackers have their heels at five yards deep as their starting point. It depends on how good you are up front. You may have to move the linebackers up some if the front three are not that fast.

St. Xavier High School does a great job with this defense. They play their linebackers up tighter at three-and-a-half yards deep. The front three are very physical, and they all tackle well. They do a lot of different things from this look.

We have visited a lot of places to talk about this defense. We went to West Virginia. We talked with Steve Specht of St. Xavier about the defense. When Todd Graham was at West Virginia, we talked with him about the defense. Todd Graham is at Tulsa now. We do not do a lot out of this defense, as other teams do. You have to find what works best for you.

We like teaching from this alignment from day one. Two years ago, we started out by teaching from the 4x4 alignment. Then, we worked on backing a man off the line of scrimmage. However, the last couple of years, we have started with the 3x3 from day one. I think this approach has helped, especially with the young kids.

I want to give you the things we expect from our personnel. Our nose is going to be an A-gap player.

NOSE

- Can be big or small and quick
- Must be tough, physical, and relentless
- Has to handle double-teams
- Unselfish

Our ends are more athletic than the nose man is. Our ends are not very big. Next year, one end will weigh 205 pounds, and the other end will weigh 195 pounds. They are not big, but they are tall and rangy.

ENDS

- Taller and more athletic than nose
- Able to handle double-teams
- Able to close on down blocks
- Able to run

Our Mike backer is an A-gap player. He plays off the nose man. He must be smart enough to read the triangle to know what is going on. He cannot be wrong in his movements.

MIKE LINEBACKER

- Physical
- Smart, can read triangle
- Able to get over the top of blocks

Our outside backers are B-gap players. They play behind the ends.

OUTSIDE LINEBACKERS

- Able to run
- Good blitzers
- Disciplined for cutback
- Able to defend inside zones and reroute receivers

You cannot just go out and tell a player to blitz the gap. You must teach him the techniques to get through that gap. They must help on disguising their moves. They must play the cutbacks and not just go flying around. They must be able to protect the inside zones and reroute receivers. The play is similar to an outside linebacker on the 4-3 defense. They can be as light as 160 pounds to 200 pounds, depending on their speed.

The Dogs are B-gap players. They play pass and run. They must be a good athlete to play this position.

DOGS (APACHE AND SAM)

- Strong safety types
- Good tacklers
- Good blitzers
- Able to defeat blocks in space

We do prefer someone who is a little taller than the other defenders. We want them to be able to get into the passing lanes. The big point is that they must be good tacklers and they must be able to blitz efficiently. We want to let the offense know that we can come off the edge on a blitz. This will keep them honest.

Our free safety must be a smart player. In most cases, we want our best athlete in this position. This year, we played free safety with a 150-pound kid, but he was tough.

FREE SAFETY

- Smart
- Ideally, the best athlete
- Good tackler
- Good ball skills

Our corner must have good ball skills. He must have good hands, and he must be able to catch the football. If he gets his hands on a pass and does not catch it, he should be upset. When we look back on the games, you have questions about those plays. They are on an island by themselves. They must be ready to play every play.

CORNERS

- Good ball skills
- Able to play man and zone

We line up in our defense, and we call "front" (Diagram #2). We are going to stack the backers behind the line and play with five secondary players.

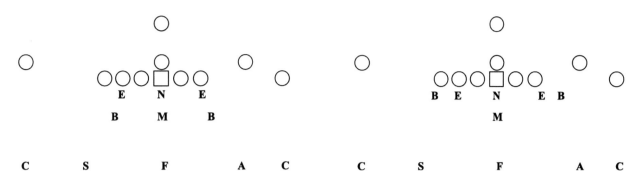

Diagram #2. Front Stack

If we call "down," we are going to bring the Dogs down. We have them labeled with S and A (Diagram #3). That puts us in a 5-3 look. This gives us a chance to blitz and to bring a defender from the edge. It is hard to ask a back to play one-third deep middle when they are up on the line of scrimmage. However, when they are eight yards deep, they can play a deep-third, or a deep-half in the secondary.

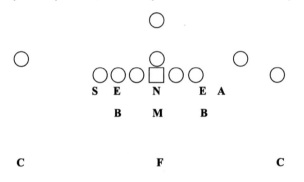

Diagram #3. Down

We run our spread look, which is our 5-1 look (Diagram #4). We walk the dogs up on the edge. When teams see us in this defense, they want to attack us on the inside. We still have the A gap covered with the Mike backer and the nose. You can mix things up and take care of the B gap. If the ball comes free in the middle of the defense, the deep-middle defenders must come down inside and converge on the play. We like to line up showing a blitz from one area and bringing the blitz from another area.

We use the nickel call on long yardage (Diagram #5). This is our 3-2 look. We have six deep defenders. We can take a lineman or a linebacker out of the lineup and replace him with a defensive back.

Diagram #4. Spread

If you have a kid who is smart enough to play outside linebacker, you could bump the linebackers over and put him outside, or drop him back in the middle. When the offense sees us in this defense, they want to run the ball because they only see five men in the box. We did well in this defense against the run by having two men, including the nickel, who could come down to support on the run. If you have five in the box and they cannot run the football, you should win the game.

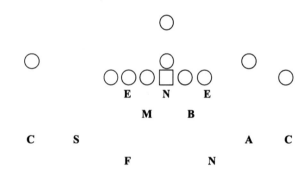

Diagram #5. Nickel

I want to move on to our coverages. Primarily we are a three-deep cover team. Our corners play the deep outside (Diagram #6). The free safety is in the deep middle. The Dogs play the flats, and the three backers drop in the middle.

We are only rushing three men from this front. Sometimes, we will bring four on the rush. We can move the linebackers up closer to the ball, which will allow you to do different things out of that look. We are unlimited on the different combinations that we can run form this defense.

We play a lot of robber coverage (Diagram #7). Against the one-back-set, you can bring the dogs to

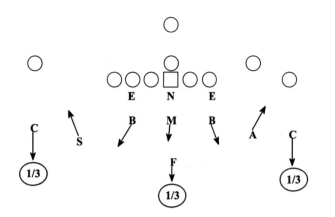

Diagram #6. Three-Deep Coverage

the flat, and drop the backers. You do not have to send the Mike backer every time you run this look. We do not run this look very much against the one-back-set, but we can. We think this defense is good against the two-backs set.

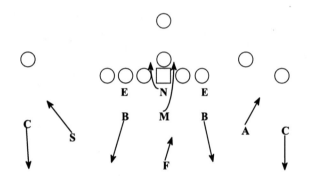

Diagram #7. Robber

On our man free, the deep free safety is deep in the middle (Diagram #8). He is free on the call. Again, this is against the one-back set. Here, the Mike backer is also free. You must know your rules as far as the man-to-man matchups. It all depends on who is blitzing on the plays as far as pass coverage. That is why it is so important to communicate on defense.

I want to talk about our fire zones for a few minutes. Here are the advantages of running the fire zone-blitz package.

• Defense can always see the ball.
• Good for run support.
• Hole player can be used to spy the quarterback.
• Fewer one-on-one tackles in space.
• Average athletes can make plays.

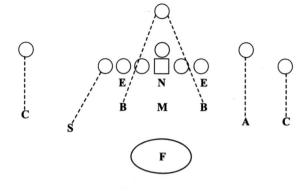

Diagram #8. Man Free

• Defend crossing routes, and picks better than in man.
• Only limited by your imagination.

I want to talk about the rules for us on the three-deep fire zone defense. It is very simple. I heard this explanation of the defense at a clinic from Kevin Coyle when he was at Fresno State. It has held up all of this time since I first heard him talk about the defense. The thing you must do, and to stress when you look at film, is to decide who the hot-route receivers are. If you can do that, you have a good chance of shutting them down. This is what you must have on this defense.

THREE-DEEP FIRE ZONE

• Two seam-curl-flat defenders
• One or two hole defenders
• Three deep defenders

We call the hole defenders the "skip" players. They defend the seam, the curl, and then the flat. We work inside-out to take away everything to the inside and work to the outside. We defend one or two holes, depending on the blitz.

I want to show you the first fire zone blitz to the split end side. We are bringing the nose, end, Dog on the backside, and Mike (Diagram #9). We want the rush end to read the backside guard. If the guard steps outside, the end goes inside of the guard. If the guard comes down inside, the end comes off the butt of the guard. We are not just running that end into the B gap. We want to know where the gap is after that backside guard moves.

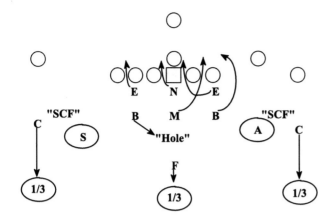

Diagram #9. Three-Deep, Split-End Side

We run the blitz to the tight-end side or strongside as well (Diagram #10). This is easier to play for us. If the tight end releases inside and tries to go vertical, the outside Dog walls him off and forces him to the outside.

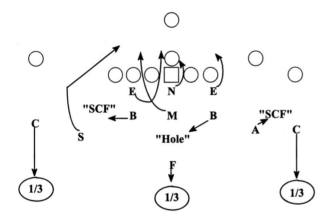

Diagram #10. Three-Deep, Tight-End Side

We also run the fire zone blitz with a two-deep zone coverage. If the offense starts throwing to the flat because we are not defending that area that well, you must have a defense to come back to stop the pass to the flat. We are bringing the Sam and Apache backs deep and have each of them play the deep half. You can run the play with the cornerbacks playing one half (Diagram #11).

This is what we need to play the defense.

TWO-DEEP FIRE ZONE

• Two flat defenders
• Two curl defenders

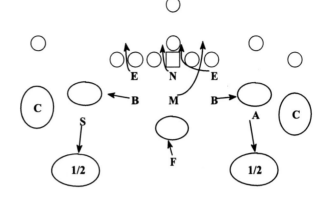

Diagram #11. Two-Deep, Split-End Side

• One hole defender
• Two deep defenders

You must coach the kids and make sure they understand where they can get hurt. The down linemen are not doing anything any different from what they did before.

On the strongside, it is the same as before with the two-deep. Because the corner is covered, he cannot play the flat. He is going to cover deep (Diagram #12). Sam and the free safety will each play one half deep. Again, the down linemen are doing the same as before.

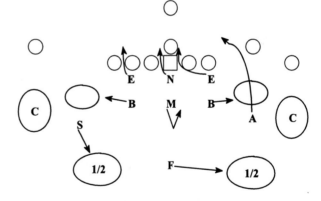

Diagram #12. Two-Deep, Tight-End Side

I do have a film that will show the defense much better than I can describe it. Again, you can contact me if you have questions on the defense. I think one of the most important things about football coaches is the amount of information that is shared at various activities. I want to thank you for your attention.

OFFENSIVE LINEMEN LEVERAGE PRINCIPLES

Silverton High School, Oregon

It is a pleasure to speak to you about offensive line play. I played 11 years in the NFL with the Giants, the 49ers, and the Jets. My philosophy is the sum total of everything I have learned from some good coaches during that time. They moved me from knowing what I needed to do technically to how that fit into the general scheme of being successful.

LEVERAGE

The whole talk today is based on leverage. There is a schematic leverage that gives us an advantage by our alignment and coordination of play. There is an instructional leverage that gives us an advantage by the way we prepare and build our skills. But, the most important thing is the physical part. Physical leverage is how we use our bodies, technique, and fundamentals to gain an advantage and become successful as offensive linemen.

SCHEMATIC LEVERAGE

You can really gain an advantage, or leverage, by simply working on your alignment. What is your relationship to the line of scrimmage, and what is your relationship to the guy next to you? If you are a team that pulls the backside guard and backside tackle a lot, you are probably going to deepen them to make them closer to your center. If you are a zone-scheme team, you might want to widen them out to create running lanes and put defenders at a disadvantage for what they have to do.

Coordination refers to how you are working with the people around you. In zone schemes especially, it is: who are you working with, and where is your help? How does everything fit together on the line of scrimmage, but also with your backs, your receivers, and even your quarterback?

Communication refers to how you get things done. Our communication is very casual on our offensive line. If we are responsible for a particular guy, we have to be precise in how we communicate, but with a tackle helping the center with a backside block, I may tell him to say, "Hey! I have your back!" The important thing is that we all get on the same page.

Schematic leverage in the passing game refers to a sense of body presence and recognition of your relationship to everyone around you. It is critical to the protection scheme and leads into the notion of interdependence. Interdependence means knowing where we have help, how that help can come, and who will bring it. Included in that interdependence are our running backs. They like to run the ball, and I like to run it, too, but if a back cannot pass protect, he will not see the field.

Recognition refers not only to seeing something, but to also communicating it. It requires that what we see must be identified. Then, when it is communicated, it unifies us as a protection unit and results in coordination of play.

Schematic leverage in the running game starts with our target and path, and gets into our zone scheme and our lead draw. If you have poor target on the lead draw, you will get bunching up in the hole. Things will close up, there is nowhere to run, and you have a poor target. The correct target and path will gain you as much leverage as anything you do.

We use combinations to gain schematic leverage. After we do our work on our individual fundamentals, the next drill work we do during individual time is combination work. We do 2-on-1, 2-on-2, 3-on-2, and all those double-teams that come off on linebackers. Each of those combinations will change schematically, according to the alignment of the defensive lineman and the depth of the linebacker in tandem with him.

Coming off of the double-team to the linebacker is called transfer. The biggest part of that transfer is finish. We have to be able to finish. It involves who comes off, when he comes off, and precisely how he comes off, so leverage is maintained on both defenders.

INSTRUCTIONAL LEVERAGE

We do not have players who are bigger, faster, and stronger than our opponents' players are, so we have to do everything right. Our personnel has to be technically sound. If we do that, we will be successful, and we have been successful because we are starting to understand the schemes. We have a ways to go but we are getting there.

In this off-season, we drew up every play in our base offensive system, listed the skills needed at each position to be successful, and followed that with the drills we will do to build up those skills. We aligned our drills, our practices, our offense, and our game plan into a unified system. That will really help us with practice planning. We can eliminate all the things we do just because we do, and we can be specific on the drills that are important in perfecting our skill sets.

Once we have aligned what we want to do instructionally, we have to build up our skill levels. Everything we do with the offensive line starts at a very elementary level. First, we want to put ourselves in a position to be successful, before the snap and immediately following the snap. Those first two steps are critical. Then, we want to use the skills we have developed, and finally we want to finish the play. All of this is taught as a skill progression.

We will connect those skills to construct the big picture for our players. If we are running zone weak, I will talk about why they need to get their heads playside, why they need to put their hands inside, and whom they are working with. I will connect those things with the roles of the people around them, and with the general philosophy of what we are trying to do.

We will build on those connections through repetition. We will do them repeatedly. When we start a drill, our kids have done it so many times they know the techniques we want. They understand the objectives of the drill, and they can see how those skills fit into the big picture.

The last thing, and maybe the most important thing, in instructional leverage is emphasis. It is not what you teach; it is what you emphasize, so I am going to give you a number of different things that are important in that progression of general, run, and pass, but the key is that you do not try to do all those things at once. You have to emphasize one thing at a time in your teaching progression.

In offensive line drills, everyone may be doing the same thing, but one guy might struggle with this and another guy with something else. You have to focus on those individual struggling points and emphasize specific points with specific players.

We start camp with just run drills. All I want to see is a correct second step. That is all I will focus on at first with all of our guys, whether their heads are right or anything else. When we get footwork down, I will shift the emphasis to whatever comes next, and develop a skill subset with my teaching progression.

Once we have those skill subsets developed, then I will emphasize big-picture concepts. Kids will begin to see a clear picture of how their correctly executed skills fit into the overall design of a play.

For example, our playside guard on the zone play is taught head placement to the outside. He knows that the 3 technique is a B-gap player and will probably try to work to the outside to keep gap control. He knows that will widen the hole to the inside and give our ballcarrier a better running lane. Our guard will use his skill set more effectively because he has a big-picture concept.

From the first day of camp until our season is over, I will tell our players why we are doing these things. I will bring that big picture into those small things, specifically on hand placement, head placement, first and second steps, hips, and eyes. You cannot emphasize all those things at once, but if players recognize why each is important, they will use them more effectively.

PHYSICAL LEVERAGE—GENERAL

The drill that goes with physical leverage is our duck demeanor drill, which emphasizes the foundation of all the things we need to do in run and pass. When a player has the correct body position for maximum physical leverage, he appears to have the demeanor of a duck.

Pad level is critical. One of my pro coaches said that for every inch of pad level, you gain 10 pounds of power. Body position is connected to pad level because getting lower does not create leverage for a player unless his feet are slightly wider than his shoulders, knees are bent and slightly knocked, and he is "sitting in that chair" with all his cleats in the ground. From that position, he can move in any direction he chooses. He could be more powerful with a forward body lean and weight up on his toes, but he could then only go in one direction—and usually that is right on his face.

He has to hedge and be in a position of leverage so he can go forward, backward, or side-to-side, move with guys, and finish blocks. Power is generated from being in a good position and doing everything else connected with it that will gain him leverage.

We want all of the parts of his feet down, with emphasis on insteps digging into the ground. In the duck demeanor, I want him to knock those knees slightly to emphasize where I want his feet to be. If he is up on his toes the only direction he can go is forward, and on his heels, the only direction he can go is backwards, so he should dig those insteps in and get all feet on the ground with a nice wide base, and keep those feet moving.

Run or pass, we want inside position with our hands, which is the position of leverage. To maximize that leverage, we need our hands out in front of us with elbows inside. Our kids will get their hands in tight like we want, but then their elbows will pop out and they lose leverage.

What the player sees is important, so it is essential to coach the eyes. If our linemen are trying to see the whole picture, we are in trouble. We want them to focus on specific points, and I will get into those in more detail when I discuss run and pass, but the eyes tell the body what to do and when to do it.

The last point of emphasis is the absolute need to finish. The quickest way off a professional team, and maybe a college team, is to not finish on a play or in a drill. You may get yourself into a bad position at the start of a play, but you can make up a lot of things with your desire to finish. That is really all about attitude.

If we could picture an offensive lineman in a pro training tape doing the duck demeanor drill, we can see the proper movements. He is in a fundamental power position for maximum physical leverage. As he moves forward and backward, left and right, he maintains that position. His feet cannot move properly if his hands are not moving, so he keeps elbows tight, hands tight, and works his arms in concert with his lower body movement. His knees are knocked slightly. He uses all his cleats, but emphasis in the duck demeanor is to really step on the insteps.

PHYSICAL LEVERAGE—PASS

Body presence goes with body relationship, and it means starting out in a good position to be successful. For example, as a right offensive tackle in pass protection, I want to keep my shoulders square and force the guy outside. We want to force him out, not just let him go outside. When I open up those shoulders and get away from square to the line of scrimmage, I have let him outside. It shortens the corner and gets me in deep trouble.

At the same time, I cannot overstep him to the point that he beats me back to the inside. If I just establish a slightly inside-out relationship and stay square to the line of scrimmage, I cut off anything that is coming inside and force him into a one-way go. My body presence is huge, and we are only talking about two or three inches there.

Most of the pass-protection problems I see in high school players are head-and-shoulder problems. Their head is forward, which means they are on their toes, and their shoulders are forward, which means their hips are high. Consequently, they have no power, they cannot move, and they are not in a position of leverage.

We want them to get down in that duck-demeanor stance with a big chest, hands on that shelf, and with their head back. From that position, they can generate all that power by popping their hips and delivering a three-inch punch. When the head and shoulders are forward, the power from the hips is eliminated.

When we talk about target, we want to focus on a small point. I tell the right tackle to look at the inside crease of the defender's shirt. That keeps good body presence and a good inside-out relationship. It also forces him to get back quicker so he can see it better. If he starts seeing the shimmy-shakes and head fakes, they are going to cause him trouble.

For the guard, the focal point might be the inside line of the inside number. For the center, it might be the outside line of the inside number, depending on which way we are sliding.

The punch is critical to a successful pass-protection block. We have our hands on a shelf, our elbows are tight, our hands are out in front of us, and it is a three-inch punch. We want to restart his heart. The first inch is contact, and two inches go through his chest.

Once we get our hands in a position of leverage, we want to leave them there, which requires you to move your feet. When you get the punch in there, grab, hold on, and stay in front of him. It is not holding if you stay in front of him. We do not want to punch and scoot back because that squeezes the pocket and engulfs the quarterback.

All of our power is generated from the hips. If we have high hips and straight legs, we have nothing to generate power with. If we sit in that chair with our hips nice and low, it will help us get something behind that three-inch punch.

There are two key points I want to make about feet. First, when moving laterally, we do not want our feet to come together. In the duck-demeanor drill, guys will bring their feet together when they move laterally because they are not in good shape or because they have poor flexibility. Second, we want to patter our feet so that when we make contact, our feet continue to move, not on our toes, but using all seven studs.

The last point of emphasis in pass-protection leverage is finish. Whether we are in a good position or a bad position, when the pass rusher starts around the corner, how fast can I accelerate my feet and widen that pocket? I will dive if I have to, or do whatever I can, but I have to make sure I finish the block. Finish the block every single time.

PHYSICAL LEVERAGE—RUN

In zone blocking, we put ourselves in a position to be successful with the second step. The first step is important in zone-blocking schemes because it puts us on the right path or angle. I do not like to call it a "bucket step" because that correlates with the notion of a false step. We open up a three-inch step to put our hips at the proper angle, but the key is that second step.

The second step is our "stick step." That second step is also three inches, also in the direction we want, and it gets us coiled and ready to unload. That is where all our power is generated.

At the same time that the second step hits the ground, our hands are inside striking. Those two things happen simultaneously. We jab and stick, our hands are inside in a position of leverage, we hold on, and we drive.

The most important thing for me, then, becomes that head placement. I have to put the defensive lineman in a bind. If I put my head backside, try to wedge, or turn and torque, I am in deep trouble, especially with smaller guys. I have to threaten his gap responsibility while maintaining contact and leverage.

As we drive, we want to continue to keep all seven studs of each foot on the ground and keep the weight on our insteps. Our base has to be wide.

We establish the angle of the block with that first step, and generate all our power from the second, or stick, step. Power comes from releasing our hips and shooting them at the target. We want to unleash our hips, accelerate our feet, and finish that block.

The defender is put in the position of making a one-armed tackle or not making a tackle at all because he is still engaged with us. We do not have to be powerful to finish blocks. We just have to have tenacity, keep moving our feet, and finish.

DRILLS

The duck-demeanor drill is the first one we do as a general drill to develop body position and movement. We get players down in a good football position with shoulders back and head back. The coach is out in front giving a four-way go. When he moves players right and left, they should pound that inside foot on every change of direction and keep their shoulders square. When they move forward and backward, they have to incorporate their hands, keep their weight on their insteps, and never on their toes. They finish with a sprint past the coach.

The mirror-dodge drill is our basic pass-protection drill. We start with our focus on shoulders and head. We set two cones five yards apart and start with a blocker and a defender facing each other in between, with the defender hugging a bag or shield tight to his body.

In the first part of the drill, the defender just moves laterally. We start in a walk-back-and-forth movement, with our shoulders back, and our eyes focusing on where they need to be. I start them off with their hands behind their backs, working to make sure their feet do not come together, their shoulders stay square, and they keep their eyes on the target.

As we progress in the drill, the blocker will get his arms on that shelf, and the defender will come in for a strike, retreat, continue his lateral movement, and then come back in for subsequent strikes. The blocker keeps elbows in tight, punches, and continues to mirror the defender. When we do the drill in pads, we do not use the bag, and we can incorporate a swim move or rip move by the defender.

The jab-stick-drive drill is the first drill that we use for teaching run blocking. We start it with a blocker and defender paired up, with the defender aligned slightly to the outside. The blocker's shoulders are square to the line at the start, but the angle he is going to take is off at about 1 o'clock or 1:30.

The first step is his three-inch jab, which redirects him to the target. The second step is the stick step, which incorporates with a punch, and the drive-steps follow. We keep a good base and finish strong.

We will start by walking through it and progress to blocking against a defender with a bag. When we do the drill in pads, we can give the defender a two-way go at the end and make the blocker fight to finish his block. It forces him to bring his hips and accelerate his feet. A final coaching point is to bring the hands from the ground to the chest. Never teach blockers to load the hands because it just gives the defender a better target.

The Crowther drill is the last drill I want to mention. We start with a four-point strike to teach how to deliver a blow. We teach hitting with the forearm rather than shoulder. That forces their hips to come forward and that forearm to come up and through the chest.

The last part of the progression on the sled is the three-point drive. Head to the playside is critical on this. On contact, they should widen the base and accelerate the feet. The sled forces the blocker to gather his feet, stay under control, dip, and take another piece.

That is it for today, men. Thank you. I will be happy to stay afterward and answer questions.

POWER RUNS AND PLAY-ACTION PASSES

Shawnee High School, New Jersey

When I was a young coach coming up, I thought you picked an offensive system and stuck with it. I thought you made the players fit what you were doing. With some coaches in our league, you always know what type of offense and defense they are going to use because that is his system and that is what he does. I found, coaching in our situation, we had to take the athletes we got and find a system that fit them.

When we get together as a staff, we want to make sure our players understand that we care about them. We want them to know we are a family and their education is important to us. I heard Jim Tressel, of Ohio State University, speak one time. He read a quote from Albert Einstein: "*Concern for man and his fate must always form the chief interest of all technical endeavors—never forget this in the midst of your diagrams and equations.*" That is something I have always remembered.

We have a great football staff. I feel we have eight head coaches on our staff. Our coaching staff has 153 combined years of coaching experience. They are great guys who love the game. They all teach and give me all the support I need. I would not be able to do all the things required of me if it were not for my staff.

When we got into our thought process about our team, we came up with a number of ideas we wanted to put into our program.

- Trademark play
- Physical, simple, tough
- Run the ball anytime, anywhere, at anybody
- Run it and run it right
- Signature play to run when the game is on the line

- North and south versus east and west, downhill running game
- Fundamental football, block down and kick out
- Toughness on both sides of the ball
- Inside drill daily pre-season, best-on-best
- Run from base formations and be good at defensive front recognition

We had a dilemma in our program some time ago. We were getting beat up by the teams we should have been beating. We lost four in a row. When we got into the big games, we were having trouble scoring. The defense was the only thing that kept us in any game. If we did not turn the ball over, we had a chance to win. That worked for a while.

In 2006, we drank the poison Kool-Aid®. What I mean by that is we went to the spread offense. We watched West Virginia play and later heard Rich Rodriguez speak on their spread offense, and we decided it was the offense we wanted to run. We went to an offense we should never have tried. We did not have the players for the offense or the players that fit with it. We could not fix the problems that occurred with the offense. We were in trouble. We opened the season 0-5.

Our staff sat down and listed all the things that were wrong with our team. We could not move the ball, and we could not stop the run. We found out the root of all the things that were going wrong went back to our offensive philosophy. We went back to what we believed in and should never have gotten away from in the first place. We began to shuffle our personnel, and that is how we arrived at where we are today.

We felt we had to simplify what we were doing and get more physical. We wanted the offensive line to get off the ball and get after people. We developed a gap scheme. We wanted to run power-type plays. We blocked down on everyone and kicked out at the point of attack.

We wanted to run the ball anytime, anywhere, and at anybody. We were going to run the power, counter, and inside zone. For us, that was our power game. We had to convince our players that we were going to have a signature play. We went to that play when the game was on the line. We wanted an offense that went north/south versus east/west.

We were going to play fundamental football. We were going to block down and kick out. That is the oldest play in football. To play fundamental football, we had to develop toughness on both sides of the ball. That is what fundamental football teaches.

Last year, in pre-season practice, we started using a toughness drill every day in practice. We worked the inside drill with the best against the best for 15 minutes every day. The only way we were going to be able to compete with the people we had to play was to get better at all those things. We ran the same plays every day and learned how to be tough and compete. This year, when we started the inside drill, the team was much better and exhibited the toughness we were looking for.

In the power football game, we had to address some issues that go with that scheme. We aligned in basic formations and ran simple plays using simple rules. We wanted no excuses for any failure of the plays. The gap scheme is as simple as it gets. The blocking is the same to either side; we block down with the offensive linemen and kick out with the fullback.

If we run the counter to the weakside of the formation, we usually kick out with the guard. The line splits are always an issue with any scheme. We wanted to put our players in a position to make a block. If you run inside, you want to open up the splits. If you are going outside, tighten up the splits. We do not go through that type of teaching.

We use standard splits and let the linemen pick the split that allows them to make their blocks. We

want him in a position to be comfortable and one that lets him make his block easier.

You have to get movement at the point of attack. We teach the shoulder block. In the fall, we start out teaching the shoulder block that goes with the scheme of down blocking. As we progress to the combination blocks of coming off to the linebackers, we let them use their hands.

In your blocking technique, the footwork is tremendously important. When we start to teach footwork, we do it in our individual drills. We spend the majority of the early season practice time perfecting the proper steps. We work on them until they are near perfect.

In your blocking scheme, you cannot allow penetration. When the lineman blocks down, he comes down with a flat angle to the line of scrimmage. We feel the shoulder block helps prevent penetration. When the linemen use their hands too much, they have a tendency to get too high.

We read the hip in our combination blocks. If the tackle and tight end are combination blocking on a defender, the tight end reads the near hip of the defender as he comes down on him. If the hip goes away from him, he goes directly to the linebacker. I do not want to sound contradictory, but in the beginning when we first start to teach the combination blocks, I tell them to stay on the block. I do not want them coming off. I want to make sure the point of attack is sound before we think about coming off to the linebacker. If the tight end is not sure what the hip is doing, he stays on the block until he is sure.

When we start to teach the double-team, we coach them to stay on the double-team and wash the defender into the linebacker.

When we talked about going to the power game, we included the inside zone play in this offense. We see a lot of 3-5-3 defensive schemes. We also have to play against the standard 50 defense. Against these defensive schemes, we were having tremendous success running the inside zone play. We had good success, particularly in the middle of the field. As we got into the red-zone areas, the play was not as successful.

When you run the inside zone play, you must get movement on the nose and the playside defensive end. The H-back is usually in motion blocking the overhangs on the outside linebackers. The fullback is running into the B and C gaps blocking the most dangerous defenders, which are usually the linebackers.

The basic scheme for the inside zone has the center and backside guard combination block on the nose. The playside guard and tackle combination on the 5-technique defensive end. The H-back comes in motion and handles the overhang of the tight end's block. The fullback handles the inside linebacker. I will get to the scheme in more detail in a minute.

I want to talk about the power-O play (Diagram #1). The first defense is a 50-look defense. The important blocks are the two double-team blocks. The center and playside guard double-team the nose to the backside linebacker. The playside tackle and tight end combo block the defender on the outside shoulder of the offensive tackle. The backside guard pulls and turns up outside the double-team in the C gap. The fullback runs a kick-out block on the 9-technique outside linebacker.

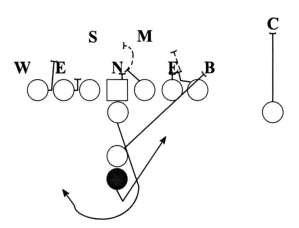

Diagram #1. Power-O

The block of the fullback on the outside linebacker does not have to be a knock-out block. Our starting fullback was 180 pounds. He was a tough player but not a pulling-guard type. We depend on the double-team to create the space in the hole. We want the double-team to be so good that it creates the running lane. All the fullback needs to do is to shield the outside linebacker from getting in on the play. If we get a stalemate with the 9 technique, that is all we can ask for. The tailback takes a drop-step to time up to the backside pulling guard and hugs the double-team block.

The backside guard, as he pulls, uses a square pull. He does not drop his inside foot back, turn, and run to the off-tackle gap. He drops the inside foot off the line and uses a crossover step to keep his shoulder parallel to the line of scrimmage. This allows him to see the frontside linebacker all the time. He can see him and attack him if he shows up somewhere other than the off-tackle gap.

The defense we see on the goal line is the 6-2 defense (Diagram #2). We still have the double-team in the off-tackle hole. A defender covers the playside guard. That is a 1-on-1 block for him. The center turns back for the defender aligned on the backside guard. The guard pulls for the frontside inside linebacker. The fullback runs for the kick-out block on the 9-technique linebacker.

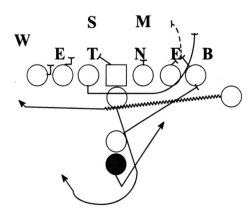

Diagram #2. Power-O vs. 6-2

The reason we go to the two-tight-end formation is the balance of the set. If we have to check off and run the other way, we have the same components to both sides. We use the wide receiver in motion to move secondary people. We put him to the left of the formation, and motion him to the defense's best personnel and run the ball to the backside.

The counter sweep is a complement to the power-0 play (Diagram #3). The formation in the diagram is a double split by the ends and a tight slot set by the H-back. Against the 50 defense, the playside tackle has to block the defensive 5 technique. We pull the backside guard and kick out the end. He does not use the square pull that he used on the power-0 play. He pulls using a trap-block technique. He wants to get his head into the hole and trap the outside linebacker to that side. The fullback goes to the backside and seals off behind the play. We tell him to go to the outside leg of the backside tackle and work out from there. The backside tackle check blocks on the 5 technique and releases inside. If the 5 technique comes inside, he blocks him.

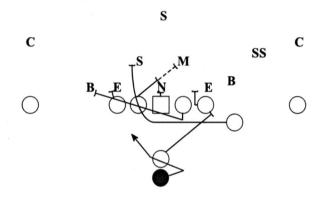

Diagram #3. Counter Sweep vs. 50

Nebraska ran this play back when Tom Osborne was the coach and Turner Gill was the quarterback. The center and playside guard use a combination block on the nose. One of them comes off for the backside linebacker. The H-back aligns in a tight slot set outside the offensive tackle. He pulls across the set and turns up in the hole for the frontside linebacker.

The tailback shuffles two steps to the backside of the play. He plants and waits for the quarterback to bring him the ball. When we run the zone play, we want to be slow to the hole and fast through the hole. We want to slow the back down on this play also. We have to get the guard across to trap and the H-back through the hole for the inside linebacker. The running back has to time up the play so he is not in the way of either component of the play.

Against the 4-3 front, we block down with the playside guard if he has an inside shade (Diagram

#4). On this play, the playside tackle blocks inside to the second level for the backside linebacker. If the defender is head-up to outside on the guard, the guard and tackle combination block to the backside linebacker. The backside guard pulls and traps the first defender outside the tackle. The quarterback brings the ball to the tailback and fakes the bootleg off the play.

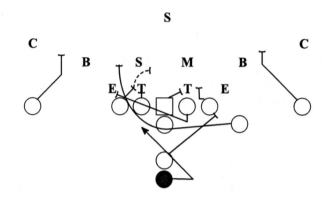

Diagram #4. Counter Sweep vs. 4-3

When we ran the zone play, we first thought we could take the tight end and tackle and double-team the 5-technique defender. We felt we could create the running lane off the double-team block. However, the better teams played a tight 9 technique and fought the tight end down inside off the double-team. We decided the best way to run the play was to expand the split of the tight end. We took the 9 technique as far as he would go without jumping back inside. We took him to a three- or four-foot split.

We blocked the tight end on the 9 technique and double-teamed the tackle from the inside (Diagram #5). We brought the playside guard to double on the 5-technique tackle. The center and backside guard doubled on the nose. We worked the center or backside guard up to the second level for the backside linebacker. If the backside guard felt the linebacker was going to blitz the backside A gap, he blocked him using inside-out leverage. The center had to handle the nose by himself.

The fullback had the playside linebacker the best way he could get him. If the 5 technique slanted to the inside, the fullback went outside through the C gap for the linebacker. If the

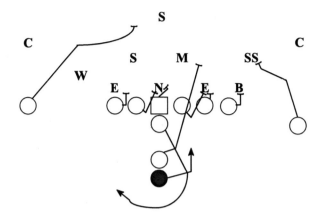

Diagram #5. Inside Zone vs. 50

linebacker scraped to the outside, the fullback mirrored his movement, shuffle stepped, and took him using whatever angle he needed. If the tackle stayed outside, the fullback went into the A gap after the linebacker.

If we ran the play against the even look or 4-3, we adjusted the double-team from the playside guard and tackle to the center and playside guard (Diagram #6). The tackle single-blocked on the defensive end. The center and guard double-teamed the defender aligned on the playside guard. The backside guard blocked the backside 2 technique, and the backside tackle blocked a check release on the defensive end.

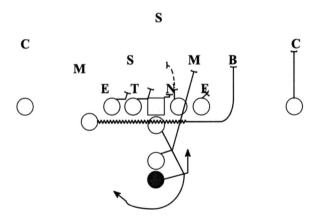

Diagram #6. Inside Zone vs. Even

As an additional adjustment, we could split the end and bring the H-back in motion. The H-back turned up on the outside linebacker and blocked him. The fullback read the double-team for his path to the linebacker. If the defense stunted their front, the fullback found the best path to the linebacker. We run this play as part of our power scheme.

The tailback takes an open step to the playside and attacks the line of scrimmage. He is thinking A gap as his original read. However, the movement of the defense will lead him to the hole. If the defensive 5 technique slants to the inside, the running back makes the break to the outside. The quarterback brings the ball to the tailback and runs his play-action fake off the play.

Our play-action passing game is based on the power offensive game. We want to run those passes off our best runs. The key to any play-action passing game is to make the pass look exactly like the run. I know everyone teaches the high hat and low hat as keys to pass/run, but high school defensive backs still look into the backfield.

These are some thoughts we use when running our play-action passing game:

- Put the player responsible for the flat/contain in a conflict.
- Put that player in a position where he cannot be right.
- If their safeties are making tackles on or near the line of scrimmage, make them pay with the deep ball.
- Run crossing patterns against teams that play cover 1.
- Run the fade in the hole against teams that play cover 2 or hard corner.
- Change up formations or personnel groupings so the same concept looks different to the defense.

In our protection scheme there are some principles and rules we follow.

- Always protect the quarterback's backside.
- Move the pocket or launch point.
- Versus an eight-man front, you must be able to control the edge (screen, naked, reverse).
- Full flow running backs to the playside, outside linebacker turn-back protection (may keep tight end in on longer routes).
- Split flow running back has backside edge rusher.
- On split-flow play, the backside guard works playside.

When we run our play-action, we have some beliefs we try to follow. We want to locate the man responsible for the flat coverage. We want to get him in a pass/contain conflict. We want to continually run at him and threaten him so that he is not sure whether the play is a run or pass. We want him to have the deer-in-the-headlights look. We want to put him in a situation where he cannot be right regardless of what he does.

We look for safeties making tackles on or around the line of scrimmage. You have to make him pay for his aggressiveness by going over the top. With teams that play cover 1, we want to use crossing patterns on them. We want to cross with backs coming out of the backfield and from the wide positions or the tight end.

Teams that play cover 2 or hard corners are vulnerable to the fade pattern in the hole on the sideline. We play teams that involve their corners in blitzes and run support. They are susceptible to the play-action pass. Anytime you run a play-action game, you can throw the same pattern but from a different formation. When you use a different personnel group and run the same pattern, it looks different to the defense.

When you talk about play-action pass, you have to talk about the protection. It is tremendously important to always protect the quarterback's backside. The worst thing that can happen to a quarterback is to be stuck in the back by a blitz coming off the edge. If we have a full-flow play with both backs going in the same direction, we have some type of scheme with a lineman coming out to protect the backside or possibly a tight end left in to block. We can also move the quarterback away from the backside with a sprint-out or stop-out type of pass. If we have a split-flow play as we do with the counter play, the tailback can block the backside on that type of play.

When you play teams that have an eight-man front, you have to control the edge blitz. The best way to do that is backside screens. On the zone play, we sneak the fullback to the backside. On the split-flow plays, we can get either back into the screen play.

When we run our play-action scheme, we run concept patterns. The formation dictates the receiver that runs the pattern. We number the receivers #1 through #4 and designate the pattern according to the concept. We match the concept with the play-action we want to run. The first pattern comes off the zone fake, which is a full-flow pattern. The counter actions are split-flow protections.

The first play-action I want to talk about comes off the zone play fake (Diagram #7). The outside receiver to the playside is the #1 receiver. He runs a flag or bench pattern. The bench pattern is a flatten-flag route run toward the sideline.

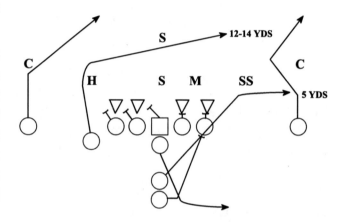

Diagram #7. Zone Pass

The #2 receiver will come from the backfield. It could be the running back or the fullback. He runs the flat pattern. We tell the flat runner as he comes out of the backfield to train his eyes on the flat defender as if he were going to block him. We try to get the receiver to go inside of the flat defender rather than cross his face. He runs at the inside shoulder as if he were going to kick out the defender. He slips by the defender at three yards and runs his pattern at five yards.

The #3 receiver is the backside slot or tight end. He runs what we call a razor. It is a crossing pattern getting to the depth of 12 to 14 yards on the playside. The backside wide receiver is the #4 receiver and runs a post.

In our protection scheme, the playside guard and tackle block the men aligned on them. The tailback has the Mike linebacker. To the backside, the center, guard, and tackle use half-slide turnback protection. The center has the A gap, the guard has the B gap, and the tackle has the C gap. If they bring the backside linebacker off the edge, the defensive end generally goes inside so all the gaps to the backside are covered. In that case, the guard picks up the defensive end in the B gap, and the tackle takes the blitzing linebacker.

We will not run this play until the strong safety starts to make plays at the line of scrimmage. We want to take advantage of his aggressiveness. If the strong safety reads the play-action and takes the fullback, we look for the razor coming across the field.

The next concept is the strongside flood route (Diagram #8). We like to run this pattern from a twins set. The outside receiver runs a fade route. The inside receiver runs a sail route. That pattern is a 12- to 14-yard out pattern. The receiver at 12 yards sticks his foot in the ground, gets his head around, and runs a turnout pattern. If the flat defender is underneath his pattern, he continues to run to the sideline. If there is no defender under his pattern, he settles into the window and stops his pattern. The third receiver runs the flat to the playside.

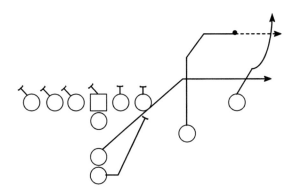

Diagram #8. Strongside Flood

On the protection, we keep the tight end in to block on the backside. On the play, we have four blockers to the backside and three blockers to the frontside. The quarterback runs the inside zone fake and brings the ball to the playside. If the flat defender blitzes the quarterback, he dumps the ball to the fullback in the flat.

We run a split-flow play-action pass. It comes off the counter look (Diagram #9). We like to bring the H-back in motion and put him into the flat on this play. He uses the kind of motion that times up with the running play. When he reaches the playside guard, he squares his shoulders to the line of scrimmage and shuffles sideways like he would if he were coming forward to block. We like to run this play when the strong safety reacts down to the motion. We run this play after he has made some stops at the line of scrimmage.

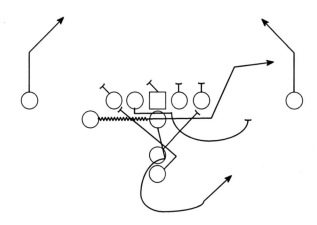

Diagram #9. Split-Flow Pass

The fullback blocks outside the tackle's block to the playside. The backside guard pulls, influences his play-action, and becomes the personal protector for the quarterback. The center turns back for the guard pull. The running back comes to the backside and makes the protection three to the back and four to the frontside of the play.

We can run this play from a trips set (Diagram #10). The H-back is the inside slot receiver to the trips side. He runs the same type of motion he ran on the split-flow pass. The tight end to the playside runs the fade route. The H-back runs the flat route off the slide motion. The outside slot to the backside runs a crossing pattern at a depth of 12 to 14 yards. The backside wide receiver runs the post route.

In the diagram, we are in a one-back set. The running back runs his counter fake and seals the backside. The backside guard pulls as he did on the split-flow pass and blocks the edge for the quarterback. The quarterback gives the counter run fake and bootlegs the ball to the tight end side.

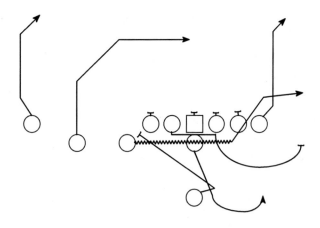

Diagram #10. Trips Play-Action

If we have an aggressive corner, we attack the outside third (Diagram #11). The outside receiver runs a curl route and the inside receiver runs the wheel. We drive the outside receiver on the corner and curl in front of him. The #2 receiver runs the wheel trying to get deep behind the aggressive corner. We feel he will react to the curl and the wheel can get deep into his third.

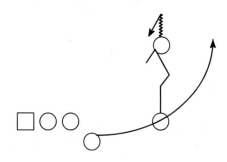

Diagram #11. Curl/Wheel

The combination we like against a cover-2 look is a fade/speed-out (Diagram #12). The outside receiver runs a fade against the two-deep safety. The inside receiver runs the speed-out and continues the pattern up the sideline into the hole in the zone. The safety plays the wide receiver on the fade, and the corner rolls up to the speed-out. The receiver makes his cut and looks to the quarterback. When he looks to the quarterback, it should draw the corner into a drop-down technique. The receiver takes the pattern deep into the hole between the safety and corner. He looks to catch the ball between 14 to 18 yards.

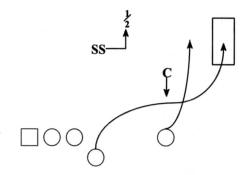

Diagram #12. Fade/Speed-Out

We play teams that play cover 1 all over the field. We use this pattern against cover-1 teams. The #1 receiver runs a razor pattern. The #2 receiver runs the flat route. The #3 receiver runs a razor, and the #4 receiver runs a post (Diagram #13). The formation is a double split for the ends with the H-back in a tight slot left.

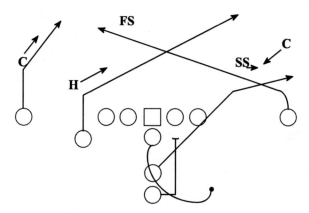

Diagram #13. Man Beater

As the playside wide receiver starts across on his razor, the corner jumps him. The fullback runs the flat pattern coming out of the backfield. The strong safety gets a natural rub with the corner and wide receiver coming inside. The fullback runs to the flat and could be wide open if the strong safety is caught in the crossover. The backside slot or tight end runs a razor from his side and crosses in the middle with the wide receiver from the other side. The frontside crossing route will be shallower than the backside crossing route. The backside guard pulls on this play to the playside. The tailback runs the counter fake and seals the backside of the pass.

We use this next pass to attack the middle of the field (Diagram #14). From the tight slot, the H-back runs his razor pattern across the field. The wide receiver to the backside of the play runs a seam route down the middle of the field. If the safety disappears, he keeps running. If the safety drops down on the crossing route and leaves the middle of the field open, the wide receiver can get behind the safety. If the safety sees the post coming, the cross by the slot should come open. The deep pattern pulls the corner deep and lets the H-back run his pattern into the outside third. If the safety drops back to cover the pattern by the backside wide receiver, the deep cross is open.

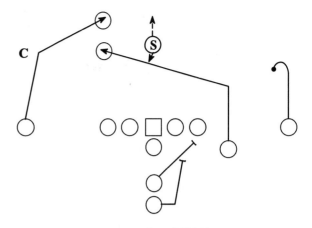

Diagram #14. Middle

I appreciate the opportunity to be here today. If we can ever do anything for you or you have any questions about this presentation, please call on us.

MOTIVATING DEFENSIVE LINEMEN

De LaSalle High School, California

Thank you. I am excited to be here. It is an honor to be here in Atlantic City. We played Don Bosco Prep last year in California, and we play them in New Jersey next year. One of our two losses last year was to Don Bosco.

I want to talk about De La Salle High School and how we achieved the success we have had. I want to share with you how similar our program is to your programs. All the public schools say we do not know what it is like to have to run a program in their situation. They think we can recruit and get anyone we want, which is not true.

I am guessing that most of you in this room have much better facilities than we do. We do not have our own field. We do have a coaching office for the entire department that would fit in the corner of this room. I am not talking about football offices. I am talking about the entire athletic department.

We do not have the technology that most of the schools we play have. We do not have an indoor camera for any of our teams. Our weight room is outdated, old, and dilapidated. However, we work as hard as anyone in his weight room does. We have not had a new sled in 17 years. We live on the sled. It is just about worn out. There are a lot more similarities between your program and ours than you care to think about or even realize.

We have a 100-yard field that we share with junior varsity and freshman programs. We also have to share the field with the soccer program. We very seldom get to work on a regulation field. When we practice, we work on half a field.

Our facilities and stadium are not very good. They are old. However, we have first-class players and a great coaching staff. With all the disadvantages we have with the physical facilities, we are blessed with

the kind of program we run and the success we have enjoyed. We have overlooked all those things and gone on to be very successful in California.

This situation challenges you as a coach. What I want to expand on is what we do and how we do it. I do not profess to be the greatest line coach in the world. I will share with you what we do. You will find it is not any different from what most of you do already. I want to talk about how we get our players to perform and get better as the year goes on.

When Don Bosco Prep came to our place and beat us, that was the turning point in our season. We were not a good football team then. We won our first two games by a few points. Those two games were not typical as to how we prepare. In the Don Bosco game, we were up 21-7 at halftime and lost the game 23-21. We totally dominated the game in the first half, and did not score a point in the second half. It completely changed what we did as coaches and the attitude of our players.

I am prouder of what these kids did this year than last year, when we won the state championship. This year, we were not a good football team, and we did not have a lot of talent up front. Those players toughened up from the Don Bosco game till the end of the season, and they worked their butts off.

They developed a foxhole mentality. We challenged our players to be the best that they could be. People use words like *brotherhood*, *love*, *drive*, and *commitment*, but they are only words unless you teach the team what they mean. Those things are a very important part of our program.

If you are considered to be part of the brotherhood, you are a Spartan. That is what every player in our program strives to be. That is the ultimate goal of players in our program. They want to be a part of the brotherhood of Spartans.

We do not talk about individuals in our program. We tell our players the most important player on the field is the player next to him. When our players start out as freshmen, we want to teach them about our offense and defense. However, we also want to teach them what it takes to achieve what they want.

It is traditional at De La Salle for the freshman to move the sleds. They actually have to pick up the sleds and move them onto the field. The sophomores carry the sled pads, and the juniors carry the bags to the field. This is a process of building team unity through performing difficult tasks together.

When we lost the state title this year, our weight program started eight days later. That was a tense and difficult time for our players. They came into the weight program with mixed emotions. The season ended on a sour note, and we were back in the weight room starting to prepare for next year. The players have rededicated themselves for next season.

I want to give you a quick overview of our defensive line. We run a four-man front. We play with a 1 technique and a 3 technique for the inside tackles. We shade the inside shoulder of the backside guard and outside shoulder of the callside guard. The defensive ends play in a 6 technique to the tight end, and a 7 technique to the openside or the weakside of the formation. We vary our alignment to the ball, depending on the scouting report.

In some situations, we crowd the line of scrimmage, and in others we play off the ball. The first game we played this season was against a team with a crazy offense. It was more like the wing-T than anything else. In that game, our defensive line backed off the ball by one yard. That gave us time to react to what they were doing.

We are a big blitzing team. When we lost to Don Bosco in the third game of the season, we had problems. Our players were not doing what they were supposed to do. Coach Ladouceur told the defense, we were not going to run anything but the base defense for the next five minutes. He understood we were not doing things right. He wanted to go back to the basics and tried to let our players play with confidence.

As a defensive line coach, we do certain things on a daily basis. However, if there is anything you get out of this lecture, remember this point: You cannot lower your expectations for your players. I found myself starting to accept mediocrity in the play of my defensive linemen. It was so bad that I began to accept poor play and bad technique in the defensive line. It does not matter at what level you coach. It could be youth leagues, little league, or college; do not accept that kind of effort.

The good thing about this season was the leadership displayed by our seniors. As coaches, we began to notice during practice that the seniors were taking on the role of player-coaches. They assisted the younger players and helped them with their techniques and skills. We talk about having ownership in the program. The seniors took on the responsibility of mentoring the younger players though tough times. We talk about that when we line up every day for practice. We get the defensive line together, and I tell them they are the most unorganized staff in America.

As the defensive line coach, I believe we have simple things to do. They have to step right and fly to the ball. We have this sled routine where we teach steps and movement on the ball. The defensive linemen have to get off the ball, play their responsibility, and fly to the ball. When we watch film, I want all the defensive linemen in the picture at the end of the play.

When we go live in practice, I stand behind the defensive line between the linebackers and coach the defensive line. I coach them every play. After we finish our individual defensive line drills, we work 1-on-1. When we work against the offensive linemen, we find out where we are in our development as a defensive line. We work a 2-on-1 drill with two offensive linemen on one defensive lineman. They work the down block and combination blocks on the defensive lineman. He plays and reacts to what type of blocking scheme he sees.

We do that every day. Our defensive line bangs for 60 to 80 plays a day. We do not have problems with anything physical. We go every day with our ones against our ones. We want to see the competition every day because we need to see where we are in our development.

We put them in two lines. I give the signal of where to go, and everyone watches the completion. When you go best against the best, you find out if you can play. In those drills, we find out who can do what you ask them to do and who cannot. After those drills, we have a live drill against the scout team. As I said, our kids bang for 60 to 80 plays a day.

I made a commitment to get our players to play better this year. I told them we were not very good, and I did not know how to make them improve on their effort. My best assessment that I learned, is never tell the kids "You are just crappy." I never tell a player that he is not worth a dime. I say, "You are not doing what we need to do, and I cannot trust you." We use the word trust all the time to express our feeling for them. Trust, responsibility, and accountability are huge pieces of everything we do.

I want to cover these things quickly. I will try to get to specific line techniques. We line up all of our kids in a four-point stance. We have the foot to the side of the shade as the balance foot. It is back in the stagger. Most people do align with the inside hand down and the inside foot back. I love to get movement in the front but still be able to play the zone play. We are very fast, so we developed our slant game. If we slant right, our right foot is back. It can change your alignment a slightly.

When you work against your scout team, it is imperative they give you a good picture and maximum effort. Anytime we work against our scout team, they must have trust and be accountable for their effort. If I ask my defensive linemen what the scout team is running and what they like to do, they should be able to answer me. Knowing our scout team is a huge part of our accountability.

When we go through our progression every day, we start out with sled work. When I got to De La Salle, we had terrible defensive linemen. All our kids were offensive linemen, and they were amazing offensive linemen. Everywhere I went, all they wanted to talk about was the offensive line. The only thing I wanted to know was "How do you get sled work?" If the offensive line uses the sled every day, how can I work my linemen on it? We had to develop a sled routine to get the defensive line on the sled. Our sled was 17 years old. We did not have a sled that really worked.

When we got on the sled, we put everything together. We worked the routine until they knew it perfectly. I broke it down to stance, start, and get-off. I talked it, got them to jog it, and then ran it. Every day, when I put my defensive linemen into drills, they should be able to do the drills without me being there. That way, if I am late, when I get out there, the kids are already going though the drills. They don't have to wait for a coach.

I know there are some things that we coach and teach that are not acceptable. However, if you don't hold them to the highest degree of accountability for their effort and performance, who will? Nobody has ever pitched a perfect game, which is what I love about football. There are no perfect games. There's never been a perfect game played. Nevertheless, there can be a perfect outcome, and that is what our kids control. We believe in the perfect outcome. That is when you tell your kids, "This is not good enough." When they stay after practice to work on timing and striking, you are getting the kind of effort you want. I'm not going to teach you guys any drill work you do not already know. What you need to focus on is effort. Defensive line coaching is a dirty job. What I like about coaching the defensive line is the dirt.

I want to talk about how we motivate and how we get performance out of our players. After I came to De La Salle High School, there was a viewpoint that became apparent to me. For our opponents, we were the biggest game of the year for them. We became a nationally known team and had our players playing in California, Hawaii, and Louisiana in national all-star games.

We have to do what we do every week, knowing we are preparing the team for the best shot our opponent can possibly deliver. We never focus on that fact, and our players never approach a game that way. Where we derive our work ethics comes from a very simple premise: We want our players to excel to what they think they can be. As coaches, we have to get our players to believe they have to give more to achieve what they want.

We want our players to become Spartans. We want all of our players to be a positive part of our program, regardless of the differences in their backgrounds. We never talk with our players about being a football star. We do not talk about winning. We talk about being the best you can be and giving the maximum effort. Winning is a byproduct of that attitude.

When we talk about brotherhood, it is not a word to be thrown around lightly. When we talk about being a Spartan, it has meaning for our players. It develops character, and it is truly a brotherhood among our team members.

To get your players to play at their highest level, you have to commit yourself to being a coach. That is harder to do than it sounds. I have two daughters at home. I have to make sure they observe my best effort. On the football field, if I am not prepared and do not work hard, how can I ever expect my players to work hard and give their best effort?

We cannot lower the bar to win and achieve. We have to raise the bar, and the wins will take care of themselves. When I looked at the Don Bosco film, I told myself, "I can live with the loss." What I cannot stand, and what came out of the game, was the effort our team played with in the second half. All the things that we did in the first half and all the things we had talked about simply went away. We dominated the game in the first half and became a failure in the second half.

The things we talked about, such as tradition and oneness, went down the tubes. If you have a great program, you do not want to finish 7-3. You want to be 10-0. We lost two games this year after going undefeated the year before. However, being everyone's biggest game was not the reason we lost two games. That cannot be the focus for your team. The focus of the team has to be on making each individual on that team rise to the maximum that they can be.

I have a family, and you have to be committed to your family, which I am, but you have a commitment to your players, also. I am a coach for the Spartans, and I care about those players deeply. I hope everyone in this room made the commitment to coach high school football to help the players on that team. I am going to coach the players on my team as hard as I possibly can. In the drills, I coach them every play. That toughness with which you coach them allows you to get more from them.

De La Salle High School began to set goals for the team a long time ago. How many of you coaches are into goal-setting? The goal-setting at De La Salle became an awakening for our young people. We wanted them to develop goals, but we wanted them to share their goals with their teammates. When they shared those goals, they are held accountable for them.

We had our young men developing goals. The coaches guided them in selecting goals that were measurable, attainable, and meaningful to them. We have a meeting where the players share their goals with the group. We give each player a 3x5 printed card called a goal card. We give the players a schedule of the goal meeting and tell them their cards are due that night.

On the goal card, we have three areas of goals. We have practice goals, weight room and conditioning goals, and game goals. Those are the three areas that are extremely important to any football program. Every player in your program has a goal card, and everyone know the goals he has chosen.

We run gassers as part of our conditioning. One of the goals a player might put down is to run all the gassers in the time allotted. He might put down that he will increase his bench press by 25 pounds. An example of a game goal is to be the best supportive player on the scout team.

On Thursday night, we have our meeting. The player stands up in front of the entire group and shares the goals he has written down. After he read the goals, he picks a player in the room. He walks over to the player and hands him his goal card. They embrace and share the brotherhood. The player who received the card is now accountable for that player's performance.

These players have written down their goals, shared them, and committed to their goals with one another. Everyone gets motivated and accepts the responsibility for the behavior and conduct of the players on the team. This has to come from somewhere. It is no longer a group of individuals or a football team. It is a whole family. They are walking around, representing their family, and their actions reflect on the family.

We also have something we call "chapel service." It is nondenominational, and we talk about ownership in our program by our players. Coach Ladouceur helps mold the character and values of our players. They choose a song with lyrics that mean something to them. They have to play the song, and pick a passage from the Bible and talk about it.

This service is a takeoff on the 300 Spartans and the courage and togetherness they shared in their brotherhood. When we gather in our meeting room, it is a very informal setting. The coaches and players sit down and take off their shoes. We discuss the meanings of the songs, and Bible verses, and what those things mean to them. We are seeking inspiration from the group and some soul-searching into their lives.

I love to see young men getting to the point where they are performing up to the level they should be. The players start to believe in the goals they have set from themselves, and their goal card become very important to them. They bring the card to you and want you to see the things they have achieved. They have a purpose of value and believe they can succeed in their goals.

Football is a game that is difficult to play. Everyone gets knocked down at some point during a game. It is not getting knocked down that builds the character in the players; it is what they do from that point forward. They have to get up and continue to struggle and play on. It is not getting knocked down that has value, it is getting up and continuing to fight and play that builds the type of character we are looking for in our players.

There is always going to be another day and another play. As coaches, we must get the players to see the best within themselves and get the best out of themselves.

We played our last game on December 20 and our players were in the weight room on January 2. We do not stop that program until the last game of the season. Not every coach works in the school where he coaches. They arrive at school at 6:30 in the morning to prepare for the day. We are not like some of the elite programs in our state where the head coach does not teach. We all teach in addition to coaching. These coaches go the extra mile to teach and coach. They do it so they can help these players. We have to take an active role in recruiting. These players come from bad neighborhoods, and they have every excuse not to play football. What we do is offer a way out of those neighborhoods.

The players come from all different neighborhoods and have to ride a public transportation to get to school. Some of them spend a lot of time on the bus just to play in this program. You have to care about the players. You have to commit your best effort to the players. I love being at De La Salle, and I love coaching the players I have. We are all a part of a big family. Your expectations you have for your players are a big part of the motivation that goes into the program. We use the goal cards, we use the chapel service, and we practice hard and are committed to the oneness of the Spartans.

We won 151 games in a row, playing all the top competition the country had to offer. NFL Films came out and did a piece on De La Salle High School. No one outside the program has ever been allowed into the chapel. We allowed NFL Films to come into the chapel to see what went on. I can talk about what goes on within those walls, but until you experience it, you have no idea the good that comes from it. The chapel changed our whole outlook and the environment within our team.

Last year, we won two games and lost the third game to Don Bosco at home. We were a terrible team. After that game, some of the players who we did not think could help us rose up and worked as hard as they have ever worked. They bought into what we were selling. That carried us to the game against Centennial High School in the finals of the state championship. We lost that game 21-16, but our players walked away from that game knowing

they had done their best. They knew they were responsible for the success of one of their teammates through the obligation of the goal card.

I just wanted to share my experience and the love for the kids and our school with you coaches today. We show the NFL film to our players as a motivational tool. The film features a lot of well-known and respected coaches and players. It has Bill Walsh and John Madden, just to mention two.

Gentlemen, I appreciate your attention. I tried to give you some idea of the way we try to motivate our players to perform at their highest level. Thank you very much. It has been a pleasure.

SPECIAL TEAMS ORGANIZATION

Jenks High School, Oklahoma

Let me tell you what a privilege it is to be here. I have been going to Nike clinics since I was a young coach right out of college. I used to be one of those coaches who did not care about special teams. I was more concerned about my individual time because I was coaching the defensive line at that time. My players were not involved in special teams, so I did not pay much attention to it.

In 2001-2002, I was a graduate assistant at the University of Houston. One of my responsibilities was to work with the special teams. I got to work with Coach Joe Robinson who is now the special teams coordinator at LSU. When I worked with him, I found he was one of the top two or three special teams coaches in college football.

I learned a great deal from him. I learned not only about schemes, but also a great deal about organization. One thing that impressed me was his passion for special teams and how he enjoyed that aspect of the game. It rubbed off on me, and I have been the special teams coordinator for five years at Jenks High School. I learned from Coach Robinson, so I gave it a shot.

I enjoy coaching the special teams. For many coaches, it is a headache, but I view it as an opportunity. I have a head coach that gives me a lot of freedom to take the ball and run with it.

I am going to talk about some different areas today. I will talk about the keys to our success. I will cover how we organize our coaching staff, how we handle our installation schedule in the fall, and how we divide what we are working on. I will talk about our practice schedule during the week and how we game plan for an opponent.

Nothing that I do is original material. It is something that I got from someone else. I will be more than happy to share it with you. I want to start out by giving you the keys to success.

KEYS TO SUCCESS (PART ONE)

- Have a designated special teams coordinator. Sell the head coach on yourself and your passion for special teams.
- Organization is key. Have no wasted time or reps.
- Involve the head coach as much as he wants to be involved.
- The special teams coordinator is responsible for all schemes but will involve all other coaches with the exception of the coordinators.

I have been on staffs where the special teams were divided up among the coaching staff—there was no coordinator. I feel, to be successful, you need a coach that oversees the entire kicking game and is the coach where the buck stops. I am that guy at Jenks High School. When I got to Jenks, I had to sell the head coach, Allan Trimble, on my organizational skills and my passion for coaching the special teams.

There is only a certain amount of time every day to get everything done. I am fortunate because I have 20 minutes a day to get everything done. That is not counting pre-practice and postpractice kicking. I want to make sure when the clock starts ticking, I do not waste any time. That takes a great deal of organization. I do not want to waste any reps, and I want maximum effort throughout that 20-minute period.

I also feel you involve the head coach in the special teams as much as he wants. Some head coaches are involved with the offensive or defensive staffs. The head coach goes through all the hassles during the day. When it comes time for practice, that puts him at ease doing what he loves to do and that is coaching. Coach Trimble wants to be actively involved with the special teams. He coaches at least one of the positions on every one of our special teams.

As special teams coordinator, I am responsible for all of the schemes, and I will involve every coach on the staff in coaching them. The exceptions are the offensive and defensive coordinators and the quarterbacks coach. The rest of the staff will be involved in special teams in one aspect or another. Some coaches will be more involved than others—it depends on how much a coach feels comfortable with and how much he wants to be involved.

KEYS TO SUCCESS (PART TWO)

- Try to eliminate as much of the work for the other staff as possible.
  ✓Meetings/film sessions
  ✓Opponent scouting/film breakdown
- Play as many offensive and defensive starters as needed in order to be successful. Sell those kids on being difference makers.
- Build your special teams philosophy throughout your program (junior high, youth programs, etc.).
  ✓Make yourself available to those programs and coaches.

When I involve the other coaches, I feel it is my job to eliminate as much of the work for them as I can. They have their own position groups, teaching schedules, and their families to think about. I do not want to burden them with the work that is involved with coaching special teams. I want to take all the responsibility away from them that I can.

I take the film breakdown and scouting report responsibilities on myself. I am a member of the defensive staff, and I have a very understanding defensive coordinator who allows me the time to work on my special teams responsibilities while we are working on defensive game planning. I coach linebackers, and while I am working on the special teams breakdowns, I am contributing to the defensive staff meeting. That lets me make the plan for the upcoming week.

I feel, to be successful, that you need to play as many offensive and defensive starters as needed in order to win. Coach Trimble feels if we need to rest a player, we rest him a couple of plays on offense or defense. We are not going to rest him on a punt or a kickoff return where one play can determine the outcome of a game.

Some players may be hesitant about covering a kickoff, knowing they have to turn around and play defense. I involve the other coaches and try to sell those players on being difference makers. You may have a player who is not being recruited heavily. If you can sell him as a great special teams player, it could improve his prospects.

I try to build a philosophy throughout our program at all levels. I do not handcuff our youth programs to do what we do, but I want them to have a sound scheme. They do not have to use our schemes unless they want to. I want them to know the importance of the special teams. We do the same thing with the youth leagues in our area. I try to make myself available to them, and we conduct a clinic in the summer for them. The kids that are playing in these programs are the same ones that will play for us down the road.

The thing I tell those coaches, and the message I have for you coaches today, is that you need to make it fun for them. There are coaches out there who are trying to rehash the "glory days" when they played—they are serious about it. In some cases, they are too serious for the kids they are working with. A good youth league coach or a bad youth league coach can make or break some of those young players. In our program, it is all about numbers. We want as many players coming into the high school program as possible.

KEYS TO SUCCESS (PART THREE)

- Head coaches must believe in the importance of good special teams play.
- As staff, you must do several things.
  ✓Sell it to your players.
  ✓Place importance on selecting personnel.

✓Understand that special teams involves more areas of the field than offense and defense.

✓Get the most out of your practice time.

✓Emphasize special teams in pre-season camp.

✓Special teams time can be combined with conditioning—it will help win early games.

✓Remember, there are many facets of special teams play to be covered prior to the first game.

The head coach has to believe in the importance of good special teams play. It cannot be lip service. Our head coach is involved with every special team, and he coaches at least one position on each of those teams. In the special areas, there is a lot to learn before the first game. It is my job to make sure we do not go into the first ball game without having covered a certain kicking situation. I have a checklist that I go by to make sure I do not forget anything before we play.

We are a 6A football program in Oklahoma and are fortunate to have a large staff. We have 13 coaches on our staff. I give this sheet to our coaches in our staff manual before the beginning of the season. This is an example of one phase of the kicking game.

Jenks Trojans Special Teams Coaching Responsibilities

Punt Return/Block	Coaches
2-5 techniques	Johnson
6-9 techniques	Trimble
Corners	Calip
Return	Riggs
Scout Team	Johnson

Also listed on the chart is a breakdown of coaching assignments for punt cover, kickoff coverage, kickoff return, PAT/FG block, and PAT/FG team. We are fortunate to have a coach who takes care of all the scout teams. When we get to the point-after team, we divide that up by offensive positions. On the point-after- and field-goal-block teams, we divide that by defensive positions.

On game day, we try to break it up so we have our eyes on every part of the field at all times. We have coaches in the box and on the field watching what is going on in the kicking game. That way, we are getting feedback on every situation that happens in the game. The first year I was special teams coordinator, I was on the field. I liked it for the excitement of the game, but I got no feedback because everyone was involved with their own particular position. The next year, I moved up to the box and it has worked out better. I can see the entire field, and I am able to make the adjustments in the scheme.

Every season, we have an installation schedule. We have a calendar of the day when all the aspects of the kicking game are to be installed. On the first day of practice, we have a team meeting and our media day. We take pictures and take care of those types of activities. On the first day of actual practice, we put in the punt team. After that, we try to install two special teams a day. From August 18 until our first game, we work on two special teams every day. We try to work 10 minutes on each team.

I have a kicking game depth chart that helps keep up with the players. That chart can fluctuate during the week. I start out on Sunday night with one version of the chart, but by Thursday or Friday, it may be entirely different. It could be affected by injuries, grades, or whatever might come up. On our punt team, I try to go three deep on the depth chart, working as many young players into the chart as possible. We have a Trojan punt team we use when backed up. We take out the bullets on the outside and replace them with additional blockers on the inside. I have a copy of the depth chart in the press box; the head coach has a copy; and two assistants on the field have copies.

My scout teams coach is my box coach on Friday nights. We have a box set up at the 50-yard line. It runs from the plus 47 to the minus 47-yard lines. On third down, anyone on the punt team comes to that box. The scout teams coach calls, "Punt team alert!" He has his depth chart and makes sure we have everyone accounted for and any injured players replaced. On fourth down, if we have to punt, we go straight out onto the field.

On the depth chart, we have the replacements on the "punt safe team." If you are not sure the offense is going to punt the ball, you can leave your defense on the field. However, most of the time, you take out your safety and replace him with the punt return man. The defense stays on the field, and we bring in the player who usually catches the punts.

We have a two-point chart on the sheet that tells us when to go for two points instead of kicking the point after.

Go for two points if	
behind by	ahead by
2,3,10,(12),16,	1,4,5,11,12,
17,18,21,(25),26	19,22,(25)

PRE-SEASON INSTALLATION

- A two-deep special teams depth chart, along with a scout depth chart, will be posted prior to day one.
- Meet with the two-deep special teams for 30 minutes before practice during the first four days (base calls/emphasize SAKR).
  ✓Day one: Protect/cover punt
  ✓Day two: Punt return
  ✓Day three: Kickoff return
  ✓Day four: Kickoff cover
- Scout team will also meet on the first day and on an as-needed basis.

We go through that routine the first week of practice. At those meetings, I usually show them some kind of drill tape of actual film footage of what we should be doing. The notation SAKR is an acronym for stance, alignment, key, and responsibility. We also have a scout team depth chart to make sure we have every position filled. We want to evaluate players on the scout team and possibly move them up into special teams positions. We want to know if a player can block a punt, be a wedge player, cover a kick, or if he has a special talent we can use. We are trying to find places for the young players to play.

Each meeting will consist of the following:

- Review of depth chart/personnel
- Goals of unit/expectations
- All teaching is done by using PowerPoint® presentations and video
- Breakdown of each position of unit (SAKR)
- Stance
- Alignment
- Key
- Responsibility
- Drills are explained and demonstrated

When we show the video, the players will see good examples that they can model themselves after.

On the first day of practice, the only special team we work on is the punt.

PRACTICE #1: PUNT PROTECTION AND COVERAGE

- Stance/alignment/key/responsibility (SAKR)
- Man protection
- Communication
- Breakdown by position
  ✓Left side: Step-and-jolt technique
  ✓Right side: Step-and-jolt technique
  ✓Bullets: Release/breakdown on receiver
  ✓Snapper and personal protection: Recognizing solid protection
  ✓Scout team: Organize/explain the look we want to see

We place emphasis on stance, alignment, key, and responsibility. We start out with a man-protection scheme. That requires the players to communicate because they will have to switch some of the blocks. We break it down by positions. We start out in small groups. One of the coaches takes the left side, and another coach takes the right side. They work on step-and-jolt techniques.

We have another coach take the bullets and work on their releases and breaking down on the return man once they get to the ball. I take the snapper and personal defenders and work with them. We do 10 minutes of individual drills the first day. We work five minutes of individuals against the scouts. We work the left side and the right side on the step-and-jolt techniques.

The last five minutes of the 20-minute period, we bring all the parts together. That gives us a look at the big picture. We have the snapper snapping the ball live to the punter. The left and right sides work on their protection techniques.

On the second day of practice, we emphasize the SAKR principles. We install our zebra protection, which is hinge protection. That is a zone type of scheme. We also put in our punt return on the second day. We break down the teaching into individual parts as we did with the man-protection scheme. The difference between man protection and zone protection starts with the splits in the formation. We cut our splits down in the zone scheme. All the coaches work with their individual groups as they did on the previous day. The last five minutes of the punt drill is a team period against the scouts.

We have 10 additional minutes to work on our punt return. The first five minutes we walk through the return and talk about everyone's responsibility. We do that in two-deep groups from the depth chart.

On the third practice, we work on the hinge or zone protection and punt coverage lanes. On this day, we introduce our kickoff return and our alley scheme, which is a man-trap scheme. During this day, we reinforce all the skills we taught the first two days. We work with our bullets on a double-team block and how to escape it. You see, each day we are reviewing the previous day's work.

The fourth day is our first day in pads. On that day, we work on the punt for five minutes in group and five minutes against the scout team. We spend 10 minutes introducing the kickoff team. We kick the ball deep middle and to the right and left.

On the fifth day, we have our first scrimmage. The punt is the only live kick we have that day. We have six live kicks at various places during the scrimmage. We have four with the first team punt and two with the second team punt.

During the season, the first thing we do on Mondays is to have a team meeting. We go over the kicking scouting report before the players go to their offensive and defensive meetings.

The first thing we do at practice is work on backed-up punting. We punt the ball from our three-yard line and have to protect it. The worst thing that can happen is having a punt blocked inside your five-yard line. I put 12 defenders trying to block the punt. I have put as many as 18 defenders trying to block the punt. The second part of the kicking practice is punts and kickoff returns.

On Tuesday in pre-practice, we work on our point-after-touchdown and field-goal teams. We also install a fake based on what we have seen on film. During practice, we work on our punt and kickoff. During the kickoff period, we install the onside kick. We work on the onside kicks live so we can get the kicker and coverage personnel timed up. We put scout team personnel to receive the kicks, but we practice precaution with them—we do not want to get anyone hurt.

On Wednesday morning at 7:10, we have a special teams meeting for the two-deep kicking members. We review the scouting report and watch cut-ups of the opponent. In pre-practice, we work on the field goal and the point after blocks. We cover fakes and swinging-gate formations and adjustments. In practice, we work on punts, punt returns, and kickoff returns. We also work on an emergency field-goal kick at the end of a two-minute offense.

On Thursday in pre-practice, we work on punt safe with the defense. We go over the punt formation with the defense and alert them to the punter and personal protector groups. They have to see any addition of the quarterback as the punt or in the protection wall. They have to notice if the punt team has inserted a running back as the personal protector. The reason they are on the field is to stop a fake punt. They have to cover all eligible receivers and not get faked out. In practice, we work our game script on all kicking. In the postpractice session, we walk through the hands team routing, and I give a tips and reminders sheet. This tips sheet comes from our game with Union High School (Tulsa).

UNION SPECIAL TEAMS TIPS 2008

Kickoff

- We must do a great job of staying in our lanes. Use great ball get-off and stay in your lane—if you get knocked out, get back in your lane as soon as possible.
- Remember, kick left/avoid right, kick right/avoid left.
- It will be of the utmost importance for us to establish field position with our kickoff cover team.

Kickoff Return

- We will use double wedge and alley check this week.
- On the wedge, we must do a great job in getting to our wedge and make it very tight. Block head-up to outside.
- On alley, we will run to the hash they are kicking from. In the middle, check to double wedge.
- Front line needs to make sure that they see the ball kicked off the tee cover; any onside kick and work to protect your teammates; expect fiddler.
- Ends should be ready for a sky kick. You can call for a fair catch if needed.
- Be alert for kicks over your heads into a dead zone. We must cover all kicks. All kicks are live once they have traveled 10 yards.
- Know your squib kick rules.
- Hands team must be ready and alert.

Punt

- We will be in spread punt unless we are inside our own five-yard line. We do have substitutions in Trojan (backed-up) punt.
- Spread/over punt calls will be automatic zebra.

On a zebra call, cut your splits down and punch the inside man to block outside. Take care of your gap responsibility. Protect first, then cover.
- We will directional kick.
- Expect to jump and try and draw you offside.

On Friday, I meet with the players two hours and 15 minutes before game time. I go through the roll call of each team so they know when they are supposed to be on the field. After pre-game and we return to the locker room, I go over the depth chart one last time. I call them by position, and we have players respond verbally.

On Saturday morning, we come in and lift. After we lift, we watch the game film as a group. We try to be constructive as coaches with the film session. I try to be as positive as I can and encourage them to get better. The films are graded, and grades are passed out to the players on Saturday.

The one thing that is true and consistent in our practice is the punting game. We work on punting the football every day. The biggest swing of momentum in a game occurs when there is a punt block. It is an instant chance for the defense to score. If the punt is blocked behind the line, there are more defensive personnel there than offensive personnel. Touching the ball does not constitute a possession. Everyone on the defense tries to scoop and score. Even if the offense recovers the ball, they lose the ball.

After the game on Saturday, I start putting together the scouting reports of the upcoming opponent (Diagram #1). I take the film we have and tag their kickoffs. I get all the cut-ups, watch them, and look for similarities in the way they kick off. I record the numbers of the players on their kickoffs and identify the safeties. I chart the depth and height of the kicks as well as the directions of the kicks. This is one of the forms I use in our scouting report.

Base Alignment	Base Coverage Lanes

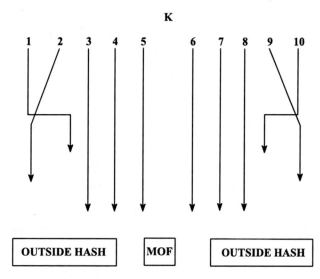

Diagram #1. Kickoff Coverage

Other schemes and alignments	
Leg strength of kicker	
Safeties	
Who is the first downfield?	
Miscellaneous	

I do alignment charts for all their kicking teams and coverage teams. I draw them up so I know where to kick the ball. I want to know where their stud is on all kicks. I want to kick away from him whenever I can.

The most frequent kick in a football game is the punt. We want to do a good job of analyzing their punter. I want to know the quality of his punts and the timing of the kicks. I want to know if he is left-footed or right-footed. I want to know how many steps he takes to punt the ball. I want to know the protection scheme and who their best cover people are. The most important aspect of the punting game besides the punter is the snapper. He is the one component of the game that has to function right every time.

On our block teams, I try to list the weak link on each team, and that is who we try to attack. On their extra point and field goal teams, I list their

most dangerous rusher and have an alert for his alignment (Diagram #2). We have to be aware of his position and make sure we block him on every play. That is the biggest thing you can get from a scouting report. In the diagram, we have their kick-blocking scheme. Following is an example of our field goal defending sheet.

Base Scheme	Base Protection Scheme

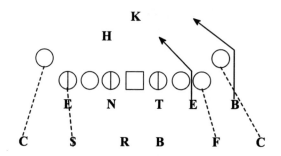

Diagram #2. Field Goal Block

Most dangerous rusher	
Number of Safeties	
Which is the blockside?	
Fakes we will run	
Miscellaneous	

One of the best things I have done was to develop a participation list. It lists the positions, player's name, and the special teams he plays on. If a player gets hurt, he has to be replaced. However, we need to know how many special teams he plays on. You can find that out from a participation chart. If you do not have a participation list, you have to go through the entire list of depth chart sheets to check for his name. Following is an example of one entry. We do this for all positions.

This shows you the teams he is on and the position he plays. Jones is on the kickoff team at the left 5 position. He is the end on the punt-return

Participation List

Position: Defensive End	Special Teams
Jones	KO/L5, PR/E, KOR,
Smith	FG/T PUNT, KOR/T
Phillips	Punt center

team, and he plays on the kickoff return. It keeps you from looking through your depth charts to find his name.

We have a goal board posted in our locker room. We list the goals in the left column of the board and keep a running total of how many goals we achieved each week. Across the top of the board, we put the name of the team we played. In the boxes under the team name, we put a Trojan sticker for each goal we accomplished.

GL   **Teams On Schedule**

	A	B	C	D	E	F	G	H	I	J
1										
2										
3										
4										
5										
6										
7										

Following are listed the goals which go in the first column on the goal board.

SPECIAL TEAMS GOAL BOARD

- Win
- Opponents average less than 10 yards on punt return
- Opponents average less than 20 yards on kickoff return
- Trojans average 15 yards on punt returns
- Trojans average 25 yards on kickoff returns
- 100 percent on PATs
- No penalties in the kicking game
- Disrupt one field goal, punt, or PAT

We went 12-2 this year. We lost to Union High School (Tulsa) in the second game of the season, and we lost the last game of the season—they were loaded. That was probably the best collection of talent I have ever seen in a high school. We did well in the other categories except on kickoff return. We had three Division I players on the return team. Anytime they touched the ball, they were a threat to go all the way. No one would kick the ball to them. We had only two games where we averaged 25 yards on the kickoff return.

I hope you got something from this. I have all kinds of material I can send you if you will email me. Thank you for your time.

Carl.johnson @ jenksps.org

THE WING-T AND THE JET SWEEP SERIES

Ridgewood High School, New Jersey

When you are invited to speak at a prestigious clinic such as this, it is a humbling experience. I am honored to share some of the things we do with you. I listened to Urban Meyer, and he was everything I thought he would be. I listened to Bill Stewart from West Virginia, and he did not say anything about football, but at the same time, he said everything about football. He did not talk about the X's and O's, but when you have the talent he has, your X's and O's are better.

I want to tell you about Ridgewood High School. Ridgewood is in the northern part of New Jersey. We are the second-smallest high school in our section. We are in an upper-middle-class area in a white-collar community. In the last eight years, we have won 65 games and had only one Division I player.

When I got the job at Ridgewood in 1984, they had never been to the playoffs. We had the reputation of being spoiled rich kids. We are the only white-collar community in our section. Our league is very urban, and we play in the same league with Don Bosco Prep.

One of the things we do very well is run the wing-T. Our offense averages well over 3,000 yards a season. In 2003, 2004, and 2005, we won state championships. I heard the coach from Minnesota speak yesterday, and he said that big plays had replaced the turnover ratio as the number-one key to success. In our last eight years, our turnover ratio was plus-108. This year, we were a plus-19 in our turnover ratio. In 11 games, we turned it over six times. That statistic is one of the things this offense gives you. I believe, in our case, the turnover ratio is the key to our success.

People are not running the wing-T offense as they used to run it. Personally, I hope no one else in our league runs the offense. The more teams in our league that do not run the wing-T, the better it is for us. Being different has a tremendous advantage over being like everyone else. It is like playing a wishbone team once a year. It is hard to prepare for that offense in three days. It is the same way with the wing-T.

When Paul Johnson went to Georgia Tech, it made a difference in that league. I asked Coach Bowden last night what effect his coming to the ACC had on the league. He said it was very difficult to prepare for Georgia Tech because of their option offense. If you are a new coach trying to decide what offense to run, I recommend that your offense not be like the teams you will compete against.

It is difficult to find teams that run the wing-T. I went into withdrawals the first spring after Tubby Raymond retired at Delaware. I had nowhere to go for a clinic on new developments in the wing-T. Gregg Perry, who was with Princeton for a while and is now at Delaware, gave us a clinic in 2002 on the jet sweep. That helped influence me to add the play to our offense. That play adds to the wing-T offense.

In the wing-T offense, when you align the wingback next to the tight end, that gives defenses problems. If people do not adjust their strong safety or cover-2 corner correctly, you have an advantage. Defensive ends are not comfortable with a blocker right outside of them. When we scrimmage against ourselves, I know how uncomfortable our outside linebacker gets with the wingback outside of him.

The formation creates secondary, read, run, pass, and interior problems for the defense. There are many methods of football. I read Bill Yeoman's book on the split-back veer. I read Darrell Royal's book on wishbone football. I am in the middle of

Urban Meyer's book right now. They run one of those offenses that have been time tested on running the football. This scheme fits our school, coaching staff, and philosophy.

There are natural conflicts in this offense. If you are a defensive tackle and the offensive tackle goes inside, what is your responsibility? The tight end could trap him, or he could down block him. Do you teach him to step out and defend the down block, or close inside and take on the trap? I know what we are going to do, but you have to figure it out.

The outside linebacker head-up on the tight end has the same problem. If the tight end releases inside, he can get trapped by the guard, logged by the guard, get kicked out by the fullback, or get down blocked by the wingback. There are four things that linebacker has to work on before they play us. There will not be another time during the season when he will have to play all those situations.

Since we are such a small school, we have to maximize everything we do. I just ran a clinic at our school for youth league coaches. We had 45 guys attend that meeting. Our youth leagues run our offense in their third- and fourth-grade programs. They are running the trap, sweep, and waggle. They run the rocket sweep. We want our players to know our offense.

I have two quarterbacks coming up who have been running the position since the third grade. One of them is a junior, and the other is a sophomore. That lends itself to lower your turnover ratio. Our quarterback this year was 5'8" and 165 pounds. You would not say he was a great quarterback if you saw him. However, he played in this league where there is tremendous level of competition and did well.

We have to shuffle the deck sometimes to come up with a quarterback, but for the near future things are coming up for us. Two years ago, we had a 6'4" and 230-pound quarterback. We went from him to the 5'8" and 165-pound quarterback. Two years ago, we won seven games and lost in the semifinals of the state championship. This year we won eight games and lost in the semifinals. That is what I love about the offense. It has flexibility.

This past year, our fullback gained 758 yards rushing the football. The halfbacks were senior and did most of the work. Next year, we will be a fullback-oriented offense. The following year, we may be a halfback-oriented offense. We have had 1,000-yard rushers at all three positions. We have had quarterbacks who have rushed for 600 yards and those who have thrown for 1,800 yards.

Our offense next year will be different from what we had this year. Everyone in the backfield will be new except for the fullback. Next year, we will be a fullback-oriented offense. This past year, we were a halfback-oriented offense, and when we had the 6'4" quarterback, we were a quarterback-oriented offense. You have to get your team involved in making plays. The wing-T offense allows that to happen.

I am a double-dot my "is" and double cross my "ts" kind of coach. I would consider myself an intelligent football coach. I focus on the fundamentals, and I am extremely anal about those fundamentals. We have extremely intelligent players. That allows us to block a play three different ways and run it three different ways because our players can handle the adjustments that go with the play.

The offense takes on the personality of our coaching staff. I love the deception of the offense. You cannot pay me a higher compliment when our parents say, "Coach, we cannot find the football." Our defensive players hate defending the wing-T during the week. The linebackers have to play the trap before they play the sweep. The secondary players have to play sweep before they play the buck trap.

I have been an offensive lineman all my life. I played tight end and tackle. The objective of playing offensive lineman is to stop the defender from going where the ball is going. We can stop the defender from going outside better from the outside than the inside. That is the entire principle of blocking in the wing-T. Everything in the blocking scheme is block down, wall through, and kick out. Teams that play us have to spend a lot of time drilling something they do not normally face.

We had a great tailback this past year, but the wing-T offense does a good job of spreading the carries around among all the backs. Our right halfback average nine yards a carry, He carried the ball over a hundred times for 980 yards. He was a tough kid and weighed about 175 pounds. He played safety and recorded 63 tackles. He returned punts and kickoffs. The fullback had 120 carries, the left halfback had 65 carries, and the quarterback had 45 carries. We spread the carries around and do not get anyone beat up. They were all about the same weight. The right halfback was 175, the fullback was 172, the left halfback was 180, and the quarterback was 165.

In all those carries, we had only six turnovers in 11 games. The wing-T offense is a lineman-oriented offense. Our offensive linemen are the best kids on our team. They are unselfish and team-oriented. On the three best plays for the left halfback, the right halfback has to make the most important block. The same thing is true for the right halfback. On his best plays, the left halfback has to make those blocks. There is no animosity between them. They are best friends. It works that way up and down the line of scrimmage. You must be team-oriented and not thinking of individual accomplishments. In this offense, all the backs block for each other.

My son asked me if I thought the wing-T helps our players to be recruited, or of it hurt our players being recruited? I think it helps our players. There are not many backs coming out of high school who know how to block. We teach those kids how to block, and they will block for each other. We spend a lot of time in the running game, and all the backs are taught to block. Coaching running backs in the wing-T is one hell of a job.

It takes a special coach to get the running backs to block their butts off, run back to the huddle, and carry the ball the next play. We did that last year and only fumbled the ball three times. That is a great ratio for the number of times we carried the ball.

I want to take a quick look at the jet sweep. The jet sweep to me is the wingback leaving in fast motion flat to the line of scrimmage, receiving the ball behind the frontside guard, and sprinting outside. This play has a number of names. Some people call it the fly sweep, and some call it a flanker reverse. If you are in shotgun, the ball is handed off forward. In the wing-T, the quarterback reverses out and hands it behind him.

Wing-T football is a series type of game. The fullback trap, halfback sweep, and quarterback waggle is a series of plays in the wing-T. All three of the plays look similar in the way they are executed. The quarterback reverses out, and the fullback dives off his left side. The quarterback gives the ball to the fullback, and we run the trap play. If the quarterback fakes the ball to the fullback and gives it to the halfback coming in motion, that is the halfback sweep play. If he does not give the ball to the halfback and keeps the ball to the outside, that is the quarterback waggle.

All three plays are off the same action. The single play is threatening three parts of the defense. That is the old way of running the series. With the jet sweep, the series progression is changed. In the jet series, we run the jet first, followed by the trap, and finally the waggle. Now, the series comes off the jet-sweep action. We call the trap the jet-sweep trap and the waggle is the jet-sweep waggle. The jet sweep is a natural addition to the wing-T series.

I have run the wing-T since 1980, and we are always looking for an open-end play. Working the sweep to the splitside is a viable option in the wing-T offense today. We used to run it only to the tight-end side.

When you run the jet sweep, the secret to running the play is getting the halfback running at full speed. The key is handing the ball to the halfback when he is running full speed. I see college teams run the jet sweep, and the receivers are running three-quarters or half speed back to receive the ball.

In the wing-T offense, we want the motion to be as late as possible and as fast as possible. The later you start the halfback in motion and the faster he runs, the less time the defense has to react to the motion. There is no strength side in the wing-T. We have a wing/tight-end side and a wing/split-end side. If the defense rolls the strength to the tight end, we attack the split-end side of the formation. We can run the same play both ways with late fast motion. It makes the defense play a vanilla defense.

We run the jet sweep in the wing-T because of its close proximity to the quarterback. That gives you fewer issues in the exchange of the ball than in the spread offense. There are less timing issues with the wingback than the flanker in the spread offense. The wingback position is the best position to start the jet sweep. Even if you are not a wing-T team, this is the best place to run the motion for the jet sweep. If you run it from a wide flanker position, everyone on the defense sees it coming and can adjust it. If you run it from the wing set, it hits so quick, the defense has trouble adjusting.

If the quarterback misses the handoff, he turns the play into a quarterback sweep. I do not know this for a fact, but I believe some of our quarterbacks have missed the handoff on purpose so they can carry the ball on the sweep.

If the quarterback misses the handoff, the halfback does not stop; he continues and becomes a blocker. We practice it that way. The split end does not crack on the strong safety. He stalks the corner. The wingback, instead of blocking back on a Sam linebacker or defensive end, he is the stalking force players in the secondary. They can do that because of the speed of the play. If you time the play correctly, the Sam linebacker is not a factor unless someone can get outside of the sweep back.

If you go back to option football at the beginning, the thing that made it unique was the arc block by the tight end. If the tight end blocked down, everyone played run. If he released, everybody played pass. The option released the tight end and ran the ball. The wingback on this play is releasing into the secondary, which tells the defensive backs to play pass.

In an option attack, the tailback is seven yards deep and begins his run at half speed. The quarterback has to avoid some defenders and pitch

the ball to the running back who is five yards deep. In the wing-T, the halfback has the ball immediately, is five yards closer to the line of scrimmage, and is running at full speed. On the jet sweep, we do not block the A or B gap for blitzing linebackers. If the defense blitzes those gaps, we run right by them.

We spend 35 minutes a week on our power running stations (Diagram #1). We have 70 to 75 players on our team at the varsity level. We are five to six deep at each running back position. We work our first- and second-team players together at one station. The third and fourth are at the next station, and the fifth and sixth are at the next station. At each station, the quarterback who is not running the play kneels in front of the quarterback in the play and snaps the ball up to him. That simulates the snap of the center. It keeps the quarterback from reversing out before he has the ball. Never run a timing drill without the center snap, or another quarterback popping the ball into the quarterback's hands.

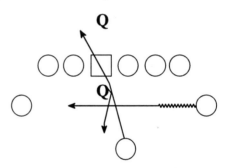

Diagram #1. Timing Drill

We use a spacing board to make sure the alignments of the wingbacks are correct. The spacing board is marked with offensive line spacing. The halfbacks and fullbacks run this drill and work on the timing with the quarterbacks. This is when we time out the motion for each back. We run the halfbacks in motion and we run the gut or counter play.

In the wing-T, the halfbacks have to learn three motions (Diagram #2). They need to learn I-back or deep motion, B-motion or dive motion, and jet motion. Deep motion sends the halfback through the position of the I back in an I formation. He goes behind the fullback. B-motion sends the halfback through the position of a halfback set to either side of the fullback. That is the position of a strong or weak fullback set in an I formation. The jet motion is a flat motion to the line of scrimmage.

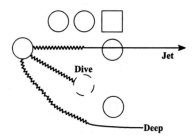

Diagram #2. Halfback Motions

We do not teach all the halfbacks to leave at the same time. Every halfback has a different speed level. The back times his motion to his speed. We want him leaving as late as he can and as fast as he can. That is why we run the timing drill. Every back has to know when to leave based on the cadence of the quarterback. His goal is to be at the near leg of the backside guard as the quarterback snaps the ball.

Our cadence has two parts to it. The first part is non-rhythmic, and the second part is rhythmic. When we run the jet sweep, we run those plays from the rhythmic snap count. The back knows when the ball is to be snapped and times his move to the cadence. Some backs will leave early, and some will leave late. The importance is not when they leave but being at the proper place for the handoff when the ball is snapped at full speed.

Every day, after we finish our warm-up and before we go to our first individual period, we do a clap drill. We come together as a team with the quarterbacks in the middle of the drill. The quarterback calls the snap count and goes through his cadence. When he says the snap count, everyone on the team claps his hands. You should hear the sound of one clap from the team. This is a good drill to teach the cadence and to react to it. This gives the second-, third-, and fourth-team quarterbacks a chance to give the cadence to the entire team. How many times does your team hear the second- and third-team quarterback call cadence? Our team hears it every day.

The first part of the cadence is a non-rhythmic cadence for any automatic we may want to use. The second part is the rhythmic count we use for our motion. The quarterback repeats the automatic twice and gives the command "Set." After he calls set, he follows that with "Go." If he called the play on "one," that is the first "go." If he calls it on two, that is the second "go." The go calls come in a rapid sequence and at a rhythmic speed.

The first thing you address is the quarterback's footwork. We stagger our stance so we can get away from the line of scrimmage. The thing that will screw the play up quicker than anything is the quarterback getting his foot stepped on by an offensive lineman. If the quarterback gets stepped on, it is his fault. If the quarterback is pivoting to his right, he gets his left foot back. We are not giving anything away because the stagger works the opposite on other plays.

On the pre-snap, we want the weight on the inside of the pivot foot. When the quarterback takes the ball, he pivots 180 degrees. He seats the ball with both hands on it. We want his back to the line of scrimmage with his feet parallel. We want the ball hidden at all times from the defense. We want the ball tight to the quarterback's body and deception from the play.

The halfback wants to be at the near leg of the backside guard when we snap the ball. We want him to get the ball at full speed and attack the flank of the defense. We do not want him to stop or turn up. He is heading for the sidelines, trying to get to the perimeter of the defense.

The halfback to that side runs to the outside number of the force defender, and the split end stalks the outside number of the corner. They are trying to get the defender blocked to the inside. They want to stay with the defender and run them up the field.

The fullback on the buck sweep has to fill the backside A gap because the guard pulls. However, on the jet sweep, the fullback has no blocking assignment in the A gap. He concentrates on his fake. He comes over the ball and rocks the baby through the line of scrimmage. If he makes a good fake, he will be tackled. If does not get tackled, we expect him to be up the middle of the field, looking to block the free safety.

After the quarterback fakes the fullback, he comes out on the waggle fake. On every play in this series, he has to come out and read the waggle. He has to know what is going on to the backside. I want them to take a mental picture every time he runs his fake. They will tell me when the waggle is there. They will see the linebacker start to cheat inside, or when the corner is starting to move across the field.

Besides the speed the halfback has to carry, his eyes are the second-most-important part of this play. The key to a great running back fake is the eyes. If the running back puts his head down, no one will believe he has the ball. He has to keep his head up and his eyes on the defense. That is the way he would run the ball. Make sure your running back's eyes are looking where they would be if he were running the play. He has to keep his eyes on the defenders to make the play believable.

On the jet sweep, you have to block three defenders (Diagram #3). Running the play to the open-end set, you must block the man over the offensive tackle, the force defender, and the corner to that side. The rest of the players on the play can fall down, and we still will have a successful play. We must have a great reach block on the outside defender on the line of scrimmage. The wingback has to get an outside block on the force player, and your wide receiver has to stalk block the corner. He works for his outside number on the stalk block.

The split of the split end is important. We want his split about five yards. If he gets too wide, that takes a defender with him and makes it harder to get to the outside. If he splits too wide, the quarterback calls "Split, split, split."

The playside guard pulls outside the reach block and turns back for the linebacker or the alley player coming from the inside. He runs a tight pull to the reach block and comes as quickly as he can. He does not belly back as he does on the halfback sweep.

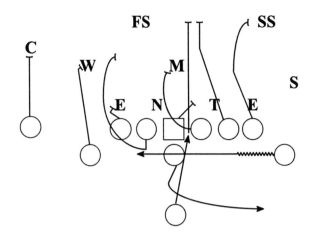

Diagram #3. Jet Sweep to Open

We do not block anyone over the guard. The 3-technique defender cannot make the play. That defender has never made a play on the jet sweep. That is if the halfback goes at full speed. If they miss the handoff, they are not yelled at. They become an additional blocker.

The center blocks the defender on him or to the backside. The backside guard pulls and turns up in the frontside A gap. His pull is the exact pull he uses on the "gut" play. He pulls around the center's block and blocks the backside linebacker. The backside tackle and tight end release inside and get downfield, trying to block the safety and backside corner. The backside guard and tackle block the gut play when we run the jet sweep away from them.

The play to the tight end, in some ways, is a better play (Diagram #4). The tight end and wing constrict the defenders. He is not split into the field. He lines up tight off the tight end, which brings the defense in tighter to the ball. If the ball is on the backside hash, there is a lot of grass to the outside for your best ballcarrier. He is going full speed, running into a wide field. The tight end reaches the defender aligned on him. The wingback blocks the force defender to the outside. We pull the onside guard for the corner or safety to that side.

The playside tackle blocks the man on him. If there is no defender aligned on him, he releases up to the second level and cuts off the backside. The center blocks the same rule he had on the play to the openside. The backside guard and tackle do the

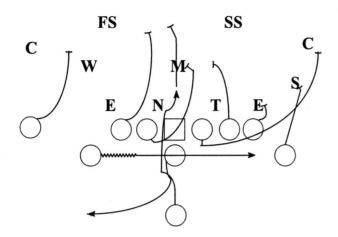

Diagram #4. Jet Sweep to Tight End

same thing. The guard pulls through the playside A gap, and the tackle releases inside to cut off the backside secondary pursuit.

The fullback runs his fake into the backside A gap. If he is not tackled, he gets up the field, looking for the safety in the middle of the field. The quarterback runs the waggle to the backside and takes his mental picture.

I want to show you the complementary plays quickly. The gut play is the fullback influence trap play (Diagram #5). The mechanics of the quarterback on all three plays are the same. After the quarterback fakes the jet sweep, he hands the ball to the fullback running in the backside A gap and continues on his waggle fake. The fullback runs off the center's block.

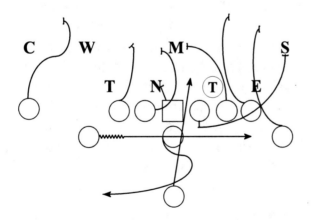

Diagram #5. Gut

The backside guard pulls around the block of the center for the backside linebacker. He has the same

block on the jet sweep. The playside guard pulls as he did on the jet sweep. On this play, the playside tackle blocks down on the inside linebacker to his side. We do not block the 3-technique defender on the jet or gut play. We feel he will chase the jet and be out of the play. We are using the gut play less and less because of the stunting defenses. If the defense guesses right, there is a chance of a fumble. The back can take an unprotected hit from an unblocked defender.

If we run the trap, it is the same play, except we pull the guard and trap the first man past the center (Diagram #6). All defensive linemen are taught not to let the offensive player release inside of them. We use a dip-and-rip technique to get inside the defender. We want our offensive linemen stepping flat down the line at a 90-degree angle. We try to beat the head of the defender inside. Once we get down the line, we rip the forearm and punch through with his backside foot. The playside tackle has the hardest block if he is covered. He has the hardest release to the linebacker.

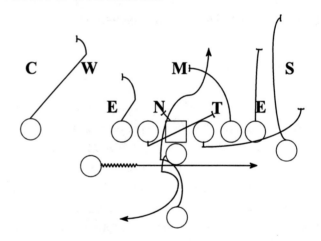

Diagram #6. Trap

The outside linebacker and defensive end begin to work outside when they see the jet motion. The trap is a nice combination for the jet sweep. We do not block the outside linebacker on this play. That is the job of the jet sweep faker. He has to hold the Will linebacker with his fake. As he takes the fake, he gets his eyes on the Will linebacker and makes him play him. We coach that. The wingback influences the Will linebacker and turns outside on the corner.

When we run the jet-sweep trap, the halfback takes the fake before the fullback gets the ball. On the halfback sweep, the fullback gets the ball before the halfback takes the fake. That makes the mechanics of the quarterback's steps a bit different. After he fakes the jet sweep, he steps back to the fullback to get the ball to him as deep as possible and to clear the fullback so he can cut the ball back.

The fullback's first step is on the midline with his playside foot. His next step bends around the quarterback and he picks up the center's cutoff block. An adjustment we may have to use is for the defender aligning in the playside A gap (Diagram #7). If that occurs, the guard gives a gap call. That tells the fullback he is blocking the shade down and the trap will be wider. The fullback bends the play to the outside behind the down block of the playside guard.

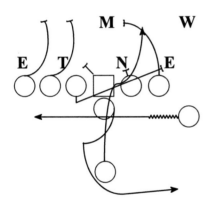

Diagram #7. Gap Call

The path the fullback takes is off the playside tackle's block. The tackle comes down on the playside linebacker and blocks him any way he can. The fullback has to run off his block.

I want to show you one last play, and my time will be up. This is the belly play (Diagram #8). It is like a lead play with a cross block. This play is set up by

the influence of the jet sweep. We feel the defender over the end will widen and come outside on the snap of the ball. The tackle blocks down on the first linemen inside of him. The guard pulls behind the tackle and cross-blocks the first man outside the tackle. The wingback folds back inside for the inside linebacker.

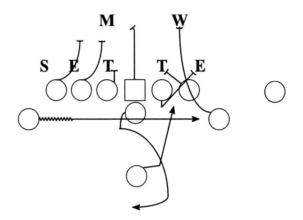

Diagram #8. Belly

You may find the Mike linebacker running outside for the jet sweep, and the block becomes easier. The jet motion impacts the defenders on the outside more than the deep or dive motion because they are threatened by that type of play. The quarterback reverses out toward the jet motion and brings the ball to the fullback, who is running a B-gap play to the side of the motion.

This play is not in the jet series. We run the play with jet motion. The motion is window dressing for the play. It moves the defenders and makes the play easier to run.

Once again, I want to tell you how much I enjoyed this clinic, and to have the opportunity to speak makes it a special one to remember. Thank you very much.

AN EFFECTIVE ZONE BLITZ PACKAGE

Christian County High School, Kentucky

Thank you. I have been fortunate to be around some outstanding coaches in my career. Everything I know about coaching I have learned from them. In addition, I am blessed to have an outstanding coaching staff with me now at Christian County. Our team this year was probably the least athletic team I have ever had. However, it was a fun year for me because those guys were such hard workers. I am an old-school guy, and I like old-school football.

WHY WE IMPLEMENTED THE ZONE BLITZ

- Confuse blocking schemes
- Apply pressure
- Disguise coverage
- Cause turnovers
- Put more athletes on the field
- Rally to the ball
- Easy to implement

The zone blitz was the safest way for us to blitz, and it allowed us to get more athletes on the field. What we found was that we could confuse blocking schemes by the various ways we could attack the offense, and it gave us the ability to apply pressure with a minimum amount of risk.

We can come out in our cover-2 shell, give the quarterback the same look every time, and disguise the coverage we are going to play at the snap. We can play cover 2, cover 3, or man-to-man out of that cover-2 shell. Our whole thing was to not give up the deep ball or the big play. We did not play a lot of it, and we screwed up some, but our kids loved it, I liked it, and we made some things happen.

We were getting the ball out of the quarterback's hand and taking the game away from the coach. If the quarterback is good enough to handle all of it, I will take my chances with him, but if the coach in the press box can call their offense, we are probably in trouble. I wanted to take the game away from the coach and put it in the hands of a high school quarterback, because it is not easy for him to make all the checks and changes.

The next thing we wanted to do was cause turnovers. We wanted to give our offense the ball, and for us, a quick change was a turnover. If we held you in our base defense the first two downs and got you into third-and-long, and then came with our zone blitz and got you off the field, that was a turnover for us. We wanted to create more turnovers, get our offense the ball, and give us more opportunities to win the ball game.

We wanted to get more athletes on the field in those situations, and our linebackers were tough, but they were not good athletes. We had some sophomores who were, so we made personnel changes in situations where we wanted to zone blitz.

A big thing for us has always been rallying to the ball. We stress that from the start of camp and throughout the year, and I tell our staff I want to see 11 blue hats to the ball when I grade the tape. If the first guy happens to miss, we are going to have the other 10 guys there to cover for him. If one man forces a fumble, we want 10 other guys coming to scoop and score. That is what we are all about.

THREE CALLS

- Sugar
- Spice
- Outside

We have smart kids, but our zone blitz scheme is not very complicated. I call it right or left, sugar, spice, or double outside. If we call a blitz on the right side, then the right side guy is going to run it. That is all there is to it.

To put it in, we took five dummies and worked on our stunts first. Then, we worked on formations. We wanted to let our guys know what they were looking at from the secondary, but we implemented from our front guys first. We did it out of a 3-4 look first, working with our nose and ends. Then, we worked on the linebacker play out of it, and we added the secondary to it last. We actually spent more time on our secondary, and that was the most important part to us, because they had to roll and do some different things within the coverages.

It was very easy to put in (Diagram #1). I put it in out of our 3-4 look because that best suited us. We could stay in the cover-2 shell, and I could take people in and out. Next year, we may run it out of some 4-3 look.

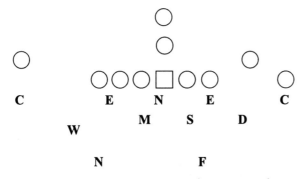

Diagram #1. Right Sugar (Alignment)

In calling the defense, the first term used is sugar. Sugar is, for us, an outside stunt. Spice is the term we use to complement sugar, and it tells the same guy to come to the inside. I could call double outside, and that brings both guys from outside and lets us play a different coverage look off of it.

We are not going to be complicated. We are not going to call it to the tight end, to the formation, or to the wideside. We are going right, and we are going left, and if I call sugar, it is the outside stunt no matter what the formation is, and we do not check out of anything. I used to be a big check person, and we used to spend a lot of time planning all our checks. I have stopped all that checking now, so we can just go out and play.

SUGAR

If we call right sugar, we are running it from the right side, and we do it two different ways with our front (Diagram #2). We will call slant or angle. When we slant, we go to the guy's hip and we want to get upfield quickly. We call angle for our guys to get to the face mask. We talk about getting one person over quickly. We went to angle because we wanted to get more lateral movement and to confuse the blocking scheme.

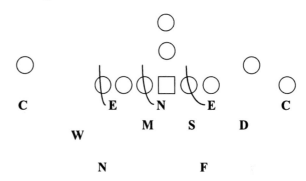

Diagram #2. Right Sugar (Down Linemen)

If we call slant, and the offensive line can step down and take us on, then we will go to angle. We want our defensive end, who is a better athlete than the man he is lined up on, to get to that face mask. We want the noseguard to get to the guard's face mask. If we call angle off of it, everyone is going to the face mask. If our defensive end does not have a tight end to his side, we tell him to angle to the ghost and become the outside contain.

When we want to fit to the blocking scheme and defeat blockers, we will call angle. If we want to get upfield quickly and not worry about the blocking scheme, then we will call slant.

We used two different stances with our defensive line. We used the three-point stance with our guys down, but we also used a two-point stance, and our kids loved that. We also backed them up a yard off the ball because we did not want to be offside.

One week we would be up, and the next week we might be down. There was no rhyme or reason for it. We did it to keep our kids interested and to have fun with it, but it did help our linemen see better.

Our Mike linebacker always lines up on the tight-end side. Our Sam linebacker is a better athlete than our Mike, and he lines up opposite him. The Dog and Will linebackers are on the outside, with Dog traveling with Sam.

They all keep their same keys and reads that they have in our base defense. In the only two film clips we have, somebody ran the ball against this defense three times. The whole thing is that we can run this even against people who were going to run the ball on third-and-long, and the reads hold up.

The reads for Sam and Mike are from guards to backs. I am a firm believer that the guards will take you to the ball, unless you are playing against the wing-T and misdirection, and then you go and play off the backs.

We are playing run first with our linebackers. If we see pass, and I am the guy who is supposed to be covering, then that is when I go to my other keys and reads.

We know which side the blitz is coming from on right sugar (Diagram #3). These two guys, Sam and Dog, know they are coming, so the Mike and Will backers fake like they are coming. We tell Mike and Will to walk and talk like they are going to blitz, and we tell Sam and Dog to be patient. We want them to give it time to open up and then hit it when the ball is snapped.

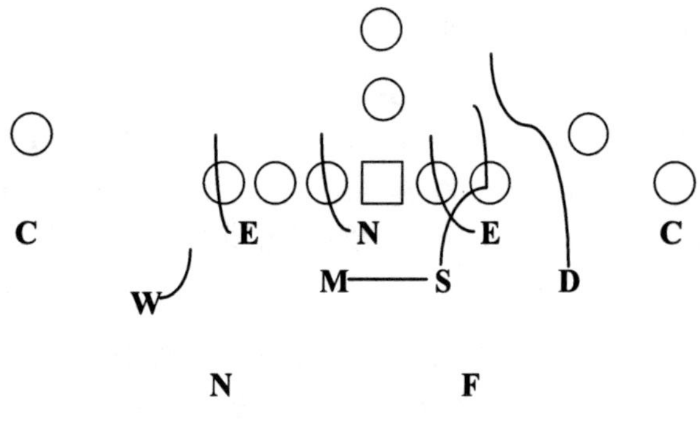

Diagram #3. Right Sugar (Linebackers)

The right end comes off through the guard's face mask. We tell Sam to read the offensive tackle and become a B-gap player. If the tackle closes down, Sam will squeeze off of his hip and just run through him. The noseguard is going to angle to the

guard's face mask, and the left end is going to get outside the tight end and keep contain.

Sam is coming to the B gap, and he goes after our end does his angle. We want the offensive linemen to see the end coming, and then our Sam is blitzing through the B gap. Our Dog is the outside contain man on right sugar. He is the last guy on the line of scrimmage who is blitzing, and that is by far my biggest pet peeve. I cannot stand giving up outside contain. If the quarterback gets outside the contain guy, a lot of bad things can happen to you on defense. So the Dog is coming off of the edge and keeping the quarterback inside.

The left end aims at the tight end's face mask. If the tight end blocks down, that is our end's key anyway. He reads from the tight end to the back. If it is power and the tight end blocks down, he will try to replace him. If the tight end releases, our guy goes to ghost. He will not touch the tight end unless he gets pressure.

This is the whole concept for me about zone blitzing. The weakness of cover 3 is the seam route, so the quarterback wants to set up and hit one of the inside receivers in the seam. Therefore, that is what our two seam guys' responsibility will be. That is what we are talking about when we say, "Seam, see the third guy." The third guy is the back out of the backfield or the #3 receiver in trips.

We are showing cover-2 right, which is our blue coverage (Diagram #4). Our secondary walks up as if they are going to press, or they may all back off, but they are all going to be moving around. We are showing blue to the quarterback, and he is getting all that fixed in his head, but we are really running right sugar, and we will be in cover 3.

I have coached enough basketball to know that the biggest thing in basketball right now is the 2-3 matchup zone defense. The concept is that I will take the guy in my area, and if he leaves my area, I will pass him on. That is what zone coverage is to us.

We do not cover grass. If we are in cover 2 and both corners have the flats, if the wide receivers run verticals, we are not going to sit there if #2 is not coming. We are going to read the second

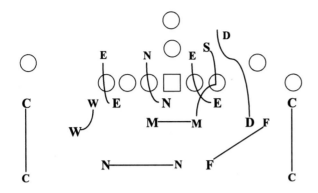

Diagram #4. Right Sugar (Secondary)

receiver, but if no one comes to the flat, we do not sit there. We will keep running vertical.

We have called right sugar, and we are showing a cover-2 look. All our inside people are showing blitz, so the quarterback most likely has a hot read. We are going to try to determine who the hot read is, and we are going to cover him. That gets us back to "seams we see in cover 3." The weakness of cover 3 is seam routes, so we want to take away the seam routes, and we want to make you think that we are in full man-to-man coverage coming after you, and then make you throw the ball quickly.

When we play blue coverage off it, we are playing cover 2, but we are still playing matchup zone. The deep safeties would be over the top, the corners are bailing, and if we do not have a threat in the flats, we are taking the guy who is in our area.

The two inside guys in our blue scheme key the #2 receiver, and the back out of the backfield becomes the third man. If that back swings to their side, they would take him. We want him to hit #2 first, then back off and see what that fullback is doing. That is how we teach it off of cover 2.

When I call right sugar and I go purple read, the purple means cover 3, and we are reading that guy. We want all our secondary guys to walk up close to the line, but before the ball is snapped, they go back to their proper depth. We want to show them man-to-man coverage and we start pointing and calling out whom we are going to cover, but we are just trying to throw the quarterback off.

Our free safety is rolling down to the seam receiver. He will take the hot read, and he is going to

carry the seam guy, so we are back to our man-to-man/zone principle. Though our corners are showing cover 2, when the ball is snapped, they are bailing. The nickel guy is getting out of there and playing cover 3. The inside guys are playing cover 3, but they will read the routes and keep the #2 receivers from getting away quickly.

The only thing about all this is that we have to be good tacklers. We want to get the ball out of the quarterback's hands quickly and run to the ball. If it is third-and-10 and we tackle the hot route for a two-yard gain, now it is fourth-and-eight.

After the inside cover guy reads #3, he will take the seam. He will take #2 and carry him. If he breaks off an out route and #1 runs inside, then we will just switch it, but we do not want #2 running a vertical. If he runs vertical, I am putting hands on him and going with him.

Our nickel guy gets over the top and becomes our free safety, and our Will becomes the same player on the left side that our free safety is on the right side. Our corners are bailing, and our Mike has third-guy responsibility.

That is our way of running the zone blitz. For us, this was easy to put in, and we liked it because we could bring pressure and still play something sound behind it. We do not have to lock up and play man to blitz you. I am not a full-blitz guy.

If I am blitzing you, we are in trouble. That means we cannot stop you in our base, and it is going to be a long night. Our offense had better score a lot of points quickly. I mean, I like blitzing, but I do not like doing it the whole game, because if we are blitzing, we are gambling.

SPICE

When we run right spice, the only thing that changes from sugar to spice is the way we come at you on the right side (Diagram #5). We are still going to angle with the noseguard and left end, but our right end is coming upfield to the outside.

The Sam linebacker will run through the inside face mask of the guard and pull him. We want to

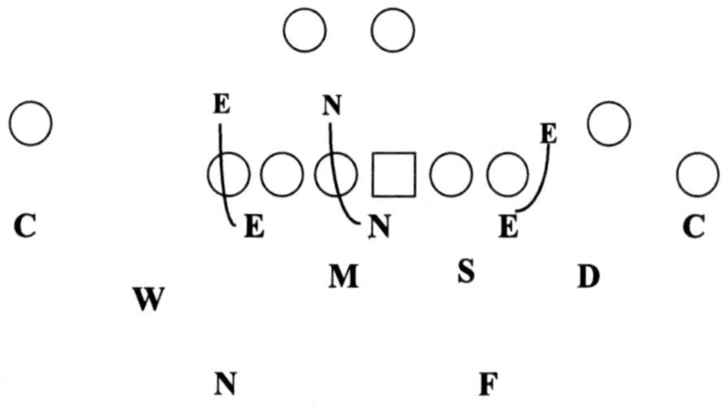

Diagram #5. Right Spice (Linemen)

make sure the guard takes him. We hope that the center will chase the nose. If the guard fans out, Sam knows he has to run over the back to get to the quarterback, and he had better get there.

Our Dog has been coming outside, outside, outside, so now all of a sudden he is coming in the B gap (Diagram #6). He walks up as if he is coming outside, and then he will stick, and here he comes.

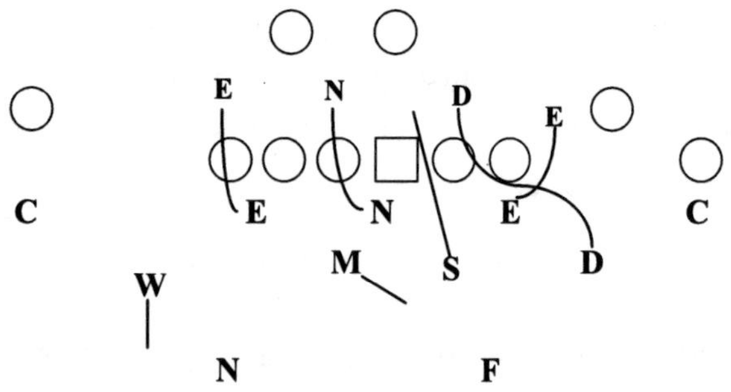

Diagram #6. Right Spice (Linebackers)

The secondary guys do not change (Diagram #7). We are still showing blitz on the left side. They are still showing it when the ball is at their belly, unless it is a run. We are going to try to sit there and play our technique and go with it. You take your chance with it. The secondary is playing purple read, which is cover 3, behind it.

In a shotgun situation, if the back is to Mike's side, he does not drop to the middle. If the back swings to his side, he is going to choke it off quickly. We want to get there and lock him on the swing route because it is 1-on-1. That is why we tell our guys we are bailing and looking. If they throw the swing route and Mike misses the tackle in the backfield, we have two more guys plus the free

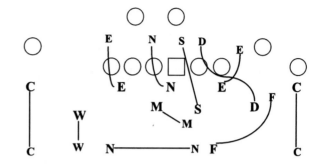

Diagram #7. Right Spice (Secondary)

safety coming to get him before he gets back to the line of scrimmage. If he happens to pick up three yards on third-and-long, that is okay, too.

DOUBLE OUTSIDE

When we run double outside, we are going to bring our Will and Dog down, and we are going to play "true blue," which is our cover 2. Our corners are going to come up and press, and everybody on the field thinks we are faking it and we are going to roll into purple or red. Moreover, that might be what we do some, but not on our double outside.

When we roll to purple or red, we are looking for the seam routes or something quick from the quarterback. In true blue, we might catch #2 running an out route with #1 running a post. We would be over the top of the post, and our corner would be sitting there in cover 2 ready to pick off the out route to the flat for six points.

When we are playing our blue coverage, our corners are outside, and they are going to bail. They are going to read the second receiver to the quarterback. Our safeties are going back to their regular cover-2 read. They will read the second receiver on both sides, open their hips, and go. Our corners are going to backpedal, and if they keep us vertical, we are all four over the top. Sam, Mike, and the nose help with the stuff underneath. We do not have to worry about that.

At the line of scrimmage, both ends are going to angle (Diagram #8). They may have to cheat a little. The right end may cheat to head-up because we want him to get there. The left end will also cheat inside. We are coming to the guard's face mask and trying to two-gap him. If the guy turns out, we will just rush the B gap, and if he steps down, we will rush the A gap. But we want to try to take that guard back.

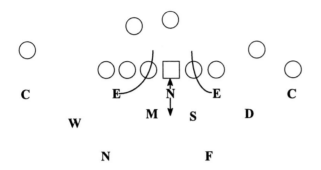

Diagram #8. Double Outside (Linemen)

We are also bringing the Will and the Dog. We tell both of our linebackers to walk up in there, but we want Will and Dog to be sneaky about it, and then both come from the outside.

Our noseguard is going to hit the center and two-gap him if it is a running play. If he reads pass, he will hit and bail out. Then, he is looking for the third guy (Diagram #9). That lets our backers read the second guy, cover hooks and curls, and help on the seam routes. These four underneath guys are trying to read these two guys, the #2 receivers. Our corners cannot help with the outside receivers if they come inside, so they will backpedal and get out of there.

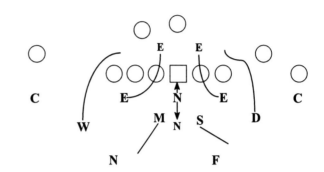

Diagram #9. Double Outside (Linebackers and Secondary)

That is about it. Anything I can do to help you, I will be happy to do. I love football, and I love talking football. I am blessed to be able to be around good people, and they have sure helped me. Thank you for your time.

WING-T OFFENSIVE CONCEPTS

Burleson High School, Texas

Thank you. On behalf of the coaching staff and members of our Burleson Elks football program, I want to thank you for the opportunity to share some of our thoughts, schemes, and philosophy of running the wing-T. I just completed my 22nd year as a high school coach in which we have used the wing-T system. We certainly do not have all the answers when it comes to installing and using the wing-T system. Nevertheless, we do have the utmost confidence in the wing-T because it has produced some high quality plays and results. As a staff, we continue to self-evaluate, analyze, and strive to improve our version of the wing-T system.

Numerous coaches have influenced our offensive design and approach over the years. Through lectures from the great wing-T coaches such as Tubby Raymond, Ted Kempinski, and Gregg Perry of Delaware, Dennis Creehan from South Dakota and Calgary from the collegiate and professional levels. Texas high school coaches: Joe Allen of North Garland High School, Joe Martin of Garland and Allen High Schools, Mike Carter of Allen High School, Randy Barnes of Ferris High School, and Gary Childress of Creekview High School. And finally, the coach that first introduced me to the system and who also provided the diagrams for this lecture, Coach Dennis Harris.

Our offensive staff has taken this information and applied it to our athletes and our program. I am very fortunate to have David Hunt as our offensive coordinator, Eddie Grimes and Jeff Cross as offensive line coaches, Kenneth Jowers as our running backs coach, and Alan Dubose as our wide receivers coach. Their interactive involvement truly en-hances our program.

Why the wing-T system? We feel that the wing-T presents the flexibility to fit your year-to-year per-sonnel. You do not have to have the great individuals to have production. The system provides the opportunity to develop specific features, but it remains variable enough not to depend on the same feature or individual model to make the offense productive. The wing-T provides a four-back attack with all backs involved in both running and catching the ball.

At Burleson, we flip-flop our line with a strongside and a quickside. We feel this feature allows us the ability to have the match-ups that can give us advantages versus any defense. We stress the importance of offensive line play to the point that we always try to have at least two offensive line coaches with each team we have in our program. We feel that it is essential that we develop productive line play in the wing-T.

The wing-T provides misdirection and a power attack. Our version also incorporates the option game. Play-action passes are a must in my opinion, and the wing-T provides numerous play-action pass schemes and concepts. Throw the three-step and five-step passing game into the system and you present a multiple-look, multiple-tempo offense. The timing of the buck series differs from the lateral movement of the belly series, which, in turn, differs from the speed of the option game. These different tempo facets lead to offensive advantages.

The system allows you to adjust during the course of a game. We have found current trends that we can incorporate into the offense that can enhance the attack. To sum things up, the wing-T is a sound, multi-pronged system that can be adapted to the talents and strengths of your team.

The following commentary and diagrams are the foundation of our basic approach. We start with our alignment (Diagram #1). We start out with two-foot splits from the tight end to the quick tackle. We back our guards and 1 techniques back to the hip crease of the center. Our wingback's alignment is a tilted 60-degree stance with an alignment of one yard by one yard from the tight end. Our line splits can be flexible depending on fronts, pressure, and offensive line abilities. Our split end will vary his splits from 8 to 12 yards from the quick tackle. Our tailback and fullback align four-and-a-half yards from the line of scrimmage. We adjust the alignment from time to time depending on speed factors from the backfield.

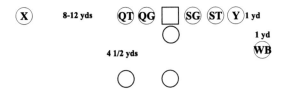

Diagram #1. Alignment, Right Formation

Next is our numbering system (Diagram #2). As others who use the flip-flop system, our line-hole numbers go with them when they are flipped. For example, right 46 (buck sweep) is run to the right side, and left 46 is run to the left.

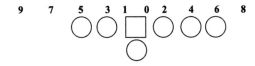

Diagram #2. Hole Numbers

We employ a lot of formations, but I am only going to share a few. Besides right and left, we use our gold formation where the tailback is in the slot that presents a balanced double-wing concept (Diagram #3).

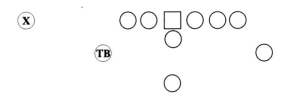

Diagram #3. Right Gold Formation

Right T-slot brings the wingback to a halfback's position while the tailback is slotted (Diagram #4). This formation allows us a lot of flexibility to run all of our offense from a different look.

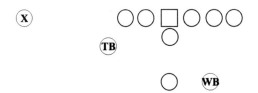

Diagram #4. Right T-Slot

Our nasty call brings our split end to a flexed alignment to the quickside. Right, gold, nasty can provide good blocking angles on both flanks and allow you to run your entire package (Diagram #5).

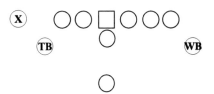

Diagram #5. Right, Gold, Nasty

We start implementing the offense by introducing the buck sweep, which is 46 in our terminology. We do this for a couple of reasons. First, we hang our hat on this play. We emphasize to our players from the standpoint that we want this play to be representative of our program.

Second, for the play to be successful, all must carry out their assigned duties and tasks to make the play successful. I cannot think of another single play that represents total teamwork than the buck sweep. The assignment for the play is easy to understand. The successful execution of the play takes time and effort. It takes skilled players to make this play go, and we are all relying on one another to make it happen.

Our linemen take great pride in this play. We have some general rules that can be flexible to play to our players' abilities. We ask our strongside players, including the wingback, tight end, and strongside tackle, to block down all the way down to the linebacker in the gap. We emphasize staying on a track with these three positions. Our strong guard pulls and kicks out or logs the flank force. Depending on the front, our center will block back versus an even or split defense, base block versus a nose tackle, or reach playside on the 1 technique.

The quick guard pulls playside, getting some depth on steps two and three, and then, he becomes a ballcarrier without the ball, reading the strong guard's path and the block. If the quick guard can read the strong guard's number, he will attack downhill to seal the first threat he encounters, which is usually the playside linebacker. If the strong guard's number disappears, he continues outside around the strong guard's log block, and he blocks the first threat.

Our quick tackle releases tight through the backside B gap, and climbs to the linebacker's depth, looking up any secondary support. The quick-tackle blocks have provided many big plays over the years. The split end stalks the cornerback aligned on him. In the past, we chased the free safety but never got the desired results. Our quick tackle has had better results with the free safety pursuing to the ball.

The backfield techniques are as follows. The quarterback seats the ball and reverses out on his playside foot. The quarterback has the midline and uses a hand fake to the fullback. On his second step, he hands off to the tailback, and then, he carries out the bootleg fake. The fullback's point of attack is the inside, backside A gap to fill for the pulling quick guard. The fullback is to block through the backside A gap to the linebacker's level if there is no down defensive lineman.

The tailback is the ballcarrier. He uses an open crossover step to receive the ball. He must then find the quick guard and follow his block. We emphasize hitting the hole north and south with his shoulders square to provide himself with a three-way cut.

With the quick tackle coming across the field, the cutback can provide huge gains. I want to show you how the base play looks versus the basic 4-3 defense.

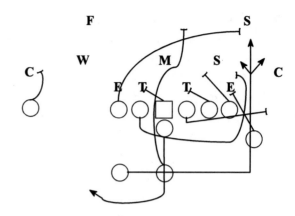

Diagram #6. Buck Sweep 46

I want to show you one adjustment we use from time to time when facing a 1 technique or shifted fronts on the strongside (Diagram #7). If the center has trouble reaching the 1 technique, we employ a l call, which has the strong tackle pulling and kicking out the force. It is good versus a wide 9 or 8 technique because of the flat angle in which he can attack. We have found this adjustment to be very beneficial.

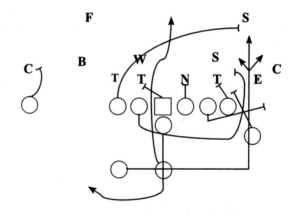

Diagram #7. 1 Call by Strong Guard and Strong Tackle

The companion play of the sweep is the trap play. Both plays play huge roles in our offense. We have multiple schemes that we use depending on the fronts and alignments of the defense. The offense must always communicate on all plays. On our trap play, we have our center block back versus the backside 1, 2, or 3 technique.

Our strong guard uses an escape step, attempting to get a clean release up to the Mike linebacker. The trapping technique employs a short

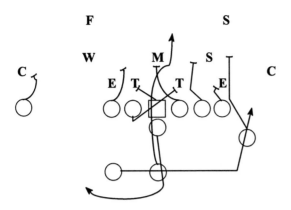

Diagram #8. 40 Trap

four- to six-inch inside drop-step that is then replaced by the outside foot. We put a lot of emphasis on "fanning the hole" with our path and eventual block on the defensive tackle.

When facing a playside 1 gap, the strong guard and strong tackle work together if the strong guard cannot get to the Mike linebacker. They employ a you/me call (Diagram #9). On a me call, the strong guard is responsible for the Mike linebacker. The you call sends the strong tackle down on the Mike. The strong guard is responsible for making the call.

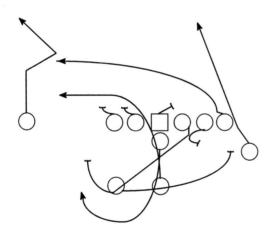

Diagram #9. You/Me Call

The split defense presents a challenge, but we will still run the trap at it (Diagram #10). The fullback may have to bend the play behind the strong tackle's block, but success on the play is achievable.

Versus double I techniques in the gaps, we can use our gap call, which has our quick guard trapping the Mike linebacker (Diagram #11). Backfield techniques differ from the buck sweep from the

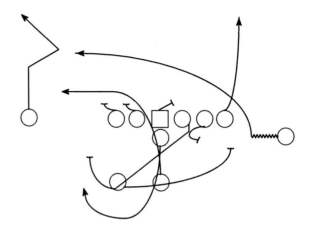

Diagram #10. Vs. Split Call

standpoint of the quarterback and fullback. On the trap, the quarterback opens slightly more to the strongside to ensure the fullback having the midline path. We encourage our fullback to get north and south as soon as possible.

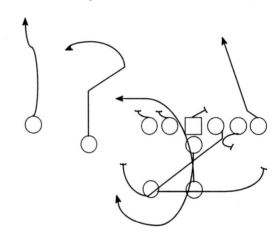

Diagram #11. Vs. Gap Call

We recently have added to our buck series by adding the buck sweep to the quickside. This has reinforced the four-back system and features our wingback as a ballcarrier. The same concept and techniques apply to the quickside as applied to the strongside.

The passing portion of the series lends itself to a natural progression. The bootleg pass off of the buck series has stood the test of time and continues to be an essential element to the offense. I know some of the protection schemes vary from system to system. In my opinion, you must design a secure protection scheme before becoming entranced with routes.

Our protection scheme has varied over the years. We have changed up from time to time by pulling the quickside guard only, pulling both guards, and pulling the strong guard only. Currently, we use the latter.

I want to look at the bootleg series associated with the bootleg passes. We start by basing on the quickside (Diagram #12). Our center will block back. Our strong tackle will use an inside plant/hinge technique. We ask our strong guard to pull playside, gaining depth to the original tailback's starting position. The strong guard's leverage on contain will determine whether he logs or kicks. The quarterback must be aware of possible pressure and adjust accordingly.

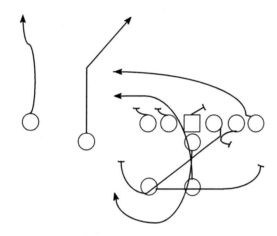

Diagram #12. Bootleg Action

Quick pressure usually results in a kick-out by the strong guard. The quarterback pulls up and goes into his progression. We like things better when we are able to log block and get the quarterback to the edge to present the option of the quarterback running the ball.

I have a few thoughts on the protection scheme that I want to address. First is the fullback's role in the protection scheme. We want the fullback's aiming point to be the outside half of the playside A gap. Sometimes, he must pick up a blitz and we lose him on the pass route. We have found over the years that this has enhanced the chances of the quarterback getting to the edge.

Another aspect that we continue to stress is the play-action pass. The tight initial path of the fullback sells the play to the defense. A wider path by the fullback can give the defense the opportunity to recognize the bootleg quicker.

The quarterback's techniques are as follows. He opens to the quickside and goes through the buck progression. The quarterback maintains the midline and fakes to the fullback and then to the tailback. After faking, we want him to think depth on his path. This helps in two areas—it buys more leverage for the strong guard and gives the patterns a better chance to develop.

For the quarterback, we stress getting the shoulders square and getting his feet in good position to deliver the pass. The quarterback's receiver progression is to look deep and work down to the intermediate route and then back to the flat. The backside route is best when called from the press box. In addition, we will ask the quarterback to take a quick look at the wingback's leverage.

The depth of the routes is critical in completing the passes. Our split end's route is a post corner at a depth of 20 to 22 yards. Our tight end's route should be in the 10- to 12-yard range. Sometimes, we shut down the tight end's route on the hash mark versus a good zone dropping team. The fullback's route is in the three- to five-yard range. He needs to be ready early in the route to catch the ball versus quick pressure. Spacing of the receivers is the key element for success. The wingback runs a vertical route toward the goalpost closest to his alignment.

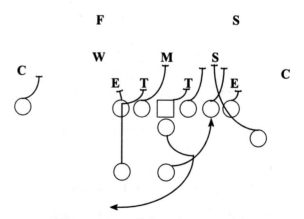

Diagram #13. Bootleg Switch

There are a lot of variations of the bootleg pass, and we use a lot of them. Our bootleg switch call is the same pattern with the exception of the wingback and tight end exchanging routes (Diagram #13).

We like both the twins bootleg and twins bootleg switch plays (Diagrams #14 and #15). They present the same multilevel approach. The majority of our bootleg routes provide three levels to defend.

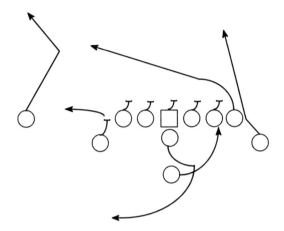

Diagram #14. Twins Bootleg

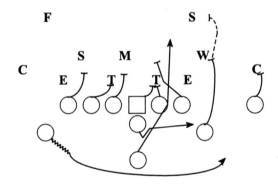

Diagram #15. Twins Bootleg Switch

The next series to discuss is the belly series. We have changed our approach to it in regard to our block schemes. We have (and still use) the traditional belly-G on the strongside. We still teach the cross block to the quickside. However, we have emphasized the belly with the zone blocking scheme for the past several seasons. It is a simple scheme in some ways, but it does rely on everyone working together for success.

All the down linemen zone playside with a big emphasis of blocking down linemen first and foremost. We want to ensure movement and control of the down linemen before we climb to the linebacker's level (Diagram #16). We ask our

wingback to fold block in the bubble to add a block to the point of attack. The backside linemen in our belly scheme use a fast-fold technique that attempts to create a moving wall to create backside cuts for the fullback.

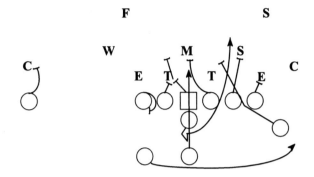

Diagram #16. Zone, Belly, Strong

Companion plays in the series are the tackle trap, the Delaware Sally play, and the play-action pass off the belly series. You can see the similarity of routes associated with our bootleg scheme (Diagram #17). The difference exists in which back runs the flat route and the fact that it is a true naked scheme relying on initial flow to the quarterback to the edge.

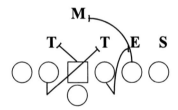

Diagram #17. Zone Naked

One key technique is the tailback's release after using a rub technique on the defensive end or outside linebacker responsible for containment. The tailback should release into the route after making solid contact on the defender. Emphasis should be placed on not releasing too quickly. The quarterback still has the option to run the ball if the opportunity presents itself.

We tie both the buck series and the belly series in together, and we pair plays from both series'. We pair the trap 40 and the strongside belly 34 from time to time. We let the alignment of the defensive tackle determine which play we run. An inside technique provides good angles for the 34 belly, while we like to run the trap versus a 3 technique.

While the buck series and the belly series each possess their own unique tempo, our option attack provides a quicker tempo for defenses to defend. We do not get into a lot of different option schemes because of time limitations, but we do use the inside veer (quick and strong), the midline option, and the zone-double option.

The inside veer scheme is used to both sides of our formations (Diagram #18). It is the basic wishbone concept that has been around for years. The more athletic a quarterback we have, the more we will run the option series. We commit 10 minutes daily to practice our option series. Our main coaching points with the play are to get movement on a 1, 2, or 3 technique and work up to the Mike linebacker or inside linebacker.

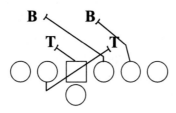

Diagram #18. Left Inside Veer

We read the first down lineman outside of the guard. The scheme sometimes evolves into a triple-team on the defensive tackle. We stress that the fullback's path should remain consistent. His point of attack is the outside hip of the playside guard. The fullback should hug the double-team and get north and south. We have found that this helps occupy linebackers and slow their pursuit. The tailback employs a technique that blocks levels. The first level is the linebacker level while working to secondary support. We feel this provides an opportunity for the quarterback to keep the ball.

The wingback's pitch path takes him through the fullback's heels. It is critical that he practices a consistent path and lets the ball bring him toward the line of scrimmage.

Our midline option helps our offense attack the middle of the defense (Diagram #19). The scheme is simple for our offensive line. Everyone (with the exception of the strong guard) fan blocks to the outside. The strong guard uses the same technique he used in the trap block versus a 3 technique. The wingback fold blocks inside. He is looking to block the inside linebacker. The quarterback keeps off the midline. The fullback's path is the midline off the center. The quarterback reads the 3 technique to give or keep.

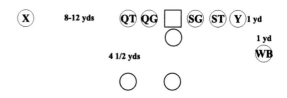

Diagram #19. Midline Options

We have paired the trap and the midline versus even and split fronts. We can also pair the midline with the veer depending on the alignments of the defensive tackles. In 2004, we led the entire state in rushing due in part to our ability to include our option series into our total package.

We also incorporate tosses to all three running backs. We also run the jet sweep series and a screen package. Our focus remains on the buck, belly, and option series that involves all of our skills positions. In my opinion, the wing-T has stood the test of time and still presents football programs a great opportunity for success.

Again, I appreciate the opportunity to share some of our thoughts and concepts on the wing-T offense.

FOOTBALL STRENGTH AND CONDITIONING PROGRAM

South Charleston High School, West Virginia

It is indeed an honor to be here. I am fortunate to be where I am today. I was away from the game of football for many years. I am a 1976 graduate of Marshall University. I played a couple years of football there. The reason I got out of football was because I became a powerlifter. I lifted in several competitions and ran a gym. The gym was Holley Strength Club in South Charleston.

A few years back, I did end up in the school system. They asked me to become a teacher and coach. At first, I told them no. I explained to the head coach that I had gone from the late 1970s to the year of 2000 without being around the game of football much at all. I was not up to date on football. It was not the game of football itself; it was the attitude of the student-athletes today compared with the way they were when I was in school. So many things had changed. I was a 1970s guy, trying to coach in a 21st century system.

It is difficult at times because of this. However, it adds to our program because the kids are starting to understand our program. They know what we are talking about when we talk about discipline and hard work.

I know all of you stress these same points in your program. I know you do. It is an integral part of every program. You can ask our players about our program, and they will tell you that our program starts with discipline and hard work.

When I did get involved in the high school program as an assistant, my influence mainly came through the weight room. For many years, I owned the Holley Strength Club in South Charleston. We not only gained national prominence, but we gained worldwide attention. We had two outstanding young men go through our program. One was Brian

Siders. He is the strongest drug-tested human in history. He has broken every record and has been world champion three times, and he has been drug-tested. He is a great individual. I have coached him since he was in junior high school. He squats 1,000 pounds and benches over 800 pounds. He was 240 pounds when we started with him, and now he is 350 pounds. He is a true testament to what our system does for the kids.

We have taken our system to the high school level. We have tweaked the program over the last few years. We initiated the program to the football players, and they are a part of the system.

The next person that has become prominent in our program is Phil Pfister. He recently won the World's Strongest Man contest. He was the first American to win that title in 20 years. He started with us as well. These two are examples of what our strength program can do.

Another prominent person to gain from our program is with us today, and that is our own Coach Johnson. He came into our program as a 220-pound sophomore. He could barely get on the field. He left our program as a 265-pound all-state football player.

It is interesting to visit a clinic such as the Nike Clinics. You walk down the hall, and you cannot help but see all of the weight equipment. Who in here has the budget to go buy all of that equipment? If you do, let me know, because I want to put in an application to coach at your school. We do not have any money at our school.

When I came to the high school to coach, the Holley Strength Club was still open and running. It was in that same building for 15 years. The owner of the building only charged me 150 dollars per month for those 15 years. It was a small room, and not as big as a basketball court. They sold the building, and we had to move out of the gym. By that time, I was coaching at the high school.

I told my principal I was getting rid of all of my weight-lifting equipment. He told me to bring it to the school. I told him I would bring the weight-lifting equipment to the school on one condition: "I am going to bring all of the 'old men' with me." I brought long-time lifters with me. They cannot come to school and train our kids, but they can come in and work out, especially on weekends if they want. Our young men see the influence the older men have with weight lifting, and they serve as good role models for them. They respect them, and they honor them for what they have done.

Our young men know that nothing these men have accomplished, or things I have accomplished, will overshadow one single thing they do in the high school strength program. A five-pound increase in a lift or a bench press is more important than having the world's strongest man lift in our gym. That is the truth, and our kids know this

The important thing in your strength program should be: "What does your student-athlete gain from the program?" I am sure your philosophy is like ours. We tell our kids, "We are here for you, to do what we can for you. You are not here to do what you can for us. We want you to be good citizens, good sons, good students, and to work hard." We tell them: that is what they can do for us. We let them know that we want to make them better students and better sons, and we want them to walk out the door with a chance to get a good education.

I know several of you have students from a diverse population. Several of us are inner-city schools. You must sell your program first to the student-athlete. Then, you have to sell yourself to the parents. As I told you at the beginning, high school football is a new adventure for me. Nevertheless, from my upbringing, I bring my old-school philosophy; I felt I knew what had to be done.

I felt I knew what the staff would have to do to get the kids' attention in the strength program.

Our philosophy is this: we are not lifting weights. We are not weightlifters; we are athletes. We are football players. We are training to be better athletes. First, you must sell that philosophy to the student-athlete.

Then, we must sell that philosophy to the parents. I can tell you this: you better sell it to mom first. Every mother is worried about her baby. The new middle school concept is bull crap. When you bring the middle school kids into the program, they are physically immature, and they are mentally immature. Coaches are just as obligated to that student, even more so than you are to the seniors in the program. The middle school program is where the program begins, and the seniors getting ready to go to the next level is where it ends.

The first thing we do is to sell to the parents that we are not going to make their son a weightlifter. We are going to make him a better athlete. We are going to do whatever it takes to make them better athletes. You must sell that to the parents every day. You pound that into their heads repeatedly. We do not lift weight; we train.

When those young players come into the program, they are about 5'8" and weigh 120 pounds, and there is not a sign of peach fuzz on their faces. The first thing you must do is to evaluate each and every one of those athletes. You take the obvious sign, and you wonder if the kid has an athletic ability. What does the kid's bone development look like? You are dealing with immature kids most of the time. You do not need to worry about the older kid who walks through the door, and he has a beard, and he is well put together. You are obligated to look at all of the young men who come into your program. We may have to use the weight program to facilitate the young kid's growth.

We do look at the kids and try to facilitate them into athletes. We look at their bone development and their physical make-up. Young bodies are full of soft tissues. Their bodies are soft, and they are still developing. The last thing you want to do is to do something that is going to impact the kid's growth in a negative way. You may have to involve your trainer and your staff. If you have a paid physical trainer, involve them in this process.

Look at the case in court where a coach at Pleasure Ridge Park High School in Louisville, Kentucky, was sued by the parents of a football player who died. The prosecuting attorney said the coach was liable for the player's death. The player collapsed on the field and died a few days later in the hospital.

Today, all coaches are in a precarious position. You are in a position of trust with the parents and the school. You are obligated to see to it that all of the athletes are properly cared for in all conditions.

Coaches are legally liable. You know that. I do not have to tell you that. They make you sign every waiver in the world when you sign up to coach. A waiver just does not stand up in a court of law. It is just a piece of paper. You are obligated to protect them as much as possible.

Go through this process. We do not want to damage the growth of any of the young players coming into our program. Ninety percent of the things we do with those young incoming kids are pulling exercises. We do lat pulls, dumbbell pulls, and we do rowing exercises. We do exercises that are going to lessen the stress on joints. We do not want to damage and impact soft tissue.

In the long run, this is going to help your program. First, you are going to stay away from injuries by doing this. I know they do get tired and hurt, and they do get stiff and sore. The two best tools to use to evaluate young athletes are your eyes and your ears. You can see when a young person is fatigued. You can watch their actions and observe the way they talk, and you will know when they are fatigued.

I tell the parents the most important part of a weight-lifting program or a training program is the recovery time. You must give these young people time to recover. We are not concerned how much kids can lift. We are concerned with quality of the lift, and we are concerned with repetition. We concerned with the movements in the weight room that are going to facilitate becoming better athletes.

We are talking mainly about football players here, but we do work with all athletes. We work with all sports, both boys and girls. It keeps me at the gym from 7:00 a.m. to 8:00 p.m., six and seven days a week. Let me tell you now, I am having a ball with it. I am having fun. I was in the coal-mining business for 25 years. I worked for someone else for 15 years, and I went on my own for 10 years. I had a health issue come up, and I got out of the mining business. I got into school teaching, and now I am really having fun.

You should be obligated to do the right thing where these young kids are concerned. Make sure you dot the is and cross the ts. If you do not do that, you could be liable, just as the coach from Louisville, Kentucky. Your job is on the line. Make sure you take care of those things at all times.

You should monitor the weight room daily. You have to be there with them every day. I see a lot of weight rooms where the head coach divides the monitoring of the weight room with three or four assistant coaches. He may make a visit to the weight room once a week, but he is not around very much. If the head coach is truly interested in the program and truly interested in the kids' improvement, you should get in the weight room and support the program, the coaches, and the players. This is not my ego speaking, but I love to be in the workout room.

I never ask our kids to do anything that I do not do, or one half of what I do. They know there is not one thing more important in that program than a five-pound increase in the bench press. You do not have to lift weights with the players, but you do need to be there for them. Make sure, if you are the head coach, that you are monitoring the program from daylight to dark.

We have to decide three things for every lift we do. The first thing we must do is to understand power. What is power? We expect them to understand speed. We start bringing the young kids over to work out as soon as our high school season is over. We were five weeks late getting to them this year, but we sure were glad of it. Being the AAA state champs is a big reward in that we did get to practice those five extra weeks.

We have two coaches who work with the new kids. It is a job for those two coaches. Our players hear the word "speed" a thousand times during a personal workout. Speed is nothing but pure physics. On all the exercises that we do, we are trying to overcome the forces of gravity. Speed overcomes the forces of gravity.

Weight lifting and power lifting has turned into a mockery and a joke. We only max lift two or three times a year. You find a lot of coaches and strength companies that will guarantee you players a 400-pound increase on the bench press if they will do their program. We know that is not going to happen.

What we need to do is to supply the kids with this information and lock it in. Speed! First, on every lift, we stress the fact that we are working on the static movement. The kids play football outside their center of gravity. You must have a strong core. Everything we do in football is from a good football position. We want to be in a good football position to make plays. We stress this to the kids repeatedly.

When you are doing a squat, anytime they are in a negative part of the lift, we want that static movement in the squat. When they are in football and they engage someone, the first thing they are going to do is to clasp the arms. As they make the hit, that is static movement. Now, they are fighting that movement. When they hit the bottom of the movement, they do not completely relax. Next is when they come with the compensatory acceleration. Speed! Overcome the forces of gravity. We are working the static portion, full range of motion, and power and speed. Speed overcomes the force of gravity. Everything we do is based on speed.

Next, we talk about the eyes. Not one coach teaches his players to look down at his feet three feet in front of him. His eyes must be up. There is no better place in your program to reinforce getting the eyes up, and to practice good stance and good technique, than a weight program. Get the eyes up! Head up; eyes up!

We do as much neutral grip work as we possibly can with our upper body. We teach the kids to block with the elbows in tight, and with thumbs up so you can steer the man you are blocking. Inside between the arms is where the power is. We do a lot of neutral grips on floor presses. Anything we can incorporate this into the lift, we do it.

The last thing we tell the players on the neutral grip work is to have control at the top. When they finish the movement, they come under control. We teach this when we teach the kids to tackle. You engage, come under control, and then drive through the man.

You can put all of these things together that you do in football and work on them nine months in the weight room to accomplish the thing used in football. You cannot just do it for four months on the football field. If we can teach these moves in the indoor program, we do not have to teach that on the football field.

We need to emphasize to our athletes why the movement is important. Why is it important that we do this exercise? We may do a lot of oddball stuff in our program. I know a lot of coaches do not have the time to do this, and a lot of you do not have the equipment to do all of the things we do.

Emphasize the full range of motion in every exercise you do. Tell the athletes why the exercise is important to football, and how the exercise is going to help football players. The perfect example of this is the squat. When I was playing football, we were taught to get into a football stance and to get up on the toes.

The first clinic I went to when I started coaching was at West Virginia University. The team split up, and we went to watch the linemen drills. In the first session, the offensive line was working on the reach block. The coach started by going over the stance. I had to check out what he was telling the offensive linemen. "We want the weight on the heels. Everything comes off the back of the heels." That was something new to me. The coach went on to say, if you are going to reach block on the defensive man in the outside gap, you must push off the back part of the heels. That made sense to me. This is the big reason that we teach in the weight room: "Everything goes through the heels."

Why is it important to develop the static part of the lift? Ninety-five percent of what a kid does on the football field is not picture perfect. We break down the films after our games. We break down film all of the time. Our kids are always in a bad position. They are high school football players.

I know we have a lot of coaches from a lot of different areas. I know Pennsylvania is a hotbed of football. We have other areas here that play good football. My idea of West Virginia High School football is this: every team has four or five football players. Each team has six or seven men who play football. You take the good players and surround them with the other players who have the heart and desire to win, and then you can be successful. We have two or three great football players. All of the other players are average football players. That is what you get in high school football in West Virginia. It is your obligation to make all of them better football players. It starts in the weight room. I live and die by this. It starts in the weight room.

Another aspect of the lift that we stress is the compensatory acceleration as part of the lift. That is football. You accelerate. You come off the line of scrimmage, you engage, and you accelerate upfield. If you are a back and you run the football, you hit someone, and boom, you accelerate. We base everything on acceleration. You can beat this into them for eight months in the off-season. It is like training Pavlov's dog; do it over and over, and they will get it, and they will not forget it.

If the players ask us what we do in our weight program, we tell them we do a few exercises, and then we do them some more, and again some more. We do them over and over in the weight room, and we do them over and over on the football field.

Let me be specific and talk about the squat. We tell our kids that when they walk out on the rack is when they gain control of the bar. How many times have we seen players walk up to the rack and then back out of the rack? We go into the rack, we get good foot placement, and then we stand up. We teach "baby sets." We pick the weight up, and take little steps. You do not have to take a trip. You can move one foot. You can take three baby steps. We set up, and slightly flare the toes outside. We do not teach the football player who is blocking the linemen to flare the toes to the inside. We want the toes turned inside. If you try to do this on the squat, the players will fall on their head every time. The only reason we flare our toes is for stabilization.

The next thing we tell them is "big chest." We want them to stick their chest out. We are doing the exercise with our legs here. The control is coming from the cord. We say to get a big breath or air, put the shoulders back, and then big lats. That is to get the elbow tight against the lat muscles to gain control of the bar.

Ninety percent of the work we do is to a box. We do box squats parallel and oblique. We do these for two reasons. You can really stress the static part, and you can see that they do not bang down on the boxes; they sit down on the boxes. I tell them I know they are going slow, but they can come down to the floor to a point where their buttocks are close to the floor. They have to flex those gluteus maximus muscles. We tell them they must tighten those buttock muscles.

We tell the players to take the weights down slow, with the heels flat on the floor. When they get to the box, they come to a complete stop. Now is the compensatory acceleration. We tell them they are not picking the weight up. We tell them to shove with the heels. Everything goes through the heels. If they are not shoving through their heels, this is what is going to happen. They come up, the back goes straight, and then they come up. What position is the player in when he comes up to the point where the back is straight and the head is up? Football position! We have eight months to teach them this movement. We do not have to repeat this come August.

The next thing we tell them is to use speed all the way through the movement. Then, it is controlled. You never take the weights to the rack in any exercise until the movement is completed. We teach all football movements to come under control before we stop the exercises.

We have a kid who just turned 17 years old this December. He is like a son to me. They are all "my" sons, and I really mean that. He is 6'3", 310 pounds, just bench pressed 460 pounds, squats 600 pounds, He practices these movements every single day. He teaches the other athletes. Sometimes, they teach him a point or two. My point is this: that kid's technique, and the technique you are teaching the younger kids, is just as important to every players right on down the line. You must reinforce every time for all of the athletes.

On 75 percent of our squats and dead lifts, we do them without a belt on. I know kids love to run out and get a belt. The reason we do this is because we want to strengthen the core. We know we are limited in the amount of time we have with those kids. We are limited from 40 to 60 minutes in our workouts. It is non-stop, and the players never sit down. We do not sit down! We want them to stand up.

We stress to them that when they are in the weight room, they are moving constantly. They are on the go all of the time. We stay away from the belts when we can to stretch the core. You cannot play football with a belt on.

One point I want to touch on concerns me a great deal. The NFL, the major colleges, and just about everyone in football relies on the bench press and the 40-yard sprint to determine the ability of prospects. I am sorry, but I feel those are two of the worse measurements in football that ever came up. Give me a lineman who can bench press 200 pounds in the first quarter, and come back and can bench press 200 pounds in the fourth quarter, If he has that type of endurance, I will take him over the other athletes who score on the two other tests. I will take him over the player who bench-presses 400 pounds in the first

quarter. Get the players in condition to thinking everything they do is important.

Take a lineman, and put him on the floor with a bench press. Give him dumbbells, and see how many times he can curl them. If he is doing that, we are going to put him on the bench. He is not going to help you doing curls.

There are a lot of new ideas floating around now. I am always reading about innovative programs. It is period workouts. They are getting players under the squat bar, and they are squatting for a period of five minutes. They are getting under a bench bar, and they are benching for a period of five minutes. They are doing dead lifts for a period of five minutes.

We have innovations that come into the school systems across the country. Things come into education that change the way we teach, and it changes the world. Don't be afraid to experiment. Try some of the new things to see what will help your program. Read, study film, take some of the ideas you hear today, and see if they will fit your program.

You can take what someone gives you related to football. You can try it, and you may not like it, but you can learn something in the process.

In talking about the big muscle group, we did not have one injury to the big muscle group. We played a 14-game schedule, counting the state finals. With 16- and 17-year-old kids, I think that is quite an accomplishment. We have taught the kids to take that kind of beating. We must know when to back off, and we must know when to hit them hard.

We have not talked about shoulder exercises and what we do. We are going to talk about the shoulder and the triceps, chest in the bench press, the trunk, core, squats, and the dead lift. I am not a big clean fan at the high school level. I know the Bigger Faster Stronger programs have been around forever. They do have several articles around the clean exercise. The longevity of a power lifter is extremely short. It is because of the impact it has on joints and soft tissue.

The first thing we talked about in this presentation was soft tissue. We do not want to impact those soft tissues and growth joints. I am not a huge clean guy. We do incorporate partial cleans. We incorporate Olympic high pulls. We incorporate portions of the lifts. Again, we do not do a lot of cleans because of the impact it has on soft tissue.

The key ingredient in a clean is speed. We talked about speed earlier. Football and athletics is built around speed. If you do cleans, incorporate the speed aspect.

In working with the shoulders, you have to work the anterior part of the shoulder, the medial part of the shoulder, and the posterior part of the shoulder. We have three separate muscle groups to work with, and you want to impact all three areas.

I have no statistics to back this up with, but shoulder injuries and knees injuries are the two leading causes for athletes missing football games. These are the muscles to work on in your strength program.

I have sent you to a different level. I have put some material up on the table for you to take if you are interested. It is material on the three methods of training, including volume, tonnage method, and the loading method. They are the three most popular methods of training as far as I am concerned. I have given examples of each of these methods.

I love talking on strength training. I love it. I have been doing this for so many years; once I get started, it just rolls out. I love it. I have always loved football. I think the dumbest thing I ever did was to quit college football. I had always dreamed about playing football. Have any of you ever dreamed about playing football? We all did. You dream about playing the game of football. The good lord spared my life, and put me in a position that I can do. I am having a ball teaching and coaching. I am very blessed and very fortunate.

I know we have some vendors here today, and I want them to know I am not trying to knock their equipment. There are cheaper ways to get things for your weight room. As I said, we have a very limited budget. One of the things we use in our program is the rubber bands that are used in weight rooms. We can never get enough of them.

When our players come into the weight room, there is a big board with a big eagle on the center of the board. Every sport has a workout listed on the board. We may have 70 people in our weight room, including boys and girls. When they come into our gym, I meet them at the door. I let them know they are not at the Holiday Inn, the Ramada, or the Marriott. It is not a singles' bar. "You are here to work out. I do not want to catch you sitting down."

They are in the program to work, and they work. Each sport has their workout program. There is a set workout for each group. It is a five-day workout.

When we finish the season, we come in to lift five days a week. However, we are not working as hard as we do later in the year. We do not want them in peak conditioning in January and February. We do not stretch or do conditioning. Again, it is part of my philosophy. It is important for them to have some time to recover from a hard season, both physically and mentally. These kids need recovery time. It is good for you to get away from the players for a while, and it is good for them to get away from you for a period.

We have a three-day workout as well for each sport. These are our workouts. We have had some success with this program. If the athletes will do four or five exercises a day for six or seven days a week, they are doing a lot of exercises. They are impacting a lot of muscle groups. We do rotate between the upper-body and the lower-body exercises.

Keep your workouts to a minimum, time-wise. Between 40 and 60 minutes is long enough. Keep the athletes moving. We allow 15 to 20 seconds for recovery between lifts. In some cases, we may go 30 seconds between reps.

When the kids come into the room and get started, they do exactly what is on the list. The kids will test you on this. We stress this to the younger kids when they first start out in the program.

The most important thing a person can do to improve the bench press is to work on the shoulder muscles and the back muscles. That rib cage has to grow. By impacting the big muscle groups, you will gain weight faster.

There are two holy places at South Charleston High School. The weight room and the football field are the two holy places at our school. They are the holy places for our athletes, except when they go home and go to church. When they are in the weight room, it is hard work. When they are on the football field, it is hard work.

We talk with our kids about this next point all of the time. There is an "in-here me," and an "out-here me." The in-here me is the community, schools, church. The out-here me is the football program and the strength program. In the weight program, I am a mean SOB! I admit I am tough on them, but I love them. They know that, and they will vouch for that. As educators and coaches, we must teach the students to distinguish between the in-here me and the out-here me. That is your responsibility.

I tell the student-athletes, if they are good citizens and good students, then they are going to be good football players. They have bought into this program. You must team them this. Coaches have a lot of influence on these kids today.

Let me talk about recovery in the weight program. Recovery is so important to these young athletes. You are dealing with young tissue and young muscles. You are teaching these athletes lifelong lessons. They are going to remember this forever. It is amazing how much the young players learn in one month.

You can add aerobic value to a workout in the weight room. We do a lot of speed work in the weight room. We will do 20 reps in one set with 15 to 20 seconds rest between sets. We do it from the squat, bench, and dead lift. It is a good conditioning exercise. We have three athletes on a station doing one exercise. One athlete does his reps and then switches with one of the next athletes. All three complete the exercise and move to the next station. It is an aerobic exercise because it is quick. If you are a no-huddle team, you can make this a great exercise.

I do want to talk about spotting in weight lifting. A spotter is just as important as a kid doing the lift. Do not let them lift without spotters. Do not leave the weight room and leave the kids in the room by themselves. Have a coach in there with them.

We try to pair our kids with other kids of equal strength and size. It speeds the workout up. It limits the amount of loading you have to do with the bar. It is a good idea once in a while to take the kid who bench presses 400 pounds and put him with the young kid who benches 120 pounds. This can have an impact on that young player and give him something to look forward to in the future. It can have an impact on the 400-pound guy because he is going to remember when he could not bench 400 pounds. We do not work these kids together every day, but at some point let them work together.

We stress to the athletes all of the time, we are not so concerned about the weights as we are the quality repetitions. We are teaching them that we want things done the right way. We put the athletes on the field to do a job, and we want them to do the job. It starts in the weight room. For eight months, we can teach them what we want them to do for the next four months.

Call the school to reach me if you are interested in any of the material I covered, or the material I laid out concerning our views on strength and conditioning. Thank you.

THE TWO-MINUTE, HURRY-UP, NO-HUDDLE OFFENSE

Rockford High School, Michigan

I am excited to be here. I hope you will be able to come away from here with a couple of thoughts pertaining to organizing a two-minute offense. A friend of mine came to see us play a number of years ago. Jim Cole from Alma College is sitting out there today. After the game we were talking, and it became clear to me that we needed more of a two-minute offense. I was embarrassed that we were not as prepared in that category of football as we needed to be. We have continued to evolve into something that would help us toward the end of a half, or at the end of a game.

In this area of the two-minute offense, or having a way to speed up the game, many people are doing this with the no-huddle offense. It is fun for the kids to practice this type of offense, and they enjoy it. Even from a coaching standpoint, it helps prevent staleness. It gives you a different gear, and it changes things up. We call the two-minute or no-huddle offense as the same. We do use this throughout the game. It does not have to be with two minutes left in a game.

We always have to start out with a philosophy. We are going to have an offense that is well prepared all of the time. We will work to have a dimension of offense that is well prepared to put an opponent's defense on their heels, raising the potential for a quick score from anywhere on the field on any given play. It is an offense we have spent a great deal of time preparing. Our objective is to put the defense on their heels. We want to increase the opportunity for a quick score. A missed tackle or a blown assignment can often lead to a score.

We are going to utilize a well-planned dimension of offense when:

- We wish to change to or create a fast-paced tempo. We want to change the tempo that is going on the field during the course of a game.
- We need to race the clock and create a scoring opportunity prior to half.
- We are in need of catching up or in the event we must come from behind to win.

The bottom line for all of us in coaching is: we are going to achieve what we emphasize. At the time when Jim Cole visited with us, we did not emphasize the two-minute offense. Now, we do emphasize it.

Here are the "musts" to consider for implementing a two-minute, hurry-up, no-huddle offense. When making the decision to turn up the heat offensively by utilizing a two-minute attack, it will require an aggressive yet calculated attitude where the game clock becomes the immediate opponent. To develop excellence in the execution phase of our two-minute attack, it will necessitate the implementation of weekly practice periods where our potential play calls are run against live defenses.

When making the decision to turn up the heat offensively, it requires an aggressive and calculated attitude. The reason for that is the fact that the clock becomes your opponent. You become oblivious to the defense. It is like "chuck and duck." You must be well prepared to do this. If you make a mistake and a pass gets picked off, the game could be over on that one play.

Another must is to develop excellence in that two-minute phase of the attack; you will have to include the offensive plays in a weekly practice period. Again, you achieve what you emphasize. We want to work on the plays that we are going to run in this offensive set. This is something I have learned several years ago on this matter. Skelly practice is not necessarily the answer.

You need to have the defensive line involved because the quarterback needs to feel the pressure. You need the offensive line to be involved so they will be in the vision of the quarterback. You may want to break it down to skelly drills, which we do, but ultimately you have to scrimmage this particular offensive system.

Another must includes practice periods that will provide the quarterback a chance to gain a valuable experience in managing the game clock when driving the ball down the field and creating scoring opportunity. This may prepare your quarterback, but more importantly, it is going to prepare your second quarterback. You better be working more than one quarterback at all times.

Here are our goals for our two-minute offense:

- Win the game in the fourth quarter.
- Score prior to the end of the half.
- Drive the football by making first downs.
- Beat the game clock.
- Efficiently use available time-outs.
- Maximize number of opportunities.
- Force opponent to burn time-outs.
- Have our quarterback's well in tune with all situations we may encounter.
- Force opponent to spend valuable practice time preparing a defensive scheme for defending our two-minute attack.
- Control the clock to where we leave little to no time for our opponent to execute their two-minute drill.

Winning the game in the fourth quarter is important; however, the bottom line is winning. You need to put your team in the best position you can to give them the opportunity to win. That is our job as coaches.

We want to drive the football but make first downs. I do not think anything is good unless you can score first downs. Move the chains. When you move the chains, you create more opportunities to run more plays. If you hit the big play, that is great, but we want to make first downs.

Beat the game clock. Efficiently, use your time-outs. I want to save the time-outs if possible, but it is best to use them wisely.

Maximize your amount of opportunities. If you are in the hurry-up mode, you are going to have more plays for your offense. This is where the coaches come into play in putting the players in the best possible position to score.

You want to force the opponents to use their time-outs as you are moving the football. Force them to kill the clock for adjustments.

Let me talk about some other things related to our goals. We want to spend time with our quarterbacks. If you throw everything at them at one time, you are applying the whole/part teaching method. We are talking about situations they may encounter. We want to put them in those situations in practice.

- We want to force the opponent to spend valuable time in preparing their defensive scheme to defend our hurry-up offense.
- We want to work on controlling the clock to leave our opponent as little time as possible on the clock.

Here are some absolutes you want to work with your quarterback on. They need to know what type of score we need to win. They need to know how much time is remaining in a half or in the game. They need to know down-and-distance. We have not been guilty of this, but every year this comes up where a team thought it was third down when it was really the fourth down. You must make sure they are keeping track of down-and-distance. At times, you cannot trust the down box. In addition, you may not be able to trust the person keeping the time and the person that is keeping the downs on the scoreboard. He needs to stay sharp on that.

He needs to know the number of time-outs available. We need to know the situations that will stop the clock. He must know how to react to the plays that keep the game clock running. We need to spend time with our quarterbacks on all of these scenarios throughout the entire season.

We want to have all the situations on stopping the clock written down. One of the assistants has a card with all of these situations written down so we know how we can stop the clock. For example, we must have a two-play package ready to go when we must call two plays, one to follow the other play when we are running out of time.

Here are some additional absolutes. He must know which plays work the sideline. On the other hand, he needs to know the plays that utilize the middle of the field. Have a handle on that as a head coach. There is a lot that goes on in 25 seconds of a game. I have one or two assistants who are on top of these situations. It is a lot better to have two people thinking rather than one.

The quarterback must know which plays will give us the best shot at the end zone. We may be in that situation where we have to take a shot to make a big play. We have those plays already in mind. We have worked on the plays that we feel will give us a chance to put it into the end zone.

We want to teach the quarterback to know when to run the clock down prior to finishing a two-minute attack. This is something you may want to consider. I do not care so much about the defense the opponents are playing, I just know we need to get the ball in the end zone. If you know what you want to run to get the ball in the end zone, there is no sense in leaving time on the clock, if you can slow the pace to a certain extent.

We think it is important to practice sideline management. You need to have the play ready on the sideline on a change of possession so they can get on the field and get the offense moving as soon as possible. We do not want to waste time with huddling up and that type of thing. If some of the offensive team is on the field, playing defense, it may be tough to get everyone on the same page at that time. Nevertheless, we need to find a way to communicate that with all of our players.

We want to practice getting on the field and getting ready to snap the ball on a change of possession. We need to practice poise and patience while under pressure. Again, that is a quarterback thing. As a head coach, I love to play the mind of my quarterback. The quarterback coach may not be happy with this. I enjoy putting the pressure on the quarterback. I do the same with the kickers and punters. I like to put them under pressure. If I can do a good job in this area, when they get in the game, it is going to be a piece of cake. To have 8,000 to 10,000 people watching us play a game is nothing compared to me standing on the field during practice.

We practice a scoring drive with no time-outs left. Put your kids in that situation in practice. Practice sending your field-goal team on the field to try an attempt with no time-outs left. All of this is easy. We do that on Thursday.

Practice the last play at the end of a half, or at the end of a game. That is not difficult to do as well.

In any hurry-up or two-minute offense, the run becomes a secondary play, but you should not forget about it. Make sure one of your assistant coaches is looking for that opportunity in the game situation. If time allows, a run is a very viable part of the offense. Obviously, avoiding sacks is critical.

The quarterback must deliver the football on time at all times. He must not mess around with the ball. He must get rid of it.

Receivers must understand the significance of spacing. That is something we are working on all of the time as well.

Receivers must run disciplined pass routes at proper depths. Proper depth is a big area of concern for us. The bottom line is that receivers must get to the proper depth so the play times up with the pass. Receivers must get vertical or out-of-bounds after the reception. They must get out-of-bounds or head north and south down the field.

We want to have all the situations on stopping the clock. One of the assistants has a card with all of these situations written down so we know how we can stop the clock. Here are the things we have on the card:

- Incomplete pass
- Getting out-of-bounds
- Penalty enforcement
- Following made first down
  - ✓ Setting of chains
  - ✓ First-down measurement
- Official time-out for injury
- Spike the football
- Called time-out
- Victory formation

I want to talk about starting points. If you are going to get into this offense, protection is paramount. It all starts with the front line. If you cannot block the defense, it is not going to be a successful offensive package. Spend time in deciding on the type of scheme you want to use. Spend time on different things the defense can run against you that you have not seen. It starts with the protection schemes.

STARTING POINT

- Protection schemes: pressure/hot
- Formations; alignment
- Hand signals/alerts uncovered
- Wristband communication method
- Snap count: eliminate error
- Gun/under center: when and why
- Pre-snap reads: best-choice receiver
- Victory: every player set/protect/official
- Defensive staff aligns opponent's defense

It is important to have a hot receiver when the defense brings more people than you can block.

The first thing we need to do once we are on the line of scrimmage is to make sure we are in the correct formation. The second point is to make sure we are aligned correctly. That does take some work.

You can use wristbands or hand signals. Either way, you need to develop a method of communicating. We have one that works fine for us, and I am sure you have your own method that works for you.

You must eliminate mistakes on the snap count. Most of the time, we are going on the sound, but we can change things if we need to.

Everyone needs to practice the victory drill. One year, our quarterback took a knee, came right back up, and tossed the ball to the official. The official was not ready for the ball, and it hit him and went to the ground. Who knows what that official could have called? We do practice the drill, and we make sure the official is aware what we are doing on the play.

PRACTICE DYNAMICS

- Daily practice of routes during individual and group periods.
- Monday: Two-minute offense leading to field goal (10 minutes).
- Tuesday: Scrimmage. Move the field and change the tempo in the middle of the script.
- Wednesday: End practice with two-minute offense, ending with touchdown (10 minutes).
- Daily practice work on pass protection and blitz pick-up.
- Pull-out periods used for teaching time. We do platoon to a certain extent. We always have some players that we can pull out of drills and work with. This gives them added reps. We want reps, reps, reps.
- Defensive staff aligns opponent's defense. I give them the alignment we want to work on. That is what I work on during the weekend.

All of these situations will help your defense when they face these offensive formations. They can improve from this practice as well.

- One coach calls out a situation and is keeping a stopwatch (our coach in box).
- One coach spots the football and whistles football ready for play.
- One coach is checking formation alignment.
- Sideline coach issues hand signals.
- Two players run set of chains—safety first. Players who are banged up hold the chains. This keeps them out of the action on purpose.

- Send offense from the sideline following the punt/kickoff return/turnover.
- Practice driving different lengths of field.

We have several coaches involved in this practice. They are not just standing around during the practice.

DRILLING THE TWO-MINUTE OFFENSE

Next, I want to talk about drilling the two-minute offense. Here are some thoughts.

- Start drive from inside the 20-yard line.
- Offense has 10 plays to score a touchdown.
- Offense has two time-outs remaining.
- Spike football during a drive when under 90 seconds.
- Use time-outs when under 30 seconds. No need to save a time-out since we need a touchdown.
- Work in official's time-out for a measurement. Have the offense on the ball with the next play called.
- Work in either an offensive or a defensive penalty. Have the offense on the ball with the next play called.

After we have worked on these things, it becomes quicker and easier as you get organized. It becomes less of a time situation.

- Start drive from own 47-yard line. You must move the fullback to the +25.
- Offense has six plays to score a field goal to win!
- Offense has one time-out remaining.
- Line up quickly and spike the football during a drive when under 90 seconds remaining.
- Work in a first-down measurement. Have the offense on the ball ready to go when the play is called ready to play.
- Save a time-out to get the field-goal team on the field.
- Work in a fourth-and-8 to -12 situation.

These are the plays we will have ready when a time-out is available. These plays will help us reach the sideline or possibly the end zone. I am only listing a few.

WITH TIME-OUTS AVAILABLE

- Condor Hyena
- Condor Saber
- Condor Panther
- Condor Ram/Slam
- Condor Rocket
- Condor Jet Sprint/Flood

PASS-PROTECTION PRINCIPLES

I tell the players up front that we have five men available for pass protection. We better be able to block five defenders. If the defense brings six or seven rushers, the responsibility is on someone else. They do not have to worry about that. Therefore, we say every protection scheme begins with the premise that we have five linemen. Should the defense bring more rushers than we have protectors, it is up to the coaching staff and quarterback to make play calls that exploit open areas left voided by the defense.

- Protection must first focus on securing the areas from tackle to tackle. Our goal is to secure the shortest and most direct rush lanes to the quarterback.
- Defensive line schemes and blitz packages must be worked on daily. Success comes from confidence and knowledge pertaining to these alignments and blitz schemes. The key is to eliminate confusion and uncertainty.
- Time must be devoted to the development of footwork and technique. Constant reinforcement is a must.
- Daily 1-on-1 and 2-on-2 drills are invaluable.

You must be working on more than just five linemen because sooner or later one of them will need to be replaced. Work on one player for each position: center, guard, tackle. One player may play more than one position.

Examples of Protection

The defense has five, and the offense has five (Diagram #1). There is no immediate need to call a back into the protection scheme unless there is a dominant defensive lineman whom we need to get help in blocking.

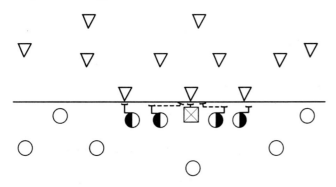

Diagram #1. Pass Protection

The center has the man on him, and that defender becomes his primary challenge. The center also recognizes that he may get help from the guards should their linebacker drop into coverage. The center must also work with the guards against any combo and cross-fire blitz. Outside blitzes are not a concern unless we are throwing routes at the intermediate or deep levels.

Next, we look at the protection when the defense has six in the box (Diagram #2). The offense has five in the box.

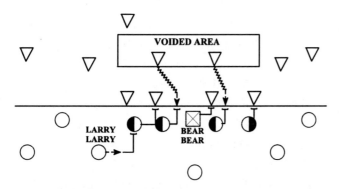

Diagram #2. Defense With Six in the Box

The offense calls into protection one back on the left side, allowing our line to slide protect to our right. The quarterback makes a "Larry, Larry" call, and the line makes a "Bear, Bear" call. The line knows they are going to slide protect to the right, and the back is going to the left side to protect.

Another example with the defense with six in the box is when we want to block the back to the right side. This time, the quarterback calls "Roy,

Roy," the line call is "Bells, Bells," and our line slide protects to the left (Diagram #3). The Roy Roy call is to the right for the back.

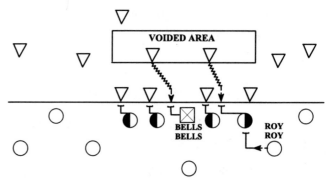

Diagram #3. Slide Protect Left

On our alignment reference, we are different from some teams. Instead of X, Y, Z, A, H, R, T, and F, we use a different system. All of those other formations are too complicated for me. We use A, B, C, and D, E, F (Diagram #4). We letter the areas outside the ends. We know that we are going to be lined up somewhere in those areas.

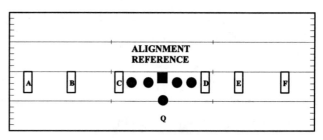

Diagram #4. Alignment Reference

Condor is one of our alignments in the bird package (Diagram #5). You can see our alignments. We are in a 3x2 set in Condor.

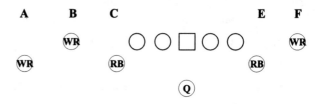

Diagram #5. Condor

The other side of that would be our Hawk call in the bird package (Diagram #6). We are in a 3x2 set.

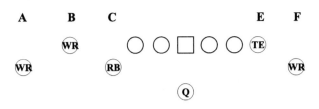

Diagram #6. Hawk Left MT

WHO ALIGNS WHERE?

- Basic rule of thumb is that he who needs to get deepest the fastest aligns on line of scrimmage.
- Press coverage often times dictates who is on or off the line of scrimmage.
- Speed of the receiver may enter into weekly game plan alignment.
- Patterns dictate routes, which dictate alignment.
- Jet motion helps determine formation alignment.

Here is how we line up on Condor trio right MT (Diagram #7). I find this easy to communicate with our players. For those of you who have been using the X, Y, Z calls for your formations, I am sure that has worked well for you.

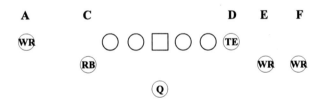

Diagram #7. Condor Trio Right MT

Here is our next formation. I do enjoy using these formations, and as long as the kids can learn them, I will keep them. Now, we want two tight ends. The call is: tight trio left MT (Diagram #8).

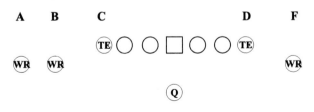

Diagram #8. Tight Trio Left MT

Wild animal package! This is what we call our two-minute, hurry-up, no-huddle offense.

- Hyena: All hitch routes
- Saber: Slant routes
- Panther: Bubble screen
- Ocelot (leopard): Out routes
- Wolf: Slant and scoop
- Cheetah: Verticals
- Ram: Rocket screen

I do not have time to go into detail on most of these, but you can see what we are doing. If you have questions, you can ask during the film session.

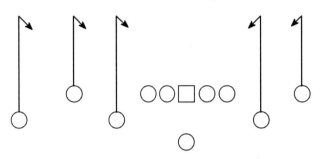

Diagram #9. Hyena Pass

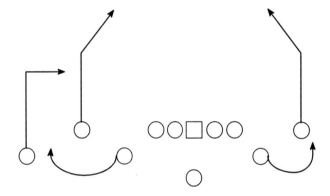

Diagram #10. Saber Pass

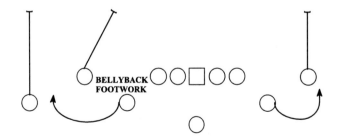

Diagram #11. Panther

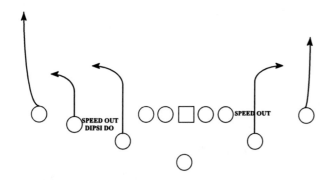

Diagram #12. Ocelot

Here are a few others that we like. They are special plays.

- Quick passes: Three steps
- Rocket: Jet sweep plays
- Quarterback draw: Fake pass
- Sally: Wing-T-type play
- Left guard special: Fun play

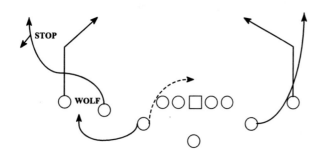

Diagram #13. Wolf

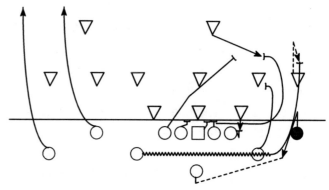

Diagram #16. Quick Nightmare Screen

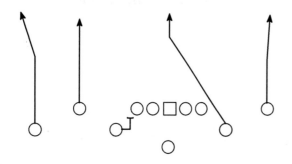

Diagram #14. Cheetah

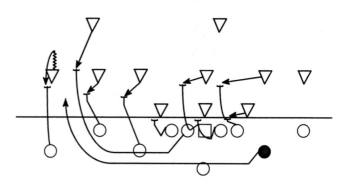

Diagram #17. Rocket Screen

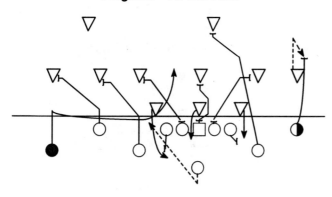

Diagram #15. Ram Screen

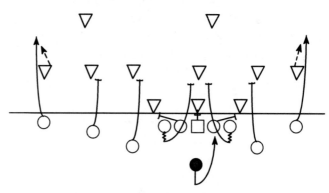

Diagram #18. Quarterback Draw

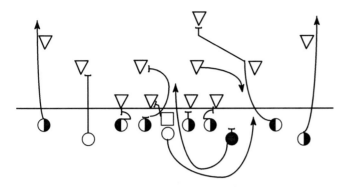

Diagram #19. Sally Bootleg Play

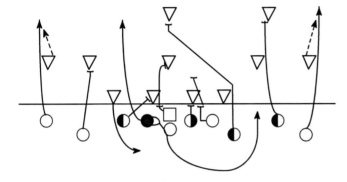

Diagram #20. Left Guard Special

We are ready for some video of all of these plays in action. I am not real big into the technology stuff, so bear with me. I am impressed that it is working up to this point.

If we call out "Bandit, Bandit", that means our receiver is uncovered, and we can stand up and throw him the ball. We try to take advantage of that case against the defense.

Our kids enjoy this offense. It is fun for them. They do not get beat up all the time running off-tackle.

Just a thought you can take with you on the screen pass. The tackles are going to stay on the wide defender. They are going to invite him upfield. They need to get a good base and work upfield. They do not have to go downfield and pancake the defenders. That is not going to happen. All we have to do is to tie them up. We tell them to get downfield, get big, and stomp the feet of the defenders. Make them "wine."

I am open for questions. Thank you very much.

OPTIONS: MULTIPLE OFFENSIVE FORMATIONS

Mountain Home High School, Arkansas

I want to thank Larry Blackmon for having me on the clinic. I do want to thank Nike for their support of the clinics. I do want to talk about Mountain Home High School before we get into the football. I hope that this will let you know where we are coming from and what we are trying to do. There are several coaches here today that are on our schedule, and that is great.

We are from the northern tip of Arkansas. We are about as un-athletic as you can get. We usually have between 50 and 60 kids out for the team. This year, we had 72 that came out for the team. We have them in the off-season program now, and our numbers are up. For the most part, we very seldom have any speed on our team. It is hard for us to put 11 on the field that can run with any speed for their position.

We are trying to take advantage of what we can do because we know the opponents have an advantage. First of all, they are good coaches, and they have some great players. We are in a tough league. When you play against West Memphis, Marion, Parkview, Jacksonville, Hall, and Jonesboro, they have great players. We do not have great players. Since I have been at Mountain Home High, we have had one kid sign a scholarship at Arkansas State. We have a player that is going to walk on this year. You can see that we have not had many great players in our program.

We are looking for the advantage in everything we do. We feel the option gives us the greatest advantage possible. We do not have the speed to run the wing-T offense. We do not have a quarterback that can hit the broadside of a barn. We do not have a passing quarterback. The thing we can do is to find a smart kid who can read the option. If we can get a little speed at fullback, we feel as if

we can be good. If we don't get players with speed at fullback, it becomes three yards and a cloud of dust for our offense.

We feel we can cut down on the number of plays we give the opponents. I was talking with Randy Coleman of Jonesboro High School earlier today, and he told me that the least number of plays they had on offense last year was against us. We feel we can control the ball at times.

Back in 2006 against West Memphis High School, we had two 18-play drives. On one of the drives, we did not even score. However, they only had three possessions in the second half. We want a ball-possession offense. We do this by running the midline, inside, and outside veer plays.

There are two theories of option teams. First is an option team that has very few formations. They are always balanced. Two examples would be the Air Force Academy and Georgia Tech. They make the defense balance up. However, they allow the defense to prepare for very few adjustments. They are going to line up the same every play.

Georgia Tech's Paul Johnson, who was formerly at Navy, runs the double-slot offense. They will change the formation, but most of the time they are double-slot formation. I am not saying Coach Johnson is wrong, but, in my opinion, that allows the defense to be prepared for what they are doing. The defense can adjust to what they are doing on offense.

The other option system is one that has many formations. That is what we run. We are seldom balanced. We want to make the defense stay balanced while adjusting to different formations. We are an unbalanced option team. We are always looking to get defenders in a bad position. If the defense is not giving us the midline, we will give them a different formation and see if we can get them to open up the midline. If they do not give us the midline, it may open up the outside veer.

Our three base plays are the midline, inside veer, and outside veer. We do add the toss sweep, a power play, and a counter play. That is it for our offense. The midline and inside veer are our bread and butter.

If we run 50 plays in a game, 35 of them are going to be one of those two plays. We run those plays over and over.

We must have a strongside and a weakside offense. The quarterbacks coach must be willing to take what the defense gives us. We will throw the ball from time to time. We hit some big plays in the passing game, and it helps our running game. When we do throw the ball, usually our receivers are wide open. The defense does not expect us to throw the ball a great deal of the time.

We want to get our best players in positions where they can run the football. The defense may be required to play out of position sometimes. If the defense overloads to one side, we still must be able to go away from it.

In 2006, we got beat in the state finals. We had three decent linemen. We had a center and two guards that were better than average. Our other players could not have been starters for many other teams. We started a right tackle that started in 13 games, and he never made contact with more than three people in a game. That is tough to do. We had to figure out a way to get our three best linemen to where we wanted to run the ball. We could end up lining up our guard to line up at tight end on one play. We had to come up with a lot of different calls to accomplish what we wanted to do on offense. Our quarterback could check off if the play we were looking for was not open.

If we can get the defense to become more involved with where they must line up, they are not going to be inclined to blitz as much. Nevertheless, we can handle the blitz as well. Teams will bring their linebackers up on the line of scrimmage and move the defensive backs up as linebackers. We want to force the defense to account for all eligible receivers.

Our offense allows us to get our best players where we *want* them and *when* we want them in those positions. We are going to give the defense several different formations to limit their blitzing.

We are trying to create blocking angles. We are doing all of this, and, still, we are only running the three running plays that we have stressed: the midline, inside veer, and outside veer.

We are always looking for blocking angles. Sometimes our backs, by the way we line them up, create these angles. Sometimes, it comes by the way we align the linemen. Very seldom are we going to try to base block anyone. If we have to base block, we are going to try to give them some help. We just are not good enough to base block 1-on-1. I do not see any value in chewing a kid out for not getting the block done when he is not good enough to make that block. "His Johns are better than our Joes." We go into the game that way.

We have over 50 formations, and we are adding to them all of the time. Formations are only limited to what you, as a coach, can develop. That is my opinion. We do all of that with formations, but we only run six to eight plays. We run mainly three plays, and really, we run only two plays.

Is it confusing running so many formations? No. We only have those six to eight plays. By changing the formation, we do not change our blocking scheme. We are doing the same thing on those six to eight plays.

Our base formation is a full-house wishbone set. We start out teaching everything from this set. We have a right halfback, a fullback, and a left halfback. If we run the inside veer on the right side, the halfback on that side is going to run through the tackle. He is going to block the outside linebacker. That is what he does on that play. We run the base 34 play.

If we move the right halfback out to a slot formation on the right side, he has the same block on the outside linebacker. He is doing the same thing, only this time he is not blocking from out of the backfield. If we put him in the wing set, he does the same thing. We do have certain tags that we use to give us a change-up, but we are doing the same thing all of the time on that play. We are doing it from a lot of different formations. We want the defense to adjust to something they have not seen.

I run the offense, and I spend a lot of time on Sunday trying to figure out what formations this defense has not seen up to this point in the season. I ask the question if adding another formation will benefit us that week against our opponent. We try to put in one new formation every week. We are trying to come up with something that will give us an advantage. If I do not come up with something that will help us, I feel I have let our kids down. The players expect us to come up with something new every week. It may be something we did two years ago and have not run since then, but we are always going to look for something.

We can run the midline from any formation in our playbook, including the shotgun. I am the type of coach that likes to run the play several years before I actually run it in a game. For four years, we have been running the midline out of the shotgun formation. We hope we will be able to run that in a game in the next two years.

We can run the midline because we can always drive the fullback in the line. We are always going to have the threat of the option. Again, the assignments do not change for the midline.

There are two philosophies on the midline. Some teams double-team the noseguard regardless of where he lines up. The other theory is to base block the noseguard. We are just talking about the midline. In my opinion, this is where it all starts. If the center cannot block the nose man, you must get him some help. Some teams will run toward an A-gap player, and some people will not. It all depends on our personnel. We have run the play both ways. We can run the play to the A-gap player and still read the 3 or 4i technique. We need backs that can make that cutback if we do run the play to the A-gap player.

When we use the different formations, we force the defense to adjust. If the defense tries to slide their line, we do not have to block the shade technique. Now, the midline is open. If they do not slide the defensive front and leave our tight end uncovered, then we are going to run the outside veer.

In review, if a balanced formation takes away our midline, then we change the formation, because the defense may then slide their front, and that opens up the midline for us. Let me go to some film that will give you a better idea of what we are doing.

A win for us on a running play is four yards. We feel good about four yards, but we would like to have more.

It does not matter what offense you run. If you have a quarterback who can run and you want to add a play to your offense, you should add the midline play. You can run the play out of any formation.

If I had to pick one play, we do the most out of this one play. We practice this play a lot. How do multiple formations help the inside veer? It is the same principle as on the midline. It makes the defense adjust to open up the inside veer. We can force changes for the defensive responsibilities:

- Defenders that are playing the dive can be blocked.
- Defenders that are playing the quarterback may need to play the dive play.
- The defenders playing the pitch may have to play the quarterback.

If the defense does not make these changes, one of our options should be open. We want to force the defense to play techniques they are not used to playing.

Changing formations can create better blocking angles for us. It is easier to block the linebackers and defensive backs. We create better angles on the linemen we are trying to block.

If the defense overshifts, it opens up the weakside veer. We do not need as many blockers on the weakside.

One thing that may force me out of coaching in 49 of the states, or force me to go Texas to coach (or to college coaching), is the rule on the cut block. Why should I have to ask my 145-pound running back to go outside and block the 6'3", 230-pound linebacker up in his chest? We cannot cut the defenders—they can in Texas and in college football. I do not believe that is a fair thing to ask my small back to block the big linebacker. I have seen our backs get clotheslined. I feel we need to do something different in that situation. The only way I can help him is by giving him some angles to block back on that linebacker. If the linebacker does not see the back coming, he may have a chance. We hope the opponents have scouted us enough to know that we will split out and bring the back inside to block on him. I hope that he will be concerned about that and will be looking outside to see if we are going to block on him. If he is not looking for us, we have him blocked. If he is looking for us, we may run by him.

In order to use formations to your advantage, you must be able to run plays to the weakside. However, you must be willing to run the ball to the weakside with one less blocker sometimes and take the three or four yards, or if they take the weakside away, run the plays to the strongside.

Our quarterbacks have 100 percent freedom to change the plays. We start working with our quarterbacks in the seventh grade. The first thing they do is learn how to check out of the midline as seventh graders. As they get older, we change a few things with them as they can do later. They know what to do when they get to that point. When the quarterback gets on the field, he is just like a coach as far as we are concerned.

I know a lot of coaches give the quarterbacks a lot to do in calling plays. I call the play, and he goes out to run that play. He knows what to do if the play is not what we have worked against. He has 100 percent freedom to change the play. If the defense gives us something better on the opposite side, he can change the play to take advantage of the defense. To us, the quarterback is always right if he gives the ball to the back on the first move. If he is

ever in doubt, he gives the back the football. Our fullback is going to carry the ball most of the time anyway.

The quarterback can check to any play he wants to go call. The thing he cannot do is this: If I call a pass play, he had better throw the football. I do not call many pass plays, and I do not want him to take away one of my opportunities on the pass. He can check to a different play or the same play to the other side of the formation.

We can call the quarterback over and tell him to run play 34 and not to change it regardless of what the defense plays. I recall one game when we were playing West Memphis away, and we had the ball on our 18-yard line. If we gave the ball back to them in the third quarter, they were going to score. It was fourth down with four yards to go, and I knew if we gave them the ball, they would score. I decided to go for it on their 18-yard line. I called the quarterback to run the veer and to keep the ball. I told him not to think about anything but getting the first down. He did what I told him to do, and we got the first down. That was the 18-play drive, where we did not score but we won the game. They did not get the ball back until the time was running out on them.

We feel we must give our players a better chance. We try to get the angles for them on their blocks. That is very important in our scheme. We can run plays from any formation. Teams know us as a wishbone-formation team. Nevertheless, we do run other formations as I have indicated.

How do formations help the outside veer? On the outside veer, we use different formations to gain an advantage as well.

It is tough to run the outside veer into a 7-techinque defender. Unless you have a great tight end that can crush the 7 technique, it is hard to run inside him. We try to find a formation that will open that area up for our running game. By using some of our unbalanced formations, the defense may adjust their 7 technique. That may give us the outside veer play. I do not care where everyone else lines up on the defense except for the 7 technique. I am not going to run the outside veer at him. We will check out of the play and run something else. If he is in the 7 technique, we should be able to run the inside veer or the midline.

Most teams adjust by sliding their line to be unbalanced. This opens the outside veer. We can run the outside veer by putting our back in a slot position. This makes the back a tight end. It creates the blockers needed for the outside veer. We go unbalanced one way, and we have a slot to the opposite side. We have our tight end, and he combo blocks down inside. We read the first man on or on the outside of the end.

When we are looking for backs, we are looking for blockers. Our fullback and quarterback are the two backs that are going to carry the ball most of the time. If we pitch the ball to the halfbacks once or twice a game, that is great. We are looking for blockers on the backs. So when he goes to the slot, I want him to combo block down inside.

If we block the defensive man we are reading, we read the next man outside of the first man we were reading. If they want to wash inside, then we read the next defender.

I want to talk about some other benefits of using multiple formations. You will see these advantages when we show the film.

Defenses adjust to stop the option game, and that should open up the power running game. The power running game consists of these plays:

• Toss
• Counter trey
• Power

The question about our splits in the line has come up. We take big splits between our tackle and guard. As long as the defensive line widens, we are going to widen. Our tackles will split over six feet. Our guards will split three to six feet. We are opening running lanes. The defense is not going to allow us to do that very long. They will come back inside and close those holes down to stop the midline and inside game.

You will not see us split foot to foot. We are going to take our splits as big as the defense will allow us to take.

I am by no means a guru. I have really studied the option game. I like it a great deal. If I were coaching somewhere else where I had some good athletes, I would still have the option game in our package. Would we do other things? Yes, we would. I actually like to throw the football. The fans and boosters back home do not think so, but I do like to put the ball in the air.

The advice I will leave you with is this: Whatever you run, believe in it, sell it to your kids, and get them to believe in it, and you will have a chance to be successful. I can tell you, Mountain Home's football team had never been successful until the last six years. Now, Mountain Home High School is competitive, where we were not competitive before. Before I went there, they had won 17 games in 10 or so years. We are doing a little better than that. We have been to the state finals, and they know what it's like to win. We build everything on a great defense. Our offense is trying to shorten the game as much as possible. Formations have become the key for us in the last several years.

I appreciate you coming to this lecture. Thank you for your attention.

STOPPING THE RUN WITH A 3-4 DEFENSE

Milan High School, Michigan

One thing I think is important to any program is to let your coaches coach and your players play. It is a team game. I had a former coaching colleague who was with the Canadian Football League, and he was the head coach at Melvindale High School in Michigan for a long time. I coached with him at Divine Child High School. The defense he brought to us at Divine Child High School was the old pro 4-3 defense. The Sam linebacker walked up on the tight-end side and played football. He had pass coverages that I still believe in today. However, we do not use it much today. It was something called levels coverage. It was a way to disguise all the different coverages he ran.

I brought that defense to Milan High School 23 years ago. We did not have the huge defensive tackles we had at Divine Child. We did not have the huge middle linebacker to play the 4-3. We ended up turning that into the old 4-4 stack defense. At that time, we actually used stand-up defensive ends. We only had two down linemen. We used a lot of multiple looks. Being an old quarterback, I did not believe in multiple looks. Fortunately for me, my defensive coordinator did. We played with two stand-up defensive ends and two down linemen. We had four small linebackers running all over the place. We had a lot of fun with it.

We developed that defense and ran it for 19 years. We won a lot of games with it and a lot of championships with it. Why we changed is what happens here. We moved into the Huron league in 2000 and had not faced many wing-T teams. We got to the Huron league, and the wing-T teams started slapping us in the face every week. The stand-up defensive ends were getting killed, and the tackles were getting trapped out of the ballpark.

We were getting beat up, and we had not been to the playoffs for some years. We thought it was time to change. The Chelsea High School coaches had been in our league when we played in the Southeast Michigan League. They ran the 4-4 defense differently. They played a 4-2 look with wide outside linebackers. Instead of building a wall up front the way we played the 4-4, they pinned their ears back and came after you.

We went to work with pads and pencils and got the defense changes done. We changed to the 4-2 defense in 2005 and got back into the playoffs. We are back in championship form and back in the playoff picture again. We used the 4-2 for a couple of years, but as we got back into the playoffs, we started to see a lot of spread teams. The spread teams were making us look silly, and we decided we needed to change again.

In 2007, we started playing around with the 3-4 defense. The thing that sticks in my mind was our Airport High School game in week two of the season. We played with the 3-4 but were doing it with personnel substitutions. We played the 4-2 look. When we wanted to go to the 3-4, we took out a defensive lineman and replaced him with a linebacker or a defensive back. The coach at Airport High School was watching what we were doing. Every time we took the tackles out, he ran the ball down our throats. When we put them back into the game, he went to the spread and threw the ball. We ended up being co-champs with them at the end of the season, but they made us look silly.

We felt if we were going to use this multiple system, we would have to have versatile athletes on the field. We now have a defensive end who can stand up and be an outside linebacker. We have an outside linebacker who can walk back and play safety. This year, we had a defensive end who could stand up and play inside linebacker and an inside linebacker who could play safety. Multiple looks and versatile personnel are very important to us.

As we progressed with the defense, we thought we were only going to use the defense against spread teams. Our league began to loosen up and throw the ball around. Today, we can run the 3-4 against just about anyone. We have a full-house team in our league, and we were able to run the 3-4 against them.

That is how we got here. Brainstorming the scheme was different. We looked at all kinds of defenses before we settled on the 3-4 alignment. We felt we could play it against the spread and the wing-T. The linebacker coaches convinced us that we could run our multiple looks without changing the linebacker reads in the 3-4. That is the beauty of our package. We play the 3-4, 4-4, and 5-4. The four linebackers in those defenses never change. The other thing we like about it is there are four defensive backs in the scheme.

We did a lot of talking with Ron Vanderlinden from Penn State when he was here two years ago. One of the things Coach Vanderlinden told us was they do not give up the big play. He told us in 2006 they only gave up 11 plays of 18 yards or more in the season. He credited that to playing cover 2 with two good safeties in the back. When we went to the 3-4, we have not given up the big play. The 3-4 has been good to us at a variety of levels.

When we installed it completely, we found it fit our personnel perfectly. We have had some great defensive linemen and linebackers the last couple of years. Fortunately for me, I am blessed with a great staff. They teach technique very well, and the good athletes we have adjusted to the defense very easily.

We are technological dinosaurs. In our 3-4 defense I like to see all four defensive backs lined up in a straight line about six yards off the ball (Diagram #1). It does not matter what we are playing; this is the way we start. We try to disguise what we are doing in the secondary. The inside linebackers start out at four-and-a-half yards off the line of scrimmage.

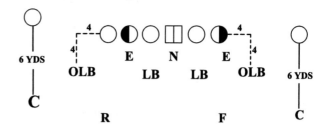

Diagram #1. Base 3-4 Defense

The outside linebackers align anywhere from 4x4 to 2x2. That is four yards outside the tight end and four yards deep. Their alignment depends on the opponent. Sometimes they are back and wide, and sometimes they are up and close. Sometimes we are in a stunt look, and sometimes we are just adjusting to a formation. The defensive ends align on the outside eye of the offensive tackle, and the nose tackle is head-up on the center. We have a lot of calls for the down front, but we did not use too many of them because of the ability of our defensive linemen.

The first game of the season, we played Ypsilanti High School. They had a tremendous wide receiver by the name of Donald Spencer, who signed with Michigan State. We thought a lot of him, and I think he will be a stud at Michigan State. He is 6'4" and 210 pounds, can run, and will knock your face off. With our small defensive backs, we did not have anyone that could cover him. He played the single receiver on the backside of the trips set. We played a 3-4 bump against him (Diagram #2). We developed it for the spread teams, but we used it against him. Everything on the defense stayed the same except the outside linebacker to Spencer's side. He walked out on him and bumped him up the field.

If a team has an outstanding back, we use the 3-4 free to match up with him (Diagram #3). We change our secondary into a cover-3 scheme. We take the free safety, which we call the fly, and he keys on that player. We felt Ypsilanti was going to run their tailback a lot. We played 3-4 free, and the free safety played a spy technique on the tailback.

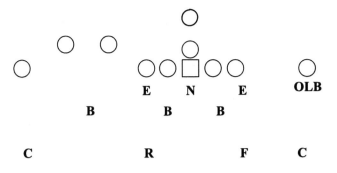

Diagram #2. 3-4 Bump

We align him between the linebackers at a depth of six yards. He shadows the tailback wherever he goes. It gives you the free player in run support and a man cover in the passing game.

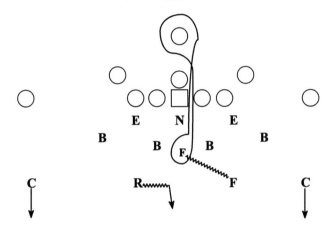

Diagram #3. 3-4 Free

We did not have to use the free that much in the first game, but later in the year; we used it many times with great success. Our free safety was a hell of a football player and is going on scholarship to Robert Morris University on a football scholarship.

The 3-4 Rover is similar to the free adjustment but is different (Diagram #4). We play a cover-3 look in the secondary and take one of the safeties, who we call Rover, and put him up in the face of the 3x1 trips look to the wideside. This is the same concept; the safety is aligned to take that receiver away.

Those are different looks we run from our 3-4 defense. We can play the 4-4 defense with the same personnel on the field (Diagram #5). When we go to the 4-4, we drop one of our outside linebackers down into a defensive end position with his hand on the ground. The Rover safety drops down and becomes

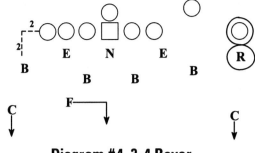

Diagram #4. 3-4 Rover

the outside linebacker. We move the defensive line one gap and play football. The noseguard moves out on the guard, and one of the defensive ends slides down over the guard. The inside linebacker stacks in the middle, and we use convention alignment with the two inside down defenders.

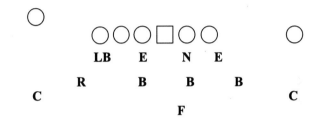

Diagram #5. 4-4 Defense

We can move them into a 1-3 stack alignment or any number of other fronts. The outside linebackers are wide in their alignment, and we play cover 3 in the secondary.

In the 5-4 defense, we bring our outside linebackers up on the line of scrimmage into 9 techniques on the tight end (Diagram #6). If there is no tight end, we align on the ghost position of the missing tight. We play this defense against teams that play with three backs in the backfield. We have some of those teams in our conference.

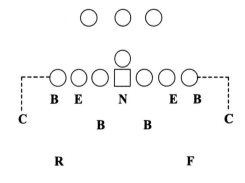

Diagram #6. 5-4 Defense

The corners walk down to a five-yard alignment on the outside. That gives us the four-linebacker look. We play with two safeties over the tight ends. We make our adjustments to whatever the offense may do.

When we went to this defense, we wanted to keep the linebacker reads the same in all the defenses. We move all the other people around in the defense, but we do not change the linebackers. This year, we were blessed with many versatile athletes who could do a lot of things. We had two inside linebackers who will get a chance to play Division I football. We had two defensive linemen who will get a chance to play Division I football. They were good football players. We had an outside linebacker who could go down and play the defensive end. We had a safety who could walk up and play a linebacker position in the 4-4 or 5-4. We were able to accomplish the multiple defenses without changing personnel.

ASSISTANT COACH CRAIG ZUPI: DEFENSIVE LINE

Running a three-man defensive line is tough unless you have some horses playing those positions. They have to be physical and strong. We had those horses. We have a philosophy for our defensive linemen. It says:

> The offensive line draws the line in the sand. That line is the line of scrimmage. We want to control the blocker and take a step over that line. We want to fight and battle them a yard to a yard-and-a-half on their side of the line of scrimmage.

If we can do that, we cut down on the lanes the backs have to run in. We used to teach building a wall at the line of scrimmage. However, that gave the back more ground to work with. We went to a slanting game, but we got too much penetration and were trapped. What we are doing now is cutting down on the running lanes, but not penetrating too far.

Because of the ability of the nose tackle, we let him go deeper across the line of scrimmage. Against

wing-T teams, he forced the center off the line of scrimmage so far the guards could not pull.

Another part of philosophy was to be quick off the ball. Since the offense knows the snap count, they had the advantage of movement. To negate the advantage, we want to be quick. We work on it every day. Everything we do, we do with a ball and a cadence. When we scout teams, we try to get their cadence. We work on that cadence, but more importantly, we work off movement of the ball. I have a ball on a stick. Someone moves that ball in every drill we do.

We have to be physical. This is football. We want to control the blocker and be strong. We want to make sure we move the line of scrimmage a yard on their side of the ball. We read the head of the offensive blockers. That tells the way the play will go.

After the lineman gets off the ball and reads, he has to react. Those three things happen almost instantaneously. He is moving off the ball and reading as he runs. He reacts on the move.

The nose tackle aligns head-up on the center and covers him up. The defensive ends align in an outside eye alignment on the offensive tackle. He wants his inside eye aligned on the outside eye of the tackle. The technique we play on the offensive tackle is jam. We want to move the offensive tackle back off the line of scrimmage one-and-a-half yards. The defensive end wants to play where the offensive tackle's feet were on his original alignment. We want the ends to play read and react from where the offensive linemen's feet were in his stance.

On the jam, I want the inside leg of the defender leading to the crotch of the offensive lineman. We aim at the V of the neck and have a good fit with the face. It is like an offensive block or a bull rush. Since we are on the outside shoulder, the offensive tackle is going to turn out on us or try to get inside to the linebacker.

If the tackle goes inside, they will try to trap the defensive end. Because we are quick and physical, we are not going to let that happen. Because we are strong and physical, we are going to drive the offensive lineman back and let the trapper run into him. We want to get a good fit into the blocker and punch him in the chest to stop his momentum. As we punch, we want to lock out and drive for a couple of steps. I want to get his shoulder going back. If the blocker's shoulders are down, he will come forward.

Sometimes, the offense comes at the 5 technique with a tight end or goes to an unbalanced set to get outside leverage. The defensive end kicks down in his alignment. He moves from the 5 technique to the 4i technique on the offensive tackle. He aligns with his outside eye on the inside eye of the offensive tackle. We call this technique a "big jam." From there, he plays the same technique he played from the 5 technique. We want to step with the foot opposite the gap into the crotch of the offensive lineman. He punches, locks out, and drives to where the offensive tackle's feet were to start with.

That movement is the physical part of the defensive end's technique. While he is doing that technique, he is reading. If the offensive tackle puts his head to the outside on the drive block, that is where the ball is going. If the head is on the outside, the defensive end wants to throw the blocker inside and step across his face. That is why you have to be physical and hit them first. You have to control them, or you get blocked.

We also use a technique called a shake. It is something we throw in to aid the defensive end and nose. The offensive lineman knows we are physical and comes hard at the defensive end. We use a shake move to avoid the blocker. We do a rip or quick swim to avoid the blocker and get on the other side of the line of scrimmage.

Our nose tackle is so physical and beats the centers up so much, we like to use the shake against the center. The center gets so frustrated and pent up to come off the ball and hit the nose that he does not touch him when the nose puts the shake on him. The nose dances around him and into the backfield because the center was not ready for it. In the shake, we are not physical, and we do not jam. We rip or swim and get to the ballcarrier any way we can.

The last technique we use is the rip. We want to be inside-eye-to-outside-eye. If we do not have as quick a player, we want to move more to the outside shoulder of the offensive tackle. The defender throws his flipper and rips up through his outside. He wants to aim at the love handles of the offensive lineman. If the offensive tackle goes down on the linebacker, the defensive end will know that because he will not make as much contact with him. If he feels the inside block, he cannot continue up the field. He has to settle down and look for the trap block coming from the inside.

When you play with a noseguard, he will be double-teamed many times. They double him with their zone-blocking scheme, or double down with the guard trying to get off for the backside linebacker. The nose tackle we had the last couple of years was physical and could take on a double-team. By letting the nose tackle go and getting physical with the center, the double-team block coming down on occasion did not get there. He can split the block and come off in between them. If you do not have the physical noseguard, get down and hold your ground. We want him to create a pile, but not to get blown off the line of scrimmage.

We have to play the trap. By getting into the offensive lineman and controlling him, we can tell if there is a trap block coming. If the defender cannot hold on to the blocker going inside, he does not want to get any more depth in his charge. He has to close down. I teach them a couple of things and let them get good at one of them. The first thing I teach them is to shuffle down, stay low, and plug the hole. If the defender does not want to do that, he can take a step back and swim inside the trap block. He makes the hit on the back or clogs the hole and makes the back bounce the ball. If that happens, the linebacker will come over the top and make the hit on the back.

Another way to play the trap is by wrong-arming. A lot of colleges teach this technique, but I do not know if I like it as well. On a wrong-arm technique, the defender takes his outside arm and leg through the inside of the trap block. He wants to get inside but get vertical at the back. That will bounce the ball, but it also gives the defender a chance to make the play. The reason I do not like that is because the shoulders get turned, and I like to stay square to the line of scrimmage. It is easier to move laterally if you are square.

ASSISTANT COACH VAUGHN PRICE: INSIDE LINEBACKER COACH

I was lucky enough to have two all-league players at inside linebacker. They were two-year starters at inside linebacker and were very physical players. When we look at the 3-4 and 4-4, the inside-linebacker rules did not change. That did a lot for them because they did not have to worry about their alignments in a different defense. Their reads and responsibilities did not change.

I aligned the inside linebackers at five yards off the ball. By the end of the game, they would creep down to four yards. That is where we wanted them to align to start with. If we started at four, by the end of the game they would be to three yards, and we did not want that.

We line them up deep because we wanted to play the run first. From that depth, they could be aggressive and be able to read at the same time. We want them playing downhill and square to the line of scrimmage. We wanted them to be able to take on an isolation block or read a pulling guard. We wanted them to align on the offensive guards. The nice thing about the 3-4 is you get a good read from the guards. We get the initial read from the guards because they are uncovered. You can see right away from the guards where they are going or whether it is a run or pass.

Being over the guard allows the linebackers to fill on the dive up the middle or an isolation block, as well as flowing outside into the C gap. The linebacker is a cut back player and does not want to overrun the ball. The 3-4 defense is designed to funnel everything to the two inside linebackers.

The first read for the inside linebacker is the guard. The guard will tell the linebacker whether it is a run or pass immediately. They can tell if the play is a sweep or trap by the way the guard blocks and pulls. After the first step, the read becomes the

ball. They have to locate the ball and handle their responsibility.

If the inside linebacker can read and pick up the teaching, he can be a very aggressive player. From their guard read, they know where the play is going and do not have to read further. They do not have to think, and it becomes an instinctive skill for these linebackers. We drill this every day.

When we drill this, I have a center and two guards on the offense, I have the two linebackers aligned over the guards. I stand behind the linebackers, and tell the center and guard where to go. We work one step in the drill. The linebackers have to tell me on their first step what type of play it is. When they become instinctive at their reads, they can become aggressive. When you are aggressive, you play with reckless abandon and play very physical.

As far as technique for the linebackers, it starts with the stance and ends with the stance. In the stance, we want the feet slightly wider than the shoulders. We want the knees bent, but we do not want the hands resting on the thighs. We want our hands in an aggressive spot.

The stance allows the linebacker to move quickly. He is focused on the key and ready to move. He can react very quickly from a good stance. In a good stance, it allows the linebacker to stay parallel to the line of scrimmage. Being parallel to the line of scrimmage allows the linebacker to play blocks better. He can blow up the block or play through them. Once you get in a good stance, you want to stay in that stance for the entire play. You want to be in the low spot because in the battle for leverage, the low man wins. When the linebacker takes on a block or makes a tackle, he wants to be in the position he started with. We want him to play with controlled aggression. We want him to fly to the play, but not fly so fast he is out of control. We want him to be able to get back to the stance he started in.

We do a mirror drill of sorts. I get in the position of a running back with the linebackers in their position facing me. I give them directions from side to side, and they have to follow the movement with a shuffle movement, working themselves forward. I want them to keep their shoulders square to the line of scrimmage. When I attack the line of scrimmage, the inside and outside linebackers attack and form a cup around me. They keep their leverage and are under control. When they arrive, I want them in the best position possible to make a tackle or take on an isolation block.

A drill we do for attacking the line of scrimmage is an attack drill. We line them up 20 yards deep. I give them directions with my hand. They have to shuffle from side to side, with the movement of the hands always working forward and keeping their shoulders square to the line of scrimmage. They want to move as fast as they can without crossing their feet. They end up around me in a cup keeping their leverage.

Leverage is what I want to talk about next. Our defense is set up for the plays to be funneled to the inside linebackers. The outside linebackers are trying to turn the plays in, and the inside linebackers are playing from the inside out. An inside-out player is a cutback player. It is critical for him not to overrun a play. He has to do his job. He cannot do someone else's job, and he cannot try to do too much. If there is an isolation block coming up the middle, the linebacker's job is to fill his hole and makes the ball go elsewhere. If he does that, he has done his job. If his flow is into the C gap and D gap, we do not expect him to make the tackle in those gaps. We expect him to be there when the outside linebacker turns the play back to the inside. When he tries to do too much, he puts himself out of position and will not be able to make the play.

When we work pursuit drills and run to the ball, we want them to have good leverage as they arrive at the ball. We do not want them overrunning the ball.

Linebacker must learn how to take on blocks. We use two different types of techniques when taking on a block. We call the first technique the "stun technique." We use this technique on an isolation block from a fullback or a guard coming out on him. The linebacker starts in a good fundamental football position. On contact, we want to punch with our hands underneath the shoulder pads. You do not have to be the strongest player to perform this technique. The punch is used along with the leg and back, which uncoils into the blocker.

Another way we take on a block is a rip technique. If the blocker is trying to reach the linebacker or cut him off, we use the rip technique to escape the block. This is the only time I let the linebacker deviate his shoulders from the line of scrimmage. The linebacker wants to get as low as possible, giving them little surface to hit, and rip through the outside of the blocker. He should end up on the blocker's back hip.

The stun technique is what I like the most, but we use a lot of the rip technique. If the offense tries to cut off the backside linebacker, he uses the rip most of the time.

There are four key points I want you to focus on:

- Stance
- Alignment
- Reads
- Techniques

Alignment and stance allows the linebackers to react and be in position on every play. Once the players get their reads down, the play becomes second nature to them. They can become aggressive if they know their reads. Proper technique allows the linebacker to make a lot of plays and keeps him from being out of position.

COACH ROBB

One of the things that happened when we went to the 3-4 was we started to blitz again. We had gotten away from stunting. Spread teams were forcing our hands with their formations, and wing-T teams were trapping us. It seemed every time we stunted, we got caught in it. With the 3-4 and the four defensive backs, we became more comfortable and started stunting again.

ASSISTANT COACH TERRY BIGHAM: OUTSIDE LINEBACKER COACH

A lot of what we do is the same as the inside linebackers. We practice together many times. The first two phases of our practice is with the inside linebacker, and after that, we split apart and do some things which pertain to the outside linebackers.

When we went to the 4-4 with the wide alignment, that became a big thing for us. We go over the technique repeatedly, but they have a tendency to play where they want to play. We have to watch them carefully from the box to make sure they stay in the alignment they are supposed to play.

When we talk about 4x4, it is important that they are four yards deep and four yards outside. If a team starts to run off-tackle, they want to get closer to the inside. It is important for them to maintain their width. We can bring their alignment in tight if a team is playing with three backs in the backfield and two tight ends. In that case, they may be at 1x1, but that is a rare occasion.

The reason the width is critical is the angle they have to take to get to the football. They are shooting for the D gap. If they align at 4x2, they will overpenetrate and get too far into the backfield. If they are 4x4, they have to pinch down. The closer they are to the line of scrimmage, the farther they will penetrate into the backfield. That opens up running lanes for the offense. The width is more important than the depth. They have to cut the running lane down, and if the angle is not good, we open lanes.

The outside linebacker's reads are simple. We read the end man on the line of scrimmage for a pass/run key. At our position, we start in a shuffle and end in a shuffle. Once they read the play, they fly up to contain it. However, they have to break down, get under control, and get into a shuffle.

Coach Price talked about that drill. We shuffle the linebackers around, show them the ball, and they break, form the cup, and shuffle. All four linebackers should be shoulder-to-shoulder around the ballcarrier.

It teaches them not to cross over. When you do this drill, it should look like all four linebackers are on a string. They should all be synced up as they shuffle.

The outside linebackers are no different from the inside linebackers. They must be physical. When we turn the play inside, we use the forearm to the hip of the blocker. As the linebacker comes to the blocker, he goes through the blocker to the ballcarrier.

The outside linebackers are not always even in their alignment. Their alignment is effected by whom we are playing and what they are doing. In this particular set, the offense sets a wing outside the tight end and a split end to the other side. We bring the outside linebacker up to a 1-by-1 alignment on the wing, and the other outside linebacker is a 4-by-4 alignment outside the tackle on the split-end side.

The most important thing for the outside linebacker is taking on the blocks with the inside shoulder. If they get to his outside shoulder, they will break the containment.

COACH ROBB

Our staff appreciate your attention. We believe in the 3-4 defensive scheme. It has paid dividends for us. We can adjust our fronts, and we have gotten back to our stunting game. If you have any questions, we will be around this weekend.

THE MIDLINE VEER PACKAGE

Webb City High School, Missouri

I appreciate the opportunity to speak here today. I think this is as far east as I have ever spoken. I grew up in Webb City and graduated from Webb City High School. I played football at Pittsburg State in Kansas, which is right down the road. We are a dinosaur in high school football. We are a two-tight-ends, split-backs veer team.

When I played at Pittsburg State, Dennis Franchione was the head coach. He was very influential in what we do at Webb City. He left, and I ended up playing for Chuck Broyles. He gave me my first job. I was a graduate assistant for one year and coached there for six years before I took the job at Webb City.

When I started coaching at Webb City, I was 28 years old. I would like to tell you how bad they were and I built them into a power and won five state championships. That is not the case. They had won three state championships before I ever got there.

We have 12,000 people in Webb City, and Friday night football is a big deal. We will have 5,000 people come to the games. When we come down to the field, 275 youth league players line up as our team walks through them to the field. They all want to play football for Webb City and be one of those players one day.

My children are that age now, and I have been highly involved with that youth program. In those programs and the high school teams, we have 400 kids practicing football in almost the same area. The youth leagues fields are in close proximity to the high school practice fields.

Webb City is a class-4 school and has been for 45 years. We have about 1,100 students. We do not have many Division I players come out of our school.

This year, we have a player going to Oklahoma State. He is not a great player; he is just 6'7" with a 250-pound frame. The majority of our players are what I would describe as good high school football players. The best linemen I have ever coached are in the 5'10" and 220-pound range. On occasion, we get a great football player, but it is not very often. We have had one play at Missouri, one at Kansas State, and one at Southern Illinois.

Most of the time, we do not know the impact we have on players. They do not talk about it, but you never know. I reflect back on my life as a player, and I remember the coaches being there with me every step of the way. It had a tremendous influence on the way I grew up and the way I think today.

One thing that is important for us at Webb City is the coaching staff has been there for eight years. We have added one coach in those eight years, and he moved up from one of our programs. The consistency in the staff has helped us tremendously over those eight years. The consistency with our kids and the summer program has been so important to the success we have had in the football program overall. The consistency helps with what we do as a football team.

We played a spread football team in the playoffs, and I talked to their coach after the game. He told me they had a difficult time in preparation for the game. They did not know how to best defend what we did. They were not used to playing teams that ran the ball as much as we did. They had trouble preparing to defend the option the way we ran it.

We are a two-tight-ends, split-backs veer football team. That is not all we do, but that is our base offense scheme. We can get into a shotgun set, spread the field, and throw the ball if we need to. Our quarterback this past year was our best athlete. When he was in the seventh grade, his coach asked me what position he should play. I told them he was the best athlete they had and to play him at quarterback. He has been a two-year starter for us, and his record is 25-1 as a starter.

I want to talk about two plays today. We call our midline series "mid." Our midline is a double-option play. The mid-veer is a triple-option play. This offense goes back to Pittsburg State. We played in two national championship games while I was there. We won one and lost one. In both of those seasons, we ran the old split-back veer.

The thing that changes the play from year to year is speed. We may block the play three different ways. If we put the wing on the set, we have one more blocker. If we split an end, we have one less blocker, but we have one less defender. Nevertheless, the thing that dictates what we do is the speed of our players.

We are running midline aiming points from a split-backs look. The aiming point for a midline play to the right is the right cheek of the center's butt. Our midline read is the first down lineman on or outside the playside guard. If the guard is covered, we read that man. If you watch film of us and see us block a man in a 2 technique, that is a scheme change. We have calls that adjust the scheme, which lets us run the play a different way.

The defense in the diagram is a 4-3 over defense. The dive back to the side of the play takes a flat step at a 45-degree angle to put him at his aiming point (Diagram #1). The luxury we have with the midline and mid-veer is that from the frontside guard to the backside end, the plays are blocked the same. If you have ever coached option football, the most important thing is timing. The amount of time you have to spend with the quarterback on his reads and meshes is large.

The back away from the call is the lead back. He shuffle-steps across the top of the formation and runs into the gap off the 3-technique defender. The playside tight end performs what we call a "rub block." He has a 6-technique defender head-up in his

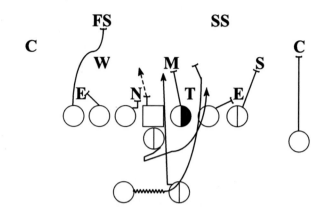

Diagram #1. Midline

alignment. He rips through the outside shoulder of the defender and turns out on the outside linebacker. The playside tackle turns out on the 6-technique defender. The playside guard rips inside the 3 technique and blocks the frontside linebacker. The center and backside guard combination block on the shade nose to the backside linebacker. The backside tackle blocks out on the 7 technique on the backside. The backside tight end releases off the line of scrimmage and blocks the free safety.

On the G-front with the nose in a 2i technique on the guard, we tell the center to block backside and get out of the way.

If the quarterback is facing out to the right, he pushes out with his left foot to the left side of the center. That gets him into the left A gap. He opens with his right foot and steps back to clear the center and path of the dive back. His eyes are on the handoff key the entire time.

These are high school players, and they need to be taught every step. They align, straddling the inside leg of the guard. The speed of the back will determine the depth off the line of scrimmage. The fast backs we move back, and the slow backs we move up. The dive back starts out running inside cones aligned on his path. Before we moved on to our turf field, I used to paint lines for them to follow. The timing on an option play depends on the backs being at the same place every time we run the play.

The defense we see the most is the 52 defense (Diagram #2). If the guard is not covered, the read is the first down lineman outside that position. It does not matter whether it is a 4-, 5-, or 6-technique defender. The playside guard, center, and backside guard triple-team the nose. Both guards are stepping to the center with their shoulders square to the line of scrimmage. The playside tackle comes inside and blocks the playside linebacker. The tight end locks on the 9-technique defender and blocks him.

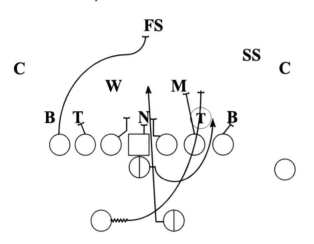

Diagram #2. Midline vs. 52 Defense

The noseguard will do one of three things. He will play to the strongside, the weakside, or slant one way or the other. The guards read his movement and react accordingly. The talent of your center will determine what type of blocking scheme they use. This past year, our center was not as good as the ones we have had in the past. When we played teams with outstanding noses, we had to build additional schemes in to help the center.

The backside tackle blocks the 5 technique to his side, and the backside tight end releases for the safety back. The lead back shuffles over and leads up on the frontside linebacker. That is the quarterback isolation.

In our offense, we do a lot of scheme adjustments to our blocking. We have a scheme adjustment on this play with the tight end covered and the guard uncovered. We use a G-scheme, which I will show you later.

Against the 5-3 defense, we have a load scheme (Diagram #3). We block the center stack like the nose triple-team. Both the guards are stepping to the center and up on the middle linebacker. This

picks up the angle stunts from the stack linebacker and nose. If the nose goes one way and the linebacker the other, we have that covered. The playside tackle releases inside for the stack linebacker. The tight end locks on the 9-technique defender and blocks him.

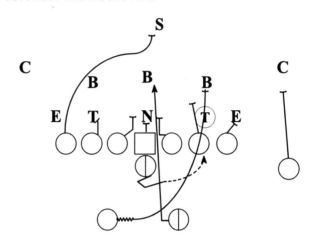

Diagram #3. Midline vs. 5-3 Defense

Our fullback is deaf. He wears a hearing aid, which gives him about 50 percent hearing. He reads lips. He struggles in school, but he is a good player. We do not have a bunch of rocket scientists playing for us. We did have a player last year who got an academic scholarship to Arkansas.

One of our blocking adjustments we use is a fold block by the tackle and tight end (Diagram #4). If the Sam linebacker is inside stacked on the 7-technique defender, we fold block the play. The playside tackle blocks out on the 7-technique defender, and the tight end folds inside for the Sam linebacker. Everything else on the play remains the same.

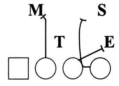

Diagram #4. Fold Block

On the mid-veer, we read the first down lineman head-up to outside the guard. The next man outside, we are going to kick out. However, if we get a 3, 5, and 9 technique, we read the 3 technique and lock on to the 5 and 9 techniques. Because of what we do offensively, it is not uncommon for us to get a six-man front or a three-man down side on the line of scrimmage.

With the mid-veer, the blocking assignments for the playside guard to the backside end are the same as the midline option. However, the quarterback reads the handoff key, which is the first down lineman on or outside the guard (Diagram #5). If he pulls the ball, he has a pitch key outside. The playside tackle releases on the playside linebacker, and the tight end arc or veer releases for the support player. In this defense, the quarterback reads the 3 technique and pitches off the 6 technique.

One of the blocking adjustments we use is to block the tight end on the 6-technique defender. That allows quarterback to bring the ball outside and options off the force defender. If teams bring the linebacker up to the line of scrimmage, we make that adjustment many times.

On the 50 front, all the blocks for the mid-veer are the same from the playside tackle to the backside end as the midline play (Diagram #6). The only difference is the tight end's block. Instead of blocking the 9-technique defender, the tight end veer releases to the force player. The quarterback reads the 5-technique defender and pitches off the 9-technique defender.

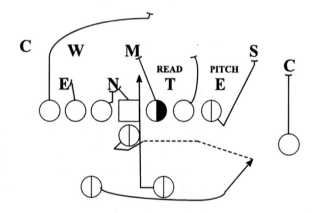

Diagram #5. Mid-Veer vs. 4-3 Over

On the backside, the center and backside guard combination block on the shade nose. The playside guard is responsible for the playside linebacker but very seldom blocks him. If the playside linebacker blitzes the A gap, he blocks him. Most of the time, he picks up the backside linebacker and the lead back blocks him on the midline. On the mid-veer, unless the linebacker blitzes the A gap, the tackle blocks him. When we first started running the veer, we double-teamed or zone-blocked the 3 technique and read the next man outside.

Most of the time, we are outweighed by the defensive teams we play against. The center and backside guard have to double-team most of the noses we play against. They may not be able to come off on the backside linebacker. The playside guard generally blocks him.

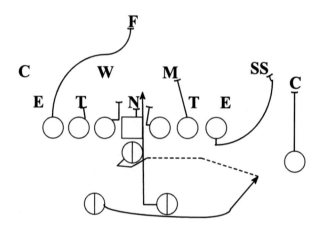

Diagram #6. Mid-Veer vs. 50 Front

The tackle's technique for getting inside the 5 technique is a rip technique. We have named that technique "Jack the Ripper." It is something our kids like and have fun with.

Against the 5-3 or 3-3 defense, the blocking is the same from the tackle to the backside end (Diagram #7). If there is no support player outside of the tight end, he takes an inside release. He knows the 9-technique defender is the force player in this defense. He inside releases and checks the 5-technique stacked linebacker. If the tackle has the linebacker, he goes up to the free safety. If the tackle has not blocked the linebacker, he blocks him.

The important thing for us is from a personnel standpoint. If the defensive tackle and outside linebacker are great players, we do not have to

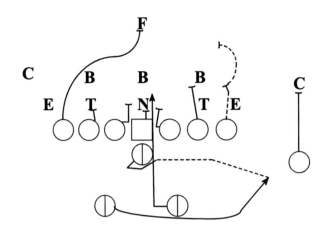

Diagram #7. Mid-Veer vs. 53 Front

block either one of them. We read the first one and pitch off the second one. We do not have to try to block a great athlete.

In our schemes, we try to keep things very simple. We rep the plays repeatedly until we can do them almost perfectly. Our normal splits for the offensive line are two, two, and three feet. That can change for the tackles and tight ends. The split between the guard and center remain two feet, but the tackle can adjust his split up to three feet, depending on what the defender will do. The tight end can use his discretion as to what split he can take. Splits in the offensive line are personnel adjustments and defensive reactions to splits.

I never want an offensive lineman to have less than a one-foot split. Tightening the splits is a security issue for the players. They feel they will not get beat inside if they tighten the split. I wear a size-12 shoe. If I cannot step between the gaps, they are in trouble.

Against the 4-3 front, if the Sam linebacker is inside in the C gap, the tackle has that assignment on him. The tight end veer releases to the outside and has the assignment on the strong safety. However, we tell him to never pass up a defender to get to another one. If the Sam linebacker scrapes to the outside, the tight end will block him.

I want to show you one thing we did against a team that beat us in the playoffs. In 2007, we were 10-0 and lost in the first round of the playoffs on a 39-yard field goal as time expired. The player made a

great play, and we lost by one point. In that game, we ran an outside veer adjustment. They played a 4-3 defense and were giving us trouble with our outside-veer scheme. We double-teamed the 3 technique and locked on the 6-technique defender with the tight end. We read the Sam linebacker on the outside veer. If he took the dive back, we pulled the ball.

Our tight end this year was a very good football player. He was 6'3" and 210 pounds. He was very smart and could execute this play well. We run an adjustment to the midline if the defender on the guard gets too tight (Diagram #8). If he moves down into a tight 3 technique or a 2 technique, we G-scheme the play and do not read. The play becomes quarterback isolation. The tackle blocks down on the 3-technique defender. The tight end rips through the 6-technique defender to the inside linebacker. The playside guard pulls and kicks out the 6-technique end.

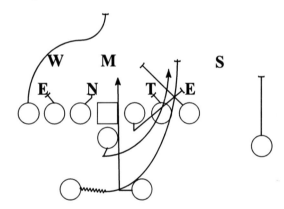

Diagram #8. G-Scheme

The dive back runs on the midline, and the quarterback fakes that play. The lead back shuffles across the top and leads the quarterback outside the down block of the tackle.

We have another adjustment we use if we think the playside linebacker is going to blitz (Diagram #9). We do want the lead back to take on a linebacker on a blitz in the hole. We exchange assignments with the lead back and the tight end. We send the tight end down on the linebacker and bring the lead back outside to load the 9 technique.

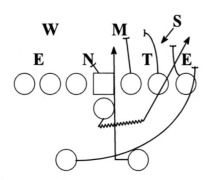

Diagram #9. Lead Back/Tight End Exchange

We have a number of scheme adjustments we make during a game (Diagram #10). If defense brings the 3 technique into a 1 technique, we can call the center playside and double-team the 1 technique to the backside linebacker. On this particular play, the center comes onside and the tight end folds inside because the linebacker was inside. We blocked the play solid, and there is no read.

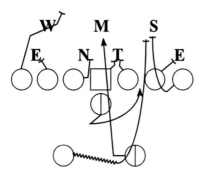

Diagram #10. Line Adjustment

We have one wrinkle off this play. We run it from the one-back set (Diagram #11). The quarterback fakes the midline to the right and brings the ball back to the left side into the B gap. It is a misdirection play with no lead back.

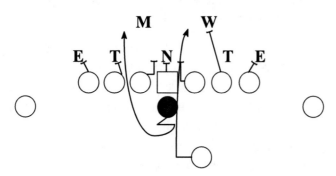

Diagram #11. Quarterback Counter

On the dive back and quarterback exchange on the midline, the dive back has to stay on his track. He cannot deviate from that path. The quarterback has to step off the midline to let the dive back run his track. The quarterback has to reach back as far as he can so he can put the ball in and ride the dive back.

On the veer, if the quarterback pulls the ball, the distance to the pitch key is important. If the pitch key is close, the quarterback has to be ready to pitch the ball immediately. When we pitch the ball, the quarterback gives a shuffle-step before he delivers the pitch.

We work our read drill every day for 20 to 40 minutes (Diagram #12). We have two quarterbacks in the drill. One is the snapper, and the other runs the play. A coach stands across the line of scrimmage and is the read key. The quarterback snaps the ball and reads the coach. The coach steps in, does nothing, and turns his shoulder or steps forward. The quarterback works on his footwork and reads the coach.

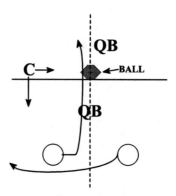

Diagram #12. Read Drill

We teach the quarterback to look for the numbers on the jersey of the defense for a key to the read. If he sees the front number, that is a give key. If he sees the small number on the sleeve, that is a pull key. If there is no movement, we give the ball. If there is movement across the line of scrimmage, we give the ball.

We want the quarterback in a balanced stance under the center. However, we do not overcoach that point. Our quarterback this past year had a broken foot at one time and felt more comfortable in a slight staggered stance.

I want the ball placed in the back's belly. I want the defender to see the ball in the back's belly. When the quarterback steps back, he has to extend the ball behind his back hip. I want him to ride the ball to the front hip before he pulls it. However, I do not want him to pass his front hip on the ride.

When we pitch the ball, I want the quarterback to carry the ball in the middle of his chest with his arms bent. When he pitches the ball, it comes from his chest in a one-handed chest pass with the thumb down. When we teach the pitch, we tell the quarterback to pitch and drift. That puts the quarterback going in the direction of the pitch. If it is a bad pitch, he has a chance to get the ball. We tell the quarterback he has to get the pitch between the waist and the shoulder pads of the pitch receiver. We do not want the ball pitched above the shoulder of the running back.

If you ever have any questions about what we do, I would be happy to show you our scheme. I appreciate the opportunity, and thanks for listening.

SELF-SCOUTING: OFFENSIVE KEYS TO SUCCESS

Perry High School, Ohio

I have been coming to this clinic for a number of years. I'll tell you, there is one reason I am standing up here today. I represent a group called *WAC*. That stands for "Wives Against Clinics." Ten years ago, I almost ended my whole clinic circuit because of the birth of my first child.

I used to go to every clinic known to man. I went all over the place. I went to every spring practice and every clinic I possibly could. I wanted to learn the game of football. I was a football junkie. I had a disease. Once you have that disease, it stays with you forever. It has been passed on to my son. He has the disease too. Poor little guy—all he wants to do is football, football, and football. It is a serious problem.

After the first child, my calendar started to fill up with birthday parties. Every Saturday, I needed to go to some kid's birthday party. One year, the Coach of the Year Clinic was coming up and my disease took over. I told my wife we needed to get away. I suggested we take the child and go to a hotel for a weekend. We could sit out by the pool and relax. She thought that was a great idea.

We got to the hotel and checked in. We were sitting out by the pool when she began to notice the big guys carrying a huge cooler of beer. The guys were talking to one another, and they were all calling each other "Coach." It dawned on her that she was at a coaching clinic. I told her it was the Coach of the Year Clinic, and I had to go. She did not speak to me for a week.

Now, I cannot go to a clinic and stay overnight without my family. It is a law and part of WAC. They are outside picketing.

Perry High School is on Lake Erie, about 20 miles east of Cleveland. It is like a college campus. We play in Division IV in the Ohio playoff system. There are six divisions. There are 600 students in our high school. The facilities are truly unbelievable, and the students are outstanding.

This past season, we ended up 11-2. We lost to the eventual state champion in the regular season and lost in the quarterfinal game in the state playoffs. Both games were extremely competitive, but we came up on the short end.

In 13 years as head coach at Perry, I have never had a Division I football player. I have had three players go to West Point. I did have a player go to the University of Florida.

This year, we had a player score 40 touchdowns. He is six-feet tall and weighs 180 pounds. He is very smart and is going to Lehigh University. At Perry, we do not have outstanding athletes. They are players that play extremely hard and with great intensity. They are what I call good high school football players.

We are a no-huddle team. I truly believe the faster we go, the better we play. We are under the center 60 percent of the time, and that is by design. The other 40 percent of the time, we are in the shotgun. We have a 60/40 percent run-to-pass ratio.

To be successful, you have to communicate with players, but you have to score points. We do some things in our offense that are considered to be unorthodox. We do it for the entertainment of the fans. Tickets are six dollars, and you have to give them something for their money. We try to entertain as much as we can with the things we do.

Coaches, if you can answer yes to any of these questions, you may have my disease. Have you ever tried to install a play in your offense because you thought it looked cool? You saw the play on TV and wanted to install it because it looked cool. Boise State against Oklahoma caused a lot of teams to install the wraparound draw play they ran.

How many coaches have installed a play on Thursday night for a Friday game? How many of you have developed a scheme and predicated your whole offense on it because you did not think the defense could align to it? If you have ever done any of those things, listen to me, I think I can help.

This is how I got help for my disease. In 1999, I read a book entitled *Developing an Offensive Game Plan* by Brian Billick. The only book I am allowed to read now is *The Little Engine That Could*. Brian Billick's book is on my nightstand beside my bed. That book changed my life and saved my coaching career. If I had not read that book, I would have been fired by now. In the book, he poses the question, "How do you know if you have too much offense?"

I had gone to clinics and had a menagerie of plays that I wanted to run. When I became head coach in 1996, I tried to do all the things I had collected over the years. In my first three years, we were 11-19. We were not winning, and I decided I had to work harder and amass more knowledge.

When I read the Billick book, it changed my life. He said to list every play in your playbook and every play you ran that year. He said to set up a chart on the running plays you ran. I listed every play I ran from 1996 to 1998.

Self-Scouting Run Chart						
Play	Total	Yds.	1-3	4-11	12+	Yds./Rush

On the chart, you list each play. Then, you list the total number of times you ran the play. You record the number of times the play lost yards, gained 1 to 3 yards, gained 4 to 11 yards, and gained over 12 yards. The last thing you list is the yards per carry the play averaged.

I filled out my chart, and what I found out was disturbing to me. In that period, I ran 25 different running plays. When I did the research, I added setting a goal as criteria to this plan. You need to set a goal for every play you have in your offense. You need to know what you are trying to achieve with the play. You need to know what the play is designed to accomplish.

Let me give you an example. Let us compare two plays. If we ran the wedge and jet plays 20 times each, here are the averages for each play. On the wedge, we averaged 2.6 yards per carry, but it never lost yardage. On the jet play, we averaged 6.4 yards per carry but 8 of the 20 times, it lost yardage on the play. Do those plays belong in your playbook? Those are the decisions I had to make.

Three years ago, I did a study on one of our best plays. I took our base run play, which is the power and used the criteria to learn about the play.

Play	Total	Yds.	1-3
Power	92 R.	9	27
	4-11	**12 +**	**Yds./Rush**
Power	36	2	7.6

The power play was 25 percent of all our running plays. It lost yardage 10 percent of the time. The play gained 1 to 3 yards 29 percent of the time. Thirty-six times, the play gained 4 to 11 yards for 39 percent. Twenty times the play gained over 12 yards, which was 22 percent. The play averaged 7.6 yards a carry. The play gained more than four yards 61 percent of the time.

The goal I had set for the play was four yards per carry. A play that averages four yards a run is a good play. It is a good play if it averages more than four yards 50 percent of the time.

If you look at our power play, it gained 7.6 yards a carry and gained four yards 61 percent of the time. That is a good play, and I need to run it. I did the same thing with my protection. That is where it started to get a bit dicey because I like to throw the ball.

The first thing you have to look at is how many times you actually call a protection. If you have more than one protection, you can look at the percentages of their effectiveness. We use the same method as we did with the run.

Protections Chart				
Prot	**%**	**A/C**	**Called**	**Int.**
Sack	**Pen**	**Scram**	**Yds.**	**Avg.**

First, we list the protection being used. The second thing we look at is how many times we complete the pass using that protection. We list the attempts and completions for that protection. The number of times we called the protection is important. The last thing we want to know is the results of the protection. We want to know if we were intercepted, sacked, had a penalty, or if the quarterback had to scramble. Then, we list the yards we got while using the protection and the average yards per catch.

When you start to factor some of these things into a protection, you may begin to wonder why you use the protection. From 1996 to 1998, I used eight protections. That, obviously, was too many. Today, we have man protection when we are in the shotgun and a three-step protection when we are under the center.

Man Protection				
Prot	**%**	**A/C**	**Called**	**Int.**
Mn	70	59/84	93	3
Sack	**Pen**	**Scram**	**Yds.**	**Avg.**
4	5	1	608	10.3

Our goal when we use this protection is to average 65 percent completions and average 10 yards a catch. In our man protection, we ran the protection 93 times. We completed 70 percent of our passes with three interceptions, four sacks, five penalties, and one scramble. The play averaged 10.3 yards per catch. In this example, the protection was a good protection.

If you are a sprint-out team, you need to know the percentage of completions sprinting right as opposed to sprinting left. If your quarterback cannot throw going to his left, why practice that protection and throw? If he can only throw going to the right, practice that and get good at it. If your completion numbers are bad going to the left, why waste the time running the play in that direction? Spend the time becoming good at going right.

From 1996 to 1998, I ran 24 different route combinations. Today, I am down to 10 routes. We'll look at our patterns. The first pattern is the *hitch*. If we cannot complete a hitch, we have a serious problem. If we are not completing 80 percent of our hitches, we have some issues. This year, we averaged 68 percent on our hitch patterns. We threw 28 hitches and completed 19 of them. Our goal on the hitch pattern is 10 yards. We averaged 14.1 yards per catch. I wish our percentage had been better, but it gained 14 yards a catch. We consider that a good route.

When you are not meeting the goals for plays, it is one of three things. It is the *talent* you are playing, the *scheme* you are using, or it is the *coaching* that is going on. If the play is breaking down, it is due to one of these things: your talent is not good enough to run the play, the scheme is not a good scheme for high school, or you do not understand the play and cannot coach it. If you will study your offense, you may have to identify some of those issues and make those determinations.

When you throw the football, you need to know where the ball is going. There are three depth areas or zones you need to be aware of. Those zones are 0 to 5 yards, 6 to 15 yards, and over 16 yards. You need to know the numbers in each area. You must take each area and look at what is going on. In each zone, there are left, middle, and right areas. You need to know where the ball is going and how good you are at completing the pass in those zones.

If you look at the examples, we were 5 to 9 to the left and 6 to 18 to the right. If you examine this statistic, you can come up with some conclusions about how efficient your pass offense is. If you are not throwing the ball to certain zones, you need to explore ways to get the ball into that area.

I am embarrassed to tell you this: In 1997, we threw the ball 120 times, and 84 of those throws were into the 6 to 15 area to the right side. I had no idea we were doing that. That explains why we were 11-19 in those three years.

I got married in 1995 and became a head coach in 1996. We did not have children at that time, and I was addicted to football. I ran 25 different running plays in those three years, and seven of them I ran 20 times. There were 18 plays in our offense that I ran less than two times in a game. I had a problem. I loved the plays, but I never ran them.

When I did run the plays, they lost yardage. The reason for that is simple. We did not run the plays enough to establish any consistency. We were spending all our time working on things we did not use. I had eight protection schemes. I only ran three of them more than 20 times a season. That tells you there were five protections I ran less than two times a game. I had 24 routes in my offense. I ran five of those routes 10 times. There were 19 routes in my playbook that I did not run once.

We went to practice every day and practiced those routes but never ran them. I averaged 51 offensive plays per game and 19.4 points in that time. I was on the verge of getting fired. I was going to more clinics trying to figure out why we were not winning. It was right under my nose. All I had to do was look at our stats. I was overcoaching beyond comprehension.

I felt I was a good communicator and teacher. I was trying to do all those different things and wondering why our players were not winning.

After I read Billick's book, I had a difficult time cutting the offense. I went from 25 to 16 running plays. I went from eight protections to six. Of the 16 running plays, only six of them I ran 20 times. Of the six protections, I ran three more than 20 times. I cut the routes down from 24 to 18. Of the 18 routes, I ran five of them more than 10 times.

In 1999, I went to the no-huddle offense. The average plays went from 51 plays a game to 57 plays a game. The points per game went from 19 to 24 points a game. During that time, our record went to 19-13, and the school made the playoffs for the first time in school history. Things were going better.

I went to the no-huddle because we were always late getting to the line of scrimmage. We started at the line and the plays came quicker.

From 2000 to 2005, I cut our running plays down to 10 plays. I figured if we did less, we would get better at what we did. I looked at the statistics of each play we were running. If it was not a good play, I got rid of it. We did well, and 8 of the 10 runs we ran over 20 times. Of the six protections, I ran five of them over 20 times. I ran 24 routes in 1996, and I am down to 13 routes, in which 9 of the 13 I ran 10 times. Our play count was up to 59 plays a game, and the point total was up to 27 points a game. In that time, our record was 30-13. We were getting better and winning football games.

I do not go to as many football clinics, and I am reading Dr. Seuss instead of football books. I am working less and winning more. Obviously, the reason is that I have simplified everything for our players. We are not running so much offense. They can concentrate on the plays we actually run in a game. We are still running 10 plays, but we run 9 of the 10 more than 20 times a game. We have four protections and run all of them at least 20 times a season. We are down to 10 routes and have run eight of them 10 times in the games.

Over the last three-year period, we are averaging 59 plays and 34 points a game. Our record over the past three years is 29-5. The only thing I can figure is the more children I have, the more games I win. I presented the issue to my wife. I told her if I have a few more children, I may never lose.

I have 10 runs which I run all the time. I have four protections that I use all the time. I have to run the no-huddle because I have to get practice done so I can get home. If I have more children, we will average about 100 points a game because I will not have time to coach all those plays I did for years.

The whole point of this lecture is we cut our offense from 25 running plays in 1996 to 10 plays in 2008. We went from eight protection schemes to four schemes. Our pass routes went from 24 to 10 routes. Now, we only coach what we run. We do not waste time in trying to do too much. You can only do what your players can handle.

If you will start to chart the plays you are running, you will be stunned. We practiced one protection eight minutes a day but only ran it five times the entire season. Is the time worth the effort? The answer is "No." When it comes down to a play to define the game, you will run what you know. You always run what you believe in.

That is all part of scouting. Find that out about your opponent—he will do the same thing. When the game is on the line, you do not run a play you have practiced five or six times. You run the staple play of your offense. You run the play that defines you as a football team.

In my conference, we have a bunch of good coaches that have been in that position for some time. We know each other. I know in a fourth-and-one situation what these coaches are going to run. They are not going to change. It is what they believe in and what they are. I like to think I am the same way. The coaches I play against in our league know me better than I know me.

The numbers are the reason we practice the way we do. Because of that, we have had some success. I want to give you some points about how you can start to figure out some things about yourself.

- Know how many snaps you take in a football game.
- Know how many possessions you have in the game.
- Know how many first-down plays you get in a ball game.
- Know the number of third-and-long and third-and-short situations you get in a football game.

We get the ball 11 times a game. That is how many times we average getting the ball. You will get 24 first-down plays in a football game. Forty percent of all your plays are going to be first-down plays. You can come up with those plays on Monday. If you have a base package, as I do, with 10 running plays, the first-down play is already done for the entire year. I do not have a game plan. I know exactly what I am going to run. The only thing I do is jazz up the formations.

When I watch film, I watch it for tendencies. We are a no-huddle team and the defense has to adjust to us. I could care less what you run. I am going to dictate to the defense. Teams can blitz me nine thousand different ways. I cannot figure all those out. All I know is the defense better adjust to what we do. I am going to run our base package and go as fast as we can.

If you are a good football team, I will set up tendencies to break the defense. Teams I know I can beat, I will do the same thing repeatedly. I know the good teams will take those plays and put them in a computer. What they come out with is a tendency. In the big football game, I will break that tendency and hurt the defense on it. You set things up to hurt good football teams. That is how you win the big games.

We went from 51 plays a game to 59 plays a game. Our average now is 54 plays a game, and that is not a bad thing. I thought the ideal number of plays would be 60 plays. I found out that is not necessarily a good thing. Larry Kehres, from Mount Union College, opened my eyes to a new concept. My entire strategy was to get to 60 plays or 11 possessions in a game. This is the law: 40 percent of all plays run in a football game are first-down plays. There will be six third-and-long plays in a game. That is, 10 percent of the plays in a game will be third-and-long. You face three third-and-short yardage plays in a football game. If you are only getting three plays that are third-and-short yardage plays in a game, you need to think about how much time you are spending on that situation in practice.

If you practice from the same place in practice, start to move the ball with relationship to the hash marks. I can tell by looking at your practice field if you are one of those coaches. If there is no grass in one spot, you are not moving the ball around.

I did the research. This is nine years of data, which comes from 5372 plays. Of those plays, 29 percent came from the left hash, 34 percent from the middle, and 37 percent from the right hash mark. When I look at these stats, I determine there will be equal number of snaps coming from all three positions on the field. You cannot practice in only one place on the field.

Here is my thinking about game planning. I know that 40 percent of 60 plays is 24 plays. That means there will be 24 first-down plays in a game. I know that eight plays will come from the left hash mark, eight plays from the middle, and eight plays from the right hash mark.

On first down, I want to be 50 percent run and 50 percent pass. How many times have you scouted a team and they are 98 percent run on first down? If they are setting me up, they will burn me big-time because I am going to play run on first down. If I am going to be 50/50 run to pass on first down, I must have four runs and four passes from the left hash mark.

If I throw the ball on first down, I have to know the protection scheme. On first down, I want to throw a high-percentage pass or play-action. That means I will be in man protection or play-action protection. That is the only protection I will use on first down. I plan the same thing for the middle of the field and the right hash mark. That is how I call the first-down play.

I leave that the same for the first five games of the year. The only thing I change is formation. I doctor the formation to make them appear different. I break the plays into gun and under positions for the quarterback. I have a shotgun run and pass and an under-center run and pass. I know exactly the plays I am going to run. There are only 10 running plays to choose from for me.

On third-and-long, I have three plays from the hash marks and the middle. There are only seven third-and-long situations in a game; therefore, I only need three plays from each hash mark. On third-and-short, I have one play from each hash mark. There are only three short-yardage plays in a game. That is how we do it. I plug those plays into the script, and that is how we practice. We practice the situations, and that is all we practice. Unless it is on the script, we do not practice it. We are not going to practice things we are not going to do in a game.

The more you narrow things down and the less you practice, the better you will be. We only run in the game the things we have practiced. On third-and-one, we are not going to pull something out of the air. On third-and-one, the players know what we are going to run. They believe in it because they have practiced it all week.

I have some things here I call "openers" and "must-runs." The openers are where I allow our players to have some fun. People think we are wide open and do all kinds of crazy things. We try to screw with teams. We create things that cause chaos and make people think we do crazy things. In reality, the players come up with the plays and goofy names, and we go out and run one on the opening play. An example of an opener is a "hook and ladder." We put them in on Thursday night. The defense stops focusing in on the base things we do and are looking at the openers.

The must-runs are plays that we absolutely have to run in a game. You have to practice situations rather than plays. The bottom line is *less is more*. The less you have, the more you will win. I call these the 10 commandments of coaching. I stole every one of them from someone.

TEN COMMANDMENTS

- Thou shalt control the tempo.
- Thou shalt handle defenses.
- Thou shalt attack any defender.
- Thou shalt run the clock when ahead.
- Thou shalt be able to play catch-up from behind.
- Thou shalt score in the red zone.
- Thou shalt attack any hole or coverage with two different plays.
- Thou shalt get the ball in the hands of our best players.
- Thou shalt handle third-and-one.
- Thou shalt handle third-and-long.

We will handle any defensive scheme that the defense runs. We will attack any defender. The only reason we watch film is to find the weak links. If we are a better team, I am not concerned. If you are a good football team, I am going to focus where you are weak.

If you do not have an idea about what to do when you are ahead, that is when games are lost. That is when they are exciting to watch. That is the situation where there is only four minutes left in the game, and the defense knows you want to run the ball. You must have the answer for that situation.

How many times have you lost a football game and realized the best athlete did not touch the ball? I make a major attempt to get the ball into our best player's hands. Everybody reads the paper. If I read a player carried the ball 32 times, I want to know where he lines up. If a player gets the ball 48 percent of the time, we want to know the plays he runs. I want to know what passes the quarterback actually completed. We work on those passes.

If I have a stud tailback on my team, I am going to get the ball to him. If I am running 60 plays a game, 40 percent are going to be pass plays. That means the quarterback has to complete 60 percent of his 24 passes. I have to call plays that will fit those numbers. If I want my tailback to get 20 carries, the fullback to get 12 carries, and the quarterback to get eight carries, I have to build that into the script. I do not want to read in the paper the next day, after we lost the game, that our star tailback only carried the ball eight times. The reason we lost the game will be my fault.

If you follow our games, you will see exactly how I have built the game plan. You have to look at how many times certain people touch the ball. We will throw the ball 16 to 18 times a game. The tailback will touch the ball 18 to 20 times. The fullback will have 12 to 15 carries, and the quarterback will have four to eight rushes.

The ninth and tenth commandments are what I had to learn the hard way. I am going to show you what Brian Billick said about those situations. We have three third-and-shorts and seven third-and-

longs in a game. On third down, Brian Billick said you should be able to convert 38 to 40 percent of the time. On third-and-short, 75 to 85 percent of the time is good. If you can do that, you are a good team. On third-and-long, the conversion rate is 20 to 25 percent of the time. If it is third-and-eight and you convert one out of four times, that is great.

In 1998, we converted on third down 32 percent of the time. We went 13-26 on third-and-short. That is 50 percent. We could not understand why we were so unsuccessful in that situation. We had to look at talent, scheme, or coaching. When I broke the play down, my play calling was all over the place.

Do you run the wedge play or a jet play? The wedge play averaged 2.6 a carry, and the jet play averaged 6.4 yards a carry. The wedge never lost a yard in 20 carries. The jet play lost yardage 8 out of 20 times we ran it. Have an idea what your plays are designed to do, and know the situations to use them.

If I am averaging 14 yards on the hitch pattern, is that the best play to run in a third-and-nine situation? The hitch is designed to gain 10 yards, but is it the best play to call? Those are things to consider. If I have an athlete at the receiver's position, I want to give him the ball and let him go. It is an 80 percent completion rate, and he can move the ball.

In 1998, we were 26 percent in the third-and-long situation. I thought that was good until I looked at the number of times we were in that situation. We were in third-and-long 72 times on average.

We are converting the third-and-short play 87 percent of the time. It is simply because of the plays we select, and they are the only ones we run on third-and-short. On third-and-long, we are up to 32 percent which is good.

I asked Larry Kehres what he did in third-and-long situations. He told me if I was struggling in third-and-long not to get in third-and-long situations. The reason you are in third-and-long is because you did not do a good job on first down. If you do a good job on first down, you will not be in third-and-long. If you are not in third-and-long, you will pick up the first down.

If you gain four yards on first down, that is the goal for a first-down play. If you run the ball on first down, you will get four yards 45 percent of the time. If you throw the ball on first down, you need to get four yards 60 percent of the time.

You have 24 first-down plays a game. You can start working on them today and have them ready to practice the first day of spring practice. Try to be as good as you can on first down.

A lot of people talk about scripting plays. I script for big games. There are certain games you know are big games. I script eight plays for the first possession. I script eight plays for the second possession. I script against the tendency I have established. In the pressure situation, I call it from the call sheet based on what we have worked on.

There is another factor you have to consider. It is becoming a big factor in today's offenses. Explosive plays are runs over 12 yards and passes over 16 yards. I created a stat called "explosion percentage." You get that from dividing the number of plays you run into the explosion plays you have in a game. My goal for 10 years was to run 60 plays a game. This year, we averaged 14 explosion plays and 54 plays a game. I would rather have the explosion percentage to be higher than the number of plays run in a game.

I am not interested in driving the ball 80 yards in 15 plays. I do not care about time of possession. If you can go 80 yards in 15 plays, it tells me you are a disciplined football team. It also tells me you do not have any playmakers. I want to score as fast as I possibly can. If you are running 50 plays a game and 20 percent of them are explosion plays, you are a good football team.

Coach Kehres and Mount Union College played SUNY Cortland in the regional finals and Cortland ran 78 plays. Mount Union ran 38 plays and won the football game. If they did not have the explosion plays, they might not have won that game. Explosion percentage is a big number for me.

The most important number I use is the "error factor." Ralph Friedgen of Maryland is the one credited with this factor. To get the error factor, you add the number of plays and divide by the number of plays run in the game. If you are under 12 percent, you will win 100 percent of your games. The plays you add together are:

- Number of negative-yardage plays
- Number of penalties
- Number of dropped balls
- Number of turnovers

I can tell whether we won or lost from the number of negative plays we had on offense and the number we produced on defense. If we had six negative plays, three penalties, one dropped ball, and two turnovers, that is 12 negative plays. If we ran 60 plays in the game, our error factor is 20 percent. If you can get that figure to around 12 percent, you will win every game.

If you can eliminate negative plays from your offense, you will win a lot of games. As I told you in the beginning, I have a disease which can lead to an epidemic. Are you thinking, *I love this play, but can our players do it?* The play may look good on paper, but can you coach that play? You have to look in the mirror, and you must know your offense better than anybody.

There is one thing that can affect everyone, regardless of your scenario. If you have players coming back on your team, you better know what they do well and have some idea of what they did well last year. If they did not do things well, find out why not. Was it talent, scheme, or coaching?

If you had all seniors and have seniors replacing them, you are a good football coach with a deep program. If you find yourself in a situation with untested players, go with a few plays and keep it basic. Take baby steps, and bring them along slowly. Know your scheme and coach them up. It is up to you and your coaches to find a cure for the ills of your team. The last warning I have for you is this: Do not get caught up in overcoaching. When you find something you like, go find the people that do it the best and study with them. Just remember less is more 99 percent of the time.

Thank you.

George Smith

TRIPLE OPTION AND COMPLEMENTARY PLAYS

McKeesport Area High School, Pennsylvania

I plan to talk about the triple op-tion and all types of option plays that complement it. If you are run-ning the option now and what you are using works for you, stay with that scheme. There are so many ways to run the option. I am going to tell you how I teach it and the plays I use in the scheme.

We start out by teaching the base option play. We do not run the base option, but we use it as a teaching tool to get everyone into the proper movement and areas. We practice the varsity and junior varsity on the same field. The days the varsity practices offense, the junior varsity practices defense. The next day, the varsity practices defense, and the junior varsity practices offense. The junior varsity may spend a week practicing the base option.

The second thing we teach is the triple option to the tight end side. We continue teaching the triple option and add it to the split end side. If we do anything that is different from most people, it is the triple option to the tight end. We run the midline option to the tight end and the split end. We run a called dive, which is the wide veer running play. We run the double option to the tight end and split end sides. We also run the quick pitch or toss to the tight end and split end sides.

KEY TERMS TO UNDERSTAND

- Read key, pitch key (Who are they?)
- Quarterback basics: Read key, pitch key
- Cadence with pitch, motion, and pitch relationship
- Fullback seal path
- Line splits and schemes
  - ✓ Base
  - ✓ Man
  - ✓ Veer
  - ✓ Loop
  - ✓ Scoop
- Wingback blocking paths

There are some key terms in the option game. You must understand who the read key and pitch key are in the option game. In the triple option, the read key is the defender you read on the dive. The read defender is the defender who tells the quarterback to leave the ball with the back or to pull it out and continue the option. The players running the triple option all know who the read-key defender is. The read key is the first man on the line of scrimmage on or outside the playside offensive guard. When we run the midline option, the read key is the first man on the line of scrimmage to the playside.

The quarterback starts out learning the basic reads. His read keys are going to be the defensive tackle and end. Every day in practice, we give the quarterback all the reads he will see in a game. Our defense will come up the field, and we come high up the field, and we sit in the hole. We show him every technique he could expect to see in a game.

When we run the triple option to the tight end side, we block the pitch key. We can use the tight end or a wingback on that block. That is one reason we have been successful. When the quarterback runs the option to the tight end side, he does not have to worry about the pitch key because we are blocking the pitch key for him. That gives him the ability to accelerate off the ride of the dive back.

The quarterback wants to start out running the option to the tight end side because it gives him a chance to see the play. The quarterback is not going to get a hot pitch to the tight end side. A hot pitch is a pitch delivered on the first step after the mesh. If you get a double-crash from the outside, which requires the quarterback to pull the ball and pitch it immediately, that is a difficult thing for a quarterback to do. When he runs the ball to the tight end side, he will never get the hot-pitch situation. He has time to read the dive key, pull the ball, and have a thought process of what he is going to do next.

When the quarterback attacks the pitch defender, he wants to attack the downfield shoulder. If he does that, it makes the defender do something. He has to fall back inside or stay outside on the pitch.

We set the pitchback in motion by using the cadence. We want him to time his movement so he does not move until just before we snap the ball. We want the pitchback to be flying when he reaches the alignment of the fullback. He comes in motion through the area behind the fullback. As he reaches that area, we want him at full speed. On occasion, the pitchback will drift away from the quarterback. If he drifts away from the quarterback, he will never be in the quarterback's line of sight. If the quarterback cannot see him, he will not pitch the ball. The distance the quarterback can pitch the ball is not the problem—the problem is sight. The pitchback has to be in front of the quarterback and running a straight path toward the sideline. The ideal pitch for the quarterback is four yards in front of his position. When the quarterback turns up, the pitchback turns up. However, he very seldom will get the ball as the quarterback moves downfield.

What we do not want to happen is for the defender to force the ball from the quarterback and make the tackle on the pitchman. That is why we want full speed. When we pitch the ball, we want to have leverage on the pitch defender, where he cannot make the tackle. We use a basketball pitch, and our quarterbacks can pitch a long distance with either hand.

The fullback has to run a straight line and not look at the quarterback. He has to look at his aiming point and run a straight line. He runs a straight line at the butt of the playside guard. He cannot reach for the ball. He opens his pocket, and the quarterback presents the ball. The quarterback reaches back, and the fullback folds over the ball on his track. Neither the fullback nor quarterback is looking at the ball. The quarterback is reading his key, and the fullback is watching the blocking. The mesh is what comes out of exact practice techniques. The timing and footwork is exact every time they run the play.

Our line splits are huge. We want a three-foot split between the guard and the center. That has to be exactly three feet because that is the proper distance for the quarterback/fullback mesh. With the quarterback's and fullback's footwork, that distance fits what they do. We try to keep the split between the center and guard exactly three feet on each side of the ball. The tackle's split may be up to four feet. We will split as wide as the defensive line will go. We do not want the defender to come back inside the tackle. Therefore, he cannot use a wild split and think the defender will go with him. He has to know how far that defender will go and take him to the maximum.

When we talk about our blocking scheme, the first scheme is base. That is man blocking. We refer to the guard's block on a defender as a base or man block. A veer block refers to the tackle's block on a linebacker. If the tackle can make an inside release across the defender's face to block the linebacker, that is a veer block. In the midline scheme, the guard could have a veer block if he has a 3 technique aligned on him. He releases inside the defender to block the linebacker.

If the defender on the outside shoulder of the guard or tackle will not let them release inside for the linebacker, we use a loop block. If the offensive tackle has a 4-technique defender head-up on him, he cannot get inside that position to block the linebacker. So, he uses a loop block and goes behind the defender to get to the linebacker. The scoop is a backside block. When we scoop block, we are trying to cut off defenders.

The wingback has to know the calls on the frontside to establish the path he needs to run to his block. He has to listen to the calls in the offensive line. He may have to fold or chip back inside an offensive tackle or switch responsibility with the tight end. The line gives their calls and comes off the line. That is the most important thing in option football. They have to explode off the ball and get movement on the defenders. That isolates the reads for the quarterback.

If you want your guards to come off the ball and get movement, do not put them on an island. Too many times, the center takes one step to the guard and goes to the backside linebacker. We want the center to snap the ball and come straight up the field, shoulder to shoulder with the guard. That gives the guard security to the inside of his block. He can come off hard and not worry about getting beat to the inside. The center comes off, and they move upfield. After they get to linebacker's depth, the center can look backside for the linebacker. The center and guard have to secure the playside A gap.

The next thing I want to go to is the triple option to the tight end side (Diagram #1). When we run the triple option to the tight end side, we run it "solid." Solid means we are going to block the pitch key on the play. In the even front, the defense's responsibility for the option is: tackle/linebacker takes the dive back, the defensive end has the quarterback, and the Sam linebacker runs to the pitch. When we block this play solid, we base block the defensive end with the tight end.

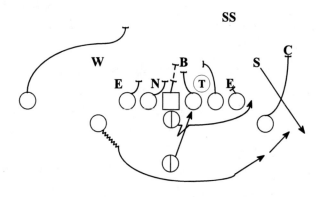

Diagram #1. Triple Option to Tight End vs. 40

The playside guard veer blocks for the playside linebacker. If he is gone, he turns back on the

backside linebacker. The playside tackle loops on the playside linebacker. The center and backside guard block the noseguard in the backside A gap with the center coming off on the Will linebacker. The backside tackle scoops to the inside. The tight end blocks the defensive end. The quarterback reads the 3-technique defender and takes the ball outside or inside the tight end's block. In any event, the defense does not have a defender on the quarterback. The outside linebacker runs for the pitch.

What this does is get the defense concerned about the quarterback carrying the ball. We had one game this past year where the fullback ran for 350 yards on the dive. When someone does not take the dive, there is no one left to make the tackle. The first year we ran this play, we put our speed back in the fullback position. If the defense made a mistake and did not take the dive, it was a 90-yard touchdown.

The defense changed and started putting the defensive ends on the dive and running the linebackers for the quarterback. If you work on that scheme, you can find the linebacker and do the same thing. We can always find who the defense has assigned to the quarterback.

Against the 5-2 defense, the end makes a Louie call, which is another word for solid (Diagram #2). The tight end blocks the 9-technique defensive end. The playside tackle loop blocks on the playside linebacker. The playside guard goes straight up to the linebacker. If the linebacker comes, he base blocks him. If the linebacker scrapes, he turns to the backside linebacker. The backside guard and center scoop for the nose, and the backside tackle scoops inside.

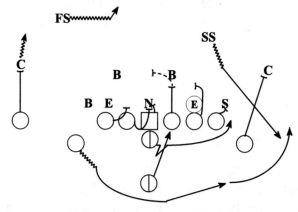

Diagram #2. Triple Option to Tight End vs. 50

The fullback has to run a straight line to the butt of the playside guard. If he is tackled, he wants to be tackled going upfield. He wants to bend his path away from the read key. If he runs at the read key, the defender will take him and the quarterback. He has to make the read key tackle him up the field and not on the line of scrimmage. He wants to pull the read key up the field so he cannot fall back on the quarterback. That way the quarterback can pull the ball and step around the collision.

When the tight end blocks on the 9-technique end, he wants to keep his shoulders square. He wants the defender to maintain outside leverage and walk out to the outside. When that happens, there is a gaping hole inside for the quarterback to turn up. I have seen those holes become as wide as five yards. The support player is outside covering the pitch, and there is only one defensive back left in the middle. It is a footrace in most cases.

If the defensive end was a 7-technique end, the tight end has outside leverage, and the quarterback will probably go outside of his block. A 6-technique end is blocked the same as the 9-technique end. If the 6 technique will walk to the outside, it gives the quarterback the option to run inside or outside the block.

If we run the play to the split end side, the quarterback is looking to pitch. Our primary formation is a double-open set. That gives us both ends split with a double-wing set outside the tackles. To the split end side from a 40 front, there can only be three defenders to that side (Diagram #3). Unless you have superhuman players, you cannot play this defense against this play. The guard and center block the nose. The tackle veer blocks on the Will linebacker and continues to the backside if he scrapes. The backside guard and tackle scoop to the playside.

If the linebacker stays inside, the tackle will block him. At some point, he will run to the outside. The wingback has a K-block on this play. If the linebacker scrapes to the outside, he blocks him. We leave the free safety unblocked and let him try to make the play. The split end stalks the corner. If

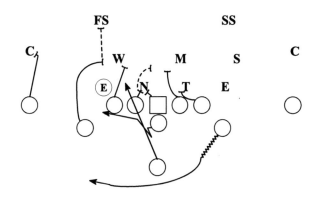

Diagram #3. Triple Option to Split End vs. 40

the Will linebacker stays inside, the tackle blocks him and the wingback blocks the free safety. The wingback and split end can switch their blocks if they need to. The split end will crack on the free safety, and the wing will block outside on the corner.

We can go to a trips set by putting both the split ends on the same side (Diagram #4). The inside split end blocks the safety, and the outside split end blocks the corner. The wingback in the slot runs the K-block on the outside linebacker. We have everyone blocked on that adjustment.

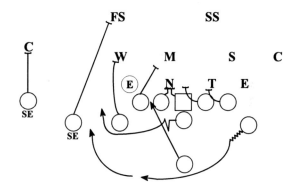

Diagram #4 Triple Option to Trips

Defenses want to keep four defenders in the secondary. They cannot play us with four defenders playing in the secondary. They play them there to prevent us from breaking a long run. They do not fly to the line of scrimmage. Defenses play us in standard vanilla fronts, and they do not stunt.

The best pass pattern we have from this scheme is a four vertical pattern (Diagram #5). We like to run it from a flex formation. The flex formation is a tight end and wingback to one side and a split end and slot to the other side. For some reason, the tight end is always open.

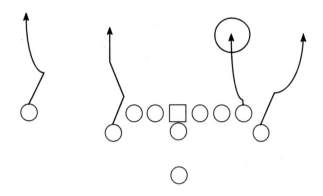

Diagram #5. Four Vertical From Flex

We run a number of different formations. Our primary set is the double open. We run a flex, trips, end over, deuce, nasty, and a variety of I-formation sets. From the I formation, we run double tight ends, slot, wing, and twins sets. We also run the pro formation.

The advantage we have on our opponents is the style of offense we run. How do you practice against something that you never see except one time a year? As the year progressed, our younger players really improved. That is what happens when you do the same thing repeatedly. Our techniques got better, and we became more intense and relentless. You can do that when you become comfortable in what you are doing.

The fact about this play is the backside wingback will probably be blocking at the end of the play. If the quarterback takes off on the run, the pitchback becomes a blocker.

The quarterback takes an open step and presents the ball to the fullback. The fullback tracks to the butt of the guard. The quarterback wants to get the ball to the fullback as deep as possible. He catches the fullback on his back leg and rides the fullback to his front hip. He is not looking at the fullback or the pocket. It is all timing and feel in the mesh area. The quarterback focuses on his read.

They have done this drill in practice a million times. It becomes second nature to them. After the quarterback and fullback have worked together for some time, the fullback can read the same thing the quarterback does. He runs the seal path to the seam. He knows when he is going to get the ball and when the quarterback will pull the ball.

We run the midline option also. This is a dangerous play (Diagram #6). In the even front, it is like taking candy from a baby. The playside guard veer blocks inside for the playside linebacker. The playside tackle fans outside on the down lineman. The tight end blocks the Sam linebacker. If there is no tight end, the wingback blocks the Sam linebacker. We tell the wingback to get to the linebacker the best way he can. He can go outside or inside to block the linebacker. The thing that could hurt the play is the linebacker blowing the B gap.

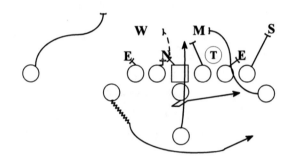

Diagram #6. Midline vs. 40

To the backside, the center and backside guard block the nose and up to the backside linebacker. The tackle fans out on the defensive end.

When we run this play against a 50, we have two ways to run the play. We can use the Roger scheme (Diagram #7). The playside tackle and the tight end or wingback to the playside block out. We do not block the 4 or 5 technique. The tackle blocks the defensive end and the tight end or wingback in the slot blocks the corner. We read the 4 technique.

If we block the man scheme, the guard, tackle, and tight end base block on their defenders (Diagram #8). We read the nose. If the nose plays straight up on the center, we take the ball backside. The center always goes to the frontside pad of the

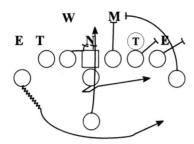

Diagram #7. Roger

nose. He does not try to reach the nose; he only wants the nose to declare one way or the other. If the nose goes backside, the quarterback pulls the ball and runs the ball to the frontside. If the nose goes to the frontside, the quarterback gives the ball to the fullback who is going backside.

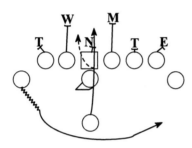

Diagram #8. Man

If you do not like this play against the 50 defense, there are tons of other plays you can run at it. We have two kinds of counters that we like against the 50. We run the counter with base blocking and the counter trey.

If we run the midline to the split end side, the pitchback might get the ball (Diagram #9). If we have a 1 technique in the playside gap, the guard tries to get across his face to the backside linebacker. He probably will not get there, but the quarterback will pull the ball. To the backside, the center and backside guard have three ways to block the play.

If the guard can handle the down lineman by himself, he calls man. If the guard calls man, the center goes to the backside linebacker. If there is a 1-technique shade on the guard or center, the guard calls call. That is the combination block between the center and guard. If the linebacker walks up in the B gap, the guard calls backer. The guard blocks

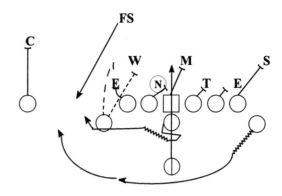

Diagram #9. Midline to Split

the linebacker, and the center blocks the shade technique. You have to block the linebacker blowing that gap. I have seen a linebacker blow the B gap and catch the quarterback from behind.

The playside wingback has the linebacker the best way he can get him. If he has to chip inside, he goes that way. The playside blocking is man scheme on the defenders. The wingback comes in motion and could get a pitch on this play. The free safety is unblocked, but we should get to him and pitch off him.

We needed a play to get the ball to the fullback. If you have a great fullback, the defense can make the quarterback keep the ball, and one of your best players may never touch the ball. We wanted to run a play that looked like the triple option. We started to run the called dive or wide veer (Diagram #10). We ride the fullback and make it look like the triple option. There is no read, and the fullback is going to carry the ball. We give him the ball, and he finds a crease to run in.

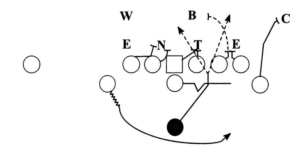

Diagram #10. Called Dive (Wide Veer)

The first thing we do is to cut our splits from three feet to two feet. In the even front, the playside tackle and the tight end "slam" the 7-

technique defender. The tight end and tackle come off together and drive the 7 technique back off the line of scrimmage.

The tackle watches the inside linebacker as he is driving on the 7 technique. He is coming off on the inside linebacker and will block him. The center and playside guard work on the 3-technique defender. If they cannot block him, they run him down the line of scrimmage into the pile.

The thing that can hurt the play is a B-gap blitz by the inside linebacker. If the tackle sees the linebacker start to blitz that gap, he comes off the slam block and blocks the linebacker. If the linebacker walks up into the gap, he calls "backer" and blocks down on him. The playside wingback blocks the first thing to the outside.

You can use motion from the wingback and make it look like the triple option. The quarterback leaves the ball with the fullback and carries out his fake. He wants to hold the secondary players on the perimeter. If the play breaks the line of scrimmage, it has a chance to go to the house. It reads like a zone play. The fullback attacks the line of scrimmage and finds a crease to run the ball.

There are three plays where we cut our splits from three feet to two feet. We cut the splits on the called dive, double option, and quick pitch. We have small offensive linemen, but they are great technicians. We have two ex-fullbacks playing on our offensive line. This offense can work for anybody.

Does anyone have any questions? We will be here all day. Thank you very much.

LITTLE THINGS THAT MAKE A DIFFERENCE

Centennial High School, Arizona

I want to thank the clinic director, John Burke, and the Nike people for having me on this clinic. The first clinic I ever attended was in 1972 at the Galt House Hotel in Louisville, Kentucky. Bud Wilkinson and Duffy Daugherty were there. Woody Hayes was also at the clinic as well. For a country boy, I thought I had died and gone to heaven. It was quite an experience.

I am indeed honored to be here today. That was nice of John to say in the introduction that we have been state champs three times. However, I do want you to know it was not always that way.

If you would visit with my coaching staff, it would not take you long to realize why I am here today. Kyle Pooler is our defensive coordinator, and he is very good. Andrew Taylor is our defensive coordinator, and he is very good. My wife heard me make the comment about how good the coordinators were, and she asked, "What do you do?" I replied that I stand around and cheer a lot. Now, my job is to go around and clap for everyone on the field.

I can assure you, it was not always that way when we first came to Centennial High School. Centennial High School opened in 1990. We were located between Peoria High School, who had won two state championships, and Cactus High School and Ironwood High School. All three of those schools had excellent coaches. For the first 10 years, we really struggled to have a .500 season. We have been working for all of those years to make our program better. I hope this can be a point that will help some of you who are struggling with this same problem today. Things can change if you are patient. Instead of struggling, now we are winning state championships.

The first question asked after our state championship this year was from a reporter. He asked, "Now that you have nine men that were starters on offense coming back, and you have five starters coming back on defense, can we count you in to win the fourth straight championship next year?" I told him: let us enjoy this championship before we talk about any four-peat. Things can change quickly in this game.

When we were struggling to compete, there were little things that we did that I thought were very good. We still do those little things today. That is going to be the focus of my talk today. I want to talk about little things that can make a big difference in your program.

One of the first things we do is to have a senior retreat. We load up in vans and go two-and-a-half hours north where it is cool. We have a staff member who has a cabin, and we stay in his cabin. The players are picking at each other, passing gas, and doing things that normal 17-year-old boys do. That is where the bonding process starts. This is when we tell our seniors what we expect for the coming season.

We started by telling the group this statement: "We have some leaders that do not talk enough. We have some seniors who are not leaders that talk way too much. You need to figure out who the leaders are, and who the followers are, if you want to win next season."

It is not just all one-way. We let them express themselves as far what they would like to see different. Over the years, we have taken suggestions from the seniors and incorporated them into our program.

One area that we discuss is helping seniors with college. I hate to hear any high school athlete say "My coach never did anything for me as far as looking into college football." I think this is the worse criticism they can make. I hope our players do not talk like that with other high school players. I think we owe it to the kid to call the college coach and tell him if the kid is good enough to play or not. We need to deal with this issue, and we need to write letters and talk on his behalf. If he busted his butt for you, then we owe it to him to bust our butt for him.

Not everyone is going to go to Division I football. However, I believe there is a place for each of our starters. It may be at a school where they have to pay a lot of money to attend. I believe there is a place where they can put on a college uniform and be on a team. I think that is our responsibility to help where we can in this process.

We also have a freshman football camp. It gives us a chance to see the new talent. Our freshman coach tells us the camp puts the freshman team ahead of the other schools by more than a week. We put in a few offensive plays, and a base defense. We believe this helps our winning tradition at our school.

We also have a California trip. It is a great time for us. We get on the bus at 10:00 p.m. We wake up the next morning, and we are in California. We stop and eat breakfast, then go out and practice. We come back, eat, and then go to the beach. We come back from the beach, go practice, and then eat again. Finally, we go to bed after a busy day. We do this for six days.

I see this as a way to have two practices in a day. The kids see this as a day to go to the beach. There is usually something going on at the beach such as a musical festival. The kids enjoy the week on the beach. In 20 years from now, our kids are not going to remember specific scores of games, but they are going to remember going to the beach. For example, last year we had an earthquake while we were there. Our kids will remember that situation. There are not too many earthquakes in Arizona.

They are also going to remember Jimmy Lewis, one of our sophomores. One day, we went to one of the parks. We got ready to leave, and we could not find Jimmy. I found Jimmy with two huge girls, one under each arm. I could not help but laugh. I noticed that one of the girls had hands larger than my hands. The other girl had an Adam's apple. I called Jimmy over, got him under my arm, and said, "Ladies, we have to go now." Jimmy had come to us after Katrina from Louisiana. I asked Jimmy if he noticed anything strange about the two ladies. He said he did not notice anything different. I told him one girl had big hands, and the other girl had an Adam's apple. Jimmy replied, "You are kidding me. You are playing!" I asked Jimmy if he had kissed them, and he said, "Not on the mouth." I told him to get on the bus and forget those girls.

I will have kids that were with that group, and they will talk about that story when they are 50 years old. When I do see that group of players, those are the stories they want to talk about.

They may talk about the time Johnny got stuck in the restroom. Those are the stories they will talk about. The bus trip was something that helped us bond, and it brought us closer together.

Before the start of each season, we write a letter to them. It took me a long time to realize it was not the X's and O's that matter the most in football. It took me 30 years to learn that. The X's and O's is not what makes the team good. It is not. Great teams are player-driven, not coach-driven. The kids play for each other. They play to keep their teammates next to them from getting knocked down. That is what great teams play for. Other teams play for individual awards, scholarships, and other things. Great teams are player-driven, and they play to not let each other down. I want the seniors to know this before the season starts.

We are allowed 10 days of practice to start the season. We cannot be in pads. It is boring, and there is not a lot to look forward to during those 10 days.

A few years ago, we made up our own game in the spring under the lights. We have a linemen's challenge, and a 7-on-7 contest. Then, we have food after the contest. The moms get together and bring the food. It is a great atmosphere and a chance for everyone to become enthused about the upcoming season. It is a chance for the boosters to do some recruiting of the freshman parents. They sell hats and T-shirts. We spice up the spring season to get ready for the fall practice.

We have spring uniforms. We believe the teams act better and play better when they are dressed alike. I do not know this for sure, but it appears to me that they do. I got tired of kids coming to spring practice with all kind of different jerseys on. I asked one kid why he was wearing a particular t-shirt, and his response was, "Because my grandmother gave it to me." What can you say now? You let him wear the shirt that grandmother gave him. We decided that we would dress them the way we want them to be dressed.

Eight years ago, I was fortunate to take an all-star football team to Australia. The Australians love Americans. It was a great trip. In addition to me going on the trip, five of our players were with the group on the trip. Each day, our players had a different shirt on with our logos on them. Another player from the United States team asked me where we got all of those different shirts. I told the answer. They get them from our schools. That kid replied that he never got a shirt of any kind from his school. He went on to say if he had known about our deal with the shirts, he would have liked to play for us. I know it is illegal to recruit, but I can tell you that works very well.

I did not believe it before, but I do now. If you look good in the uniforms, you play good in them. Years ago, I thought that was a hoax. Now, I tell the players to get in front of a mirror to make sure they look like they want to look. The kids with the biceps want to roll up the sleeves to show those guns, and the fat kids want to tuck the shirt in so their gut will not show. This is fine with me. That has nothing to do with the character the kid is in that uniform. He just wants to make sure he looks good. We have been fortunate in that we were selected as a Nike team, and that is the reason we are wearing those jerseys. I want the team dressed in the best uniforms we can put them in.

A few years ago, we were playing one of our big opponents. They had won three of the last four state championships. We were in our ragged, nonmatching uniforms, and the opponents came out on the field to warm up in great-looking uniforms that matched. Our players stopped and watched the opponents' warm-up. It was unbelievable. They were awestruck. I could not believe the expressions on the faces of our team. One of the assistant coaches came over and said, "Coach, we will have those same features on our uniforms next year." I cannot tell you how powerful that is when you run out on the field and everyone is dressed the same. It is something the kids like and think is cool.

We also have a captain's book. We allow our kids to select the captains. Once we have them selected, we give them the book. Normally, the players do a good job of selecting the captains. The book outlines the duties and responsibilities of the captains. It gives practical solutions to problems that captains may encounter. It is not a matter if someone is going to break a team rule, because team members are going to break a team rule. The captain must know how they are going to deal with that situation. I give them some practical solutions for those situations.

We have goals for each game. They are pinned on a board for everyone to see. The most important thing we stress is turnovers. The team that takes care of the ball the best is going to win. The team that takes the ball away from their opponents the most is going to win. I stress this point several times per practice. I do not think we can stress this enough. We set goals in our turnover ratio.

We have a tip sheet for our team. For the last state championship game, it was 31 pages long. We had listed every play from every formation our opponents ran. The tip sheet is a condensed version of the scouting report. The scouting report is fine, but if they do not know what is in the tip sheet, it does not help anyone. For every question they miss, they are going to do some physical activity on

Monday. Their responsibility is to know what is in the scouting report and what is in the tip sheet. The way you make be plays is when you know what the opponents are going to do. By using the goal chart, it has helped us a great deal in this area.

We want our players to use their brief "fame," if you will, for good. I was very proud of our guys when we worked with HopeKids. HopeKids is a group in our valley that helps kids with cancer. They are small kids that love football but are never going to get to play the game. We brought football to those young HopeKids. Our cheerleaders were also with us on the project. Our kids intermingle with the HopeKids and play with them and make the day better for those HopeKids.

We worked with the Special Olympics this year. We had the kids raise money for a Thanksgiving Day dinner for a family. We adopted a family for Christmas and helped them. Our players gained so much more than those they helped. Service takes the focus off us and on to someone else. That is what you must do to have a team.

NFL players doing all of the celebrations that the kids can see each Sunday is not a good thing for teams. They celebrate, and our players think this is the way it should be done. It takes away from the team concept. We need to take the focus off the individual and put it someplace else. Where else can we focus on others, than to help the Special Olympics individuals and the needy families?

When we walk out of our locker room to the field, it is special. We have a two-and-a-half minute walk. Our band drum line has this beat going. By the time our players take the field, their feet are no longer on the ground. They love the band drum line. The band also loves the march. I would advise you if you have a drum line at your school, use them.

We feed our players after the game. Some people say the players are more dangerous to themselves and to others right after competition. We want them to stay around for a while, and we have food and drink for them. They can relax and calm down a little before they leave school.

We all have been guilty of saying things to the players in the heat of battle that we are sorry for later. This postgame meeting gives us a chance to make things right.

A good example of the type of things we may correct is an error by the staff that was one of the worst things that ever happened to me. A player who did not get into many games came up to me and asked me if it would be possible for me to put him in the game Friday night because his grandmother was coming to see him. I assured him he had practiced hard and that he would get into the game.

On Friday night, I forgot to put the player in the game. He did not get to play. After the game when we were all together eating, I went up to that player and apologized to him. I told him I had made a mistake, and that I was very sorry for not getting him in the game. I did not make excuses. I told him that I forgot about the earlier conversation. He was okay with that explanation.

I do not think that player would have come back to the team on Monday if I had not talked with him on Friday night. You can make a lot of things right after the game. It is not good to allow them to go home and hear their dad say, "I told you about those coaches." It is better to fix the situation as soon as possible after the game is over, if you can. This is something that feeding our players allows us to do.

BOB WYLIE'S TIMER

(BEEEEEP) I am not a relative of Bob Wylie. This is not a paid advertisement. To buy this horn is the best money I have ever spent on anything related to football. There are hundreds of ways to make use of this beeper. On offense, one of my pet peeves is wasting time and wasting reps. It takes forever for the players to get into the huddle.

To speed this up, I tell the team from the time they break the huddle to the snap of the ball, they have 3.8 seconds. After they come up and have not snapped the ball, I beep the horn. "Sorry, you did not make it in time. You have one up-down after practice." The next time, if they do not make it, they have two up-downs. After five or six of the up-downs, they decide they better speed it up and make the snap before 3.8 seconds. They do not want to even do one up-down. It is not the severity of punishment; it is the certainty of punishment.

Before we implemented the beeper, I would encourage the players to speed it up. They would work hard for a couple of plays, but soon they were dragging on the time element. Now, they bust their butt to get ready to go.

On defense, we do not take the ballcarrier to the ground. We thud, and when the whistle blows, the play is dead. Then, they hear the BEEEEEEP! They have 3.8 seconds to get ready on defense to play the next play. That outside corner has a hard time to get back to the huddle and to get ready to go on the next play. I have had players tell me they have dreams about hearing that BEEEEEEEP at night. Our kids are not big, but they will run to the football. If they cannot beat the horn, they will get on each other. They will not get on the far side corner if we go away from him.

We have an ax handle that we use on our sideline as a logo for working hard. We use it for big games. We give the ax handle to the player that has the biggest hit for that week. He gets the ax handle for the next week. He can carry it around with him the next week.

We have a senior scrapbook. I got this from my nephew in Detroit. He liked this more than the letter that he received. We assign a girl to take a scrapbook and collect articles on the games and anything he did in a game. She collects this information and builds the scrapbook for a particular player. They give the scrapbook to the player at the banquet. That is a lot of hard work. Usually, we find a girl who likes every player on the team. All you have to do is to find the right girl. Ask her if she will make a scrapbook for Bobby. It is amazing what they will come up with.

We have a voluntary pro/college-type chapel service before our games. We think that humbling ourselves, and giving thanks to our creator, brings perspective and peace to our players. It relaxes them, and we feel that relaxed players will play better. We do not force any of the kids to do this. Some kids chose not to take part in our chapel service.

We are fortunate in that we have a person from the Fellowship of Christian Athletes who puts on great chapel services for us. They relate what is going on in the lives of the players in football to their everyday lives, and to what is going to take place in the next one-and-a-half hours.

We also have a character coach on our staff. Strength in our minds begins with strength of character. How many of you have had great players who would not do their homework or come to school, or whom you could not trust? The players have a lack of character, and we believe that strength begins with strength of character.

On Monday, we give up 20 to 25 minutes for our character coach to talk with our players about the right thing to do, caring about others, and giving credit to others. I think we are missing a great opportunity if we do not try to help our players become better men. I believe we have had players that became better men, and in the long run became better football players. It is a win-win situation.

My high school coach, David Conrad, would turn over in his grave if he could hear what comes out of our locker room today. Back in 1965, to get ready for a game, the players had to sit still, or they had to stare at the wall, or they had to be pounding on their body to get ready mentally for a game. We found not every kid gets ready for a game in that manner today.

In our locker room, we have the tall speakers and the music is coming out of them at a high volume. They go out in the gym and dance with each other, and they are having a great time. My old coach would have said, "They are not ready to play." I feel they are relaxed and ready to go. Not all kids participate in the dancing. They like to go off by themselves, and they do. Whatever they want to do to get ready for the game, I am good with it.

Let me talk about our website: www.coyotefootball.com. Coach Hal Borhauer started this website, and soon the website was so valuable the parents took it over. If you get a chance, look at the website. We have had hits from 48 states. We have hits from all over the world. Our kids check the site every day for a lot of different reasons. They put all of the players' pictures on the front of the page. They list the results of all games, a preview of the games next week, and they have other items of interest. [Editor's note: One of the best high school websites I have seen. It is worth viewing the site.]

The website is an easy way to keep everyone informed. We go to Concordia University in Irvine, California, for our camp to start the season. We have a hill near the area where we practice. We run up to the top of the hill; well, some people run up to the top. I have to walk up to the top of the hill. They have pictures on the website of the team at practice on the hill. The people who run the website would be glad to assist you if you are interested in setting up a website.

We all lift weights in our off-season program. The big difference in our program is to give the players grades for the work they do in the program. We give them A, B, C, D, or F. If they are getting a C, it means that half of the teams they are going to play are better than that player. If a player gets an F, it is something we must look into. We do not give them that much to do that they should get an F. We ask them these questions: Are you a football player, or are you not a football player? Do you want to win the state championship or not? It is clear for us and for the players. We take those grades and put them on coyotefootball.com. No parents come to us wanting to know why their son is not getting to play in the fall. We tell the players and parents that hard work pays off eventually.

Lifting competition gives the players an incentive to shoot for. However, we have not done much of this in the past two years.

We have a wall of accomplishments for the players in the weight room. Seeing your picture or hearing your name is the strongest thing in the world. If you do not believe this, call someone by the wrong name. "It is not Jim; it is Richard!" They will straighten you out real quick.

Seeing their name on the wall is even better. If the girls get to see the player's name on the wall, that is twice as good.

We also have a board with goals for the players to shoot for. We have a record board to show them what the other great players have done. We keep a record book of all lifts.

The next point I want to talk about is a shame. In our school district, and in our state of Arizona, the cafeteria food has to be sold, or they have to throw it away. They cannot give the food away. So I go to the cafeteria manager and ask if we can buy the food. We take the food to the weight room and sell it to the players for a small fee. It helps to have something to eat when you are lifting weights. We get rid of the food, and that is a lot better than throwing it away.

Here are some things we do out of season. We have the board on the wall with players' pictures on it. They are on 8x10 pictures. You have to get up close to see the pictures. We are going to blow them up larger and put them up so everyone can see them. I see young kids staring at those pictures. They are planting a seed with the idea that someday they are going to be up on that board. I have had kids ask me what they would have to do to go to college. "What do I have to do to get my picture up on that wall?" I give them the same story. First is grades, and then I tell them how strong those players were, and how hard they worked to achieve the goals to get up on the board. It is a great motivator.

Isn't it sad that we have to recruit our own feeder schools? We have 32 feeder schools in our district. We have seven high schools in the district. A certain number of schools are supposed to come to our school. We have to go visit those schools, or they will be convinced to go to another school in the district. We go to our feeder schools, and we take our captains and trophies, and we wear our special shirts. We are getting most of the athletes we are supposed to be getting now.

In talking about our coaching staff, we try to get most of our work done by Saturday. When I first started coaching, we would work all day Saturday until 7:00 p.m. Then we would work all day Sunday until late that night. We worked on the game plan. Most of the time was spent on what-ifs. "What if this happens? What if that happens?" A lot of it was wasted time. Today, our coaches know we are going to be out of the meeting by 4:00 p.m. on Saturday. One of the reasons our staff has been together so long is the fact that we understand what we need to do. In addition, I value the time the coaches need to spend with their family. I want the coaches to be with their family on Saturday and Sunday.

We have been together so long now that we could have spring practice without having a meeting. We could walk out to spring practice and ask Kyle what he wanted to add to the offense. Kyle would tell us he wanted to add the I-formation plays, and the deuce-formation plays. He would tell us he wanted to put in three running plays and three pass plays. Everyone knows what we are going to do. I want to keep the coaching staff together. The team is better for it when you have a staff that has stayed together for a long time.

We have a techno-guru who puts together individual tapes for us. He goes home on Friday after the game, and he has individual tapes for us. In the old days, we graded the tapes together, and it took forever.

Head coaches must recognize that the time of the assistant coaches is very valuable, and they must respect them and give them some time to be with their family on weekends. If mom is not happy, no one is going to be happy. Those individual tapes have helped us a great deal in this regard.

I do not think you win unless you have principles that are on your side. I do not think you win unless parents send you kids who are hard-working, responsible, humble, and willing to be a part of the team. I do not think you win unless you have teachers who are supporting the program as well.

We send a message to the faculty at the start of the school year, letting them know we are going to work with them. This is what the message states: If you have any football player that is a problem in your class or is not doing his work or is giving you a problem in any way, you just let us know, and we assure you it will not be a problem any longer.

The first time you approach a player on a problem the teacher sends you, be reasonable, and ask him what the problem is. He may tell me something simple, such as he had a bad day, and he will do better. We will try it out and see what happens. If we do not hear from the teacher, then everything is fine.

If we do hear from the teacher the second time, we are going to take serious matters in hand. We give them extra exercises to do after practice. One thing we found is that players do not like rolling on the ground as a punishment exercise.

We have a special seating stand for our faculty down in the end zone. They all sit together, and it is great seeing them at the games supporting the team. The players like this because they know their teacher saw them play on Friday night. Our teachers like it because they can be with their families.

It is important to give spirit shirts to the important people in your school. I do not know who they are, but you do. We have a social studies teacher who started a club called Coyote Chicks. They are a group of girls who support the football team. They go to all of the games, and they wear their Coyote Chicks t-shirts. We want those types of people supporting our program. Those are several of the little things that we do that we feel has helped us become successful.

We try to make connections with the kids. You can tell when those connections are made. It all comes back to me in some type of response. We all know we can coach the kids hard when they know the coaches care about them. We believe football gives us an opportunity to teach valuable life lessons if we would just look for them. I believe these things are true by the example we had a few years ago.

We had a kid who had been a part of our program for a couple of years. He never missed a practice and he never missed a game. He was a tough kid. He came up to me and said, "Coach, I think I will have to miss practice tomorrow." I asked him why he would have to miss practice. He took off his shoe, and his sock was full of blood. I asked him to let me look at his foot. He had the ugliest ingrown toenail you would ever see in your whole life. He went to the doctor, and the doctor found it was very serious. The doctor looked at the young man and asked him why he had not had him look at this earlier. "What is more important to you, football or your toe?" Without hesitation, the player said, "Football, and I cannot let my teammates down!" When they make that type of connection, and they play for each other, you have a chance of winning.

In conclusion, I would like to say I appreciate your time. Good luck, and God bless you.

UNDER THE HELMET: DEPRESSION AND MENTAL HEALTH

Liberty High School, Pennsylvania

Thank you for allowing us to be here with you today. All you have to do is be around the Larry Blackmon family to know how welcome we feel sharing our story with them and others. It only takes one sentence to realize that I am not from the South.

To start, I want you to watch a 30-second video. I need you to concentrate on every line on the video. That is the first thing we are going to do, and then we will get started. Please look at the video.

BO TKACH

- Two-time first team all-state football player
- Two-time District XI javelin champion
- ESPN's 2000-2001 Academic High School Football All-American
- Youth volunteer
- 2007 Wilkes University magna cum laude graduate
- Lifelong battle with obsessive-compulsive disorder (OCD) and depression
- July 2007: Lost to suicide

That is our son. I want to introduce my wife, Sandi. We are here to spread some awareness about a problem we face in America today. You can see the things Bo Tkach achieved in his short life. We lost him in July of 2007 to a miserable disease called depression. I want to show you today that depression is a disease, and that it is not a state of mind.

Our first indication that Bo had a problem was when he was in kindergarten. He was five years old at the time. His teacher sent him to the guidance counselor and told her Bo was having bad thoughts. She told us he should not be having these thoughts at five years old.

We summed up the situation and were led to believe that it was because Sandi was going to give birth to our third child soon, and perhaps there was some jealousy going on.

In the seventh grade, things got worse. We noticed he was pulling his pants up tight. I told him to pull his pants down, and I looked at his waistline. He had on four pairs of underwear.

He was diagnosed as having an obsessive-compulsive disorder caused by a chemical imbalance in his body. Through all of this, it created a whole life of uncertainty. In spite of all of this, he was able to have an unbelievable imprint on life.

Two nights after his death, they had calling hour at the church, and in our small town, they had to call out the fire department and police because there were over 1,400 people who came in to pay their respects. They included college coaches, high school coaches, and players from around the tri-state area.

Sandi and I decided we would try to do something to make an imprint on young people and coaches in the area of depression. As a result, the Bo Tkach memorial "Under Every Helmet and Hat Is a Child Who Needs Us" was developed.

Our daughter, Tristin, and our other son, Tyler, convinced us to use this name for the project. Tristin is a schoolteacher, and Tyler is a defensive end at the University of Pittsburgh.

Both of my sons played high school football for me. If you have coached your own son, you know that can be stressful. When I coached my sons, it was the best seasons we ever had. Our house was filled with kids during that time. Football has been very special to our entire family and has affected the manner in which we conduct our lives. I have been fortunate to have been in football for 30 years. I continue to go to as many clinics as I possibly can because I am still learning about the game of football.

The second part of this story comes about three weeks after we lost Bo. In 2005, Matt Millen, the former president and general manager of the Detroit Lions, called me up to talk. We grew up 20 miles from each other, but I did not know him. In 2005, I was the coach of a very good team that was undefeated. I found out that 15 of our players were out drinking the week before. I benched those 15 players that were guilty of drinking. We lost the game by three points. We missed a fourth-and-one by just one inch, and we lost the game.

Matt Millen called me up and let me know that he thought it took some stones to do what I did with those 15 players. It was a very controversial decision. The rule I had to follow was the fact that anyone who was caught drinking would have to sit out the games for two weeks. I did not talk with Matt Millen again for the next year or so.

After losing Bo, Sandi and I started going to some regular counseling. We did not feel it was going the way we wanted it to go. We would go to the meetings, and after the meeting was over, they would tell us they would see us the next week. That was not strong enough for us. We wanted to go to a Christian counselor. Matt Millen called again and said, "I just heard about what happened." A newspaper reporter that used to be in our area had given the message to Matt about our Bo.

I told Matt that we were looking for a counselor. He replied, "Jim, that is what my wife does." Two weeks later, we were sitting in his home, and we began the process of counseling. Every two weeks, we met at his house with him and his wife and went through a series of biblical studies to try to help us with the pain of losing a child.

I did not know anyone who had ever lost a child through a suicide. I emailed the Indianapolis Colts because I knew what had happened to Tony Dungy's son. What were the chances of getting through to Coach Dungy? The very next week, he called me. He called me on my cell phone and said it was Tony Dungy. I knew that no one who knew me would try to play a joke on me after what had happened.

Tony Dungy talked to me for about 45 minutes. He told me two things that stuck in my mind. He told me that my marriage would go into the 80th percentile in regard to divorce because my wife and I may not deal with this in the same way. He went on to say that our own children may not deal with it in the same way.

My daughter was a "day counter." We were going to see the University of Pittsburgh play one day, and she called me up. I answered the phone, and she asked me if I knew what day it was. I told her I was not sure what she meant. She replied, "It has been 30 days since we lost Bo." Before the call, I was having a "good hour," and that got me upset again. Sandi reminded me what Coach Dungy had told me about this kind of thing happening. Everyone is going to interpret it differently. We need to understand that everyone is trying to help in this regard.

We had a lot of people come up to us and say the stupidest things you can imagine. They did not want to hurt us, but they were just not used to dealing with this topic.

The morning after the first call from Coach Dungy, he called back. He said, "I forgot to tell you something. If you really believe in heaven and that your son is better off in heaven, then it is almost selfish to want him back." The thing about this is the fact that Tony Dungy called me back.

My son, Tyler, came home for the Labor Day weekend. He told me that he was not going to go back to Pitt unless I went back to coaching. I had been out of coaching for one year. I asked him what he meant by those comments. He told me he thought I would die if I did not do something to get my mind off the situation. He said, "All you are doing is crying." He was right.

I had some coaches ask me to come back to coaching and I did. It was good for me until I was driving home from practice one night. I could not stop crying. It was on a Monday evening, and I called Coach Dungy. I told him that I was struggling to keep from crying. Tony talked to me for several minutes until I got back home. I walked in the door at home, and the TV was on. The announcer on the TV said, "The Colts will be kicking off to start the game." I could not believe it. Tony Dungy took my call an hour and a half before the kickoff. I make that point to tell you that football people take care of football people. We all need to be examples to start reaching out.

After breakfast this morning, we returned to our room, and we had an email from Matt Millen. (In the Super Bowl last week during the pre-game show, Matt Millen was sitting next to Tony Dungy.) Matt's email said, "Jim, Coach Dungy asked how everyone was doing."

We are from a small town in Pennsylvania on the edge of the coal region. We are not everyday "newspaper-headline" type of people. The point is Matt and Tony could have forgotten about us and not called us or said one word to help us. They did not do that, and that is what I want to get across to you today.

I coach hard. Don't think this is going to be a "soft-soft" type of talk from this point on. If kids are not doing things right, I am going to crew them. If they make mistakes, I am going to rip them. I am a line coach, and I coach hard. No one is saying you cannot coach kids hard. The thing you must do is to love the kids you are coaching. They are the only kids you have. Football is in a position to have an influence over more kids in this country than anything else.

A *USA TODAY* headline read: *The U.S. Army sets a record for suicides in the month of January.* We lost more soldiers to suicides than we lost in the war in January. Perhaps, there is another enemy we need to fight. They do not have enough therapists to help the soldiers that are returning from the war. In addition, we do not have enough people to recognize we are dealing with a disease.

One of my former college teammates called me up one day and he was telling me about his two sons. He has one son that is signing a scholarship with West Virginia University, and the other son is a Division I basketball player, and he is a junior. He has an obsessive-compulsive disorder just like my son had. My friend asked me, "How did this happen?" We talked some more, and he kept coming back to how this happened.

I asked him, "If he had been diagnosed with diabetes, would you question what had happened?" He said he would not question this if it were diabetes. "If the situation was diagnosed as cancer, would you question it?" Again the answer was, "No." No, we do not question these diseases. Depression is a disease! Until we recognize this, we are going to have a problem on our hands.

In August, I spoke to the Lycoming College football team. The coach told the team that I was coming in to talk to them about depression. When I walked into the room, I had over 100 kids looking at me as if they had lost their best friend. I got up to speak, and the first thing I said was this: "Listen, you young and restless—give me your eyes." The players sat up and listened to what I had to say. I had to get their attention.

This worked out to be a neat exchange because after the talk, we had two kids come up to talk with us. We had a big kid that was a lineman come up crying his face off. He said, "Coach, my best friend in high school just shot himself before I came to camp." I did not know what to do or what to say. I called the head coach over, and we arranged for him to see the college counselor. We got the process started.

I am not a doctor. I am not a therapist. I am a football coach. That is what I am. Larry Blackmon introduced me last night. He said, "This man coached for 30 years, and after he retired, he realized he did not have any hobbies." I can't golf, and I can't fish. I am a coach. Therefore, this is what we have decided to do.

Because of the unfortunate circumstances, this is what the good Lord has led us to do. We are taking this challenge. I want to go through this program that we have put together.

Under Every Helmet and Hat Is a Child Who Needs Us

Bo Tkach Memorial in Conjunction With the University of Michigan Depression Center

University of Michigan Depression Center

This program was written with Eric Hipple, former quarterback for the Detroit Lions. He lost his son six years ago to suicide. We were introduced to Eric through Matt Millen. We started talking, and I talked about the coaching aspects of what needed to be included, and Eric included the aspects related to the suicides. Then, the University of Michigan put their stamp on it, which simply means I am not a nutcase coming to talk with you. It is a legitimate educational program. That is why the University of Michigan has their seal on our material.

Eric Hipple is the outreach coordinator for the University of Michigan Depression Center. It is the first depression center in the United States on a college campus. They are doing some great work there, and we will cover some of the information they are covering.

When I go out to talk to kids at schools, I will not show Bo's picture to the kids. A kid in the audience may recognize the picture and see it as "the attention Bo is getting." Believe it or not, kids will hurt themselves for that kind of attention if they are having this problem.

Here is what we are going to try to do. Here are our goals.

MISSION (PROGRAM GOALS)

- Promote mental health awareness in athletics; holistic care
  - ✓High schools, colleges
  - ✓Coaches, parents, student-athletes
- Encourage relationships; establish trust
  - ✓Coaches and student-athletes
  - ✓Team members
- Educate communities and provide resources/support
  - ✓Outreach
  - ✓Tools for everyone involved

We are working with Nike on some information we can give to football coaches to start out with some things they can do if they are faced with a kid that has this problem of depression. What do you do if a kid comes in to see you and tells you, "I just don't know if I want to live anymore?" What do you do? We are going to try to spread that information to help educate coaches about the depression disease.

I want to stress one thing about coaching. I am a tough coach. I rip them when they make silly mistakes. However, I do not name call them. You do not want to call a kid a name. Criticize what they are doing wrong. If you are going to yell at a kid, teach them something. Coach them if you are going to raise your voice.

One thing we did this year at Liberty High School was to meet as a "book-of-the-week club." We met at a pizza house and talked about books. We had 14 kids a week that came to the meetings. We had some quality football players come to the meetings. The first book we took up for review was *Season of Life* by Jeffrey Marx. The conversations we got into were amazing. I would recommend doing that if it is something you can do. If I had called the program an FCA group or a Bible study, it was going to flash a red light and we might have scared some of them away. It worked fine for us. I let them guide the intensity of the meetings.

The mission we are doing personally has been great. We had a golf tournament last summer. Two of my former students put it together. They both work in TV and in the Internet industry. In one day, they raised $55,000. If anyone in our area under the age of 25 does not have insurance to cover the cost of a mental health assessment, we pay for that, and we pay for their counseling. Last month, we had 15 people that we helped with counseling. The cost is $250 per hour. We did get a special counselor to come out to help us, and he only charges us $125.00 per hour. That is what Sandi and I have been doing.

We had a flag football game between two rival schools. Each group made $10,000. People want to help with these projects.

I want to mention awareness. The University of Michigan did a study of Major League Baseball. They found that winning percentages were very low when teams traveled. Why is it lower? Is it the ice machine out in the hall? Is it the different bed they are sleeping in? Is it a different sleep pattern they are in?

Take a look at high school football players. They are up late on Friday night after a game. On Saturday night, they are out doing what high school kids do. On Sunday night, they are trying to get to sleep, but they have slept late that morning and have a hard time going to sleep. Come Monday morning, they are rolling out going to school early in the morning. Take this kind of schedule for four to six weeks. Most school principals can tell you that most problems start four to six weeks after school starts. The records are starting to point to the fact that the sleep patterns of kids is one of the reasons they are having problems.

Here is something I have a hard time trying to figure out. Young kids usually wake up early. Those young kids will be up at the crack of dawn. We send the young kids to school at 9:00 a.m., and the older kids go at 7:30 a.m. in many cases. The high school kids want to sleep in, and we get them out early. Over 15 school districts in the United States are looking at swapping times to get kids back on a better sleep track. That is only one thing. However, a lot of little things add up. Sleep is one thing you need to address with your players.

AWARENESS

- The Importance of Recognizing Stress, Sleep, Depression, and Substance Abuse Issues
- High schools/colleges
  - ✓ Different levels of competition require different approaches
  - ✓ Division I vs. Division III
- Coaches
  - ✓ How can you encourage positive mental growth and development?
  - ✓ Activity and discussion
    - → Your role as a coach
    - → How do you impact your student-athletes?
- Parents
  - ✓ Open communication
  - ✓ Summer meeting for parents and coaches to maintain contact
- Athletes
  - ✓ Encourage accountability
  - ✓ Promote responsibility for self
  - ✓ Discuss sleep schedule/nutrition

It has always been interesting how I deal with most parents. I bring them into a summer meeting. I sit them down, look at them, and say, "Unless I do something illegal or immoral, do not talk to me about your kids' playing time. Let your kids play. You go out and cheer for them." If you run that through some situations, you can keep yourself out of a lot of crap. I would tell the parents that if they wanted their kids, they could take them home with them. If they are going to grow, the parents must leave them with the coaches.

You have to teach the kids how to dress, how to walk, how to talk, and how to sleep, and you must teach them how to eat. We tell our kids to be on time, follow rules, and make no excuses. I put it back on the kids. It has worked for us, but I am not saying this is the only way it will work.

Let me talk about relationships. We need to establish relationships, and we need to be around the kids. Here are the things we discuss.

COACHES AND STUDENT-ATHLETES

- Act as a mentor and friend with a shared respect
- Develop trust
- Make a commitment to the individual and the team
- Stay positive
- Fairness and integrity
- Strong work ethic coupled with maintaining balance
- Learn from mistakes

Here is a quote from basketball coach, Rick Pitino: *"Everything I've learned about coaching, I've learned from making mistakes."*

TEAM MEMBERS

- Delta Force mentality: No one gets left behind
- Cohesive, coordinated team
  - ✓Coaching staff is on the same page
  - ✓Shared respect for each other and the team vision
  - ✓Team spirit: motivation and inspiration

Next, we need to discuss education for those that need to become involved in depression awareness.

- Targeting athletic programs nationwide
- Outreach efforts
  - ✓Speaking engagements
  - ✓Implement mental health awareness training

The following athletes struggle with depression. These athletes have come forward in the last three to four years to speak publicly about their problems with depression:

- Boris Becker, tennis
- Vin Baker, basketball
- John Howell, football
- Barret Robbins, football
- Dan Cody, football
- Jim Shea, skeleton racing
- Terry Bradshaw, football
- Russ Johnson, baseball
- Picabo Street, skiing
- Julie Krone, horse racing
- Pat LaFontaine, hockey
- Pete Harnisch, baseball
- Nikki Teasley, basketball

And, there are many more names that could be added to that list.

WHO IS AT RISK WITH DEPRESSION?

- Depression impacts all income levels, men and women, all professions.
- One in 10 people will experience some form of depression or bipolar disorder between the ages of 13 and 19.
- Fourteen percent of you will have depression at some point in your lives.

WHAT IS DEPRESSION?

Depression is not:

- The blues, being sad, stressed out, or upset
- Caused by a bad day
- Normal for anyone
- A weakness or a character flaw

Depression is:

- A chemical change in the brain involving: neurotransmitters, genetic vulnerabilities, and environmental stressors
- Accompanied by intense, persistent symptoms, which prevent optimal functioning

INTERACTIONS AMONG GENES, BIOLOGY, AND ENVIRONMENT (JON-KAR ZUBIETA)

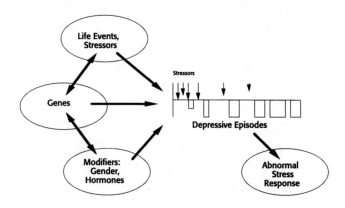

INTERACTIONS RESULT IN CLINICAL DEPRESSION

- Depressed mood (blue, gloomy, tearful, sad)
- Diminished interest/pleasure in most activities
- "Slowed down," anxious, irritable
- Trouble sleeping or too much sleep
- Increase/decrease in appetite/weight
- Unexplained physical symptoms, fatigue, loss of energy, pain
- Feeling worthless, inappropriately guilty
- Trouble thinking, concentrating, making decisions
- Recurrent thoughts of life not being worth living, death, suicidal ideation, specific suicide plan or attempt

INTERACTIONS CAN ALSO TRIGGER BIPOLAR DISORDER

- Inflated self-esteem, grandiosity
- Decreased sleep
- Pressure to talk
- Flight of ideas, racing thoughts
- Distractibility/lack of focus
- Hyperactivity in the workplace/socially, spending sprees, sexual indiscretion
- Irritability

Note: We cannot currently diagnose depression based on brain images. We do know that treating depression makes a difference. We can show that depression is a disease. When the brain is scanned, these depressions do show up, but, as we said, we cannot diagnose them at this point.

FACTS

- Suicide is the third leading cause of death of individuals in the 15 to 24 age range.
- Every year four to eight percent of adolescents experience a major depression.
- Children of depressed parents are three times more likely to experience a major depression in their lifetime.

Suicides per 100,000 for those 15 to 19 years old, compared with the rate for the entire U.S. population (*USA TODAY* 2/9/2000)		
	15-19 years old	*U.S. Pop.*
1956	2.3	10.0
1961	3.4	10.4
1966	4.3	10.9
1971	6.5	11.9
1976	7.3	12.1
1981	8.6	11.5
1986	10.1	11.9
1991	11.1	11.3
1996	9.7	10.8
1997	9.5	10.6

WHAT CAN YOU DO TO HELP?

- Awareness
  ✓Stay vigilant; be aware of what's going on with your team
- Relationships
  ✓Continue to build trust, open communication
- Education
  ✓Have a list of resources on hand
  ✓Coordinate a support system with parents and teachers
  ✓Educate yourself to counteract stigma
- When someone is showing signs/having symptoms
  ✓Encourage talking
  ✓Seek treatment (make referrals)
  ✓Offer support and follow through

RESOURCES

- University of Michigan Depression Center: www.depressioncenter.org
- Depression and Bipolar Support Alliance: www.dbsalliance.org

- National Mental Health Association: www.nmha.org
- National Institute of Mental Health: www.nimh.nih.gov
- National Alliance of the Mentally Ill: www.nami.org
- American Foundation for Suicide Prevention: www.afsp.org
- National Suicide Prevention Lifeline:(800)273-8255

RESOURCES FOR PARENTS

- Mentor Research Institute
- www.steponeforparents.org
- www.incrisis.org
- Consult with your local mental health department for services in your community.

Have any of you seen the video by Randy Pausch entitled "*The Last Lecture?*" He was a professor at Carnegie Mellon University. You should look at the book. We use that in our book club. The University picked a profession to do what they call "The Last Lecture" to give to the kids. No one knew this, but he only had six months to live. He got up and gave the lecture and it is incredible. One point that stood out with our kids in the book club was this comment: "*The brick walls are there to give us a chance to show how badly we want something.*" That line stood out with our kids. I was once one of those guys that always wanted to know what life is throwing at me next. You should teach kids that life is up and down, especially in football. One week you are happy, and the next week you are down in the dumps.

If you will take one or two points from here and stress them a little more next year, I guarantee you will see a difference in your program.

When Eric and I put this together, we did not want to give football coaches the impression we were going to wear pink gloves and be soft. We talked about the Delta Force mentality. The Delta Team has a motto that is interesting: "We all come back out of this mission together. No one is left behind."

We started this with our kids. Our team is only as good as the weakest man. We tried to sell it to the kids that they had to take care of each other. Just because a kid is not a starter, it does not mean that we cannot pay respect to that kid that is out there every day. If the coaches will let the players who are not starters know that they are proud of them for busting their tails, I am sure it will boost those athletes. Do not leave those guys behind. I am going to tell you, you will need them later in their careers. You can take negatives and turn them into positives.

The website, www.botkach.com, has a lot of information about mental health problems, depression, obsessive-compulsive disorders, and much more. Two former students set this up for us, and they maintain the cost through the local TV station. The video that I showed earlier was played on the local TV football show every Friday night. We feel that helped get the message out because we have had a lot of people come to us for help. Football coaches were starting to ask questions.

I will tell you this: Sandi has been the rock that has held everything together for our family. I was the football coach that everyone knew, and I was the loud, tough guy. However, she was the one that stood in my shadow. She kept the whole family together. She made it possible so we could continue to move along. I come up and speak, but Sandi is a very strong lady.

We had a commercial made promoting the need for awareness to mental health and depression. Football people were behind making that commercial.

I want to thank you for listening to a different presentation. It is hard to separate some of the football with the other areas of this lecture. I hope you got something out of this lecture. Just go and coach the heck out of them.

Thank you very much.

COVER 2 AND SECONDARY DRILLS

Pittsburgh Central Catholic High School, Pennsylvania

Let me start by saying it is an honor for me to have this opportunity to speak at the Nike Coach of the Year Clinic. I am always happy to represent Central Catholic. I want to give you the basics of cover 2, and then introduce my secondary coach, Coach Rick Capretta. He will break down some of the drill work for the corners and safeties.

When you become a head coach, they throw a lot of stuff on your plate. You lose contact with your athletes on the day-to-day intricacies of their positions. It is great to see so many coaches here that I know and have learned from.

In today's game, teams are spreading the defense with four wide receivers. We play about 35 percent of our snaps in cover 2. When I came to Central, I was a 4-3 stack, cover-2 coach. We were running around in shorts, playing in passing leagues, and I thought everything was going fine. We got into the first game, and I found out something real quick. I found out we were playing a two-back offense instead of a one-back set. I found out I did not have a two-gap middle linebacker. That is tough to have in high school football. What I did was adapt to a 4-4 cover-3 scheme.

I wanted to play someone in the four gaps on either side of the ball. As the season progressed, we played a bunch of one-back teams. I felt we had to get back to the cover-2 defense.

I want to go over the basic 4-4 defense with the cover-3 secondary (Diagram #1). With a 4-4 defense, you have an eight-man front with all the gaps covered. You have a three-deep secondary, which is sound. In the four-man front, we play with a 3 technique to the tight end and a shade nose to the openside. The ends play in a 7 technique to the tight end and a 5 technique to the openside. The strong

safety walks down to the outside as a D-gap defender. The Sam linebacker is a strong A-gap player, and the Mike linebacker is the weakside B-gap player. The Will linebacker is the D-gap player to the weakside.

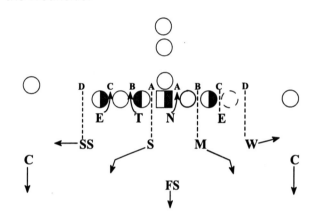

Diagram #1. 4-4 Cover 3

The weakness of the three-deep zone is the underneath zones. You have four underneath defenders and five zones to cover.

When we go to the 4-3 cover-2 defense, the gaps change a little (Diagram #2). The 9-technique end to the tight end is a D-gap player. The Sam linebacker has the C gap to the tight-end side. The 3-technique tackle has the B gap to the tight-end side. To the backside, the nose plays the backside shade on the center and plays the A gap to the backside. The backside end plays a 5 technique on the offensive tackle and is a C-gap player. The Will linebacker is the D-gap player to the openside. The Mike linebacker has to play two gaps. He plays the strong A gap and the weak B gap.

The offense went to a one-back set. That forced the Mike linebacker to play two gaps, but the offense lost a blocking back. When they go to the

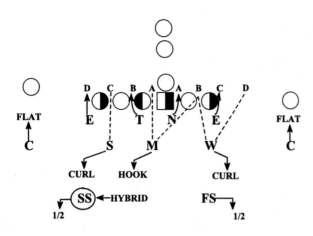

Diagram #2. 4-3 Cover 2

one-back set, they lose their blocking back and cannot isolate the Mike linebacker.

If we call "Central 23," that call adjusts to the offensive formation. If the offense is a one-back set, we play cover 2 in the secondary. If the offense comes out in a two-back set, we play cover 3 and walk the strong safety down to play 4-4 defense with cover 3 in the secondary.

We are fortunate to have a player who can play on the outside in the D gap as a force player and be able to play on the hash mark in a half-field scheme. He can also go out and help the corner with a jam technique on the wide receiver. To make this kind of adjustment, you must have a hybrid player in your scheme. He is the type of player who can play the outside linebacker on the 4-4 defense and play the half field in the cover-2 secondary.

From scouting a team, you know that 88 is their third receiver and 89 is their fourth receiver. If number 89 is not in the game, you can call cover 3. If the fullback leaves the game and 89 enters the game, you call cover 2. Those are all personnel issues, which you can address relatively easy. However, in high school football, the personnel groups are not clearly defined. High school teams change their formation, but not necessarily their personnel.

You cannot call the coverage until you see the set. That is why we double call the defense. We can adjust when we see the formation. If the formation comes out of the huddle as a one-back set, we fly into our cover 2 look and play the coverage. If they come out in a two-back set, the strong safety rolls up, and we play cover 3.

One of the things I do when I put in coverage or a defense is to let the defense know the strengths and weaknesses of that defense. When we talk about the strengths of the 4-4 cover-3 defense, we have eight defenders in the box and three deep secondary players.

When I put up the 4-3 cover-2 defense, we have a nine-man front with the force corner rolled up. The corners are the force players on this defense. We make it clear to our defense: if you are a flat player, you are also a force defender and a pitch player on the option. It all ties together. In this defense, I have the five-underneath zone covered. I have the corners rolled up in both flats. The Sam linebacker has the strongside curl zone, and the Will linebacker has the weakside curl zone. The Mike linebacker has the middle hook area.

I also have defenders in position to stop releases off the football. In high school, that is a critical point. The last thing the offense wants to see are their receivers getting jammed off the line of scrimmage. The weakness is the three deep zones covered with two defenders. That is something the defense has to work on to make their job easier.

When you play underneath zones in cover 2, you have to define the zones (Diagram #3). The flat zone is 10 yards deep on the tips of the numbers. The curl players are 12 to 14 yards deep and two yards outside the hash marks. The curl player's drop in cover 2 is different than it is in cover 3. In cover 3, there are only four underneath zone players instead of five in cover 2. In cover 3, the curl players had to work from inside the hash marks to outside, trying to close the large hole in the curl/flat area. The Mike linebacker is 12 yards deep and four yards inside the hash mark. The Will linebacker has the same drop as the Sam linebacker, and the backside corner has the same drop as the frontside corner.

The safeties are half players. I have an alignment rule at 11 yards and a hash mark rule. I

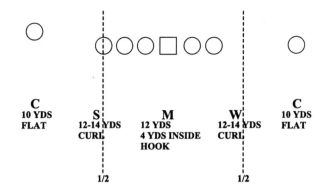

Diagram #3. Underneath Zones

want the two safeties to balance the field because there is a lot of field to cover. If the ball is on the far hash mark, I do not want the safety to align on the tackle in the tackle box. I do not want him any wider than two yards inside the hash mark.

Before the snap of the ball, the entire group of underneath defenders is aligned at five yards off the line of scrimmage. The corners align with outside leverage on the wide receivers. The Sam and Will linebacker align so they can control the second vertical receiver to either side.

I do not only play cover 2 to a one-back set. It is a game plan decision. If we play a team with a potent outside zone game, we will not be in a cover-2 shell. We will have the box loaded with defenders. We want the quarterback to show the defense he can throw the ball all over the lot before we go to a cover-2 defense. If the one back is a great tailback, you may want to stay in the 4-4 look.

I always start to teach the drops in a cover-2 defense in the middle of the field. Before they snap the ball, I want the linebackers to peek at where their drops are going to be. They have to see their landmarks on the field. When the quarterback sets up at five yards, they should square up in their zones. We want the relationship between the defenders so they can break and converge on the ball thrown between the zones.

After we work from the middle of the field, we go to the hash marks. Their angle to their drops will change from the hash marks. The Sam linebacker into the field has a long way to go to get to his curl area, which is two yards outside the hash mark. The

Will linebacker aligned into the boundary is almost backing straight up to get to his area. The Mike linebacker has a steep angle to get into the strongside hook area.

I add three things into the teaching of coverage. There are the three bastard looks the defense has to be aware of. The three looks are three-step drops, bootleg, and full-flow sprint-out. There are special responsibilities in cover 2 for those types of plays.

On the three-step drop, the defenders drive on the immediate threat. The corner has the three-step patterns right in front of him. Those patterns are generally a hitch or a slant. The corner sees the hitch pattern right in front of him. On the slant, the Sam linebacker on his drop should drive through the slant of the outside receiver to his side. The Mike linebacker has to find the tight end, the most immediate threat to him. The Will linebacker is playing like the Sam linebacker. He is driving on the most immediate threat to him.

The safeties take more teaching to play their techniques. On the three-step pass, the safeties want to freeze their feet. He has three routes to cover immediately. They have to play the slant or get off the hash mark to cover the fade route. This is a great defense against the quick passing game. We roll up in the receiver's face, ready to play the quick game. The hole in the cover-2 defense is the fade route at 18 yards on the sidelines. That takes some teaching for the safety to play the fade on the three-step game.

The bootleg is a whole other story. On the bootleg pass, there will always be a flat route, clear-out route, drag route, and backside post pattern. As soon as the defense sees the bootleg pass, they have to find those routes. I want to see the defense react to the pattern when they recognize the bootleg. I walk the linebackers through their reaction. I start them to the line of scrimmage to react to the play-action. When they see the bootleg, I want them to scramble to their zones and find those receivers.

On the bootleg, the corner jams the outside receiver running the clear out and settles into the flat, waiting for that pattern to come to him (Diagram #4). The safety to that side has to get off the hash mark to cover the clear route. The Sam linebacker reacts up to the fake. As soon as he recognizes the bootleg, he wants to drop to his curl. I do not want him to expand with the flow of the quarterback. He is the curl player, and the corner is the flat player. He settles into the curl, looking for the drag pattern from the other side. We do not want the Sam linebacker to get in the quarterback's face. He settles and waits on the drag route coming across the field.

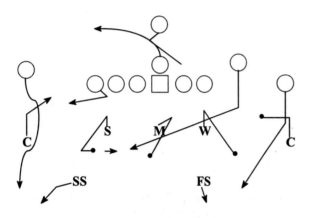

Diagram #4. Bootleg

The Mike linebacker steps up and retreats through the frontside hook area. The backside safety will handle the post pattern coming off the backside. The backside corner squeezes in from the backside flat. You have to work the bootlegs and let your defenders know they have a three-level route to handle. They cannot leave their zones on those types of passes. They have to get to their zones, and the patterns will come to them.

The third bastard look is the full flow sprint-out pass (Diagram #5). We define that pass as both backs and the quarterback going in the same direction. It could be one back and the quarterback in the same direction. In the diagram, the sprint is to the right with both backs and the quarterback outside the offensive tackle. We are going to squeeze the field. The Mike linebacker becomes the secondary contain defender on this play. He works laterally to the line of scrimmage and then goes to force the play. The corner stays on the flat route, and the Sam linebacker stays on the curl. The

safety to that side gets off the hash. He expands his two-yard hash rule by two yards.

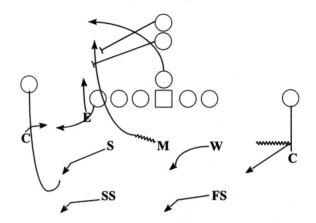

Diagram #5. Sprint-Out

The backside safety on action away from him runs two yards inside his hash mark. The backside corner squeezes to the backside hash mark. The Will linebacker squeezes the field and replaces the Mike linebacker. Both the safeties are off the hash marks, squeezing the field to the side of the sprint-out. I tell the linebackers they will not believe how fast a linebacker can get to a sprint quarterback. The linebacker forces more high throws than anything else. The quarterback does not want the linebacker in his face.

If the 9 technique does his job and contains the play, both backs will be on him. The alley to the quarterback is wide open for the Mike linebacker. He can get there in a hurry.

Our counting system is like everyone's. We number the receivers from the sideline to the backfield. In a double-wide slot formation, the wide receiver to the field is #1 strong; the second receiver going to the inside is #2 strong. The #3 receiver is the one-back in the backfield. The inside slot to the backside is #2 weak, and the wide receiver to the backside is #1 weak. We use the numbers in our cover-2 and man reads.

The corner has a read on the #1 receiver, moving to the #2 receiver. The Sam linebacker and strong safety read the #2 receiver, moving to the #1 receiver. The Mike linebacker reads the #3 receiver in the backfield. After I teach the defenders their drops, we start to read receivers. All the underneath players and the safeties are on a #2 to #1 read. Everybody looks at the #2 receiver to get into their coverage. The corner is lines up on the #1 receiver, but he looks at the #2 receiver.

The weakness of this defense is trying to cover three-deep zone with two defenders. We can play this coverage if all the underneath defenders do their job. The corner has to jam and funnel the #1 receiver to the inside. The Sam linebacker has to jam and wall the #2 receiver to the outside. If the underneath players can funnel their receivers into the half player, he has a chance to cover them.

If the defenders allow the receiver to get free releases, the half player has to cover from the hash mark to the sideline. That is a tall order. The underneath coverage has to collapse the receiver and funnel him into one area. If they do that, we can play the coverage.

The most dangerous thing that can happen to a cover-2 defense is four vertical routes (Diagram #6). When the corner sees the vertical release by the #2 receiver, he knows the safety has to cover. That tells him he has to jam the #1 receiver, funnel him inside, and get ready to run with him if he goes vertical.

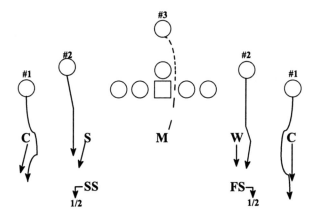

Diagram #6. Four Verticals

The Sam linebacker reads the #2 receiver and sees him going vertical. He looks through his curl and sees the #1 receiver going vertical. There is no threat to his curl zone from the outside. He continues to wall him outside and run with the #2

receiver as long as he goes vertical. This is match-up zone coverage.

If the #3 receiver would happen to go vertical, the Mike linebacker would play him like the Sam linebacker. If the #3 receiver was in a trips formation, he has to wall him out of the middle and run with him if he goes vertical.

If the #3 receiver swings out of the backfield, we do not attack that route. We have a no-cover zone up to five yards. Once the ball is thrown, we rally back to the tackle. The corner does not break back to the swing route and let the offense complete a pass on the sideline for the first down. After they throw the ball, the corner reacts up to make the tackle. If they ran the swing pattern out of three-receiver trips set, you will have to game plan for that.

The second most dangerous route is the smash route, which is a hitch by the #1 receiver with a corner route by the #2 receiver (Diagram #7). The corner reads the #2 receiver on a vertical route. He jams the #1 receiver, looking to see if he is coming vertical. The #1 receiver runs the six-yard hitch pattern in front of the corner. The corner does not jump routes run by the #1 receiver. He sinks into the dead zone behind him. He knows the #2 receiver has released vertical, and he has to play him coming in behind him.

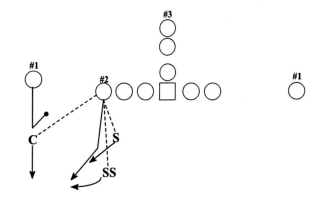

Diagram #7. Smash Route

The safety to that side reads the vertical release of the #2 receiver. He knows he has coverage on the #2 receiver. He forgets about the #1 receiver and plays the #2 receiver. The Sam linebacker reads the vertical release of the #2 receiver. He sees the hitch by the #1 receiver, but it is not coming inside to threaten his curl. He concentrates on the #2 receiver, trying to get him outside the hash mark.

Since Sam linebacker is walling the #2 receiver off the hash mark, the safety knows he can widen off the hash mark because the #2 receiver cannot get back inside to run a post cut. The safety plays over the top of the Sam linebacker. The Sam linebacker can continue to run with the #2 receiver to the corner because the #1 receiver never threatens his curl. If the quarterback throws the hitch, the corner reacts back to make the tackle and stops the receiver from making the first down. We want the corner to look through the receiver to see the quarterback as well. He wants to know if the quarterback is throwing the hitch or coming downfield with the ball.

You might think this is a lot of teaching. It is. It is what we do in the summer, playing touch football. We play the coverage, and we teach these reads. You have to get the reads and reps to play this kind of coverage.

If the offense puts two wide receivers in the formation, they like to run the curl/flat combination (Diagram #8). Everyone in the coverage is reading the #2 receiver. If he goes to the flat, the Sam linebacker knows he does not have a threat from the #2 receiver. His eyes go to the #1 receiver. He knows he will be the next threat to his curl zone. He matches up on the #1 receiver coming inside. We tell the Sam linebacker the curl zone is 12 to 14 yards deep and two yards outside the hash mark. However, the curl is wherever the #1 receiver runs it.

When the corner sees the #2 receiver start to the flat, he has to leverage that pattern immediately. The safety to that side sees the #2 receiver go to the flat, and his eyes go to the #1 receiver. He plays the #1 receiver on the post, and over the top on the rail route by the #2 receiver turning up the field.

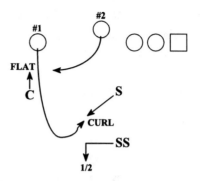

Diagram #8. Curl/Flat

We all face the bubble screens and three-step hitches. We also get the jet sweep from this formation. I think this coverage is great for defending those types of plays. We are going to be physical and aggressive on run and pass with this coverage. If the offense's third and fourth receiver can block the Sam or Will linebackers on the perimeter, they are going to be standing next to me on the sidelines. Those linebackers cannot let that happen.

If the offense goes to the empty set, we make an empty call. We put the nose and 3 techniques into the A gaps so they can play the quarterback draw.

I play the cover-2 look against four wide receivers. I have to play two gaps with the Mike linebacker, but there is no threat of an isolation play. The blitzes come out of our cover-2 shells. When we get in the cover-2 alignments, we disguise what we are doing in the secondary. The linebackers walk in and out on the #2 receivers, blitz on certain occasions, and play coverage on other occasions.

To teach the coverage, I get them to spot drop to landmarks. You can only spend a day or two on that in camp. By the end of the second day, we are into reads. I think it is a great defense against the bubble screens, rocket screens, quick-game passes, jet sweep, or speed option. It allows us to be physical on the wide receivers.

ASSISTANT COACH RICK CAPRETTA

What I am going to do is review what Terry just said, and talk about some of the techniques we use to play the coverage. To play this defense well, your corners and safeties must have good feet and hips.

Every drill we do emphasizes the players' feet and hips. We have a great trainer/speed coach, who constantly emphasizes all those ideas.

We want to play with our shoulders over our knees and the knees over the feet. We do not have the 4.4 or 4.5 defensive back, so we must be technically sound. The corners are five yards off the ball. We can loosen to seven yards based on his experience and skill. We want the corner to get his feet moving before the receiver does.

In our stance, we want the shoulders over the knees and the knees over the feet. The feet are slightly wider than the shoulder-width. He has one eye on the quarterback and one eye on the #2 receiver. If there is no #2 receiver, he has one eye on the running back in the backfield. He wants to find the football. You can play this defense, but you must get tons of reps.

The corner aligns with an outside leverage position on the outside shoulder. When you play the technique in an off position, it is difficult to get hands on the receiver. When we drill this, we have the corner put his hands behind his back. We want him to put his face on the receiver. We use a shuffle and get the facemask on the receiver.

On an inside release by the receiver, the corner gets his hands on the receiver and pushes him to the hash mark. The thing he cannot do is be outleveraged by the #2 receiver. He never wants to be outleveraged to the outside. The inside release is easier because you have the #1 receiver, #2 receiver, and the quarterback in your vision.

The outside release by the receiver is a hard release to play. The corner has to shuffle his feet and jam the receiver. We want to fight him and make him release inside as much as possible. If the receiver gets outside the corner, he has to get his head back around to the quarterback. We do not want to be at the mercy of the receiver. We never want to turn our backs to the quarterback in a rolled-up cover 2. The corner shuffles, keeps the receiver in front of him, jams with the outside arm, and sinks to a point.

We want to discourage the three-step game with our alignment. The outside release has to be met with the shuffle as if you were playing man-to-man in basketball. The most difficult thing to teach a young corner is to turn inside. He wants to chase the receiver.

We disguise our defense quite a bit. When we are playing man-to-man, we want to show cover 2. When we play cover 2, we want to show man. We walk up in press coverage and bail out.

The safeties align at 10 to 12 yards, depending on their skill. Their landmark is the hash marks of the field. The safety has one eye on the quarterback and one eye on the #2 receiver. He pedals for two steps, shuffles, and freezes to find out what is going on. If the safety gets a drag or flat by the #2 receiver, he gets off the hash because the #1 receiver becomes the most dangerous receiver to him. The speed of the wide receiver will determine the distance off the hash the safety moves. The faster the receiver, the further off the hash the safety comes. He can come off the hash three or four yards.

We know the offense wants to attack our cover 2 in the middle of the field and on the sidelines between the corner and the safety. The drills we do are vertical drills, featuring the post and corner routes. We run receivers up the field straight at the safety.

The alignment of the safeties will vary according to down-and-distance. The strongside safety has to be your best tackler because he is involved with the run game. Cover 2 allows you to communicate and trust your teammates. Everyone involved with the coverage must communicate. The safeties have to talk to the corners and linebackers. That is critical in cover 2 because you are constantly getting drag routes and complementary routes. You develop that communication and trust in the summertime, when you are working in passing leagues and summer practice.

When we first start to teach the defense, we sink our defenders into the skeleton drop areas. If you want to run a good cover-2 defense, you have to be in position. Playing cover 2 is not as difficult if you are in the right place.

The next drill in teaching the cover-2 defense is to run routes into the coverage. Cover 2 is good against teams that have blazing speed at the receiver positions. On a running play, we want the corners to attack the receivers, defeat them, and squeeze the lane. That allows the safety to come up into the alley and play football. This defense attacks in the running game.

That is what a spread team likes to do. They want to spread the defense so they can run the ball. We constantly work on this idea in the summertime. It is not a pass-happy type of practice. We concentrate on run support from the cover-2 alignment.

Players want to do more than they are asked to do. They do not think anything is going on in their zone and stray out of their area, following a receiver. When something happens in their zone, they are out of position to stop the pass. If the corner squeezes inside, that is the time the offense will throw the screen to the backside.

To get as many reps as we can in practice, we go with a half-field drill (Diagram #9). We have an offense on each side of the field. We run two- and three-man patterns in the drill. We run every combination of routes imaginable. The things we work on in this drill are switch routes. That is an important route because we have corners who want to chase receivers instead of backing off and sinking over the top of the #1 receiver.

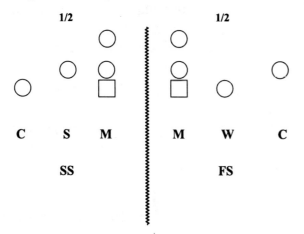

Diagram #9. Half-Field Drill

You can draw up any route in practice. This is the time to work on the game plans against the offense's favorite plays. If you are organized, you can get a surprising amount of routes in a short amount of time. This is generally a 15-minute drill. After 15 minutes of dropping and chasing the ball, the players are spent. This is the best form of coaching because everything is right there in front of you. You can threaten any defensive back or linebacker you want.

In the drill, we have two sets of offenses and defenses working. We have a center, quarterback, running back, and two receivers on the offense. On the defense, we have the corner, outside linebacker, Mike linebacker, and safety. The coaches work from one drill to the other. The offenses stagger their plays so one side goes and then the other side. At the beginning, we use cards with the routes draw on them. Our scouts learn the patterns very quickly, and that increases the number of plays you can run in the 15-minute period.

You have a lot of people working. If you wanted to, you could turn the drill into a man-to-man drill. That is great for identifying athletes early in the summer when you have your young players working. You have receivers running routes and the quarterbacks throwing. You get a good quarterback/center exchange on every rep.

When we get into the season, we use the drill as a support drill. That lets us see the corners, linebackers, and safeties working their support, pursuit, and fits on the running game. We get to see the safeties running the alleys and linebackers fitting inside the support player.

Another pattern I like to work on the corners during this drill is the #1 receiver on a go pattern and the #2 receiver on an out. We want the deep out at 10 yards. We want the corner to jam the receiver, force him inside, and find the hole under the #2 receiver on the out pattern.

You can incorporate the shed blocking with this drill. We work the corners on stalk blocks from the wide receivers. We work the safeties on the tight end or a #2 receiver. These are 1-on-1 drills. The good thing about the drill is you get the reps you need to play this defense.

The drills you need to work with the corners are shuffle drills. (Diagram #10). In the shuffle drill, we work it with two receivers and a corner. The corner aligns on the outside receiver. He jams that receiver, forces him inside, and has to find the other receiver.

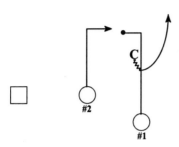

Diagram #10. 2-on-1 Shuffle Drill

Another drill we incorporate into our scheme is the get-beat drill. We line up the defensive back and a wide receiver on a line. The wide receiver breaks downfield, and the defensive back chases him. He gives the receiver a head start and tries to catch up as they run down the field. We later incorporate the free safety into the drill, covering over the top.

A drill we work with the safeties is to put a receiver on the sidelines and the safety on the hash mark. We snap the ball, and the safety begins to pedal. He goes into his run and has to break to the sideline when the ball is thrown. That is all I have. I am going to turn the program back over to Coach Totten.

COACH TOTTEN

When we play cover 2, all the secondary players have their eyes on the #2 receiver. However, we want to try to emphasize—in every drill and every play—to find the football. The secondary player cannot make a play without finding the football.

With one back in the backfield, we want to know who he is and where he is aligned. If the back is a fullback aligned three yards deep, you get trapped. If it is the tailback aligned at five yards, it will be the zone play if they run the ball. I want to keep as many linebackers in the box as I can. If the #2 receiver is in a wide split position, I tell the linebacker to get into a position where he can wall

him out of the middle. We play down-and-distance. If it is a run situation, we do not walk the linebacker out on the #2 receiver. If the #2 receiver is split outside the hash marks, the linebacker will only go to the hash mark. The #2 receiver has walled himself out of the middle by his alignment.

The linebacker drops to the hash mark so he can meet the #2 receiver if he tries to threaten the curl or the middle of the field. We do not want him walking all the way out and opening the middle.

If the offense comes out in a trips set, we stack the linebackers in a 30 alignment. We make a "bump" call. We bump the linebackers across to the trips side (Diagram #11). The Sam linebacker walks out on the #2 receiver and plays his wall technique on the #2 receiver. The Mike linebacker moves over and aligns on the outside shoulder of the guard. He is in position to play inside of the #3 receiver in the slot. He has to control the #3 receiver. The Will linebacker moves over into a 30 alignment on the backside guard.

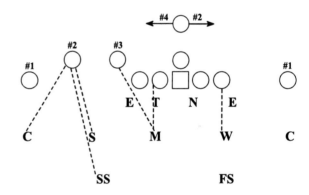

Diagram #11. Trips Adjustment

The Will linebacker has to be aware of the #1 receiver to the backside. He has to help the corner on the slant inside. The offense puts their best receiver at the single receiver and tries to exploit the soft coverage into the backside. We do not check to cover 3. We play cover 2 and play the stud receiver in a 3-on-1 scheme. We have the safety over the top of the corner. The corner plays a tough jam technique on him, and the Will linebacker give support on the inside. The Will linebacker has to be aware of the one back in the backfield because he is the #2 receiver to the weakside. He is also the #4 receiver to the trips side.

If the offense runs the trips set as part of their regular offense, I put the Will linebacker to the trips side and the Sam to the single-receiver side. The Will linebacker is the better pass coverage defender.

If they align in a double set and motion into the trips set, the linebackers bump over. The Sam linebacker moves out on the #2 receiver, and the Mike and Will linebackers bump to a 30 alignment.

If the offense gets into trips set with the tight end as the #3 receiver to the trips side, we make a "switch" call (Diagram #12). That tells the 9-technique defensive end to move into a 7 technique on the tight end. The Sam linebacker bumps out onto the #2 receiver. When he moves out of the box, you do not have a C-gap defender. We move the defensive end into the C gap on the inside shoulder of the tight end.

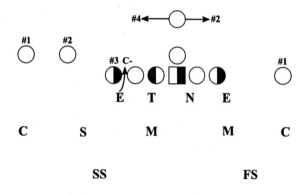

Diagram #12. Tight End Trips

With no tight end in the game, we bump the linebackers. If they run an empty set, the Will linebacker plays as he normally would on the #2 receiver to his side (Diagram #13). The defensive tackles move inside to the A gaps to protect against the quarterback draw, and the Mike linebacker moves outside to 30 technique to control the #3 receiver.

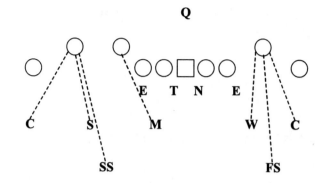

Diagram #13. Empty Set

I hope this gives you an alternative defense to play against teams that want to spread the field. The biggest problem is young corners playing the jam technique on receiver. You have to train them on the outside release. He wants to turn and go with the receiver instead of shuffling outside and forcing him inside. When he turns and chases the receiver, he loses his vision on the quarterback and is at the mercy of the receiver.

It is hard to get the safeties to trust their technique in the half-field. They want to get off the hash mark too quickly. They have to trust their technique and react to what happens in front of them. If the safety aligns and takes a step toward the #2 receiver, he is one step off the hash mark on his first step instead of being on the landmark.

The other technique you have to coach hard is the technique of the outside linebackers on the inside route by #1. The linebacker has to wall off the #2 receiver, but he has to see the #1 receiver. As he runs with the #2 receiver, he sees the #1 receiver plant and come into his zone from the outside. He has to release the #2 receiver, settle into his zone, and play the #1 receiver. That is hard to teach and execute.

One of the problems we had with our corners was being too aggressive on the wide receiver. We were continuing to jam the receiver on the hitch with the ball in the air. We have to learn when to release the receiver and when to beat him up.

Thank you, coaches. It has been fun, and I hope we helped you find an alternative coverage.

THE 4-3 DEFENSE AND STUNTS

Orchard Park High School, New York

I want to thank you for being here today. I hope you get a lot out of this lecture. We had a great year this year. When we started this program, we had 35 players on the team. We now have three teams with 40 players on each of those teams, and we have 300 kids in our program. This year, we graduated 26 players who started with our program seven years ago.

I am going to talk about four things today. I am going to talk about the power play, zone play, play-action, and the quick game. Those are the staples of our offense. The great thing about all of the plays is the simple blocking schemes. With our blocking scheme, it does not matter what the weather is or what the defense runs. We can handle zone blitzes and pressure.

That is critical, especially in Buffalo. The last three or four games of the season are bad-weather games. We had turf this year, which helped us. We are very simple in our schemes, but we are very multiple in our approach. Our blocking has its background in the wing-T and double wing. From there we went to the power I and the pro I, and the last two or three years we have been in the spread offense.

Our offense is A to Z, from the power I to the spread offense. This was unique for us, but more recently, I have seen some high schools in Oklahoma running quite a bit of pro I with a combination of the spread offense. I think what we are doing is great. If you win the turnover battle, you will win 90 percent of your games. If you average over 200 yards rushing, you will win 94 percent of your games. If you do all those things and have a big special-teams play, you will win 97 percent of your games.

We are not going to turn the ball over. Our quick game is safe, the power game is safe, and the zone scheme we have developed over the last three years is safe. Our play-action passing is great with regard to turning the ball over.

In our power-I sets, we run the stack I. That is two tight ends and three backs aligned in the I formation behind the quarterback. We can break the I and get into a wing set with two tight ends. We align in a tight slot to one side and a flanker/tight-end alignment to the other side. That is a one-back set in the backfield. We can get into the trips tight-end set. We also align in a spread formation. When we get into the spread formations, we align in double slots and trips sets.

This year, we used a different formation. We called it our "rhino formation" (Diagram #1). I think it is a better alternative than the power I. You have the same blocking as the power I, but you can run either side with the play. We set two backs behind the guards one yard off the line of scrimmage. The quarterback is in the shotgun with the tailback behind him. You can run power either way and counter either way.

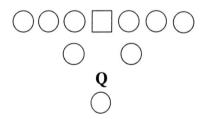

Diagram #1. Rhino

We like to get into the wing outside the tight end with a flanker to that side (Diagram #2). We can throw our choice routes to the one receiver on the backside of this formation. We run the zone from this formation.

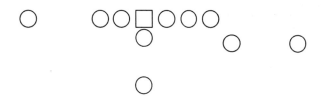

Diagram #2. Trips Wing

We also run a no-huddle scheme that speeds up the offense. We have names and numbers for our players. Our power scheme is based on a down block with a kick-out and a lead block. We also run a block down, kick-out, and double lead. On occasion, we lead two blockers through the hole, and at other times, we lead one blocker though the hole.

The blocking rules are down and bump. The last man on the line of scrimmage is the down blocker. If the tight end is the last man on the line of scrimmage, he blocks down. If there is no tight end, the tackle has the down block. In a 50 defense, the tackle has a man on his outside shoulder, and the guard is uncovered (Diagram #3). The tackle does not have a down block because there is no defender from head-up on the guard to head-up on the tackle. The tackle's rule becomes bump.

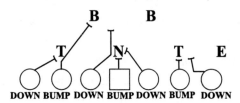

Diagram #3. Down/Bump Block 50 Front

If the tight end has the down block, he picks up his inside foot and takes a three-inch step. He picks his foot up and puts it back down. His next step is up the midline of his body. We use that same footwork on our zone play. It is like a dance step with everyone taking the same steps.

In a bump block, the offensive tackle takes an up-and-down step with his outside foot. He steps and punches the man on his outside shoulder with his outside hand. He is in a temporary double-team with the tight end who has a down block. That is the double-team we use in our power and zone plays. The tackle's eyes are to the inside at the second level of the defense. If the linebacker runs through the B gap, he comes off the block and has a down block on the linebacker.

In the 40 front, the tight end has a down block on the 7-technique defender (Diagram #4). If for some reason the tight end cannot handle the 7 technique, we give an "I" call. He blocks out, and the fullback or guard kicks out the 7 technique. The tackle has a down block on the 3 technique. The guard has no down block and bumps the 3 technique. He and the tackle are in a temporary double-team on the 3 technique. The guard's eyes are to the inside on the second level. He stays on the double-team as long as he can. The tackle and guard walk the 3 technique until the guard has to leave for the linebacker. We practice the double-teams repeatedly.

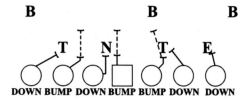

Diagram #4. Down/Bump Block 40 Front

We start each practice with a punting drill. We punt four out of five days a week. I think the punt is the most critical play in football. You can dig a hole with one bad punt. We have not had a punt blocked in eight years. The biggest part of that fact is the snapper. We have great snappers. Our punter is our quarterback. He is a good athlete and can kick it 45 yards.

While we are working the punting game, the offensive linemen are on the side, working their steps. They work on their footwork and double-team every day.

On our power play, we pull the backside guard. Our blocking rules for the pulling guard are simple. We pull the guard, and the center, backside tackle, and tight end block what we call "zone to the puller" (Diagram #5). The center has a down block and blocks back for the pulling guard. The backside tackle rule is to zone-step to the puller. The backside guard pulls and the backside tackle zone-steps into that gap and blocks whoever is there.

The backside tight end zone-steps to the puller. He zone-steps toward the pulling guard and blocks his gap. Those rules allow us to be very aggressive.

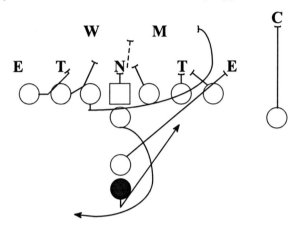

Diagram #5. Zone to the Puller

The splits in the offensive line are anywhere from 6 to 18 inches. If we think a blocker needs help, we cut our splits down. In short yardage, we cut our splits down. The 18-inch split makes our first step the right distance. That distance makes the step seem as if it was built for our zone scheme.

We run the G-scheme, which has been a great scheme for us (Diagram #6). If we are having trouble with the defensive end crashing on the fullback and wrong-arming him, we have a solution. We use a G-scheme to make the block. Our alternative power scheme is to pull the frontside guard. It is a good scheme because the end so many times does not see the guard coming, and it is an easier block for the guard. The center and backside blockers zone to the puller as their rule.

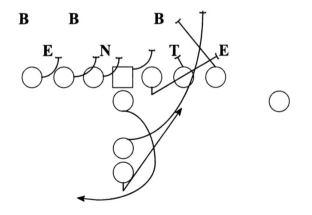

Diagram #6. G-Scheme

Our other power scheme is the counter (Diagram #7). We pull the backside guard and tackle. The playside is blocked the same as all the power plays to the playside. On the counter, the fullback comes to the backside to cut off the backside. The guard kicks out at the tackle, who turns up in the hole looking for the frontside linebacker. If we do not want to pull the tackle, we add the word "cat." In that case, we can put one or two blocking backs into the hole, depending on the formation. We have a number of 26 plays. We add the word to name the scheme we want to use. If we call "26 cat," that is the counter without the tackle pulling.

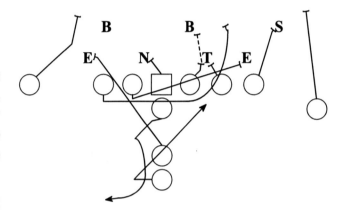

Diagram #7. Counter

We can use motion off the backside as a puller or align in the backside slot and pull him. We use the H-back, fullback, another tight end, or a lineman with an eligible number to pull off the backside (Diagram #8). Most of the time, we double-team block at the point of attack on the power play.

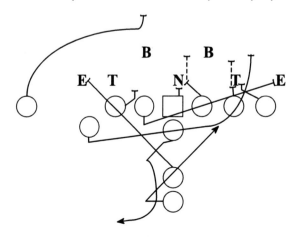

Diagram #8. Openside Pull

When we name things in our offense, we try to use three-letter words. We call 30 hot, which is an outlet pass. We call 26 cat, which is a counter with no pulling tackle. We use the term "Bob," which means big-on-big.

We became good at deceiving the defense. We use motions and formations to confuse the defense. My son was a running back for me. He rushed for 2,000 yards the last two years. Our quarterback is going to Bucknell because he was a great runner. That gave us the ability to have two backs in the backfield running our I-formation blocking schemes. We sat in multiple formations and motioned into sets that we wanted to run our offense. We made sure to break the tendencies so that people would not be able to set their defense according to our motion. We ran plays away from the motion and not just toward the play.

We keep running the same blocking scheme with different linemen pulling. We pull the onside guard and the backside guard with the same blocking. The big plays come when the receivers block downfield. We work hard on stalk blocking in practice.

When we run the zone play, it is the same blocking and the power, except you do not pull anyone. When we first started to run the zone play, I was leery about running it. I did not think it would be an effective play for high school players. I got some tape from Jim McNally of the Buffalo Bills and watched how they blocked the play. That was the theory behind the play. The zone and the power was the same play. The zone play is all about the steps in the offensive line and steps the back takes syncing up on the play.

When we run the zone, the aiming point for the back is the playside leg of the center. The only time we read the zone play is from the shotgun. If we are under center and the quarterback calls "back," that means the fullback will block the backside away from the play. That keeps the backside defender from coming down the line and cutting the play off.

From the shotgun, that is the defender we read. Against the 50 defense, the center and backside guard work a temporary double-team on the nose (Diagram #9). The guard, tackle, and tight end run a zone scheme for the linebacker, 5-technique tackle, and the 6-technique end. The backside guard and tackle cut blocking on defenders in their gaps.

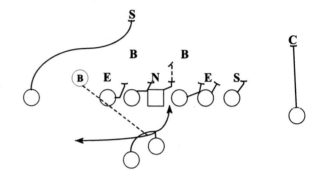

Diagram #9. Zone Read vs. 50

With any zone play, it is important to keep contact on the defenders. The zone plays work if you can get the defense to move. The chop blocks on the backside are the thing that creates the seams on the play. We want to stay with the double-teams as long as the defense will let us. We do not come off for linebackers until the linebackers begin to press the line of scrimmage. The frontside linebacker is the linebacker that will least likely be blocked. He generally overruns the play, and we end up behind him upfield.

In the 3-3 stack defense, we have to use our zone rules (Diagram #10). The playside guard and tackle block the 5-technique stack. The center and backside guard block the nose stack. The backside tackle and tight end cut block on the backside B and C gaps. If there is no tight end and the quarterback is in the shotgun, we read the outside defender on the backside. If he plays the quarterback on the bootleg, we run the zone play. If he comes flat down the line of scrimmage, trying to make a play on the tailback, we pull the ball and run out the backside of the formation. On some of our zone plays, we have as many as three double-teams.

Against the 4-2 defense, the center and playside guard work a double-team on the 2-technique defender (Diagram #11). When we have a double-team block, I want four hands in the

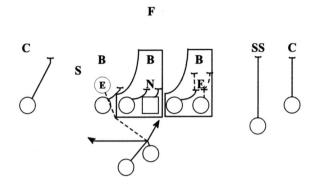

Diagram #10. Zone Read vs. 3-3

defender's chest. I want four eyes on the linebacker. We walk the down lineman up into the face of the linebacker. If the linebacker tries to get across the top of the double-team, that is the movement the back wants to see. We have a double-team on the 3-technique defender. The linebacker tries to get over the top into the outside gap. That opens the cutback lane for the running back.

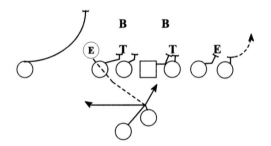

Diagram #11. Zone vs. 4-2

If the backside double-team does their job, we have a big running lane on the cutback. The backside tackle and guard are working the double-team on the backside 2 technique. They have four hands on the defender and four eyes on the linebacker. The tackle and tight end to the playside zone-step and work for the 6-technique end and outside linebacker.

We are not big in the offensive line. Size does not matter with the zone play. You must have movement and no penetration. It is important to use the momentum of the defender to get him to move.

The beauty of the scheme is that it is not bothered by blitzes. The more defenders that the defense sends, the better the play is for us. The

coaching point for the back is to be slow to the hole and fast through the hole. The back cannot get in a hurry to get into the line of scrimmage. The key to zone running is to explode once you make the cut. The zone play is not a shake-and-bake type of play. The running back's moves must be quick and decisive. He presses the line of scrimmage, but once he decides where to run, he explodes through the line of scrimmage.

The quarterback reads the backside defender. If he comes down the line, the quarterback pulls the ball. If the defender stays at home, the quarterback gives the ball to the tailback. If the defender comes up the field, he gives the ball.

If you run the spread offense, you must have an answer for pressure. The play-action fits right into our offense. From the shotgun, you can run the naked bootleg or pull the backside guard to secure the throw (Diagram #12). The offensive line blocks the zone play to the right. The pattern is a three-level stretch pass. The outside receiver to the playside runs a corner route and takes the top off the coverage. The H-back in the tight slot to the playside blocks down on the man to his inside for two counts.

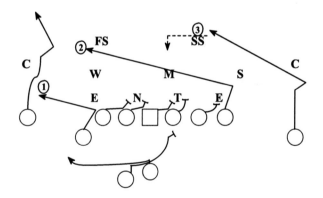

Diagram #12. Naked

After he blocks down, he releases into the flat at three yards. The first receiver to the inside on the backside of the play runs a drag pattern across the field, getting to the depth of 10 to 12 yards. The outside receiver runs the center-of-the-field read. If the middle is open, he runs his pattern into the center of the field. If there is anyone in the middle, he hooks over the center at 10 yards. That is our concept for the naked or bootleg passes. If we call "back" on this play and the fullback goes to the backside to cut off on the defensive end, he runs the flat pattern.

The quarterback makes the play look like the read play. He has to put the ball in the tailback's stomach. It is a better fake to place the ball in the belly of the tailback. The quarterback pulls the ball and comes out on the fake. His read depends on the amount of time he has to throw the ball.

If the defense is fooled, he has time to look deep first. If he has a defender in his face immediately, he gets rid of the ball to the flat right away. If that pattern is open, we take it because it is an easy throw and catch. The flat read is the first read, the drag is the second read, and the center read pattern is the third choice.

The tailback makes a good fake and cuts off to the backside. The tailback needs to look at the defenders on the fake. We do not want him to put his head down. That looks so unnatural. We want the naked to look exactly like the run.

If we want to tag the pattern of the playside wide receiver, we can get him involved. We can bring him back to the quarterback on a comeback. We can do a number of things, but they are all scouting-report material. If we want to protect the quarterback, we pull the backside guard. The running back fakes and fills for the pulling guard. We can get the backside guard to pull by saying, "Boot."

We can run the power pass out of a number of different sets. The one I am going to show you comes from a stack-I formation (Diagram #13). The line is blocking, turning back in their protection. The first back in the stack runs his pattern into the flat. The playside tight end runs a corner pattern. The backside tight end runs a drag across the formation. The quarterback has a flood pattern to the playside. We run a both backs to the playside and fake the off-tackle power. The quarterback looks to the flat first, drag second, and the flag if it is a touchdown.

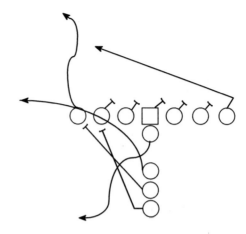

Diagram #13. Power Pass

Our three-step game is our 30 series. The protection scheme is big-on-big (Diagram #14). Our center is right-handed. When he snaps the ball, his hand is between his legs. He always blocks the left A gap. If there is a man in the left A gap, the center and left guard get four hands on him. They have their hands on the down man, but they look at the linebacker. If the linebacker comes, one of the blockers comes off on the linebacker. The back blocks the inside linebacker to his side.

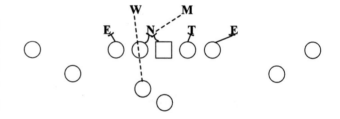

Diagram #14. Three-Step Protection

If we see an immediate threat in the A gaps by the linebackers, we get a "jacket" call. The line seals their inside gaps, and the back is an edge blocker on the defensive end. If the back is opposite the jacket call, he has to come to the other side. If the linebacker comes late, the back blocks him, and there is no jacket call.

We run a play called 27 show (Diagram #15). The show stands for shovel option. The playside guard and tackle block down on the nose and backside linebacker. The backside guard pulls and wraps around the center for the playside linebacker. The H-back moves up the field and stalks the safety. The corner stalks the corner. The quarterback is the kick-out blocker. He does that by sprinting out with the ball. That should bring the defensive end to the quarterback. The tailback steps up and follows the pulling guard into the gap. The backside blockers apply their rules and zones to the puller.

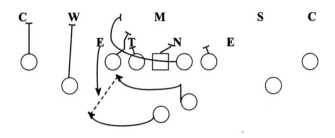

Diagram #15. 27 Show

We have an opposite call that is helpful for us in our running game. If we come to the line of scrimmage and the playside is loaded with more defenders than we can block, we call opposite and run the same play to other side.

We have some simple rules for the quarterback in throwing the ball. If he has a choice of receivers, he wants to take the shortest throw. The second thing he wants to consider is the softest coverage. If the shortest throw has a pressed coverage on him, that is not an easy throw or the safest. He takes the longer throw to the receiver into the wideside of the field, with a soft corner on him. We want to take the safest throw. Turnovers are killer for the offense's team. You lose possession of the ball and field position, and, generally, it leads to a score.

I hope you got something out of this talk. Thank you for your attention.

THE 4-3 DEFENSE AND SECONDARY COVERAGES

Westfield High School, Virginia

Most people do not know where Westfield High School is. We are a large school right outside of Washington D.C. We are excited to be here. I want to introduce Kyle Simmons, my defensive coordinator. We are going to be working together and, hopefully, we can give you something that will help you. The good thing about speaking at a clinic is that it is great for your staff because we all work together.

I want to tell you some things about our school. We are in Chantilly, Virginia, outside of Washington D.C. We have been there nine years, and we have 3000 students in grades 9 through 12. We play in the toughest conference in the state of Virginia. Our conference consists of six schools, and they are very big schools.

The first day of practice this year, we had 240 players out for football. We do not cut anyone, but some, obviously, cut themselves. The 240 players included freshmen, but that is still a lot of people. We have a large number of players, and we do things a little different from other people. We have been relatively successful. We have been 88-18 over the last nine years. We have won five district titles, two regional titles, and two state titles over those nine years.

Five of my assistants have been with me for over 20 years, and the other coaches I have known for a long time. We have a staff that has been together forever. We have 16 coaches on our staff including the freshman staff. That has been a big part of our success. The second thing that makes us successful is that we have good athletes.

We came to talk about defense today, but before we can get into X's and O's, I want to talk some philosophy. You must have a philosophy of how you are going to run and manage the game.

The first thing we talk about is our offense, defense, and special teams working together to put the other groups in the best situations. You will understand more about that in a minute—it is huge to our success. We always start talking about being as good as we can be on defense. The offensive coaches get the first picks from the talent base we have on our team. They pick their quarterback, wide receiver, and running back. The running back and wide receiver may play some defense, but the quarterback never will.

After the offense picks their quarterback, wide receiver, and running back, the defense gets the rest of the athletes. Doing that brought our program around. The guy who is playing tailback for Penn State, Evan Royster, was our tailback. However, when it came to a critical situation on defense, he played defense. We talk about our offense helping our defense.

On offense, we need more than 12 first downs a game. If we can get 12 first downs on offense, our defense will be good. The offense does not want to turn the ball over. We want to limit the penalties. On offense, we want to take care of the ball, run the clock, and score points. In the last seven years, we have averaged over 39 points a game.

On the special teams, we want no blocked kicks. We want to return every kickoff outside the 35-yard line. When we kick off, we want to keep the receiver inside their 25-yard line. Probably the most important thing is catching all the punts. If we can do all of those things, we can help our defense to be successful.

On defense, we want to allow no rushing touchdowns. Our philosophy is to stop the run. In every game we want to have at least four three-and-out series. We want to get two turnovers per game.

Turnovers on offense and defense are tremendously important to us. On offense, you must practice ball security. We do not fumble the ball. Practice is not a very pleasant place for someone who fumbles the ball. The other part of "no fumbles" is having the quarterback throw the ball away. We do not want him to take a sack or force the ball into coverage and put our defense in a bad situation.

On defense, we constantly coach our players to get turnovers. We practice strip drills at every position and work with our defensive backs and linebackers to catch the football. For us to be successful, we have to turn people over in games.

When we get a turnover, we want to get to the near sideline. If we get an interception, the first player we block is the intended receiver. If we can take him out of the play, we can get a big return. When we get the turnover, we want to know where we are going with the ball. That is something we do not do very well, but we are working on it.

I included some things in this lecture because I think it proves a point. In 2005, we did not have one of our better teams. However, we had some good players and a great tailback. In the first nine games that year, we were 9-0 and did not lose a fumble. In the first nine games that year, we had four interceptions but two of them were Hail Marys at the end of a half. We really had two interceptions. In the 10th game, we had two fumbles and one interception and lost the game.

We went into the playoffs having to play the same team we lost to in the 10th game in the first round of the playoffs. In the first game, our defense played great. In the second game, the defense played great. In the second game, the offense had no turnovers, and we won the game 31-7. That is the point we are talking about in our philosophy.

We feel like time of possession in a game is important.

THREE-AND-OUT BY THE OFFENSE

- Wears out your defense
- Defense cannot make adjustments
- Defense gets into panic mode
- Loss of field position

If your offense comes on the field and throws the football three times and does not pick up a first down, you have to punt the ball. The defense does not have time to rest. If that happens too many times, it wears out your defense.

If the offense turns the ball back to the other offense too quickly, the defensive staff does not have time to make the coaching adjustments. We have to make those adjustments in the course of the game. If we cannot get those adjustments made, the defense goes into a panic mode. If the offense cannot move the ball, the defense feels the pressure to stop the other team right now. That kind of thinking leads to mistakes and risk taking. If you cannot get first downs, you will lose more field position with every possession. You must move the football, or you put the pressure on your kicking game and defense.

When you get three-and-outs by the defense, there are some positive things that come from that.

THREE-AND-OUT BY THE DEFENSE

- Offense gets multiple possessions
- Defense stays fresh
- Causes offensive mistakes

When the defense forces the offense to give up the ball in three downs, it gives the offense more possessions. The more possessions the offense has, the better chance they have of scoring. When the defense plays fewer plays, they stay fresher, which allows them to play with greater speed. We feel like the offense falls into that panic mode and tries to make something happen, which causes them to make mistakes. They try to do something instead of simply punting the ball and playing defense. It causes a change of field position in your favor.

We concentrate on our special teams. In practice every day, we have one to two special teams periods. We spend 20 to 25 minutes at every practice working on special teams. When we play special teams, we use defensive players. We want speed on the field. We may not play them on the first defensive unit, but they are defensive players with speed. This gives the players more reps, and they are contributing and getting ready to play next year. Our defense feeds off big plays. Special teams can turn the momentum of a game faster than any other play in football. If our team makes a big play on special teams, they go crazy. Special teams are the key to field position.

We want to make our opponent drive the length of the field to score. In 2007, in the state semi-finals, we had to play the number 18 team in the country, Oscar Smith High School. I do not know how to describe the amount of talent that team had. We could not match up with them athletically. They were unbelievable. In that game, we averaged 43 yards a punt, and they had zero return yardage. Oscar Smith averaged 25 yards a punt, and we averaged eight yards a return. That led us to a 24-21 win. We won the special teams/field-position battle and won the game.

DEFENSIVE PHILOSOPHY

- Kill the run.
- Know your scheme; be able to make adjustments.
- Keep player jobs as simple as possible.
- Allow athletes to make plays.

When we played Oscar Smith in 2007, they were averaging 400 yards a game. We did not allow them to rush the ball and made them one-dimensional. If you allow a team to run and pass the ball, you stand no chance to win the game.

You have to know your scheme and make adjustments. When we set up the game plan, we think we know what we have to do. However, until the game, you do not know what adjustments you will have to make to that plan. I think Bud Foster at Virginia Tech is a tremendous defensive coach. They are good every year. I talked to him, and he shared an eye-opening statement. He told me they did not change much on defense from year to year. They know what they need to do and know how to adjust to what everybody does. That is what we try to do. Know the scheme well enough to handle anything the offense may do.

We want to make the jobs of our players as simple as possible. We do not want them to have to learn too much. We want them to play and not be thinking about what they have to do. If the players know what to do, it speeds up their play. We want to allow our athletes to make plays on defense. That is something that is important to us. We had a player who played linebacker for us who was player of the year his junior and senior years. He was 5'8" and 165 pounds. We did not coach him much. We aligned him and told him to go make plays.

Our base defense is a 4-4 with a cover 5, which is robber coverage in the secondary. We feel some things are most important for the defensive linemen to do. The first thing is to get off the ball and change the line of scrimmage. We are a zone-offensive team, and the thing that hurts us is teams that get off the ball and penetrate.

We are a gap-control defense, and we want to maintain control of our gaps at all times. We can maintain the integrity of the gap and still get upfield. When we play defense, we want the defensive linemen to attack one half of the offensive blocker. Playing in the defensive, the defenders must use great hand quickness. You must be active with the hands and play with the hands at all times.

In our base defense, our nose is aligned in a 1 technique and shaded on the center (Diagram #1). He wants to attack the V of the neck of the center. If the play is toward the nose, he has to force the guard to his outside to block him. He cannot allow the center to block him. We do not tell our defensive linemen they are there to keep blockers off the linebackers. We want them to make plays whenever they can.

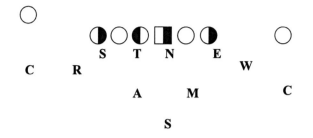

Diagram #1. Base 4-4 Defense

If the play goes away from the nose, he has to force the center to turn back on him and block him. He cannot allow the guard to scoop him from behind. Most of our nose players are short, squatty players. They have some thickness, but they do not look like much. They have quickness and play very well for us. If the nose gets a double-team, we do not want him to give ground.

The tackle is a 3-technique player. He is in an outside shade on the guard to the strongside of the formation. He attacks the V of the neck of the guard. If the guard blocks down, the 3 technique turns his body and goes down with the guard. He grabs cloth and does not allow him to release free to the inside. He plays down the line of scrimmage and wrong arms any blocker coming to block him. He is going under all blocks and bouncing the ball to the outside.

If the play is toward the 3 technique, he wants to force the block of the tackle. He cannot let the guard reach him. He has to make the tackle come down on him. The type of body we want in that position is a big, strong, wide body. The tackle we played in 2007 was 6'4" and 290 pounds. He was not just big, he could play.

The Stud is the strongside defensive end. He is one of our nastier players. We have a good way of playing this position. He aligns in a 7 technique on the tight end. His primary job is to destroy the tight end. We tell him we want him to enter the mouth of the tight end and come out his rear. That is exactly what we want to do. We want the tight end taken care of. We tell him to raise hell in the C gap. The player we played at this position was 300 pounds plus, and he was not an athlete. He would do what we coached him to do.

The Stud end cannot allow the tight end to get across his face. If the tight end arc releases, the Stud will step to the release but will not chase it. He looks back to the inside for anything coming at him. If he gets a pull, he attacks the pulling lineman. He does not wrong arm the blocker, but we want him to force the ball to bounce. He wants to close ground and attack all blocks coming at him. We do not want to slow play anything. We want to attack all blocks and destroy them.

The end is the weakside end and plays in a 5 technique. He attacks the V of the neck of the offensive tackle. If the tackle down blocks, he attacks down the line of scrimmage and wrong arms all pulls. If the play comes to the end, he is not the contain player, but he maintains outside leverage on the blocker. He is a pass rusher and can play in coverage on the zone blitz scheme.

The Mike linebacker aligns on the offensive guard's outside shoulder at a depth of four-and-a-half yards. The Mike linebacker's fit is off the end or the nose. The biggest thing the Mike linebacker has to read is the guard pull. His pass coverage technique is under or inside all receivers going to the curl. We do not want him behind any receivers.

The adjuster is the other inside linebacker. However, he has to adjust to the formations the offense gives the defense. He is a hybrid type of linebacker. He has to get outside and play against a trips formation. He fits off the Stud and nose. In his pass coverage, he plays under or inside the wide receiver going to the curl. He is a scrap linebacker, so he may have to come all the way across to the outside.

The Whip and Rover are the outside linebackers. The Whip aligns to the weakside and the Rover to the strongside. They play two-yards outside and one-yard deep outside the defensive end. If a running play comes to them, they are the contain men. If the run goes away from them, they are the cutback players. On pass coverage, they punch to the #1 receiver and play the slant, curl, or flat. They want to play the slant first, so they do not punch out to the flat and overrun the slant.

The Rover is protected to his side. The difference in the Rover and the Whip is, on certain situations, the Rover has to play the deep half. He has to be disciplined, and he plays more pass coverage.

The corner plays at a depth of eight yards with an inside leverage on the #1 receiver. The corner is in a zone backpedal and is a deep-half player. The most important thing we have to teach the players in that position is not to turn zone coverage into man coverage. We are counting on the corner to be a deep-half player. We are not counting on him to play the run. We are not asking him to play the bubble. All we want him to do is get his butt back and play the half-field. The player who is now our adjuster was a corner. We had to move him because he is too aggressive to play the corner position.

The safety is the toughest position on the field to play. This is a player you want to start playing safety as a freshman and play that position for four years. The safety on our team is like the quarterback. He does not play any offense. He is a one-way player. He has to know how to mix into the coverage and the stunts we run. He has to adjust to the formations and get us into the proper coverage.

In our base defense, if the tight end blocks, he becomes the extra run player in the box. We do not give him a gap responsibility. He is run support, and the point we make to him is not to follow his own jersey. That means, do not pursue directly behind one of his own teammates. That is the rule for the entire defense: When you pursue the ball, always be on a deeper path than the player in front of you is on.

If the #2 receiver goes vertical, he plays him in man coverage. If the #2 receiver runs across the field, the safety carries him as far as he needs to. However, he always stays over the top and maintains his cushion.

If the #2 receiver runs outside, the safety robs the #1 receiver. If #2 runs the shallow cross, the linebackers get involved in the coverage, and the safety plays center field over the top.

DEFENSIVE COORDINATOR KYLE SIMMONS

Offenses are putting us in a bind with the spread formation and the running quarterback. We love our base defense, and that is what we would prefer to stay in, but we have to make some changes. What I am going to share with you today is something we are in the process of developing. We ran it some last year and plan to make it a big part of what we do.

We are looking to get the extra defender in the box. Against a double formation, our adjustment was to get into a 4-3 defense. We are not playing 4-3 as a base, but our players know when they see the double formation, that is our adjustment. We can play cover 2 and cover 3 out of that look. With the running quarterback, we have to make some adjustments.

We call *Will spin*, which is a hash-mark defense (Diagram #2). If the ball is on the defense's right hash mark and we call Will spin, we run a weak line slant. We are trying not to add different terminology other than what we already do. The Stud, tackle, and nose are slanting to the weakside of the defense. The Stud slants to the guard, the tackle slants to the center, and the nose slants into the weakside B gap. The end starts up the field keying the offensive tackle. If he gets a run key, he contains the football.

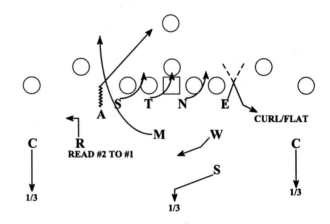

Diagram #2. Will Spin

If he reads run away, he becomes the cutback player to the backside. If he reads pass, he drops into the quick slant area under the #1 receiver to that side. This is a defensive end, and we must practice with him to get that done. He is not a defensive back, and all we want him to do is get in the quick passing lane. If nothing shows in the slant area, he runs to the curl and reacts back to the flat if anything threatens that area.

The adjuster comes off the fieldside edge. He is a spill player on all running blocks. The Mike linebacker works to the #2 receiver to the strongside for anything quick. If there is no threat from #2, he continues on his scrap path outside. If the ball goes away from the Mike linebacker, his fit is outside of the adjuster.

This technique is something you have to work with your linebacker on to get it right. They are used to being a hard run player and fitting into the gaps. In our base defense, if the line slants, the inside linebackers have to be much more patient. They have to be patient and sit on the backside. If the defensive line does a good job, the ball will cut back.

The corners run to the deep outside thirds, and the safety goes to the middle third. The Rover is now in a strong safety position. He spins down and takes the place of the adjuster. He keys #2 to #1. If #2 goes vertical, the Rover collisions the #2 receiver, but he does not run with him. If we cannot get to the quarterback by the time the Rover collisions him, we should not be running this stunt.

If the #2 receiver runs the bubble to the outside, the Rover goes from #2 to #1 and takes away any quick inside pattern runs by the #1 receiver. The Rover works through #1 to get to #2. If it is run away from him, he squeezes the inside seam.

The Whip linebacker on run to him fits off the nose. If it is a pass, he plays the low-hole area in the middle of the field. I am not saying there are no holes in the coverage, but the offense has to catch us in the stunt to do something about it.

If they come out in a trips formation to the left side of the defense, we align as we would in our base defense (Diagram #3). The Stud, tackle, and nose run the Will spin to the right side of the defense, and nothing changes for them. The field corner aligns on

the #1 receiver at a depth of eight yards. We will be in a cover 2, and the corner will roll down to the flat on that side. The adjuster aligns inside the #2 receiver. The Mike linebacker bumps his alignment to the trips side and keys the #3 receiver.

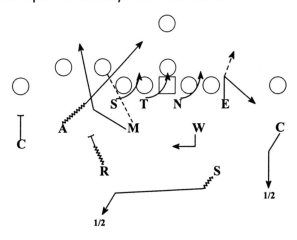

Diagram #3. Will Spin vs. Trips

The adjuster, Rover, and Whip all have to be good athletes to do what we ask them to do. The defensive end keys the run first and drops into the flat/curl area if there is no run threat to him.

The adjuster comes off the edge as he did before. The Mike linebacker does not run an all-out blitz. He looks at the #3 receiver as he starts to the outside. If #3 is coming inside on a quick route, he plays through him. If the #3 receiver disappears, he looks for #2 coming inside on a quick slant. If there is no threat coming to him, he continues on his rush pattern outside the adjuster.

The Rover comes down and replaces the adjuster keying the #2 receiver. We play cover 2 behind this defense. The safety plays the half-field to the strongside, and the boundary corner plays the half-field to the boundary. In our base defense, the corner plays the single receiver into the boundary in man coverage. That is the look he wants on this defense. He wants to give the man read and bail out to the half-field. He aligns at six yards and works back to eight.

On the slants of the Stud and tackle, if the guard and center block out on the slants, they have to get across the faces of those blocks. They cannot let the offensive linemen keep them from getting to their gaps. They have to go under all blocks. The Stud has to be into the B gap. If the guard blocks out on him, he goes under that block. The tackle plays the same technique. They cheat their alignment after the quarterback starts his cadence.

If you run these kinds of movements, you have to disguise what you are doing. You have to be patient and not move too quickly. We did not do too good of a job of that last year. We were too impatient.

We run a blitz from the Whip called *quick fire* (Diagram #4). We give a Sam call to the defensive linemen. That tells them we are slanting to the strongside of the defense. The Stud to the strongside starts upfield reading the offensive tackle. If he reads run, he is the contain player. If he reads pass, he drops to the outside under #1 and looks for the slant, curl, and flat. He is not covering a receiver; he is getting in the throwing lanes.

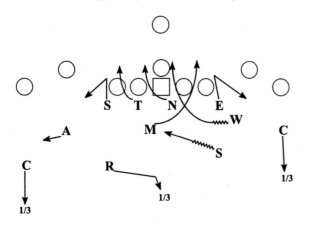

Diagram #4. Sam Quick-Fire Spin

The 3-technique tackle slants to the inside shoulder of the offensive tackle. In our base defense, if we do not have a tight end, we do not want both the Stud and the tackle outside. The end plays the same technique he did on the Will spin. He comes across looking for the run. If there is no run, he drops as he did before. The nose slants across the center's face into the strongside A gap. The adjuster widens his alignment slightly. I want him wider because he has the flat on a pass, but he has a read on run to him. Anytime we have a lineman slant to the outside, the adjuster wants to be able

to see whether the lineman has contain. If the lineman has containment on the run, the adjuster can fold inside. If the lineman does not have contain, the adjuster is outside for contain.

The Whip linebacker cheats inside and blitzes through the A gap. The Mike linebacker comes off his butt and blitzes through the B gap. The safety cheats down and replaces the Mike linebacker in the box. Last year when we ran this stunt, I blitzed the safety and left the Mike linebacker in the middle. The safety cannot get there soon enough without showing the blitz. We changed the stunt and brought the Mike linebacker. When I blitz the inside linebacker, on occasion it puts us in a terrible bind. If the play goes away from where you blitz, you do not have the middle backer. Too many times, you are screwed even when you do everything right. We do not play a lot of man coverage. It is not our best scheme for our players. Bringing the safety down into the box is better because he is not accounted for in the blocking scheme. The corners and Rover are in three-deep cover. The corners have the outside thirds, and the Rover rolls into the middle third.

The Whip reads the guard as he blitzes. If the guard blocks down, he comes off his butt. If the guard blocks out, he comes underneath the block. The Mike linebacker reads the tackle. If the tackle blocks down, he straps outside. If the tackle opens to the defensive end, he tries to beat the block inside the tackle.

When the defensive ends drop off the line of scrimmage, I do not care if they turn their backs to the quarterback. They can see the receiver and get in the throwing lane. When the quarterback sees the blitz coming, he wants to get rid of the ball. If the defensive end is in the passing lane, he has to hold the ball. That may be all the time we need to get to him.

Sometimes when I listen to other people speak, I get bogged down with their terminology. Sam, to us, means our defensive line is slanting to the strongside. Quick fire is an outside linebacker stunt to us. If we called Sam quick fire in our base defense, we would be in man coverage.

Against the trips set, we have to make some adjustments to get where we are supposed to go (Diagram #5). Our alignment is just like the alignment shown in Diagram #3. The defensive line runs their line slant the same way they always do. The Stud plays run first. He comes across the line and reads the tackle. If it is a run, he is the containment. The tackle slants through the inside shoulder of the offensive tackle. The nose crosses the face of the center. The end comes upfield and reads. If it is run, he plays containment. His technique is the same on the pass. He tries to get in the throwing lane.

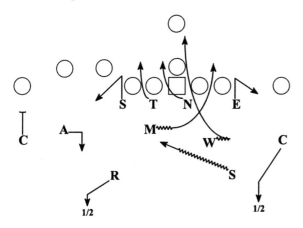

Diagram #5. Sam Quick-Fire Spin vs. Trips

We want to give the same look every time. We are in a cover-2 look on this play. We want the Whip to cheat to the weakside to improve his angle on the guard. The Mike linebacker has farther to come because he aligned into the trips side of the formation. He has to cheat to get in a better position to get into the B gap to the weakside. I am not crazy about the alignment, but it does cause the offense some issues with him coming from that position. The angle the safety takes is different because he has to go to the trips side to replace the Mike linebacker.

The adjuster plays his normal technique in trips. The field corner rolls into the flat, and the Rover and boundary corner roll into the half-field coverage.

If we align to the empty set, we play cover 2 to both the three-man and two-man sides (Diagram #6). The Rover and safety run the half-fields, and the corner, adjuster, and Mike linebacker play the trips side. The corner and Whip play the two-man surface. We slant the defensive line to the trips side. That puts the end into the B gap. That allows the Whip to play the #2 receiver to that side and play contain on the run his way. When we slant the line, it allows the Whip to slow down his run pursuit and keeps him to the backside if they run the ball to the trips side.

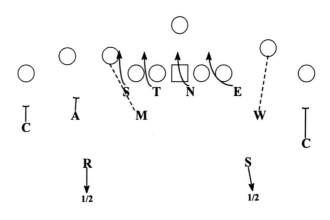

Diagram #6. Empty Set

We can double-call the line movement. If we call Sam/Will spin, we get outside movement by both sides (Diagram #7). The tackle and Stud run the Sam movement to the strongside. The nose and end run the Will movement to the weakside. The Mike linebacker fakes to the B gap and blitzes into the strongside A gap.

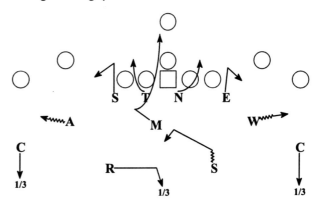

Diagram #7. Sam/Will Spin

On pass, the adjuster and Whip cover the curl/flat area. The corners drop into the outside thirds, and the Rover goes to the middle. The safety drops down and replaces the Mike linebacker. They use the same techniques they used on the other movements.

When we align to any trips set, it is important that we are consistent with the way we line up. Regardless of the coverage we play, we want to line up the same way every time. This blitz has a better angle for the Mike linebacker in his alignment in the trips formation (Diagram #8). The alignment is the same, and the coverage is cover 2. We look like man coverage to the single receiver, but we are in cover 2. The safety drops down and replaces the Mike linebacker. He has to take the right angle because of the Mike linebacker's alignment.

When we blitz, we want it to be as sound in the run game as it is in the pressure game. The corner and adjuster funnel the receivers into the hash-mark areas. That makes it easier on the half players to cover. We do not feel the half players can cover from the hash mark to the sideline. We have to force the receiver into an area he can cover.

If the offense motions a second back into the backfield, we want to go to our base 4-4 defense. That requires us to communicate with each other.

Our time is up. I hope you got something from this presentation. They have us set up in a breakout room. If you want to come down and talk some more, we will be glad to share.

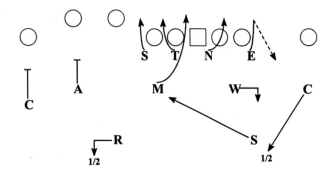

Diagram #8. Sam/Will Spin vs. Trips

SPREAD FORMATION PASS OFFENSE

Plant High School, Florida

When you come to clinics, you hope to learn some things that will help you. You know the only reason I am here speaking to you today is because of the personnel I had and the success we enjoyed this year. I had an All-American quarterback. At the tight end, I had a 6'3" 230-pound tight end who ran a 4.5 and refused to be tackled. I had three other wide receivers, and two of them ran 4.4s. We had an offensive line that in nine games allowed only three sacks. I am up here talking about offense because I had some tremendous players. It is not because I reinvented the wheel or had some special magic dust that we poured over us.

You can trace the success in the program right back to the assistant coaches. I have a tremendous staff of coaches. Everything in football has different parts. I watched an NFL program the other day, and they were interviewing Herman Edwards. They were talking about the computer and all the advancements made in pro football. When they asked Herman Edwards about his slant on that viewpoint, he said, "All I know is somebody has to draw the cards." He was referring to the computer generated play cards used at so many NFL team practices.

You can put that stuff on a computer, and it comes out professionally done, but somebody had to put that material into the computer. That somebody is the assistant coach. We still draw them manually. When the week starts, we have 50 cards ready to go with the opponent's offense and defense, and they are all in the right order. The key to winning football games is the scout teams. You win football games because of what your scout teams do Monday through Thursday. The scout-team offense is the main reason you win.

The approach to our practice is based on what we see in films on the opponent. We practice whatever is in films. We do not try to guess what the other team will try to do to us. We feel, after four or five weeks, we have put together a volume of work. Should we see something they did not show us on film, we probably saw it two weeks ago.

In our first game of the season, we practiced against the 3-5-3 defense. In week four of the season, we will see another 3-5-3 defense. If sometime in between that time someone plays the 3-5-3 as a surprise defense, we have already practiced against it. We do not try to chase myths. We practice against things we think they will do to us. We practice what we see on film, and we know it will help us. It may not help that week, but somewhere down the road that practice will help. That is our offensive philosophy and approach about practice.

We won the championships in 2006 and 2008. There were big differences in the way we won in 2006 and 2008. In 2006, nobody knew much about us, and we felt we were always behind the eight ball, which made us play with a purpose and gave us an edge. I had players who had a chip on their shoulder every day. Every single day became a challenge to them.

In 2008, they were the greatest group of players I have been around. However, being great players does not win you football games. If you have players with good character but they are passive, that does not win you football games. Somewhere along the line, each team has to find their identity. My quarterback was setting records week after week. He set records for most touchdowns and yards in a half of football in the state of Florida.

We were going along and winning, but I did not feel we were getting where we need to get. We had no edge. We could not find an identity in eight touchdown passes in a half. In week six, our quarterback, Aaron Murray, broke his leg and was out for the season. In the second quarterback, when our starting quarterback got hurt, this team found its identity. It happened on that play. As coaches, we did not know it. All we were doing was coaching the next play. We had a sophomore quarterback, Bill Neely, step in to play. He won seven-and-a-half games for us. Aaron Murray played seven-and-a-half games and won six-and-a-half of them.

Bill Neely had never been in a varsity game except for some mop duty at the end of a game. That night, in the second half of the football game, he threw for 173 yards. In seven-and-a-half games, he threw for 19 touchdowns and 1,900 yards. I think the fact that we were close in the locker room was what won us that state championship. We pulled together after the injury to Aaron, and found resolve in ourselves. Bill Neely was not the only one who stepped up. Orson Charles, our tight end, said to Bill, "I've got you." That meant: "Do not worry, and lean on me. I have your back." Our defense started swarming all over the place. At the beginning of the year, our offensive line had given up six sacks, and Aaron Murray was hit 24 times. The last nine games, we got sacked three times. Those five linemen who were playing football were no longer playing football. They were protecting the sophomore. They were protecting their friend.

Our team came together that day in the second quarter. From that day on, there was never a game they thought they were going to lose. We knew we were talented, but we did not think we had a chance to win the state championship. There was never a doubt in those players' minds that they were going to win.

There was a moment in the championship game that tested our character and won the game for us. On a punt in the first quarter, we snapped the ball over the punter's head, and they recovered at our five-yard line. One of my players got in my face and at the top of his lungs he said, "We got you, coach. They will not score!" He made the first tackle for a loss, and sacked the quarterback on the second down. The third down was an incomplete pass, and we blocked the field attempt on the fourth down. They did not score, and the game was over. We lead 28-0 at halftime and won the game 34-14.

You must be committed to whatever you do. That does not mean we are a team that runs the ball, and that is all we are going to do. Coming down the stretch in our season, we won some games because we ran the football. In the championship, we had an 11-play, 80-yard drive for a touchdown. The touchdown that put the game away came on a 13-play 63-yard drive. Some people do not think we run the ball at all. We throw the football a lot, but we use the passing game as part of our running game. We look at those passes as long handoffs. In our passing game, we want to use the entire field. We teach our quarterback to make full-field reads on certain plays. We are one of a few teams that do that. We want to keep it simple for our quarterbacks. I may give Aaron a full-field read, but with Bill, I gave him one read.

Philosophically, we want to play the game fast. We talk in terms of 10-yard explosions. We want to do everything fast, and that goes for practice also. When we do our conditioning drills, we do them in 10-yard explosions. That goes back to the old adage of "You play like you practice." We want our receivers to be 10 yards fast, but we want the linebackers to be that fast, too. We want to dictate the game's tempo and pace.

VARYING SPEEDS OF OFFENSE

- Green
- Yellow
- Red

The yellow speed is the sugar huddle. When we go to the sugar huddle, I am calling the plays. If we play teams that show late on their defensive schemes, we have a series of plays for them. We develop a number of plays that go against a cover-2, cover-3, or man defense. We use the yellow tempo for teams that change up on us. If we have a team that declares the defense and sits, I read the defense and signal the play to the quarterback. The quarterback and receiver have their own vocabulary to communicate the play. An example would be "Orson, Orson." Orson is our tight end, and he wears number seven as a jersey number. The play would be number seven. The red tempo is the regular huddle call. When you want to run the clock, you use the red tempo.

The green speed is the no-huddle offense. The quarterback calls the plays at the line of scrimmage. We do not necessarily use the green tempo as a hurry-up offense. We have two different modes of offense in the green tempo. We have green and green go. The green go is the hurry-up, two-minute offense. We practice the two-minute offense every day. We practice all the speeds and tempos every day.

We throw the ball 200 times a day in practice. The wide receivers have to catch 200-plus balls in practice every day. I have three wideout coaches. I have 23 coaches on my staff. All our coaches are great coaches. Our quarterbacks look terrific because the four wide receivers make them look great.

We want the defense to play as fast as the offense. In practice, we run a double whistle all the time in drills and scrimmages. The first whistle is to stop the play, and the second whistle is to get everyone to the tackle. Everyone keeps coming after the first whistle. They have to be around the ball by the time the second whistle blows.

PHILOSOPHY

• Dictate pace and style of the game. Make opponent adjust to us.
• Timing
• Spacing and separation
• Protection

We want to dictate the pace of play to the defense. We are going to dictate where the defense aligns and dictate what defense you play. We have plays in our offense that will beat everything the defense can play. We make teams adjust to formations/motions/different looks and run the same plays.

TAKING FREEBIES

• Quick screen
• Bubble screen
• Scats
• Hots

VARYING LEVELS (PROGRESSIONS) OF THE PASSING GAME

• *High (deep passes):* Must take shots down the field (particularly early)
• *Intermediate (middle range passes):* Particularly against zones
• *Low (short passes):* Acts as this offense's version of a running game

Every defense gives the offense certain areas as a no-cover zone. We want to take advantage of what the defense will give. We want to take the easy completions and freebies the defense gives us. To keep the defense from setting on a certain pattern, you have to vary the levels at which you throw the ball. The key notes are to throw the ball deep, and do it early in the game.

I want to show you a couple of things that worked for us. Each year, the personnel are different and you have to change. We changed our offense a lot as the season went along this year. We had the receivers with the ability to do that. Orson Charles could play tight end or fullback, and get down the field. We had another player who was 6'3", 205 pounds, and ran 4.5. We used him at the tight end also. This season, we used a lot of tight end sets in our offense. That let us create a new protection scheme.

At the end of the season, we had one of the greatest defensive lines I have ever seen assembled in high school football. When we worked against them, I wanted to make sure we showed them something different every time we faced them. We had to create different protection packages against them.

In the spread offense, it is a new day. Football is an adjustment game. The defenses are starting to adjust to the spread offenses. We talk about dictating the pace of the game and dictating the defense played against us.

When teams play us, they feel that they must change their defense to cover what we are doing. We prepare for the defense we saw, and they change the game plan. Our main goal is to dictate to them what defense they have to play. We have not snapped the ball, and we have told them they are not going to play a 4-3 cover-2 defense against us.

This is not like Peyton Manning in the early part of his career. The defenses felt they could blitz him. They could not, and he threw for a tremendous amount of touchdowns. They thought he was too smart and they could not blitz him, so the next year, they rushed three and dropped eight into coverage. That coverage might be all right because those players are professionals.

We have played teams that were a 4-4 front and cover-3 in the secondary on film. When we came out in our set, they rushed three and dropped eight into the secondary. This is a high school team. They have dropped eight defenders, but they do not have eight defenders. We are extremely safe with that because we know they have eight in the secondary, but they do not know how to cover. To compound the problem, they have no pressure on the quarterback. I know the defensive coaches in this room will disagree with some of what I am saying.

We teach our quarterbacks against cover 2. We feel like there are certain spot to attack against cover 2. When we have experienced quarterbacks, we teach them eight different cover-2 situations they may face. I start with the basic cover 2. There are three hot spots in the basic cover 2.

In the summertime, I take my players around to different colleges to passing camps. I know what I will probably see in the upcoming season in coverages from our opponents. This was our

second year in the spread offense, so I wanted to know about cover 2 or cover-2 man. I ask all the college coaches what their best play is against that defense. This play is called "gamecock" because we picked it up in South Carolina (Diagram #1). The formation is a trips set to the right side. The X-receiver runs what we call a "show corner." The receiver starts on a slant to the inside, breaks straight up the field, and runs the corner route.

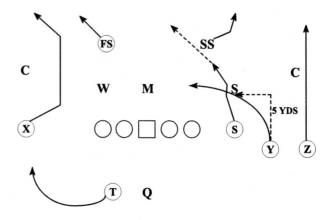

Diagram #1. Gamecock

The slot receiver, who is the inside slot, runs the post into the middle of the field. The Y-end runs a shallow route into the middle. The Z-receiver runs the go pattern, and the T-back runs the swing.

We teach high principles the first day of practice. Some people will think that puts you in a five-man protection scheme. I do not look at it that way. I look at it as the wide receiver being in the protection scheme. The objective of spread protection is to have fewer defenders in the rush area. If you bring another blocker into the box area, you also bring another defender into the box to block. By spreading the formation, there are fewer defenders to protect against. With five receivers in the pattern, there are more places to put the ball. That is our approach to pass protection.

The responsibilities of the underneath coverage in a cover 2 is standard. The corners roll into the flat areas. The outside linebackers are seam/curl players. The Mike linebacker has the middle hook. The safeties are half players. The pattern we want to beat this coverage with is the seam-post route.

That is a skinny post into the middle. In the gamecock, the skinny post is run by the inside slot receiver in the formation. The wideout base their reads on the safeties in the half-field.

The wideouts and quarterback always reads the safety opposite the seam-post pattern. We drive the X-receiver inside into the view of the free safety. He wants the free safety to see him as he drives up the field and into the corner. That is why we call the route a "show corner." The harder the free safety goes to the corner route, the deeper the slot receiver runs the skinny post into the middle of the field. The further the safety gets from the middle, the more to the post the receiver runs.

The slot and quarterback are reading the free safety and feeling the strong safety. We swing the tailback to the weakside. If the Will linebacker goes with the swing, the quarterback knows he has man coverage on the swing pattern. If he stays, we have a chance to get a fast running back in space against the defense.

The Y-end has the hot route if the Will and Mike linebacker blitz. If they blitz, the Y-end gets to the hot pattern immediately. He dives to the inside at five yards, looking for the ball. If they fly out into coverage, he runs his hot pattern five yards up the field and into the inside on a shallow cross. The quarterback reads the free safety and feels the linebackers. The Y-end wants to break up the field to get the Sam linebacker's attention so the slot can wiggle inside of him up the seam. The Z-receiver runs the go route and holds the strong safety with his route. He wants the strong safety to take a step toward his pattern.

We give our quarterback free rein to check the play at the line of scrimmage. We grade our quarterbacks as to their checks. There is more than one right answer to a checked play. In 2006, our quarterback graded 97 percent on his checks. So many times, the quarterback has a much better view of the defense than we do on the sidelines. When you teach the quarterback to play in the spread offense, he is the triggerman and the key to the offense.

You must have a catalog knowledge of the offensive playbook:

- Automatics
  - ✓Based on defense
  - ✓Keep them simple
  - ✓Based upon game plan
- Audibles
  - ✓Number system and language tied in to two-minute/green offense.
  - ✓Let the kids (led by the quarterback) create additional code words and signals.
- Knowledge of every player for every play
  - ✓Formations
  - ✓Responsibility: Know all positions.
  - ✓Nuances: Draw up every running and passing play with full explanation.

On Saturday and Sunday, we sit down with the quarterbacks and go over the game plan and checks. We show him what we have seen on the film and give him a list of the checks we like. We give him three or four checks against the cover-2 secondary. We also give him three or four checks against man, cover 3, and anything else we might see. We give him a list of automatic calls against something the defense may do. I do not want to sound cocky, but I want the players to know those plays are going to work.

We do these things daily in practice. We call them "things we do every day without fail."

DAILY PRACTICE:
THINGS WE DO EVERY DAY WITHOUT FAIL

1-on-1

- Go to combos, 2-on-2s, and such.
- Play it as a game.
  - ✓Make everything competitive; the players love it.
  - ✓One point for a catch, six points for touchdown, two points for defense for incomplete, six points for interception, 12 points for intercepted touchdown.
  - ✓Usually play to 30 with penalty for losing.
- Run some reps where the quarterback does not know what the wide receiver is going to run (no tells).

Scramble Drill

- High comes low.
- Low comes high.
- Shadow parallel.

7-on-7 Period: Play It as a Game

- 7-on-0: Dummy reps with no-huddle, two groups, 20 reps in a 10-minute period
- 7-on-7: High tempo, enthusiasm, trash talk

Two-Minute Offense: Bingo

- Dummy it in every day.
- Play it live on Wednesday nights (best-on-best).

We run a number of 1-on-1 drills. We work it down to 2-on-2 combination routes against two defenders. They can use zone techniques or man techniques. Every time we do the drill, we want to make it competitive. We want to put something on the line. The loser has to do some penalty. It does not matter whether it is a push-up or an up-down, but someone has to do a penalty exercise.

We work a 1-on-1 drill called "no tells." No one knows the pattern except the receiver who is running it. We do not tell him what to run, and he does not tell the quarterback what he is running. The quarterback takes the three-step drop and has to read the body language of the receiver. This builds the unspoken ties between the receiver and the quarterback. He reads his moves without knowing his pattern.

We run the scramble drill with the quarterbacks and receivers. We have some simple rules. If we run a slam pattern and the quarterback scrambles out of the pocket, the receiver running the corner or high route breaks his pattern and comes back to the quarterback. The receiver running the hitch route or low pattern breaks his pattern and goes long. The shallow pattern runs parallel to the quarterback.

We do a drill called "9-on-4" as a scramble drill. There are nine defenders and four wideouts in the drill. It is a free-for-all drill. All the defenders are defensive backs. There are no linebackers in the drill. We put four defensive backs man-to-man on

the four wide receivers and the other five defenders are in a defensive shell, reacting to receivers coming into their zone. The defenders can grab the receivers. They can knock them down. If they get him down, they can jump on him. They can grab the jersey. The receiver runs a pattern, the quarterback scrambles, and he has to find a receiver.

The 7-on-7-period is a high-intensity period. We dummy the drill for 10 minutes with two groups. After that, we go 7-on-7 with the receivers against the defensive backs and linebackers. We want it competitive and enthusiastic. We want the offense and defense to get after one another.

Every day, we work our two-minute offense. We dummy it every day. The real deal comes on Wednesday night. We practice under the lights and at 8:00, we have a live two-minute drill. We play two-minute offense against two-minute defense. We go the best against the best. It is a battle. We do it every Wednesday night.

In our pass-protection schemes, the center is responsible for making the calls at the line of scrimmage. We want to keep the protection scheme simple. If the front is a four-man front, the offensive line blocks big-on-big (Diagram #2). The offensive line is responsible for the four down lineman and the Mike linebacker. The center designates the Mike linebacker that fits the protection. He may designate the Will linebacker as the linebacker the five offensive linemen are responsible.

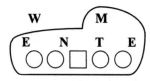

Diagram #2. Five-Man Protections

If we release everyone on a pattern and the defense brings six rushers, the quarterback reads the hot receiver on the play. We have a number of special protections. We can unbalance the set by bringing the X-receiver to the trips side and moving the quarterback into the trips side. The single back blocks to that side, and we slide toward the sprint-out. We release the backside defensive end since we are sprinting away from him. We can deliver the ball before he can get to the quarterback.

On play-action pass, we use turnback protection with the offensive line. The back blocks the edge to play-action side. The big thing in a protection scheme is to make sure we are all on the same page. The center is in charge of all offensive line calls, but there must be communication down the line of scrimmage.

The rule of thumb to follow in the protection scheme is to protect the weakside. Any pressure release has to come in the face of the quarterback and not to his backside. If the one-back is included in the protection scheme, the quarterback is in charge of that adjustment. The quarterback's mobility can always help the offensive line. Being able to avoid rushers is a plus in any protection scheme. If the quarterback has to vacate the pocket, the receivers know they are to help him find a receiver.

A drill we use with our pass-protection techniques is a 3-on-3 drill (Diagram #3). We have a center, two offensive linemen, a wideout, and the quarterback. There are three defensive linemen and a defensive back. We do eight reps of all-out pass rush. It is man-on-man blocking for the offensive linemen. The quarterback has to work on his techniques and keep his head and eyes downfield. The receiver works 1-on-1 with the defensive back. This drill exhausts the offensive linemen. The actual plays we run in practice will be 50-50 run to pass plays.

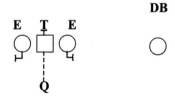

Diagram #3. 3-on-3 Drill

Question: How do you protect against the 3-3 stack?

The 3-3 stack defense is a man-protection scheme (Diagram #4). With a three-man front, we use a two-man rule. There are five offensive linemen and six defenders in the box. If they all come, the quarterback has to throw hot. The hot receivers are aware of who they are responsible for in the protection scheme. We assign two offensive linemen to two defenders. If we are going to read hot to the outside linebacker on the right, the tackle to that side blocks the defender who is the greatest threat. He cannot block both of them and takes the most immediate threat. If both the linebacker and down lineman rush, the B-gap rusher is the man he blocks.

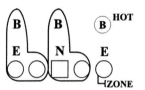

Diagram #4. 3-3 Stack

The playside guard and center block the middle stack. The backside guard and tackle block the outside stack. If we want to secure the pocket, we keep the one-back in to block the playside linebacker.

In the off-season, we work on our protection packages. You cannot pass the ball if you cannot protect the quarterback.

I have enjoyed my time, and I appreciate your attention.

OFFENSE: COMPLEXITY THROUGH SIMPLICITY

Geneva High School, Illinois

It is a pleasure to be here to talk offensive football with you. At Geneva High School, we run a power-I scheme with multiple formations. It is actually an I-formation attack with a power-game twist to it. We call what we do "complex simplicity." We believe in it, and we have had some success doing it. I believe there are three main ingredients needed to be successful in our offense. They apply to any scheme that you might run.

First, I think turnovers are critical. We practice preventing turnovers every day. I do think there is a lot of luck involved in this aspect of the game. We have been on the plus margin when we were losing, and we have been on the plus margin when we were winning. All in all, having those turnovers and getting that extra possession is critical, especially for field position.

Next is first-down efficiency. A lot of guys talk about third down and how important it is on third-and-long or third-and-short. We believe that first down is critical. We really like to get four or five yards on that first-down play. That sets us up offensively, and it puts the defense in a bind. Therefore, we really concentrate hard on first-down efficiency. We do not just run the ball on first down. We like to throw it some on first down, but what comes with that is that if we are unsuccessful, we're looking at second-and-10.

Third, talent plays a key role—no doubt about it. I once heard Vince Dooley talk about the difference his great tailback made in how he designed his I-formation attack. Talent is critical, and it has played a big part in our success. We have been fortunate to have several all-state players, and they have made a major difference in what we have been able to do.

HISTORY OF THE FOOTBALL PROGRAM

I have been at Geneva High School for 10 years, after coaching at a previous school for five years. I have been in the desert without any water—we had the longest losing streak in the state of Illinois. There are not too many boosters knocking on your door when that happens.

The first five years at Geneva, we won about 22 percent of our games. In the last five years, when things began to click, we have won 85 percent of our games. I will get into how we changed the mentality there. If you are a new coach, you do not walk into an established program. That is what you are going to start with. You have to stay on top of it and be persistent.

Here is a 10-year history of our record. It gives you an idea of where we are now. It is important to note that we went to a two-platoon system in 2003. I think our offense has a symbiotic relationship with the defense. I think the point totals are very, very important.

Year	Record	Total Pts.	Pts./Game
1999	0-9	61	6.8
2000	1-8	128	14.2
2001	2-7	157	17.4
2002	2-7	121	13.4
2003	5-4	229	25.4
2004	11-2	368	28.3
2005	7-4	302	27.5
2006	11-2	434	33.4
2007	11-1	382	31.8
2008	13-1	502	35.6

We were not doing things a whole lot differently in those first years, but we were persistent. We made decisions about what we wanted to do and what kind of offense we wanted to be, and we stuck with it.

For us, 2003 was an important year. We got over the hump. In that year, we went to a two-platoon system. We were not ready to do that with just 40 players, but we made the decision to change. It was a tough decision because we were right on the borderline numberwise. Now, we have 75 or 80 players, but then, we had to make a commitment, and that is what we did.

Our offense now has a symbiotic relationship with our defense. We were very good on defense that year, so we played a lot of field position. We did not take chances with the ball, and we ground it out. In previous years, if the defense was not so good, I would take some chances. The point is: Your offense needs to coincide with your defense.

TURNAROUND IN THE PROGRAM

When we got to Geneva, we had to change the attitude, and, for us, that began with weights. Our kids built their confidence in the weight room. They took positives from setting goals and achieving them. That carried over to the football field.

We talk about "Pete" and "Ralph" in our program. All these kids want to belong, and that is why they are there. It takes some effort for them to be in the football program. I hope that you have a Pete in your program. For us, a Pete is a kid who has it all. You do not have to do anything with Pete. He plays, he gets it done, and he is the man. If you get two Petes, you are really in business.

What we have to win with are the Ralphs. The Ralphs are the guys who never tuck their clothes in, their hair is always a mess, and they do not even know a girl, much less date one. That is Ralph. As a coach, you have to make Ralph a player. We talk about the Ralphs all the time because they make your program. You have to make a place for the Ralphs.

We also talk about six positives for every negative. Kids want to hear good things, so we need to say good things. If you have to chew a kid out on the field, then as you come off the field, you need to find him and give him a hug. The kid cares, and he will take that with him all night. That is not healthy for anybody.

We have very few rules at our school. The ones we do have are as follows:

- Do nothing to get you in trouble.
- Do not lie.
- Go by the golden rule.
- You look us in the eye when we talk to you.

In our offense and defense, we have very few rules. We are not so smart, and we can only do so much, as you will see.

I want to go back to the weight room. The weight room was a key difference for us. We are fortunate that as we started to win a few games, people got excited in the community. We were able to come up with $100,000 for a weight room. We had started with a 10x10 room that we could only fit a few players in at a time. Some guys would be doing stations or running, and we rotated guys in and out. You make do with what you have. We are very fortunate that the community is now backing us up, and we now have a large, first-class facility.

I want to mention some basic principles to success. First, we preach discipline. We ask for loyalty, and we try very hard to earn our players' trust. We are going to be fair, and we are always going to do what we say we are going to do. That is very important.

You must have commitment. Decide what you want to do and how you want to do it, and make a commitment to it. Once you make a decision, believe in yourself and be persistent—just keep pounding.

You have to love your guys. You have to love your coaches, and you have to love your players.

After our breakthrough season in 2004, my neighbor came to me and said he could help me with our program. In his work, he helped businesses find ways to work smarter, not harder. He went on to show me how to organize for success. He told me we had to have a vision for our program. He said that every kid who comes into our program should have a vision of success.

I thought about that, and it made a lot of sense. I got my coaches involved, and we came up with "champions through character." That is what we believe in. We posted it on the walls, put it on our letterhead, and now, when those kids come into our program, they know what is expected of them. They are going to be a champion, and they are going to do it with character.

Finally, we talk about controlling your "dash." You have no control over when you are born or when you die. However, you do have control of how you live in between those two events. On your tombstone under your name, you will have a date of birth, a dash, and a date of death. You have no control over the two dates, but you can control the dash. This is what we teach that the letters for that dash stand for in our program: The D is for *discipline*, the A is for *attitude*, the S is for *sacrifice*, and the H is for *habits*. We use the word dash as an acronym for theses traits, and we talk to our kids about controlling their lives by controlling their dash.

OFFENSIVE THOUGHTS

On offense, if I had my way, I would get into two tight ends and a power-I backfield and we would go at it. We would just put the fists up and go. That is what we played when I was in school, and that is what I grew up with. However, we did not have the personnel to do it when we first started. We still do not have all the personnel we would like, so it has been a slow evolution. It is a matter of things borrowed and things stolen that we have built into our attack.

I always ask myself what is critical now. We do not want to get caught-up in the minutia. What do I have to take care of right now? You have to keep your focus on what it is that you are up against right now and make the strategic adjustments you need to be successful.

The off-season is very critical. How can we get better? What are our problems? What assets can we accentuate? The best thing I have done to get answers is to watch the game tapes from the start of the season straight through without stopping them or rewinding them. I just get a feel for the season by doing that. It is the best thing I ever did. It gives me a sense of what we did well, what we did not do so well, and what we need to work on.

You must keep in mind that your offense must fit you. We might be able to spread out and throw the ball more, but that is not me—that is not what I do. We will be flexible enough to take advantage of the weapons we have, but it is not me to start winging the ball all over the place. Your offense must fit you first. Within that, it must fit the players, and, to a lesser degree, it must fit your conference.

OFFENSIVE PHILOSOPHY

You get to a point in every game where the game is on the line. It could be early on, or it could be late in the game. Whenever it comes, when the game is on the line, you cannot flinch. You have got to hold the course. Do not flinch. Do the things you did in practice to prepare for that situation, and do not let your kids see you hesitate.

A sidebar to this point has to do with defensive game planning. You have to adjust your plan to the threats posed by your opponent, but you have to stay within your base defense. Just because you face a different offense each week, you do not change your defense each week. It is a mistake to change your defense for a different opponent each week. You made the decision about what defense you wanted to run, so stick with it. Obviously, you have to game plan, but do not outsmart yourself.

As far as our running game goes, we run trap, power, option, and counters. We will run option a little more if we have a quarterback that can run it. Now, we have an outstanding tailback, so we run a little more power. In the passing game, we run the play-action offense including the three-step drop, the five-step drop, and the sprint-out.

The offense was set up so we do not have to outman our opponent. That was critical when we first got going. At times, we do have a small personnel advantage where we can muscle up and outman some people. However, the whole offense is designed where we do not have to do that. We have been able to use formations to create vulnerabilities in the areas that I want to attack and run the plays that I want to run.

Essentially, we use formations and threats to make the cover guys tackle and make the tackle guys cover. We do not have very many plays. We stress execution from a lot of formations.

What we strive for is a ball-control offense with a great trapping package, which takes the pressure off the offensive line. I do not have to outman any people to do that. We can "formation" them to create gap opportunities and to create big play capabilities. We do not throw the ball to move the chains. We tell the quarterback that when we throw the ball, we are going down the field looking for the big play.

BASE OFFENSE

The first key to our offense is our approach to first down. I have to be able to pass the ball on first down. If we run it, then I have to have four or five yards. Turnovers are always bad, but they are devastating on first down. Finally, we look for a 60/40 run/pass ratio. This past year, we were more like 70/30 ratio.

We only have eight base running plays, but we run them out of all different formations. In every formation that we have, we can run any play that we have. It cuts down teaching time. The offensive line does not have to do a lot of thinking. The moving around is done by our backs. We try not to make it too complicated.

We have seven base pass plays and all are play-action off of my eight base run plays. That is 14 play-actions, two three-step passes, and two five-step passes.

Being creative with formations is where the fun is for me. We have 40 different formations, and I do not know what the math is, but consider that we can run every play from every formation, and then figure how many ways we can attack a defense.

FORMATIONS

We have our own terminology and you have yours, so I will just say that we get into all variations of the standard I formation and shotgun sets. We will be in standard pro sets, twins sets, and wing sets with I or offset backs. We will be in one-back sets with three and four wideouts, and we can shotgun any of those. Of course, we can also come out with three backs and two tight ends. Finally, we have shifts and motion out of every set. You get the idea. We try to be creative with our formations and use them to gain advantages, but, of course, we do not go into a game with all of them.

POWER

I want to start with our power play to make sure I get that covered, and then, I'll come back and talk about the trap (Diagram #1). The guys always kid me that our offense is 33 percent power, 33 percent other runs, and 33 percent pass, and I am all right with that. That is what we do.

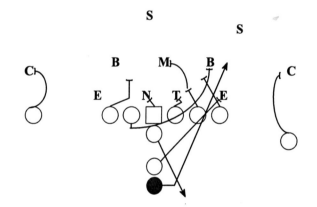

Diagram #1. 44/45 Power

I put our quarterback in a staggered stance, and whichever foot is back is the one he pivots on. There is so much movement on and around the line of scrimmage that I want him off the line, because we have guards and tackles coming through the gaps all the time.

My fullback's hand is at three yards. If you do a lot of zone stuff, you will not like where we align our fullback and tailback. My fullback's hand is at three yards, and he is up in there with attitude. My tailback's heels are at five yards. I got that from the time when I was not very good and my linemen could not hold their blocks very long. I just felt I needed to scoot them up so they could get through there. The tailback's attitude is to get downhill hard and fast and to not think about making a cut until he gets through the line of scrimmage.

The key to our blocking on the power play is the combo block between the guard and the tackle. It is very similar to a kind of inside-zone mentality, except we are really off the ball. A lot of your zone teams talk about a bucket step or more of a lateral step, but we want to get off the ball with this.

The idea is that these two guys are responsible for these two: the defensive tackle and middle linebacker. Where we were getting in trouble a few years ago when we first started dabbling with the zone concept was that we initially manned it up on the tackle. Then, if the linebacker shot inside, our guard was not reacting quick enough to come off. So we really emphasized that you do not have a guy, you have these two, and, depending on what they do, you either stay on the tackle or you come off on the linebacker.

We want to get off the ball, we want to stay on the double-team for as long as possible, and we want movement. That helps our guard who is pulling around for the playside linebacker.

On the pulling guard's first step, we are not big on throwing the elbow open. We just want to get there. Most of the time, he does a quick pivot. He pivots on the foot, points to where he wants to go, and then works upfield. He is looking for the first hole through the line.

We have it drawn up going through the B gap. However, it might not be in the B gap. If the end really squeezes hard, the B gap can close. If the 3 technique is a real man, he might make a pile as he is taught to do. You may have to go more outside, or you may have to go to the A gap if that is where the seam is. Simply put, the guard is responsible for that linebacker, and we get him there.

The backside tackle's block is a scoop block. The tight end's block is critical. Our fullback is kicking out the end man, so our tight end has to step hard, rip through, and get to this linebacker if available, and, if not, to a double-team on the Mike. We rep this in practice, in half-line drills, and in team period so we can time it up with the backs.

The fullback's block is what we call a J-block. He really gets up inside, and he is looking for the last man on the line of scrimmage, whether a 9 technique or a 7 technique.

When we get an inside shade on a tight end, we can go foot to foot with the offensive tackle and turn the inside shade into a 5 technique. He is right there, and now we will double-team him.

I have never had big fullbacks, so we do not expect much movement on the J-block. We try to get up in there tight and get our head on the inside. If the kid comes down, we look at walling him to the inside and bouncing the ball to the outside.

As far as formations go, I want to cover two of them. This is our twins left tight formation with the tight end on the backside (Diagram #2). I really want to get a lot of guys in the hole here. It is crowded in there. I will "bomber" the slot, and he and the fullback will switch responsibilities. The guard coming around has the first man in or inside the hole, and the fullback has the first man in or outside the hole. Otherwise, nothing changes, and if we run it out of gun, it is the same deal.

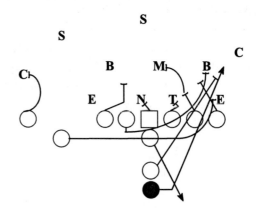

Diagram #2. Alternate Formations and Motions, 44/45 Power

TRAP

I want to talk about the way we run the inside trap play (Diagram #3). What we do is not a lot different except maybe with the step of our pulling guard. Instead of throwing his elbow and really opening himself up as he might do on power, he just pivots and goes right downhill because the fullback is at three yards, and he is there in a heartbeat. We tell our guard he is right if he is running into the center. That means the center really needs to get his butt off the ball.

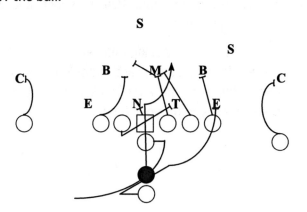

Diagram #3. 30/31 Trap

We do not jab step with the fullback. We want him straight in the hole as quick as possible. If we are running 30 trap, which is a trap to the right, the fullback steps with his playside foot straight downhill and opens up his pocket on the second step. We used to do it the opposite way but the fullback's thigh board kept getting in the way, so we changed it and it straightened out the mesh. We tell the fullback to try to beat the guard to the hole, so everybody is really trying to make the play hit fast.

The quarterback opens with his butt to the zero hole on 30 trap, and we call it the big dish. We want him to bend up and down with his legs. We want him to dish the ball as if he is serving dinner. We do not want him swinging it.

His next step is straight back. The tailback is coming off a counter step and faking 44 trap, and we want the quarterback to go at least two steps with his back to the defense.

Here is how it would look out of a different formation (Diagram #4). I do not like to move too much in the trap series. If I initially put my formation out there, I can pretty much find the 3 technique. We have trapped the 1 technique before, but, of course, we want to trap the 3 technique.

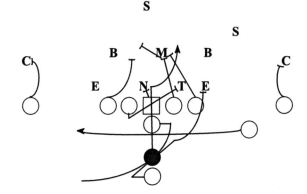

Diagram #4. Alternate Formations and Motions, 30/31 Trap

We will call "trap, check-with-me" in the huddle and then check it to the 3 technique at the line. If I monkey around too much with formations and the defense starts sliding, it puts too much pressure on my quarterback and line. I would rather find you, sit the defense steady, and run the play.

Our counter off this is 44/45 trap and everything is the same (Diagram #5). The only guys who change are the quarterback and our trap man. Everybody else does exactly the same thing. Instead of trapping the 3 technique, now we are trapping a 9 technique or a 5 technique.

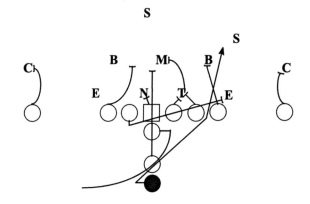

Diagram #5. 44/45 Trap

Before we run out of time, I want to show you a couple of boots (Diagram #6). I could spend all day on just "boot" alone. It is a great play for us. We call it 16/17 boot, and we run it out of all formations.

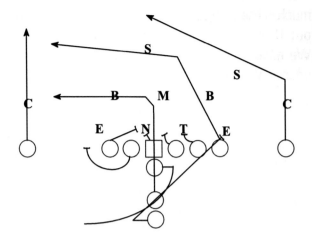

Diagram #6. 16/17 Bootleg

In our base boot package, the fullback has to get to the flat at two to three yards. The tight end runs a drag pattern at 12 yards, and the backside receiver runs a post. The frontside receiver, depending on the coverage, runs a deep out or a takeoff. We will run it out of every formation, and I have some tags to the routes.

We may have 15 different boots, but the line does not change at all. We are a little different in that we pull the frontside guard instead of the backside guard, and it has not hurt us at all. The guard really gets depth and looks for the last man on the line of scrimmage.

The play was originally designed as a run. We tell our quarterback to look for the run first. Then, if we throw, we always look long to short, and we want the big play first.

Let me close by saying that you have to love what you do as coaches and have a passion for coaching. I hope you got a feel for what we do in our offense. Thank you for your time.

GAME PLANNING VS. 2X2 AND 1X3 SETS

St. Augustine High School, Florida

First, I want to thank the Nike people for having me here. Before I get into my topic, I want to say how fortunate and blessed we are as coaches. The effect we have on kids is amazing, and I hope every coach understands that.

St. Augustine is a 3A high school, 30 miles south of Jacksonville. We have about 1,500 students in a very diverse student population. We have a number of kids in our program with learning disabilities, so we try to keep everything simple.

IDENTIFICATION OF SPREAD STRENGTHS

When you identify a spread team, you have to ask whether they are a Northwestern type of team, where they want to run the ball first, or a Purdue type of team that wants to throw it first. You have to find out what they do so you can decide what you are going to stop, and what you want to emphasize in defending them.

Against a running quarterback, you have to be gap sound. People use the spread to create run lanes and identify defenses. The formation takes the pressure off its offensive linemen, and it creates mismatches for its athletes. Finally, most spread teams are all good perimeter-screen teams, so what we do defensively is geared to all those particular things.

PHILOSOPHY: DEFENDING SPREAD SETS

We see spread teams that run all manner of shifts and motion out of one set and into another, and it is tough when you have to adjust your alignment and your coverage to match strength with all of it. You have to have answers that will hold up. We have one coverage that is our fail-safe response. No matter what anybody lines up in, we can line up in this, and

we are okay. You have to be able to line up right, and then you have to handle motions and shifts. I will show you how we do it.

You have to be able to play a five-, six-, or seven-man box. There will be times when we play teams that are big run teams, so we will want to be in a six-man box. There will also be times against teams that throw the ball first, and are just okay running, when we will want to be in a five-man box. Then, obviously, there will be times when we want to be in a seven-man box and play cover zero. If somebody is just running the ball over us, we are going to commit to stopping the run first.

Some spread teams run the triple option. I am not going to get into how we cover that. It is tough when you have to handle a running quarterback who can run the pitch outside or the shovel pass inside. That is another clinic talk.

You have to be able to play some form of man coverage because you sometimes have to get into a six- or seven-man box. It does not have to be press man, and we are not a big press-man team. It can be some form of off man and still fit to the front you are playing.

As you go through a season, I think you have to have two answers for every single set, and you must be able to pressure, but above all, you have to keep it simple. If you are going to face spread teams that are running all over and trading all over, your guys have got to sit there and play. They cannot be worried about all that stuff.

The last point concerns something we do in practice. We are going to set an offense on each hash, and our defense will be ready to line up in the alignment that is called. The first offense lines up and runs a play against our defense. Then, as soon as that play is over, the other offense breaks the huddle and lines up on the other hash. Our defense has to run over to get to that offense. When that play ends, they have to get back to the other hash for the next play, and so forth.

We are firing two offenses at our defense during team period. We do the same thing in inside drill and in skelly. I always ask the defensive guys what it is like, and I want them to say that it is slow. The game is slow. They are standing there waiting for the offense to come up. That is great because it gives our defense a real sense of confidence. The pace of the drill is so fast that we actually get one rep every 25 seconds.

PALMS VS. 4 WIDE

This is what we play versus anything (Diagram #1). We play it versus 2x2, we play it versus 3x1, against slot, and against empty. We will probably see three I-formation teams, two wing-T teams, one triple-option team, and three or four spread teams. Whatever we see, palms is our big thing.

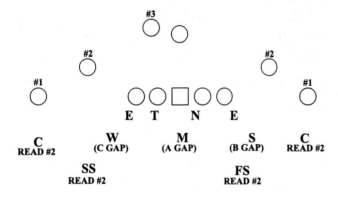

Diagram #1. Palms vs. 4 Wide

The corner and free safety read #2. In our terminology, we say that we are "palmsing #2." We have debated whether to pedal or shuffle with our corners. I like the shuffle because I think it is easier to read it that way, but some of our guys would rather pedal, so we let them.

If #2 is vertical, the corner plays #1—period. If #2 runs a flat route, the corner comes off on #2, and

the free safety handles #1. That is easy for those guys to understand.

We always work a lot of half-line coverage stuff. Even if it is cover 3, we will get half line and run every cover-3 route possible out of twins at our guys, and we do the same thing here. We will run every route combination we can in a half-line situation at palms coverage.

The Sam linebacker will apex the #2 receiver and the offensive tackle. Depending on how good #2 is, sometimes we begin to creep him in a little bit. The free safety will split the Sam and the #2 receiver. You can play him at 10 yards, but we back ours up to 12. You just have to be sure the free safety can get to the #1 receiver on a vertical route if he gets a flat route by #2. We play our corners at about seven yards.

Sam has some responsibility on him. His alignment gives the appearance of a five-man box, but we tell him it is a seven-man box. We invite people to run on us here. Sam takes a straight backpedal for three steps and settles there. We do not want him opening and letting the #2 receiver underneath, and the only thing that will take him from there is #3 to the flat.

To summarize, the corner and free safety handle #1 and #2, Sam handles #3 to the flat, and Mike handles #3 vertical. This will all make sense when we are done.

On the other side, everything is identical. Will is apexing #2, the strong safety splits the Will and #2, and the corner is over #1. The corner and strong safety read #2, just as I explained on the other side.

If you already play cover 2, then cover 2 is your combo to this. If your corner bails on every play, then the offense will throw hitches all day, so you can line up just like this and play cover 2, or you can line up like this and play palms.

I want to show you how the box all fits up when you are a five-man box as we are here (Diagram #2). Any time we are in a five-man box, the first thing we will run will be tango because that gaps us out.

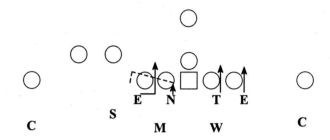

Diagram #2. Tango, Run With Five-Man Box

The end on the right will take a lateral step and run a rip. The tackle is in the B gap, the nose is in the opposite A gap, and the left end is in the B gap. In the five-man box, Mike is obviously the A-gap player.

The concern on the left side is obviously containment. In tango, the nose fits in the A gap and plays the A gap first against the run. If he gets pass, he becomes the contain man. Versus run, we are gapped out, and with the end coming inside, everything is going to spill to the Sam linebacker. We are in good shape. If we face a sprint-out team, we end up secondary containing with our Mike linebacker. The running back is involved in protection there, so we bring our Mike.

Here is how it looks against a spread team (Diagram #3). It is still 2x2, so we are palmsing #2 on the twins side, Will has #3 to the flat as always, and Mike has #3 on a vertical. Nothing changes on the twins side.

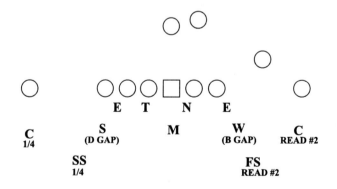

Diagram #3. Palms vs. Spread

On the other side, our defensive end is an automatic 7 technique against a tight end and one back. He is a C-gap player now, so that moves Sam out. The tight end is the #2 receiver, and he is so far

inside now that it would be difficult to play our palms read on him, so we just play our cover 4 to that. Sam is the flat cover guy, and the corner and strong safety are playing quarters.

For us, an Ace formation is a 2x2 set with two tight ends and two wideouts. Against that, we just play our quarters coverage on both sides, just as we do on the tight-end side against spread.

I want to show you what happens when we play palms against a trips formation (Diagram #4). In palms, the rule against the single receiver on the left side here is to play cloud support, so the corner rolls up at five, and the free safety is over the top at 12. On the trips side, the corner and strong safety are palmsing #2 exactly as they always do. Sam has #3 to the flat, and Mike has him on a vertical route, also just as before.

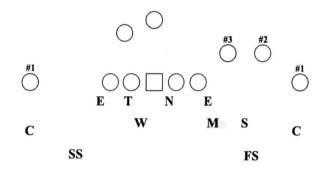

Diagram #4. Palms vs. Trips

What I do not like in this is that we have to get the Will linebacker in the box because Mike has to get width and depth. We hip Mike with the defensive end at a depth of six yards. He has to run with #3 on a vertical route, but if #3 goes flat, he will level off and look for a crossing route. That puts pressure on Mike if #3 is a good receiver. You have to decide if your Mike can end up running with that guy, but as far as lining up, you can line up against everything in palms.

Against empty, we simply play the three-man side as we play trips and the two-man side the way we play twins. We would obviously tango that. We have other things besides tango, and we would do something inside on Will's side so he would not have to come all the way down to the A gap and play that fit.

When we do not like Mike running with the vertical, our answer is trio (Diagram #5). If we want to play palms trio, we can call "slide palms," or "slide tango palms," or "slide spear palms," or whatever it happens to be. But if we call palms, we play palms, and we do not check out of it. If we double call it, we will go slide palms trio, but against any 3x1 set, the Mike knows he does not have #3 vertical anymore on only trio call.

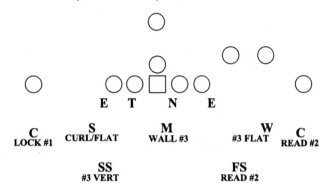

Diagram #5. Trio

Here, the corner, free safety, and the Will are all playing palms. The only difference is that Mike will now wall #3, and the strong safety will handle #3 vertical. We do not really try to disguise it. We will go ahead and line the strong safety up on it.

Mike can move back in the box, Sam can hip up on the defensive end, and the weak corner locks #1 backside. Of course, we will have a movement for the front with it because we still consider it a five-man box.

Let me show you another thing real quick that you might like against trips. We are going to call this "mini," and that term refers to the coverage (Diagram #6). On the single-receiver side, we are going to go ahead and play our half-field stuff as we do. Then, we will take our corner, our Sam, and our strong safety over the trips side, and put our Mike and Will back in the box. We will probably replace Sam with a nickel back.

It gives you six in the box, and if they try to single you up, you have 2-on-1 with a jam, funneling him to the inside. On the trips side, we will lock our corner up with the #1 receiver. The only thing he will

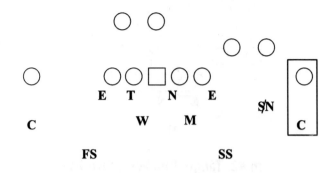

Diagram #6. Mini

not do there is carry #1 on a shallow cross. Hopefully, Mike will pick that up. The nickel and strong safety will then play palms on the #2 and #3 receivers. Essentially, you are taking #1 out of the game, and we are palmsing #3.

The #1 receiver is usually the booster club president's son. They run him on takeoffs all night while #2 and #3 run combination routes. Our only concern is coming up with a Sam or a nickel, who can play that position and cover #2 on a vertical.

MOVEMENTS

I want to cover the movements we like, and then I will get to the film. Thumbs is something we run out of a six-man box (Diagram #7). We can run thumbs and tango together. On this, the tackle is going to racehorse through the inside hip of the tackle, and the end pushes two steps hard to get the tackle turning his shoulder, and then he is coming straight back under.

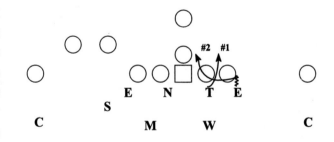

Diagram #7. Thumbs

Spear is real quick. Here it is run on the nose side (Diagram #8). The end is one quick flash and he is coming up under, and the nose flashes and he is wrapping. We can call double spear and do it on the tackle side, but normally it is run with the nose.

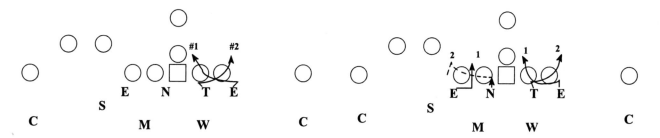

Diagram #8. Spear

Pirate is a movement that everybody has (Diagram #9). The thing about pirate that we are concerned about is the containment issue. The nose has to contain on the side where the tackle and end are coming up under.

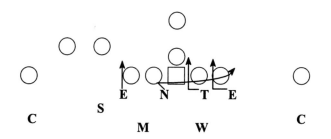

Diagram #9. Pirate

We run a movement called Gator, which is simply a combination of thumbs and spear (Diagram #10). We like to run it with a six-man box.

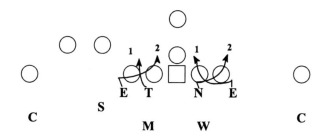

Diagram #10. Gator (Thumbs Plus Spear)

I covered tango, run with a five-man box, so a great movement I want to show you now is tango, spear with a five-man box (Diagram #11). This is one of our best movements, and we have generally found that our four-man games are as effective as or even more effective than the full blitzes.

It took all the worry off of our guys when we started running this defense. It is simple, it is sound, and it gives us multiple ways to defend the spread sets.

Diagram #11. Tango, Spear With Five-Man Box

In the time I have left, I want to talk about some specific blitz calls. First, I want to talk about the advantages of the zone blitz versus spread sets:

- Ability to overload a side for pass or run
- Easily adjusted to get the most out of pressure
- Can change who enters each gap easily
- Field defense so alignments and adjustments are locked in
  - ✓Note: Whichever zone blitz you choose to run, you should have a base defense out of it.
- Be careful of having too many zone blitzes
- Must have a reason for running the blitz

Coaches, remember this: It is not what you know; it's what your players can execute.

Here we run a stunt to the field. We can run this against most spread sets. Against the pro set with the tailback in the deep spot, we can bring six rushers by calling "field sooner 3" (Diagram #12). We are bringing the end, nose, and tackle, and the Sam and Mike backers. The field end has the #2 man to the flat. We have the corners deep, with the strong safety coming down to take #2 to the flat, and the free safety has the deep middle.

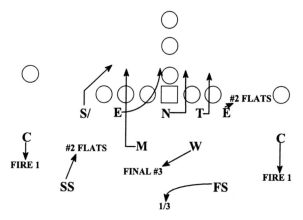

Diagram #12. Field Sooner 3 vs. Pro

Against the doubles set with two twins, we still can run the field sooner (Diagram #13). Now we bring the field end back to the inside to cover for the Mike backer. Will takes the flat and hook areas. The secondary plays the same as they did against the pro set.

The corner locks on the #1 receiver. On the backside, the corner and free safety read the second receiver. They play palms on that side.

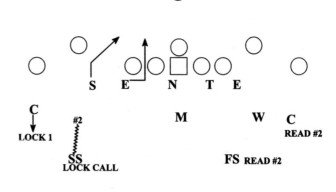

Diagram #15. Slide Palms Weak Alert vs. Doubles

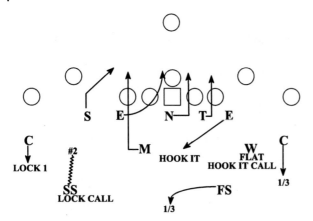

Diagram #13. Field Sooner 3 vs. Doubles

Against the trips look, we can still run the sooner blitz (Diagram #14). The field end must take #2 to the flat. The Will backer takes the deep-middle area behind the Mike backer, looking for the third receiver in his area. The strong safety must read 2/3. The three deep play the same as on the other two calls.

Against the trips formation, we run the slide palms weak alert (Diagram #16). On the three-man side, we want to read the #2 receiver with the corner and strong safety. The Sam backer has #3 to the flat, and the Mike backer has #3 vertical. We bring the tackle and weak end on the alert. The Will backer stems up to the line of scrimmage and comes on the blitz. The free safety comes up to replace the Will backer.

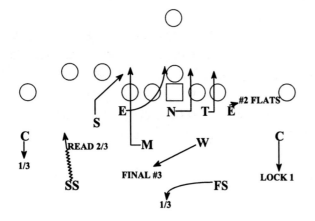

Diagram #14. Field Sooner 3 vs. Trips

We can run the zone blitz to the boundary. Against the double-slot formation, we bring the end and Sam backer on that side (Diagram #15). The strong safety must lock the call on the #2 receiver.

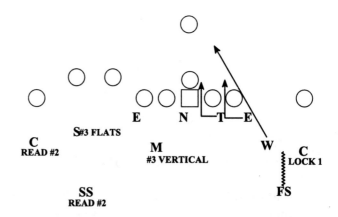

Diagram #16. Slide Palms Weak Alert vs. Trips

That does it. Thank you for having me.

2009 COACH OF THE YEAR CLINIC NOTES
LECTURES BY PREMIER HIGH SCHOOL COACHES

NEW!

EDITED BY EARL BROWNING

2009 CLINIC NOTES
Lectures by Premier High School Coaches

Edited by Earl Browning.

$29.95 • 272 pages • 978-1-60679-065-6

Also available:

2005	2006	2007	2008

1-58518-934-0	1-58518-982-0	978-1-58518-074-5	978-1-58518-740-9
264 pp. • $24.95	256 pp. • $24.95	268 pp. • $24.95	256 pp. • $24.95

NEW!

2009
COACH OF THE
YEAR CLINICS
Football Manual

Featuring lectures from several of America's most renowned coaches. Edited by Earl Browning.

$29.95 • 288 pages • 978-1-60679-062-5

Also available:

Title	Item #	Price	Qty	Total

Tax on materials for California residents only. Shipping & Handling: $7.50 for first item $1.50 for each additional item	PLUS	CA Tax 8.25%	
	PLUS	Shipping	
		TOTAL	

Name _____ Organization/School _____

Address _____

City _____ State _____ ZIP_____ Phone ( ) _____

Method of Payment: ☐ **VISA** ☐ **MasterCard** ☐ American Express Cards ☐ **DISCOVER** ☐ Check #_____ ☐ P.O. #_____

Account # ☐☐☐☐ ☐☐☐☐ ☐☐☐☐ ☐☐☐☐ Expiration: ____ / ____ CVC #: __ __ __

Signature: _____ Email Address: _____

★★★★
COACHES
≣**CHOICE**™
www.coacheschoice.com

Send check or money order to: **Coaches Choice**
P.O. Box 1828 Monterey, CA 93942
or call toll-free: (888) 229-5745 or fax: (831) 372-6075